A Rebel Book

SERMONS IN STONES

OSHO

www.osho.com

Printing: Lightning Print Inc.

A Rebel Book

Publisher: Osho International, 570 Lexington Avenue,
New York, NY 10022
Copyright © 1987 Osho International Foundation,
All rights reserved.
Osho ® is a registered trademark of Osho International Foundation,
used under license.

ISBN 0-88050-012-3

SERMONS IN STONES

Spontaneous talks given
to disciples and friends in
Bombay, India

OSHO

CONTENTS

1 I belong to my own category

BELOVED OSHO,
MANY CONTEMPORARIES AND ENLIGHTENED ONES –
RAMAN MAHARSHI, MEHER BABA, GEORGE
GURDJIEFF AND J. KRISHNAMURTI – HAVE WORKED
WITH PEOPLE, BUT PEOPLE GET MORE OFFENDED BY
YOU THAN BY ANYBODY ELSE.
OSHO, WHERE DOES YOUR TECHNIQUE DIFFER FROM
THAT OF OTHER ENLIGHTENED ONES?

The question is very fundamental. It arises in many people's minds, and it needs a very deep insight into the workings of different masters. We will take each of the masters named in the question separately.

Raman Maharshi is a mystic of the highest quality, but a master of the lowest quality. And you have to understand that to be a mystic is one thing; to be a master is totally different. Out of a thousand mystics, perhaps one is a master.

Nine hundred and ninety-nine decide to remain silent – seeing the difficulty, that whatever they have realized is impossible to convey in any possible way to others; seeing that not only is it difficult to convey, it is bound to be misunderstood too.

Naturally, one who has arrived to the ultimate peak of consciousness will most probably decide not to bother with the world anymore. He has suffered for hundreds of lives living with these miserable people, living with all kinds of misunderstandings, groping in the dark and finding nothing. And these blind people who have never seen the light all believe they know what light is.

From ancient days, a philosopher has been defined as a man who is blind, in a house that is completely dark, searching for a black cat which is not there. And the search goes on....

After a long, long, tedious journey, someone has come to the sunlit peak of relaxation, for the first time is at ease with existence, and decides not to get involved with all kinds of blind people, prejudiced people, deaf people who are going to misunderstand you, who are going to misinterpret you, who are going to crucify you, who are going to poison you, who are going to do every nonsense that is possible against you. Why bother?

You cannot blame those nine hundred and ninety-nine mystics who decide to remain silent. It is not their responsibility, it is not their commitment. They owe nothing to the world; why should they get unnecessarily into the mess, into the madhouse the world is?

Raman Maharshi remained in his cave in the mountains of Arunachal his whole life, unconcerned with the world. He simply tired of it. Naturally, nobody is against him.

He never says anything against any superstition, against any belief that is based on lies. He never criticizes any religion, any politics. He is not a revolutionary. He is not interested in transforming human beings, creating a better society.

He is not even a little bit interested to share his experience. He is just like a well – if you are thirsty, you will have to find the way, you will have to find a bucket, you will have to find a rope, you will have to reach the water. The water is not interested in you or in your thirst.

Naturally there is nobody who will criticize Raman Maharshi. He lived silently, peacefully – not against any vested interest, not in any way proposing a new man, a new humanity. He is fulfilled and contented; he is finished with the world.

Meher Baba is not finished with the world in the same sense as Raman Maharshi. But he is interested *only* in your spiritual growth – as if spiritual growth is something separate from the whole structure of society, religion, education, past, all the traditions, conventions.

So he remains interested in your spiritual growth, but spiritual growth is a complex phenomenon – it is connected with many other things. Unless your conditionings are changed, unless your belief systems are changed, unless your mind is unburdened of the past – there are so many things to be cleaned – only then can the still small voice of your being be heard.

Meher Baba takes spiritual growth out of context. Naturally nobody is against it. In fact, all the vested interests are tremendously respectful of such people, because they are continuously giving – without any intention on their part – opium to the people. They are giving the idea – which is false – that your spiritual growth is possible without going through a deep psychological revolution.

Secondly, Meher Baba remained silent his whole life; he never spoke. All that is written in the name of Meher Baba is written by his secretary. Now, there is no way to know whether the secretary is writing from his own mind.

He had come to see me, and I looked directly into his eyes when I asked, "Are you certain that whatever you have written is not from your mind? Can you give me any evidence that these messages have been telepathically given to you by Meher Baba?"

He felt a little embarrassed and he said, "I cannot say it with absolute certainty, but this is how I felt – that these were messages given by Meher Baba."

"But your feeling.... Have you ever tried in some way to get the consent of Meher Baba, his signature? He was not speaking, that is true, but he used to give his autograph. You could have taken your book.... He was not speaking, but he could hear. You could have asked him: 'I have written this book in your name, and my feeling is that this is your message. Just give it your signature so that I can tell world that Meher Baba agrees with me.' This would have been a simple method."

Meher Baba used to have a small board with the whole alphabet on it just for small messages and things. You would ask for his blessings, and he would put his finger on the letters, "b-l-e-s-s-i-n-g" – blessings are given. If he could give blessings on the board, he could have said yes or no on the same board, but he was never asked. In fact, the secretary may have been afraid he might say no.

Now, who will be against this man? – who has not spoken, who is not against anything, anybody. His whole business is to help you spiritually – and that too only in silence; you can sit with him in silence. Now, there are very few people in the world who can understand silence. A master first needs to teach you how to be silent, and unless he is satisfied that now you are capable of listening in silence, listening to that which is not being said vocally, verbally, but only telepathically....

Meher Baba had never prepared anybody for telepathic transference of ideas. And to me it seems to be absurd. What is the need? – because even in telepathy you will have to use the same language. If I want to say something to you – whether I say it aloud so that you can hear or I say it silently so that you can hear only telepathically, it makes no difference. Unless I am trying to give messages which are secret, unless there is a certain conspiracy.... But around Meher Baba, nothing has happened. The man himself was of great importance, but he remained silent for the same reason as Raman Maharshi.

But he could not stay in one place. He did not abandon the world completely. He was still thinking that some way could be found to approach seekers. He moved around the world in search of seekers, but I don't think he found any. He found only worshippers who sang devotional songs to him, because they had their desires.

And in the East it is believed that if the person who is enlightened blesses you, any desire is bound to be fulfilled. Existence can never say no to the enlightened consciousness. For the enlightened man, existence is always 'yes'; there is a deep synchronicity.

So the people who gathered around Meher Baba were not seekers, they were people who wanted position, power, money, prestige – all the wrong kinds of people. And because he was engaging people in wishful dreaming and not saying anything, he was not against the vested interests. Why should any government be against him? Why should any religion be against him? There was no question – these people were harmless people.

The third man on your list is George Gurdjieff. He is the most unique master the world has ever seen, but his uniqueness created a distance between him and the normal humanity. All his methods were valid methods, but the journey was long and he made it even longer by the way he propounded it. In fact, that was one of his devices to find the real seekers.

Are you ready to go to the very end of the world, or are you just a curiosity monger? – you will go a little way to know what this man is all about, waste his time, and then you will be back in the world. He would choose only those who are ready even to die if that is the only way to find the truth. Naturally he was surrounded by only a very small group of people.

And he was also not interested in any social revolution. His whole interest was to crystallize a few individuals who were courageous enough, to give them their original face, to help them to know the ultimate ecstasy that existence makes available. But it is only for the chosen few. Not that somebody chooses them – but because only very few people are courageous enough to risk everything to find themselves, they become the chosen few by their own courage and their own daring.

And Gurdjieff was not interested at all in the fast asleep humanity. Raman Maharshi was not interested. Gurdjieff was not only not interested, he had all the condemnation possible for those who have been sleeping for lives together. He is the only man in the whole of history who said, "These sleeping people don't have souls, and unless a man becomes enlightened he *cannot* have a soul. A soul is a reward: you don't come with a soul at birth, you achieve it by your effort."

Naturally, no government was offended, no church was offended. If a man has collected two dozen people, the pope is not worried, the *shankaracharya* is not worried – he is not a competitor. And he worked personally with each individual – naturally he could not work with millions of people.

So these people were just in the margin; their names can appear only in the footnotes. They don't belong to the vast humanity – just on the fringes. Having small groups, they were not a danger to anybody.

And the fourth man, J. Krishnamurti, could have been a danger, could have been crucified – he had a far higher intelligence than any Jesus Christ, and far more intellectual genius than any Socrates – but because of a certain obsession, he became very much against organization. He was against all organizations. Naturally you would think that if he was against all organizations then all organizations would have been annoyed by him. But this was not the case, because he never created any organization of his own.

A single individual for ninety years continuously went around the world. Who cares? Seven hundred million Catholics are going to bother about a single individual who is talking against organizations? And who is listening to him?

In India he used to speak in New Delhi, Bombay and Adyar

Madras. This is not India. Nine hundred million people don't live in these three cities. And how many people in Bombay were listening to him? – never more than three thousand. And these three thousand were almost always the same people who had been listening to him for forty years, fifty years. He was saying the same thing all through his life, and the same people were listening. In fact, nobody was listening.

He became a sort of entertainment, and that's what he said to one of my friends who went to see him just before his death: "The thing that hurts me most is that I became just an entertainment for a few people and nothing more. A few people enjoyed my logic, and that was all." And now that he is dead, ninety years' effort has simply disappeared into the air.

Governments are against me because I am against them. Religions are against me because I am against religions. Political leaders are annoyed with me because I say they are mediocre, because I say only psychologically sick people become interested in power politics. People who suffer from an inferiority complex are the people who seek power, prime ministership, presidency. These people need to be in psychiatric hospitals, and they are running the world.

I am against all religions because I am for religiousness, and religions are barriers to creating a humanity with a quality of religiousness. A Christian is not needed, nor a Hindu, nor a Mohammedan. These are the barriers to religious progress.

What is needed is truthfulness, sincerity, silence, lovingness... a life of joy, playfulness... a life of deep search, inquiry into one's consciousness. And these qualities have nothing to do with Christianity or Judaism or Jainism or Buddhism. Meditation is needed, but meditation is nobody's monopoly.

Naturally, all religions are against me, annoyed. Because I am the first man in the whole of history who is saying that religions are the barriers preventing humanity from becoming religious. They are not the vehicles of God, they are the enemies of God. Popes and Ayatollah Khomeinis and *shankaracharyas* – these are not the representatives of God; they may be representatives of the devil. Because these are the people who have divided humanity, and who for centuries have been continuously creating conflicts, bloodshed, wars, crusades, *jihad*, holy war, and all kinds of nonsense. In the name of religion, these people are oppressing humanity.

I am against nations because I don't see any need for there to be nations. Why can't the whole planet earth be one single humanity? – which would be saner, more scientific, more easily controllable.

Right now things are such that you can only say we are living in an insane world. Every three months the common market in Europe is dumping so much food in the ocean... mountains of butter! Last time they had to destroy so much food that the *destruction* cost was two hundred million dollars – it is not the cost of the food, it is the cost of destroying it. And just nearby in Ethiopia, one thousand people were dying every day. What kind of humanity are we living in? Half of humanity is dying in poverty.

Every six months, America goes on throwing billions of dollars worth of food into the ocean, but they will not give that food to Ethiopia or to India or to any other country where people are starving and dying.

Nobody cares about human beings; everybody cares about money. These money-minded people cannot be called sane: that food has to be destroyed; otherwise the market prices will fall, and they don't want their prices to fall. They want their prices to remain stable, so the food has to be destroyed. If the whole world is one, things can be very simple.

At one time Russia was burning wheat in its trains instead of coal because coal in Russia is costlier, and they had an overproduction of wheat. In India, people were dying because wheat was not available. Coal we have enough of, but you cannot eat coal. If the world were one, then the coal from India could go to Russia and the wheat from Russia could move towards India.

There is no need to destroy mountains, exactly mountains of butter. And why did they have to destroy it? Before, they had been selling it to Libya. In Libya, butter was available at half the price of butter in Europe. The butter was coming from Europe, but they were selling it at a throw-away price, just to get rid of it. Otherwise they would have to arrange dumping it and that takes money.

Just to save that money, they were giving it to Libya.

But President Ronald Reagan started going insane against Libya for no reason at all, bombed the poor country, bombed Kadaffi's three houses, killed one of his daughters – for no reason at all – and pressured Europe so that all the supplies that they were giving to Libya would be stopped. Mountains of butter collected in Europe. Now you need space, cold storage... so the old butter had to be thrown into the ocean for the new butter to come in. There is no need of nations. These are the hang-ups of the past.

And if there are no nations, there is no need for armies. Right now, seventy percent of the budget of every country goes to the military; seventy percent to the military which does nothing except left, right, left, right, polishing their guns, their shoes, their buttons – that's all they do. And all over the world, seventy percent of the budget goes to the military and whole countries have to live on thirty percent of their budget.

If the nations disappear, one hundred percent of the budget is available for the whole country – because the armies are useless. Right now there is no problem of there being any war with any planet. With whom are you going to fight? So what is the need to polish your guns every day? to polish your boots, and morning and evening, left and right? All these idiots who are doing this can be put into creative work. I don't want any nations in the world. The world is one single humanity. I don't want religions in the world.

Religiousness is enough, more than enough. As religions disappear, millions of monks and nuns who are just parasites.... They do nothing. That is another army that is sitting on the chest of humanity. They should disappear. They have renounced the world, but for their food, for their clothes, for their housing, the world has to work. It is a very strange thing: they will earn the virtue of having renounced the world; they will enter paradise. You will go to hell, because you provided food, clothes, shelter to these saints. And they have been simply condemning you! Strange logic.

These people should go to hell – who have not been doing anything except condemning, calling everybody a sinner, creating guilt in everybody, destroying everybody's integrity and self-respect. But these people will go to paradise.

With religions disappearing, all these people can be put into creative work. There is no need of monasteries, there is no need of churches, temples, mosques. All these houses of God – and there are millions of men who don't have any houses, who live their whole life on the street. The houses of God are empty – there is no God. All these houses of God can be made available to the homeless. All these monks can be put into creative work, all the armies can be put into creative work.

And when there are no more nations, all dirty politics will have to disappear. Different arrangements can be made for managing the whole world – a world government based on merit, not dependent on votes. In the whole world there are thousands of universities. The world government can be left in the hands of the universities, and all the universities should choose their best people for the world government. An education minister should be a man who really understands education and who can bring new forms of education into the world. Many departments of government will have to disappear, there will be no need. For example, the defense ministry – defense against whom?

The universities could choose the most meritorious people – the Nobel prize winners, the great vice-chancellors, the great artists, the painters, the poets. There could be a different kind of government which is not dependent on the vote of a sleepy humanity, of those who don't know what they are doing.

And we can make this world *really* a Garden of Eden. Adam and Eve will not have to go back to the Garden of Eden. And one day you will hear a knock on the door – God wants to come in! Because you have managed to create a far better garden than his old one. But we can keep that garden too, as a museum piece.

Naturally, Raman Maharshi, Meher Baba, Gurdjieff, Krishnamurti belong to a different category. I belong to my own category. There is no category to which I can belong; I have to create my category. Naturally they are all against me because I am going to take away all their powers, all their conspiracies against humanity. Naturally, they are together against me.

And they are a little puzzled: what to do with a single man? It looks awkward to them also. All the governments of the world, all the religions of the world have to decide against a single individual. Certainly that single individual must have something significant; otherwise there would be no need of so much fear, paranoia.

I am for man's spiritual growth, but I understand spiritual growth in its whole context. It is not something separate, one dimensional; it is a multi-dimensional phenomenon. It needs a revolution in society. It needs a revolution in society's economic, political structures; it needs a tremendous and radical change in everything that has been dominating us up to now. We have to create a discontinuity with the past.

Only then a new man – a really spiritual man, a man of cosmic dimensions – can be born. I am certainly blessed because I am the first who is opposed by all. This situation has never happened before, and will never happen again. And you are also blessed because you are fellow travelers with a man who is not just an old dead saint, a goody-goody. I want you to be the very salt of the earth. Too many goody-goody saints have created so much diabetes. We need a different kind of saintliness. I have called that different kind of saint Zorba the Buddha.

BELOVED OSHO,
YOU HAVE MENTIONED IN THE PAST THAT THE
WITCHES BURNED BY THE CHRISTIANS KNEW,
AMONG OTHER SKILLS, HOW TO HYPNOTIZE. IT
SEEMS THAT IN ANCIENT EGYPT TOO, HYPNOSIS WAS
PRACTICED. IT HAS EVEN BEEN SUGGESTED THAT
JESUS WAS A SKILLED HYPNOTIST. WAS HYPNOSIS
ONCE A RESPECTED FORM OF HEALING? HOW DID IT
EVOLVE, AND HOW DID IT FALL INTO DISREPUTE?

The science of hypnosis – and remember, I am calling it *science* of hypnosis, not *art* of hypnosis – is one of the most ancient sciences. It was practiced in the lost continent of Atlantis. Its literature was saved in Alexandria in Egypt. Pythagoras, a great seeker and searcher from Greece, visited the library in Alexandria and he refers to great literature on the science of hypnosis that has come from the lost continent of Atlantis, which sank into the Atlantic ocean in some natural calamity. The name 'Atlantic' comes from 'Atlantis'.

Perhaps Atlantis had the greatest and the most ancient civilization. And Egypt tried to learn as much from the teachers and the universities of Atlantis as was possible, because the pharaohs – the kings of Egypt – were tremendously interested in collecting all possible sources of knowledge.

The library of Alexandria was perhaps the greatest library that has ever existed. Even the library of the British Museum is just a small library in comparison to the library of Alexandria. The library of the British Museum is a big library. If we put books on the ground just as we put them on the shelf, they would make three rounds of the earth – that many books are in the British Museum library. But the library of Alexandria was many, many times bigger than the British Museum library.

It was burned by Mohammedans, by Khalif Omar. It took six months to put the fire out. That can give you an idea of the bigness and the vastness of the collection. And why did the Mohammedans burn it? I am mentioning it knowingly because it refers to your question. The library contained many things side by side with the science of hypnosis. If they had remained, Mohammedanism would not have survived.

Christianity burned living women in thousands, calling them witches. The word 'witch' is not a bad word; it simply means a wise woman. But Christianity converted the word, gave it a wrong connotation, created courts all over Europe, a great investigation to destroy witches, because witches are directly connected with the devil. This was the strategy to destroy those wise women.

The real fact was that if those women had remained alive, Christianity would have looked very poor as a religion. They knew far deeper truths than Christianity, far more refined religious flights, methods of hypnosis and meditation – which always go together. By destroying the witches, Christianity was trying to destroy hypnosis and meditation both. It was a question of survival.

Mohammedans destroyed the library in Egypt which contained literature of immense value, and Christianity destroyed living human women. And the courts tortured those women, forced them to confess before the court that yes, they had a sexual relationship with the devil.

There is no devil anywhere. After those witches, the devil has not approached any woman. And strangely enough, it was only in Christian countries that the devil was having sexual relationships with women – in no other country.

And they tortured them so much that they had to confess – knowing perfectly well that once they had confessed then they would be burned. Before confession there was torture, and once they confessed before the court then the court would declare that this woman was a witch and she should be burned in the central place in the town so the whole village can see what happens if you are in a sexual relationship with the devil. Thousands of women were burned. Their only fault was that they were still carrying the science of hypnosis and the science of meditation. And they were teaching in small, hidden schools.

It was a great danger to Christianity, because Christianity has nothing comparable to hypnosis or to meditation. Christianity, Judaism, Mohammedanism – these three religions are very poor. They don't deserve even the name of 'religion'. They don't have anything of what you will find in Lao Tzu, Chuang Tzu, Gautam Buddha, Bodhidharma, Nagarjuna, Shankara. You will not find anything of any fundamental value in them.

The science of hypnosis and the science of meditation are two sides of one coin. Meditation you have to do alone – because there are two types of people, just as there are men and women. The science of meditation is more suitable for men, and the science of hypnosis is more suitable for women; hence the witches – they were all deeply into the science of hypnosis.

Hypnosis needs somebody else to take you into your inner center. The meditator goes alone. He goes to the same center, but he goes alone. That is something... part of the man's psychology. Hypnosis also takes you to the same place, but it needs a hypnotizer. A woman going alone feels afraid. That is against the feminine nature. She needs someone she loves, trusts; she needs someone to be with her on the deepest journey to herself. The hypnotist was a master or a great friend or a great lover, someone with whom the woman was able to relax without holding anything, with no fear, knowing that she is protected by someone better than she can protect herself.

This is a general division, but there are men who may have a more feminine nature, the qualities of a woman – for them hypnosis will be more helpful than meditation. And there may be a few women who have characteristics of men – like Joan of Arc or the queen of Jhansi, Laxmi Bai, women who can fight with a sword in a war – for them meditation will be easier than hypnosis. But both are exactly the same processes.

In meditation, you simply relax yourself. It is auto-suggestion. In hypnosis, it is hetero-suggestion – it is suggestion by somebody else who is sitting by your side. And just his closeness – if you love, if you trust – is enough for you to relax.

And if meditation and hypnosis can both be joined together.... And that is my effort, that's what I have been doing. If they both can be joined together.... Just as my effort is that men and women should not remain separate because they are halves of one whole, they should come closer and become one. Love should be nothing but a deep merger with your other part, so deep that there are two bodies but only one soul.

Meditation and hypnosis also can be together, one. In fact, they are halves of one whole. And the moment you try the whole process – either beginning with hypnosis or beginning with meditation, that is simply your preference – you are moving into the same space from two doors towards one center. That center is your being.

And all the religions have been trying to prevent you from reaching your center because that is the only way to keep you miserable and to keep you enslaved, to exploit you, and not to give you any chance of revolt.

This mystery school will try its best to bring all opposites together as complementaries. And if they can be made complementaries, the progress happens in leaps and bounds. Then you are not moving with only one leg, you are not flying with only one wing. You have both wings, you have both legs; you have a totality.

BELOVED OSHO,
MODERN SCIENTISTS LIKE KARL PRIBRAM, DAVID
BOHM AND OTHERS, HAVE BEEN STUMBLING ON
RELIGION. THEY HAVE BEEN STATING THAT OUR
BRAINS MAY BE HOLOGRAMS, INTERPRETING A
HOLOGRAPHIC UNIVERSE; THAT CERTAIN CIRCUITS
IN THE BRAIN ARE THE TRIGGER OF CONSCIOUSNESS
WITHOUT A CONTENT, THAT IT IS THE ANALYTICAL,
THE THINKING PART OF THE MIND, THAT CREATES
SEPARATION AND FRAGMENTATION WHILE THE
INTUITIVE PART EXPERIENCES REALITY IN A HOLISTIC
WAY; THAT ENERGY IS A LIMITED TERM NEEDING TO
BE REPLACED BY A WAVE CONCEPT. THEY ARE
PROPOSING 'RESONANCE' AND 'SYNCHRONICITY' AS
MORE APPROPRIATE TERMS. BELOVED OSHO, WHEN
YOU ARE TALKING ABOUT THE MIND DO YOU
MOSTLY MEAN THE THINKING PART – THE ONE
WHICH CREATES OUR BELIEF SYSTEMS AND
PERSONALITIES? IS IT ENOUGH TO TOTALLY
DISIDENTIFY WITH THE THINKING, OR DOES THE
MIND ALTOGETHER – INCLUDING THE CONSCIOUS
AND THE SUPERCONSCIOUS – NEED TO BE TRANS-
CENDED? IS THE UNIVERSE, IS EXISTENCE MADE OF
MIND STUFF? ARE THESE SCIENTISTS CONTRIBUTING
TO A SCIENCE OF ENLIGHTENMENT, AND CAN ONE
DO SO WITHOUT BEING ENLIGHTENED?

No, that's impossible; nobody can create a science of enlighten-ment without being enlightened himself. That would be just like blind people creating a science of light, or people who have never known love creating a science of love. Enlightenment is absolutely necessary for any understanding of what it is.

Listening to your question... the scientists are trying something which is beyond their field. Enlightenment is not of the mind. Enlightenment is freedom from the mind; it is transcending mind, it is going beyond mind. And all these scientists you mention are talking about mind. Enlightenment has nothing to do with mind;

it has something to do with awareness *of* the mind. It does not go into the details of the mind, what it consists of, how it functions, all its mechanics. Awareness is simply disidentification with the mind; mind is left behind as a mechanism. The moment the mind is completely left behind and there is only pure awareness, just a luminosity, it is enlightenment.

And existence is not made of the stuff mind is made of, no. Existence is made of the stuff called God; to be more exact, of godliness, which is even beyond enlightenment. Enlightenment is beyond mind. Mind is beyond matter. Godliness is beyond enlightenment, and godliness is simply beyondness. Then this beyondness goes on and on with no end to it.

Any scientist who is trying to understand enlightenment without becoming enlightened is proving himself a laughing-stock. It is not an object that you can study from the outside. You can study a roseflower from the outside without becoming a roseflower. Of course, it is simple – if you yourself become the roseflower, who is going to study it?

The scientist studies objects, but enlightenment is not an object – it is your subjectivity, it is the scientist's very soul. He cannot put it on the table and dissect it and try to find out what it consists of – who will do it? Science has a limitation. The limitation is that the objective world is its world. Beyond it, any scientist trying to approach the subjective world is just being a Don Quixote. He needs his nuts and bolts tightened – or maybe loosened. Science has no way beyond objects. Beyond objects is the world of religion, or more exactly – of religiousness.

BELOVED OSHO,
A CONSTANT COMPARISON WITH YOU, WITH
ENLIGHTENMENT, HAS MADE MY LIFE VERY
DIFFICULT. DEEP DOWN, I HAVE A NEARLY CONSTANT
GUILT FEELING FOR NOT BEING ENLIGHTENED. MY
CLOSEST FRIENDS HAVE POINTED OUT TO ME THAT
IN A WAY I AM ALWAYS COMPARING MYSELF TO
YOU. THEN MY INTELLIGENCE DOESN'T LOOK SO
INTELLIGENT, MY HAPPINESS SEEMS SHALLOW AND
FALSE, MY LOVE A PRETENSION, AND MY
UNDERSTANDING JUST A JOKE. FOR YEARS I HAVE
HAD THIS STANDPOINT THAT I AND EVERYBODY
ELSE IS AN IDIOT – EXCEPT FOR YOU AND PERHAPS A
HANDFUL OF OTHERS, THE BLESSED ONES. HAVE I
SIMPLY FOUND A NEW WAY TO TORTURE MYSELF? IS
THIS COMPARISON WITH YOU A STRATEGY TO
SUFFER AND REMAIN UNENLIGHTENED?

For tomorrow....

2 You are the world

BELOVED OSHO,

"YOU ARE THE WORLD." THIS IS ONE OF THE
CONFUSING STATEMENTS OF KRISHNAMURTI. WE
DON'T THINK THERE IS ANYBODY ELSE PRESENT ON
THE EARTH EXCEPT YOU WHO COULD HELP US TO
UNDERSTAND IT, SO WE REQUEST YOU TO SAY
SOMETHING ON IT.

Yesterday, there was a question left, left for tomorrow; but just now I realized that tomorrow never comes. Unless tomorrow comes sometime, that question will have to wait.

J. Krishnamurti's statement that "You are the world" is not confusing at all. It is very simple; just a little intelligence is needed to understand it. We can try to approach the statement from a few different directions.

The world is only a name; the individual is the reality. You can go on trying to find the world all over the world, and you will not find it; you will always find the individual. Words like the 'world', the 'society', the 'religion', the 'nation', are mere words with no content behind them – empty containers. Except you, there is no world.

This is one way of understanding the statement: that the individual is the only reality. And the world is nothing but the collectivity of individuals, so whatever it is, it is a contribution of individuals. If it is ugly, you have contributed to its ugliness. If it is full of hate, jealousy, anger, greed, ambition, you have contributed to this whole hell in which we are living. You cannot throw the responsibility on somebody else; you have to accept the responsibility on your own shoulders. That is another way of understanding the statement, "You are the world."

We are continuously shifting the responsibility. If there is war, if there is an Adolf Hitler, a Ronald Reagan, it becomes easy for us to point to these people and say that they are responsible. But who creates them? Adolf Hitler is our contribution. Without us, he is nobody. Ronald Reagan is nothing but our opinion. It is *our* vote, it is *our* support. So the moment you condemn anybody, remember: you are condemning yourself. However indirect your contribution may be, your contribution is there.

It is possible to live like a Jaina monk or a Buddhist monk or a Catholic monk in a monastery, completely closed as far as the world is concerned. There are monasteries in Tibet... there used to be many in China before the communist revolution. There are a few in Europe with a strange and long history.

The monastery at Athos in Europe is one thousand years old. In one thousand years, whoever has entered the monastery has not come out living. You only enter: once a monk, forever a monk. And the monastery does not allow its inmates to come out into the world; they are brought out only when they are dead. Do you think they are not responsible for Adolf Hitler? they are not responsible for world wars?

Apparently it looks... How can you make these people responsible? – who have left the world, who have never looked back, who have disconnected themselves with the world. But still I say to you they *are* responsible. They are responsible by escaping – they escaped their responsibility. It does not make any difference. The Buddhist monks, the Jaina monks, the Hindu monks are not participating in worldly activities. But you can contribute in a positive way or you can contribute in a negative way.

You can set fire to this house – that is the positive way, the active way. You can stand by the side of the road and not do anything to put the fire out – that is the negative way. But both are responsible. The negative person does not look so responsible, but his responsibility is absolutely equal – because in life there is a balance.

You may be against war, you may be a pacifist, you may be a chronic Protestant – always with a flag protesting against war, against violence. Naturally you can say, "How can I be held responsible?" But life is a complex phenomenon.

Your protests, your pacifism, your fight against warmongers is still part of war; you are not a man of peace. And you can see it when people protest – their anger, their violence is so obvious that one wonders why these people are protesting against war. They should join some camp *in* the war – they are full of anger, rage. They have just chosen to have a third camp behind a beautiful name – "peace". A good mask, but inside is the same anger, the same rage, the same violence, the same destructiveness against anybody who does not agree with them. They are contributing as much violence to the atmosphere as anybody else. They may be talking about love, but they are also saying that you have to fight for love.

Hazrat Mohammed had words written on his sword meaning "peace is my message." He could find only a sword to write on, that "peace is my message"! And he gave birth to a religion he called Islam. *Islam* means peace, and Islam has done more violence in the world than any other religion has done. In the name of peace, at the point of a sword, Islam has been killing, converting millions of people. You can choose beautiful words, but you cannot hide the reality.

J. Krishnamurti's statement that "You are the world" simply emphasizes the fact that every individual, wherever he is, whatever he is, should accept the responsibility of creating this world that exists around us. If it is insane, you have contributed to that insanity in your own way. If it is sick, you are also a partner in making it sick. And the emphasis is important – because unless you understand that "I am also responsible for this miserable and insane world," there is no possibility of change. Who is going to change? Everybody thinks somebody else is responsible.

One of India's great emperors was Akbar. There is an incident in his life recorded in *Akbar Mamaz* – "the biography of Akbar." One day he was just chit-chatting with his friends.... And he had around him the very best, wisest, most creative people chosen from every part of the country. His court jester was standing just by his side.

By the way, you should understand it: in all the courts of all great emperors there used to be a jester, whose whole function was to keep the court from becoming too serious, to keep the court light, playful – once in a while, an explosion of laughter. It was a great insight to have a court jester, and he used to be one of the wisest men of those days – because it was not an easy phenomenon.

Birbal was Akbar's court jester. And as they were discussing,

Akbar slapped Birbal – for no reason at all. Now you cannot slap the emperor back, but the slap has to go somewhere – so he slapped the person who was standing next to him.

Everybody thought, "This is strange!" There was no reason in the first place. Suddenly, as if a madness had got hold of Akbar, he slapped poor Birbal. And that man is also strange. Rather than asking, "Why have you slapped me?" he simply slapped the man who was standing by his side!

And that man, thinking perhaps this was the rule of the court, slapped the next person. In a chain, it went all over the court. And you will be surprised: that night, Akbar's wife slapped him! And he said, "Why are slapping me?"

She said, "That is not the question; a game is a game." He said, "Who told you that this is a game?"

She said, "We have been hearing the whole day long that a great game has started in the court. The only rule is you cannot hit the person back, you have to find somebody else to hit. And somebody has hit me – so your slap has come back to you, the game is complete!"

In this big world, thousands of insane games are going on, and you are all participants – of course in very small measures, according to your capacity. But remember, the slap is going to come back to you sooner or later. Where else will it go? Whatever comes to you, remember, it is your doing. Perhaps you have forgotten when you started it. The world is big, it takes time. But everything comes back to its source – that is one of the fundamental rules of *life*, not a rule of a game. So if you are suffering, if you are miserable, if you are tense, full of anxieties, anguish, don't just console yourself that this whole world is ugly, that everybody else is ugly, that you are a victim.

J. Krishnamurti is saying you are *not* a victim, you are a creator of this insane world; and naturally, you have to participate in the outcome of whatever you have contributed to it. You are participating in sowing the seeds, you will have to participate in reaping the crop too; you cannot escape. To make the individual aware so that he stops throwing responsibilities on others – on the contrary, he starts looking inwards to see in what way he is contributing to

this whole madness – there is a possibility he may stop contributing. Because he has to suffer too. If he comes to know that the
whole world is nothing but his projection on a wider scale....

Because millions of individuals have contributed the same
anger, the same hatred, the same competitiveness, the same violence, it has become mountainous. You cannot conceive that you
can be responsible for it: "I may have contributed just a small
piece..." But an ocean is nothing except millions and millions of
dewdrops. A dewdrop cannot think that it is responsible for the
ocean – but the dewdrop *is* responsible. Without the dewdrop
there is going to be no ocean at all. The ocean is only a name; the
reality is in the dewdrop.

To accept your responsibility will change you, and your change
is the beginning of the change of the world – because you *are* the
world. However small, a miniature world, but you carry all the
seeds. If revolution comes to you, it heralds the revolution for the
whole world. And when J. Krishnamurti says "You are the world"
he is not saying it only to you; he is saying it to everybody: You are
the world.

If you want to change the world, don't start by changing the
world – that is the wrong way humanity has followed up to now:
Change the society, change the economic structure. Change this,
change that. But don't change the individual. That's why all revolutions have failed. Only one revolution can succeed, which has
not been tried up to now – and that is the revolution of the individual. You change yourself. Be alert not to contribute anything
that makes the world a hell. And remember to contribute to the
world something that makes it a paradise. This is the whole secret
of a religious man. And if every individual starts doing it, there
will be a revolution without any bloodshed.

In Akbar's life there is another incident. He had built a very
beautiful marble pond. He was bringing swans from Mansarovar,
from the Himalayas. And he decided that in the pond there should
not be water. This is the emperor's pond – instead of water, there
should be milk. Everybody in the capital was to be informed that
just one bucket of milk, not much, from every house had to reach
the palace early the next morning, before sunrise.

Birbal told Akbar, "You don't understand human mind at all. Your pond will be full of water." He said, "What nonsense...? It is my order!"

Birbal said, "Your order, or anybody's order – I understand human mind."

Akbar said, "Let us wait; tomorrow morning it will be decided who is right."

And the next morning both went to the garden, and the pond was full of water. Akbar said, "This is strange. How did it happen? Catch a few people from the street, whoever is available, and ask how it happened." And the people were threatened: if they spoke any lie, their life would be at risk; if they said the truth, they would be set free.

They said, "The truth is, we thought the whole capital would bring buckets of milk. One bucket of water would be completely overlooked, nobody would ever know. But now I see that the pond is full of water; it seems that everybody had the same thought – the whole capital! Not a single man was different." The human mind functions exactly the same.

So if the world is such a tragedy, it is our human minds which are creating it; we are contributing our bucketful of misery.

No revolution can be successful unless the human mind is understood by human beings and they start behaving in a different way – not hoping that "My bucketful of water is not going to be noticed at all." If everybody understands that this idea is what will come to every human mind, and decides, "At least I should bring a bucketful of milk. I should not behave in such an unconscious way as all human beings are behaving...." It is possible to have the pond full of milk.

"You are the world" simply means: whatever it is, we cannot save ourselves from responsibility.

Our monks, our saints have tried only this. What they were try-ing to do, if you go deep into their psychology, was to say that, "We are no longer responsible for all this nonsense that is going on in the world." But they depended on the same world. For their food they were dependent on the same people; for their clothes they were dependent on the same people. They were not in any way separate from the world; they had only stopped being *active* in the world. They were silent partners in the whole insanity that is going on. And they should be condemned more, because they were more intelligent people, wiser people. Still they could not see the point that just standing aside is not enough; you have to do something against the normal human mind.

Escaping to the Himalayas is not going to help, because even in the Himalayas your mind will remain the same, just you will not have the opportunity to know it. And it is better to know the enemy than not to know it, because by knowing there is a possibility to change. Not knowing is very dangerous. When a disease is diagnosed, it is half cured. When a disease is not diagnosed, then comes the real problem. Medicine is not the problem; diagnosis is the problem.

One man lived for thirty years in the Himalayas. His problem was anger, and he wanted to get rid of it. In the Himalayas for thirty years he was not angry for a single moment – there was no reason. The wife was not there, the children were not there, the parents were not there, the society was not there – there was no provocation.

His name became famous by and by, and people started coming to worship him. Now it was even more difficult to be aware that the anger was still there. When people are worshipping you, there is no question of anger.

Then came the *Kumbha Mela* in Allahabad. People said, "You are such a great saint. Without you, the *Kumbha Mela*, the greatest gathering of people on the earth in one place, will be missing something. You have to go." And by now he was convinced that he had become a great saint. People were coming from far away to make the difficult, arduous journey through the mountains just to pay respects to him.

He went to *Kumbha Mela*, but there were millions of people – nobody knew him. Somebody stepped on his foot, and immediately he slapped the man, took hold of his neck and said, "What do you think you're doing?"

Suddenly he remembered that he was a saint. He said, "My God, what am I doing? What happened to thirty years? The anger came in such a flash, so instantaneously, not even a single moment of thought." He was going to kill the man. That was the reason he had gone to the Himalayas – because he was afraid he would murder somebody and would be crucified or have to live for his whole life in jail. Even his family had said, "It will be good if you go to the Himalayas because you will kill somebody, and that means you have killed yourself too. This way two lives are saved. You go." But thirty years...What happened?

It is simple fact: the people who have escaped from the world are not to think that they are not responsible for this world. By escaping, they have not changed the world. By escaping, they have not contributed anything to make it more beautiful, more human, more intelligent, more meditative. Neither have they changed the world nor have they gone through any inner change themselves. Hence I am against renouncing the world.

Be in the world, however difficult it is – because it is only in the world that you will be reminded on every step what kind of mind you are carrying within. And that mind is projected on the outside, and it becomes huge because so many minds are projecting in the same way.

"You are the world" is not a mathematical statement. "You are the world" is a psychological insight. And it can become the very key for the only revolution that can succeed.

BELOVED OSHO,
HAVE YOU ANYTHING TO SAY ABOUT 'CHANNELING'?
SUPPOSEDLY A SPIRIT BEING SPEAKS THROUGH A
WILLING HUMAN HOST. THIS IS A GROWING
PHENOMENON THAT IS HAPPENING RIGHT NOW,
PARTICULARLY IN CALIFORNIA AND NEW YORK.
THERE ARE FAMOUS ONES – SETH, RAMTHA AND
LAZARUS. BUT NOW THEY ARE SPRINGING UP
EVERYWHERE – PEOPLE CLAIMING TO CHANNEL
KWAN YIN, BEINGS FROM OTHER GALAXIES, ETC., ETC.
A COMMON THEME SEEMS TO BE THAT THEY HAVE
COME TO HELP THE PLANET EVOLVE RIGHT NOW.

THE WORD 'CHANNELING' IS ABOUT AS COMMON AS
'COCA COLA'. EVEN SOME SANNYASINS ARE
CLAIMING TO CHANNEL THIS ONE OR THAT ONE.
THERE IS ALMOST AN ATTITUDE THAT IF ONE IS NOT
CHANNELING SOMEONE, ONE IS NOT OPEN TO
SPIRITUAL POSSIBILITIES. IS CHANNELING A REAL
PHENOMENON? WHY IS THIS SPRINGING UP RIGHT
NOW, AND WHY ARE PEOPLE SO ATTRACTED TO
CHANNELED BEINGS AND INFORMATION? IS THERE
ANYTHING FOR OUR SPIRITUAL GROWTH IN THIS?

David and Kaveesha, California needs all kinds of idiotic ideas. It seems all the idiots of the world are born in California. It is the land of sex, drugs, and rock and roll. Everything is possible in California. But it remains only for a few years – three years, four years at the most; then the fashion changes.

In California everything is a fashion – and when something is in fashion everybody is involved in it, because not to be involved in it means you are out of date, lagging behind, not belonging to the contemporary world. Channeling is simply a new name for an old disease. In the past they used to call it 'being possessed by a ghost'.

Channeling is the new name for being possessed. Then the ghost speaks – but that is a very old idea, not very appealing. In old countries, it still continues to happen. There are people in villages in India who become possessed, and when they are possessed you can ask questions and they answer – and they answer in such a way that you can make anything out of it. It is never a certain, meaningful statement. Channeling is an American translation of the old idea of being possessed.

There are many people in America – particularly in California and New York – who become possessed and start talking to you, answering you. And certainly their language is different from the old; it is more scientific. The very word 'channeling' has come from television – channel number one, channel number two.... Now, the poor old countries cannot think of channeling, that word is not yet meaningful to them.

And the idea of channeling has given a scope... you are channeling to a certain planet, a certain galaxy – and you can say any nonsense, there is no way to prove it right or wrong. Even scientists know nothing about galaxies. There are at least fifty million galaxies. Scientists are still working with very refined instruments to count how many galaxies there are.

And one galaxy means... One sun and the planets that are attached to the sun is one solar system. A galaxy means millions of suns, millions of solar systems – which are moving around a certain unknown center of gravity. Each galaxy is so huge.... Science has not been able to find out all the facts about even one galaxy, the galaxy in which we live.

Now there are the cunning and there are the stupid, and there are idiots who are channeling to other galaxies and bringing messages to humanity. Books are printed with their messages.

But the whole thing is that a person goes into a deep hypnotic sleep – if it is authentic. Out of ten, nine are not authentic. If somebody is authentic, then all that happens in reality is that he relaxes, his conscious mind goes to sleep, and from his unconscious mind, collective unconscious mind, cosmic unconscious mind, things start coming up. You can say they are coming from ghosts. You can talk about them in psychological terms and say they are coming from the unconscious. Or you can talk about them in Californian terms: they are coming from channel number one, channel number two. But they are all coming from your own unconscious mind. This is about the authentic cases.

And when so many people are channeling, it becomes a competition. If somebody else is channeling, why can't you channel? No talent is needed, no intelligence is needed; all that is needed is insincerity, cunningness, fraud.

Every year in India, Mohammedans have their holy festival, *Muharram*. And during *Muharram*, holy spirits possess people. Those holy spirits – because Mohammedans, just like Christians and Jews, believe only in one life – those holy spirits will always be around until the last judgment day, which goes on being postponed, and I don't think it is going to happen ever.

I had a center in Jabalpur near a Mohammedan graveyard. And

they reported to the collector that because of our meditations, the spirits in their graves were very much disturbed. The collector called me: "Why are you disturbing their spirits?"

I said, "This is strange. What report have you received? Who has come?"

He said, "Mohammedans – and it may create a riot unnecessarily." Jabalpur was one of the most vulnerable cities in India for Mohammedan and Hindu riots, any excuse....

And their excuse was that because when we were doing our meditation we would use the Sufi mantra "hoo." So the Mohammedans had said, "Because they say, 'Hoo, hoo, hoo' the Mohammedan souls lying in their graves wake up. These are dangerous people – because nobody has ever heard of such a meditation. And after one hour these people are gone, but those spirits roam about and torture Mohammedans, and many are becoming possessed."

The collector said, "You stop. At least this 'hoo' mantra should be stopped because it can create trouble. And in your own book you have explained that 'hoo' is part of 'allah-hoo', it is a Sufi mantra. So they have certain grounds against you, that you are disturbing the souls. They are sleeping well, and you 'hoo, hoo' every morning, and they get so disturbed that they start torturing Mohammedans." So I had to close that center.

In my childhood in my village... Each time that Mohammedans celebrate the holidays of Muharram, some people are "possessed by the holy spirit." The holy spirit is called *wali*. There are a few people who are thought to be very saintly – they are possessed by walis – and they dance and they shout, scream, and you can ask questions.

And they should not run away, so their hands are tied with ropes, and two persons keep them in control. There are many walis, and each wali has his own crowd, and people come with sweets and fruits – somebody has received a blessing last year and has got a boy, a child; somebody has got married, and somebody has come to get a blessing for the future. Only Mohammedans participate in it.

But I always enjoyed every kind of entertainment. My parents used to tell me, "Listen, that is the Mohammedans' festival, and you are not supposed to be there."

I said, "I am neither Hindu nor Mohammedan nor Jaina nor anybody. What do you mean – that I cannot enjoy anything? All festivals belong to some religion. In fact, I belong to *no* religion so I can participate in all festivals." So I would go there.

Once I managed to hold the rope of one wali who was just an ordinary man and a fraud. I had told him before, "I will expose you if you don't allow me to hold your rope."

He said, "You can hold my rope, and you can share a few sweets also, but don't say anything to anybody."

We both used to go to the same gymnasium – that's how we became friends, and he himself told me that it was all fake. So I said, "That means I am coming; if it is fake, you have to share it."

I went there with a long needle, so I could make him jump. He became the most famous wali because no other wali was jumping so high! He could not say anything about what was happening – because he is possessed by the wali and the wali cannot be afraid of a needle. So he could not say anything, and I went on sticking him with the needle. He managed to get almost four times more sweets, more fruit, more rupees... more people came to get his blessing.

He said, "That is great, but you tortured me so much!"

I was in such demand from that day – every wali wanted his rope to be given to me. Because whoever got me as his assistant would become the greatest wali – immediately, the very same day. For ten days the function continued, and no wali wanted me again the next day! They would say, "I will escape from town if you come again!"

I said, "There is no need. I am in so much demand by other fools who don't know what is happening.... You just give me half your share – because you will still have double."

And I found that almost everybody was a fraud – because I could make everybody jump with my needle. Not a single one in the whole town was an authentic person who was possessed or anything. They were just pretending – shouting, screaming, saying things that you cannot understand, but you have to make sense out of it. And the *maulvis*, the Mohammedan scholars, will explain to you what the meaning of it is – "You have been blessed, your desire will be fulfilled." And who bothers about whose desire is fulfilled or not? If a hundred people come, at least fifty people's desires are going to be fulfilled. These fifty will come back, and these fifty people will spread the idea. The other fifty will also come back – not to the same wali, but to other walis who are there, because the first wali they went to doesn't seem to work: "Perhaps he was not powerful enough."

And my walis were the most powerful, and their power was decided by how high they jumped, how much they screamed, how much they shouted. And everybody asked me why my walis were making such gestures towards me....

I said, "That is a spiritual language – you will not understand."

In California, Kaveesha, you can start a new game. Don't bother about this channeling – within two years it will be past. California is good. It has money, it has the young generation, unemployed, and it has a tradition of changing everything – changing the job, changing the wife, changing the town, changing the house. In two or three years they become bored. So rather than being worried about their channeling... It is absolute fraud.

And if there is someone sincere, that means he is relaxing to the point where the unconscious mind starts throwing up its repressed contents. It has no spiritual value. But it will be good to check. Go to any person who is channeling with the galaxies, but keep a good needle with you! With the needle, the person will start dancing, jumping, and his galaxies will start going higher – from one channel to nine channels. You can check: if your needle does not work, that means the person is at least not a fraud, but is simply falling into unconsciousness and allowing his unconscious to reveal its contents. But they have no spiritual value.

But before you leave, try the needle – particularly on the famous ones!

BELOVED OSHO,
DO YOU REALLY SAY YES TO ME TOTALLY JUST THE
WAY I AM?

Yes, I say yes totally to you as you are because that is the only way I can transform you. My acceptance does not mean that you have to remain what you are; my acceptance means that whatever you are I respect you, I love you. But at the same time, my acceptance means that you can be much more, that this is not the end of your journey. In fact, you have not even begun yet, but I can see the potential.

For centuries, this has been the way to challenge you to seek and search: you have been condemned; whatever you are, you are wrong. The emphasis has been that if you are proved to be wrong, a sinner, then you will start changing. But that whole technique has failed. People have accepted that they are wrong, they are sinners, and it is beyond them to be saints. So relax and be sinners – of course not in a joyous way, but with sadness. Their whole life becomes unworthy in their own eyes: guilty, sinful, sad... a long, dark story... useless, futile.

The past has condemned you with the hope that it would change you, but their hope has proved wrong. I am going to try a totally different method. I accept you as you are, but that does not mean that I want you to remain as you are. I love you as you are, but I love you because you have so much potential in you, such a great possibility of growth, that with just a little effort you can become a light unto yourself.

Whatever you are, enjoy it. But there is much more, so don't stop at it. You are on the first rung of the ladder – it is perfectly good, because without being on the first rung, how can you be on the second and how can you be on the final, the ultimate? Nobody is a sinner.

Yes, there are people who commit mistakes, but nobody is a sinner. And everybody has a right to commit mistakes – because that is the only way to learn. And everybody has to stumble in the dark. That is nothing special to you; everybody falls once in a while, and it is good training.

To me, whatever existence makes available to you is for your good. Just use it, and keep your eyes on the faraway stars – they belong to you. However far they are, they are not beyond your reach.

BELOVED OSHO,
IN RECENT YEARS, SCIENCE HAS BEEN DISCOVERING MORE AND MORE THE ELEMENT OF SUBJECTIVITY IN EXPERIMENTS IN PHYSICS. ALSO, IN MEDICINE TODAY, WE TALK ABOUT THE SUBJECTIVITY OF THERAPY; THE SAME MEDICINE HAS DIFFERENT RESULTS WITH DIFFERENT DOCTORS. PLEASE CAN YOU COMMENT ABOUT THE SUBJECTIVITY OF A SCIENCE THAT CLAIMS TO BE AN OBJECTIVE ONE?

Anything that has to do with human beings can never be totally objective; it will have to allow a certain space for subjectivity.

It is not only true that the same medicine from different doctors has different effects; it is also true that the same medicine has different effects on different patients from the same doctor. Man is not an object. First you have to understand the word 'subject'.

A piece of stone is just an object. There is no interiority, there is no innerness to it. You can cut it in two; then there are two objects. You can cut it in four, and there are four objects. But you will not find any interiority.

Subjectivity means that from the outside a man is just as objective as any other object – a statue, a dead body, a living body, what is the difference? The statue is simply an object, it has no subjectivity. The dead body has once been a house for a subjective phenomenon, but now it is empty. Now it is an empty house; the person who used to live in it has left it. The living man has all the objectivity of the statue, the dead body, and something more – an interior dimension – which can change many things because it is the most powerful thing in existence.

For example, it has been noted that three persons can be suffering the same disease, but the same medicine will not work. On one person it is working; on another it is just fifty-fifty, working and not working; but on the third it is not working at all. The disease is the same, but the interiorities are different. And if you take the interiority into consideration, then perhaps the doctor will make a different impact on different people for different reasons.

One of my friends was a great surgeon in Nagpur – a great surgeon but not a good man. He never failed in his surgery, and he charged five times more than any other surgeon would charge. I was staying with him and I told him, "This is too much. When other surgeons are charging a certain amount for the same disease, you charge five times as much."

He said to me, "My success in many other things also has this basis: when a person gives me five times more, he is determined to survive. It is not only because of money that I am greedy. If he is willing to give me five times more – when he could get the operation at cheaper rates – he is determined to survive whatsoever the cost. And his determination is almost fifty percent of my success."

There are people who don't want to survive; they are not willing to cooperate with the doctor. They are taking the medicine, but there is no will to survive; on the contrary, they are hoping that the medicine does not work so they will not be blamed for suicide, yet they can get rid of life. Now, from the inside that person has withdrawn already. Medicine cannot help his interiority, and without his interior support, the doctor is almost helpless – the medicine is not enough.

I came to know from this surgeon.... He said, "You don't know. Sometimes I do things which are absolutely immoral, but to help the patient I have to do them." I said, "What do you mean?" He said, "I am condemned by my profession...."

And all the doctors of Nagpur condemned him – "We have never seen such a cheat."

He would put the patient on the table in the operating theater – doctors are ready, nurses are ready, students are watching from the gallery above. And he would whisper in the patient's ear, "We had agreed on a fee of ten thousand – that will not do. Your problem is more serious. If you are ready to give me twenty thousand, I am going to take the instruments in my hands; otherwise, you get up and get out. You can find cheaper people."

Now, in such a situation.... And the person has money; otherwise, how can he say yes? And he accepts it: "I will give twenty thousand, but save me."

And he told me, "Any surgeon could have saved him, but not with such certainty. Now that he is paying twenty thousand, he is absolutely with me; his whole interior being is supportive. People condemn me because they don't understand me. Certainly it is immoral to agree on ten thousand and then put the person in the operating theater and whisper in his ear, 'Twenty thousand, thirty thousand... Otherwise get up and get out – because I had not realized that the disease had gone so deep. I am taking a risk, and I am putting my whole reputation on the line. For ten thousand I will not do that. And I have never failed in my life; success is my rule. I operate only when I am absolutely certain to succeed. So you decide. And I don't have much time, because there are other patients waiting. You just decide within two minutes: either agree, or get up and get lost.'

"Naturally the person will say, 'I will give you anything you want, but please do the operation.' It is illegal, it is immoral, but I cannot say that it is unpsychological." Anything to do with man cannot be purely objective.

I used to have another friend, a doctor who is now in jail because he was not qualified at all. He had never been to any medical college; all the degrees that he had written on his sign were bogus. But still I am of the opinion that an injustice has been done to the man – because it does not matter whether he had degrees or not. He helped thousands of people, and particularly those who were becoming hopeless, going from one doctor to another – who all had degrees – and getting tired. And this man was able to save them.

He had a certain charisma – no degree. And he made his hospital almost a magic land. The moment a patient would enter his office, immediately he would be surprised. He had been everywhere... because people used to go to him only as a last resort. Everybody knew that the man was bogus, it was not something hidden. It was an open secret. But if you are going to die, what is the harm in trying?

And as you entered his garden – he had a beautiful garden – and then his office... He had beautiful women as his receptionists, and it was all part of his medical treatment – because even if a person is dying, looking at a beautiful woman his will to live takes a jump; he wants to live.

After the reception, the person would pass through his lab. It was absolutely unnecessary to take him through the lab, but he wanted the person to see that he was not an ordinary doctor. And the lab was a miracle – absolutely useless, there was nothing significant, but so many tubes, flasks, colored water moving from one tube into another tube, as if great experiments were going on.

Then you would reach the doctor. And he never used the ordinary methods of checking your pulse, no. You would have to lie down on an electric bed with a remote control. The bed would move far up into the air, and you are lying there looking up and hanging over you there are big tubes. And wires would be attached to your pulse and the pulse would make the water in the tubes jump.

The heart would be checked in the same way – not by ordinary stethoscope. He had made all his arrangements visual for the patient – so that he could see he had come to some genius, an expert. And the man had no degrees, nothing at all. His pharmacist had all the degrees, and he used to prescribe the medicines because the man had no idea about medicine.

In fact, he never did any criminal thing. He never prescribed medicines, he never signed for them. This was done by a man who had degrees, who was absolutely qualified to do it. But because he arranged all this, and because he had written strange degrees on his sign... and since those degrees don't exist I don't think they can be illegal. He was not claiming any legal degrees, he was not claiming that they were from any university that exists. It was *all* fiction – but the fiction was helpful. I have seen patients half cured just in the examination. Coming out, they said, "We feel almost cured, and we have not taken the medicine yet. The prescription is here – now we will go and purchase the medicine."

But because he had done all this.... This is when I saw that the law is blind. He had not done anything illegal, he had not harmed anybody – but he is in jail because he was "cheating people." He has not cheated anybody.

To help somebody to live longer, if that is cheating, then what is medical help? Because of human beings, medicine can never become an absolutely solid, hundred-percent objective science. That's why there are so many medical schools – ayurveda, home-opathy, naturopathy, acupuncture, and many more – and they *all* help. Now homeopathy is simply sugar pills, but it helps. The question is whether the person believes.

There are people who are fanatic naturopaths – nothing else can help them, only naturopathy can help them. And it has no connection with the disease. One of my professors was madly into naturopathy. Any problem... and a mud pack on your stomach. I used to go to him to enjoy, because it was very relaxing, and he had a very good arrangement – a beautiful bath and showers.... And without any difficulty I used to go and say, "I have a very bad migraine."

He said, "Don't be worried. Just a mud pack on your stomach."

Now a mud pack on the stomach is not going to help a migraine. But it used to help me, because I had no migraine! A mud bath, the full bathtub, and you are drowned in the mud, just your head is out – it is very comfortable and very cool.

Soon he realized that, "You come again and again with new diseases."

I said, "That's true. Because I have got a book on naturopathy – from the book I get the disease, and then I come to you. First I read it, to see what you will do. If I want it to be done to me, I bring that disease; otherwise, unnecessarily lying down in the mud for half an hour...." He said, "So you have been cheating me?"

I said, "I am not cheating you. I am your most prominent patient. In the university everybody else laughs at you, I am the only one who supports you. And the others who come here, come here because of me – because I say that my migraine disappeared."

He said, "My God, now I am suffering from migraine. Go!"

People used to become angry with me. They would tell me, "My migraine, instead of going, has become more intense – because a cold stomach does not help migraine!"

I would say, "Then your system must work differently. With my system, it helps me!"

There are homeopaths, fanatics who believe that homeopathy is the only right medicine and all other medicines are dangerous – particularly allopathy is poison. If you go to a homeopath, the first thing he will do is inquire about your whole history from your birth up to now. And you are suffering from a headache.

One of the homeopathic doctors used to live near me. Whenever my father came to see me, I would take him to the homeopath. The homeopath told me, "I pray you don't bring your father because he starts back three generations, that his grandfather had a disease...."

I said, "He is also a homeopath. He goes deeper into the roots."

He said, "But he wastes so much time, and I have to listen – and he just has a headache! About his grandfather and all his diseases, then his father and all his diseases... then himself. By the time *he* comes, almost the whole day is finished. My other patients are gone, and I am listening to him telling what kind of diseases he has suffered from his childhood, and finally it comes out that he has a headache.

"I say, 'My God, why didn't you tell me before?' and he says, 'Just as you are a homeopath, I am also a homeopath. And I want to give you a complete picture.'"

The first thing they will ask is about all your diseases because they believe that all diseases are connected, your whole life is one single whole. It does not matter whether you had something in your leg or your head – they are part of one body, and for the doctor to understand, he has to know everything.

The homeopath will ask you what kind of allopathic medicines you have been taking – because that is the root cause of all your diseases; all allopathic medicines are poison. That is the attitude of naturopathy too, that allopathy is poison. So first you have to do fasting, enemas... just to clean you of all allopathy. Once you are clean of allopathy....

One of my relatives was very much interested in naturopathy. His wife had a small problem and that was that her hands once in a while would get what you call "pins and needles." It was not much of a problem, because for two, three minutes the sensation would remain, and then it would be gone. I told her many times, "Don't make much fuss about it. Enjoy it when it happens – it is not a pain, you just feel pins and needles. So enjoy it!"

But the husband was a naturopath, so he brought a bigger naturopath and they started working on her. I tried hard to stop them: "There is no need, it is not much of a disease, and it happens only once in a while. She is almost fifty – twenty years more she will live. In twenty years it will happen maybe sixty times, not more than that – just drop the idea and enjoy it."

But they were going to the very roots. They started putting her on a fast, enema, vomiting... they cleaned her completely. And when she was completely clean, she became mad.

And I told the husband, "I was afraid you would kill the woman! You cleaned her so much, she is just a skeleton. And because she is just a skeleton, all is cleaned, those pins and needles are now happening all over her body. You have succeeded!"

But they insisted that it was not naturopathy that was responsible for it; it was allopathy, she had been taking allopathic medicines for years. Finally she became mad. The last time I went to see her.... She used to love me very much. I had been chosen by my university to go with a delegation to Saudi Arabia. She was not in her senses, but when I told her that I had been chosen to go to Saudi Arabia with a cultural delegation, she heard it, she understood it, and she said, "Only two things you have to remember – don't forget."

I said, "I will not forget. You just tell me what those two things are."

"First, don't use wooden sandals" – because I used to wear wooden sandals in the university just to torture the whole university. I would be at one corner of the campus, and the whole university would know that I had entered, I was in the university. Wherever I was, I could be found just by the sound.

I said, "Why are you worried about my wooden sandals?"

She said, "It won't look right in a foreign country. What will they think of wooden sandals? No, you don't do that."

I said, "Okay, I will not use wooden sandals. What is your second advice?"

She said, "Second advice: You are going to a Mohammedan country. Don't speak against the Koran." And the same night she died. And for perhaps three months those had been the only words of sanity from her. My own explanation is that she loved me so much that even in this insane state her love took over her madness to give me suggestions – don't speak against Mohammedans, against the Koran, and don't use the wooden sandals.

Man is a subjective being. If the patient loves the doctor, then water can function as medicine. And if the patient hates the doctor, then no medicine can help. If the patient feels the doctor is indifferent – which is ordinarily the case with doctors, because they are also human beings, the whole day long seeing patients, the whole day long somebody is dying... they slowly, slowly become hard, they create a barrier to their emotions, sentiments, humanity. But this prevents their medicine from being effective. It is given almost in a robot-like way, as if a machine is giving you medicine.

With love, the patient is not only getting medicine; around the medicine something invisible is also coming to him. Medicine will have to understand man's subjectivity, his love, and will have to create some kind of synthesis in which love and medicine together are used to help people. But one thing is absolutely certain: that medicine can never become entirely objective. That has been the effort of medical science up to now, to make it absolutely objective.

3 Old age: A new beginning

BELOVED OSHO,
SOMETHING FEELS DRASTICALLY WRONG ABOUT THE
WAY SOCIETY LOOKS AFTER – OR FAILS TO LOOK
AFTER – THE ELDERLY. YOU HAVE SPOKEN OF THE
LEGALIZATION OF EUTHANASIA FOR THOSE WHO
ARE SO MENTALLY OR PHYSICALLY DEBILITATED
THAT THEY CAN HARDLY BE SAID TO BE LIVING AT
ALL. BUT WHAT CAN BE DONE FOR THOSE WHO ARE
NOT PHYSICALLY OR MENTALLY INCAPACITATED, BUT
ARE RETIRED FROM THEIR PROFESSIONS, AND WHOSE
FAMILIES HAVE GROWN UP? IN THE PAST, FAMILIES
OFTEN FELT OBLIGED TO HAVE ONE OR BOTH
PARENTS LIVE WITH THEM – OFTEN WITH
DISASTROUS RESULTS. ABUSE OF THE ELDERLY, CALLED
'GRANNY-BASHING' IS AN EPIDEMIC PROBLEM IN
AMERICA. ALTERNATIVELY, THE ELDERLY ARE PUT
INTO HOMES, WHERE THEY ARE VISITED AT
WEEKENDS OUT OF GUILT AND A SENSE OF DUTY; OR
THEY ARE ENTIRELY NEGLECTED. THE HOUSING
COMPLEXES PROVIDED FOR THE ELDERLY ARE OFTEN
DEPRESSING AND LONELY, LIKE A STATE OF LIMBO
BETWEEN LIFE AND DEATH. IT FEELS SO UNGRACIOUS
AND INHUMAN THAT SOCIETY USES PEOPLE AND
THEN CASTS THEM OFF INTO ANONYMITY. WOULD
YOU PLEASE COMMENT?

The problem of the elderly has arisen because man is living longer than he used to live before. All the old skeletons found in India, in China and other ancient countries prove one thing: that nobody used to live more than forty years, hence the problem of the elderly never arose in those societies.

It is because of this fact that the scriptures go on saying that in our country people never became old. It was not something great, it was simply that before old age they were dead. Death came before old age; now it comes after. And as a country is more advanced, people are living longer – ninety years, a hundred years. In a few countries, there are thousands of people who have crossed the boundary line of one hundred and fifty. And in a few special places, because of their food, their climate and their genetics, a few people have reached the age of one hundred and eighty. And they are still young, they are working just like anybody else.

But the problem for the society is that employment is limited. The population growth is tremendous. New people are coming in such great numbers that we have to vacate places for them, we have to retire people. And as time passes, we will have to retire people even earlier than we are retiring them now. Now in a few countries it is sixty years, in a few countries fifty-five years, but soon this will not be possible. People will have to retire by the age of around forty-five – because the pressure of the new people coming will be so great that if you don't give them opportunities they will create chaos.

But to retire somebody at the age of forty-five is dangerous, it creates many psychological problems.

First, a person needs some work, some creativity, to feel that he is needed. This is one of the most essential psychological needs of man – to be needed. The moment you feel you are no more needed, suddenly something starts dying within you, shrinking within you – as if the will to live has lost all its power, energy, hope. Tomorrow is nothing but darkness.

And the person who has become useless to the society – that's what retirement is.... We make it as beautiful as we can by giving a beautiful pocket watch, celebrating it – it is just a cover-up. The reality is, we are throwing the person in the junkyard: "You are no longer needed, your work is finished. Now younger people, more educated, better educated, who know the latest scientific developments, are going to replace you. You are out of date." Suddenly, you have become a posthumous person.

You will go on living, breathing, eating, but it will be just like an appendix to a book – the book is finished, and nobody reads the appendix. One starts losing dignity, self-respect; one starts feeling out of place everywhere – one is no longer connected with the society, with who is now in power; a great gap has arisen.

These people are going through a tremendous inner turmoil and crisis. To keep them in the family, as has always been done in the past, is to create a nuisance for the new ones – because these people have nothing to do except criticize. They are ready to get angry, easily annoyed, irritated, ready to fight.

In fact, these are their ways of making the society and the family feel that they are alive, that you cannot just ignore them. They are doing it in a wrong way, but whatever they are doing should be understood with great compassion: they are simply asking for a little attention. For their whole life they have been paid attention to – in the offices, in the shops, in the government, wherever they were they were somebody. And now they are nobody – not even to their own children.

And the problem becomes more complex because the children have no obligation to be bothered with these old people. They have a small life span of their own; soon they will be retired. Before retirement they want to enjoy life – to eat, drink and be merry. And these old people are sitting there, continuously watching what you are doing; they suddenly become very spiritual, moralistic disciplinarians; they start finding loopholes in everybody's life – and nobody likes it. Nobody wants to be interfered with. Their independence to live their life in their own way is their birthright.

And these old people, to the younger generation, look like idiots for the simple reason that the younger generation knows more, it is better educated. Science is progressing in leaps and bounds. Every generation comes with the latest developments, canceling all old knowledge as false, as mistaken.

It was not so in the past. Things have changed so dramatically that unless we take the whole into account, we will not be able to solve the problem.

In the past the situation was totally different, diametrically different. There was no gap between the younger and the older generation. The gap has only been created in this century. In the past, by the time he was six or seven the young child would start following his father – if the father was a carpenter, he would start carrying his wood, his instruments. If the father was a woodcutter, he would go with him to the forest – whatever small help he could give, and whatever small amount he could learn... because profession came by birth. You were going to do the same thing your father did and your forefathers had been doing for centuries, there was no mobility.

It was not that a shoemaker's son would become a carpenter, or a carpenter's son would become a goldsmith – the profession came by birth. So from the very beginning the child knew what he was going to become: he was going to become exactly a replica of his father.

The question of a gap did not arise. And the father always knew more, and the child always knew less – because the only way of knowing was by experience. A carpenter's son had to learn by doing carpentry. Naturally the father was much more knowledgeable about the art, the craftsmanship, and at no time could the son say, "You are out of date."

This is why all the old civilizations respect old people, because the old people always knew more than the young people. Old people expect the same today also, but it is not possible – they have forgotten that the basic root was that the older knew more than the younger. Now the situation is just the reverse: the younger know more than the older.

Your father may have come out of the university thirty years ago. In thirty years, everything has changed. And when you come out of the university, the father cannot expect – *should* not expect the same respect that was always given to him in the past. The situation is completely reversed. Now the son knows more; the father has to ask the son for his advice because he is coming fresh from the university, bringing the latest research on any subject. Now, experience is not the only way of learning.

We have created schools, colleges, universities – an alternative way of learning, far quicker.

The way of experience is slower. Now, how quickly you can learn depends on your intelligence. Libraries are available, books are available, teachers are available. If you are just ready to learn, you can learn so much by the time you come out of the university that it is natural at many points to think: "My father is behaving stupidly, my father is doing things which are out of date – they should not be done."

Your father may be a doctor – he is giving medicines which

you know, because you have come from the university, have been abandoned; they are not to be given, they are dangerous. And he is still prescribing them because in his time he learned that those were the right medicines. Such drastic changes have happened.

The younger generation has come for the first time to a higher knowledge level than the older.

If he is considerate, a young person may respect old age – but it is going to be just formal, not real. In the past it was a real phenomenon, not formal – he really felt it. Now he cannot feel it. I know from my own experience.

My teachers in the university had passed their examinations, their post graduation, their PhD's twenty years before. In those twenty years everything had changed.

It does not change for the mediocre – because they never go to the university, they are not bothered. But what has happened in the world of knowledge is that people still go on listening to a man who is teaching everything wrong.

Because I have been interested in books from my very child-hood, it was a constant problem and conflict in every class. I could not pay them respect; I said to my teachers, "Formally, I can pay respect to you, but don't expect it in a realistic way – because what you are saying is no longer true. And to give real respect to you means to accept what you are saying as true.

"I respect truth – that's why I cannot respect you. For twenty years you have not been in contact with the developing knowledge. Once you came out of the university, you never read anything about what has happened in your subject."

And the rate of research in all subjects is such that now big books – particularly in physics, in chemistry, in biochemistry – are not written, because by the time you write a big book of a thousand pages most of it will have been proved wrong. So only periodicals, papers are published. And in that too you have to be very quick because you are not working on the subject alone.

Albert Einstein was asked once, "If you had not discovered the theory of relativity, do you think it would have ever been discovered?"

He said, "Within three weeks – at the most."

It was very shocking because people thought that you had to be an Albert Einstein.

He said, "That is true, but there are many Albert Einsteins around the world who are working along the same lines. It is only a question of who comes first, it is a race."

And it was found that another German physicist had already discovered everything about the theory of relativity, but he was late in publishing his paper; otherwise, Albert Einstein would not have been the first man to bring light to the whole subject. This man had discovered everything, he was just a little lazy about writing his paper – but his discovery was earlier than Albert Einstein's.

People are researching small details – not big subjects, because big subjects take a longer time. People are taking very small pieces of subjects so that they can finish them quickly before anybody else does, and then they can give the paper to the university, or to whoever publishes the paper.

Now there are thousands of universities around the world working on the same subjects, thousands of scholars. And I found that my teachers, without exception, were twenty or thirty years behind the times. And because I said so, it became a constant trouble. Colleges, universities would not accept me, would not give me admission, and they would not give the reasons. Somehow I had to convince a principal. I still remember the scene....

This principal was a little crazy. He was a devotee of the mother goddess Kali of Calcutta, and every morning from four o'clock he would start....

He was a very big man. He was a wrestler in his youth, and the rumor was that in the early days the famous wrestler Gama was defeated by him – but by that time Gama was no longer famous. And this principal had the body of a great wrestler; he was black, looked dangerous. And from four o'clock the whole neighborhood was tortured by him – "*Jai Kali.*" And he had a real loud voice, no loudspeakers needed.

When I was refused from a few places, I thought perhaps this crazy person could be persuaded. So I went early in the morning, five o'clock. He was in his temple – in his beautiful bungalow, he had a small temple, and the whole area was sounding, resounding,

"Jai Kali" – victory to Kali.

I went into the temple. He was alone. I also started shouting, "Victory to Kali."

He looked at me. He said, "You are a believer in Kali?"

I said, "Anybody who has any intelligence *has* to be a believer in Kali. And you are the greatest man I have come across."

He said, "Everybody thinks I am crazy."

I said, "*They* are all crazy."

He invited me for breakfast. And he said, "What are you doing?"

I said I was studying in a certain college, although I had been expelled from that college.

He said, "You leave all those colleges and come to my college. I will give you all the scholarships, every kind of help, because you are the first person who has recognized me."

In that way I got entry into his college. But once I was in, he was in trouble – professors started coming to him.... He called me, and he said, "This is not good. It seems you bluffed me."

I said, "This is true, I bluffed you – because there was no other way."

He said, "Then you will have to do one thing: you should not come to the college at all; just come to take your examinations."

I said, "What about my percentage for being present in the lectures?"

He said, "I will take care of it. You will get ninety percent for attendance, but don't come to the college! Because every professor is complaining – it is not a question of one professor; you are torturing everybody. They all say, 'Now we cannot compete with this young man. He has read the latest – and we can see that we are twenty years behind, but we cannot manage to read all that has happened in twenty years. We have to take care of the children and the wife and the whole family. And he makes us so embarrassed. He brings facts and we know that he is right, but we cannot tolerate this constant embarrassment. And because of him, other students are losing respect. They are all thinking that we know nothing. He has created the atmosphere in the college that all the professors are idiots.'"

I said, "It is true, you have got first-class idiots."

He said, "Listen, I am giving you all the facilities for not coming to the college."

I said, "That's a perfectly good arrangement, but once in a while can I come to your temple just to participate in the worship?"

He said, "Now there is no need to bluff me. I was also surprised that nobody in my whole life had said that I was a great man. Only this young man has recognized my spirituality. You bluffed me once, that's enough."

For two years I did not go to the college, but I was going to the university library, getting ready for my post graduation so I could torture the post-graduate professors.

Today, every young person coming from the university is ahead of the older generation. His lifestyle has changed, his thinking about the world has changed, his values have changed – and the old people are constantly poking their noses into it. So the only way that has been found is to put these old people in houses for the old.

Out of duty, out of guilt, the children go to meet their parents there, but not for love, not for joy. And most often they are neglected; nobody ever goes there. Their lives are certainly very miserable.

They have lost their jobs, and with their jobs their respect, with their jobs their worth, with their jobs the feeling that they are somebody. Their ego is punctured. They have lost their family.

Their children are grown up and don't want to live with them – because they would like their children to listen to the music of Mozart, and the children are interested in the Beatles. The old people think, "Beatles? – this is not music. This is simply madness, this is not dance!" The gap is so big that it is unbridgeable. The solution is sad. The children are gone, the family is gone.

These old people's houses look sad; they seem to be waiting rooms for the graveyard – dull, depressed, dark.

Certainly there is a great problem, and this problem is going to become bigger every day.

My suggestion is: first, the moment old people retire and their families send them to the houses for the old, their marriages should also be canceled – because love can bring a new spring again. It doesn't matter whether you are fifty or sixty.

They have produced children, they have lived together; now it is time. They are departing from the family, they have departed from the job; they should depart from the marriage also – because their sadness has much to do with the situation of the husband and wife left alone. No friends, no children, no job – and they are tired of each other, they don't seem to take any interest in each other.

It should be optional: if some couple wants to live together, that is up to them, but if couples want to separate they should be respectfully separated so they can start their lives anew – and for the first time without worries. They have their pensions, money is no longer a problem; they can find new partners, new lovers. And it has been psychologically established that if even an old man falls in love with a woman, his life is lengthened at least by ten years – because love gives juice to your roots, you again become young, you again start looking at flowers, thinking of poetry, thinking of painting, writing love letters.

So the first thing is that love should be given another chance. And what is the harm? – if you can have two springs in your life....And now you are more experienced. You will not reproduce children again – that phase is over, you have tortured yourself enough. You will take every care that children are not produced.

And it is a strange phenomenon: the moment somebody falls in love, many things change – his face has a different glow, his eyes become more shiny, he smiles more. He may go and dye his hair – life is taking a new beginning – get a beautiful set of teeth. He has to become a little younger.

To me, love is a kind of chemistry – it *is* chemistry. Your body starts functioning in a different way. He will start thinking, if he is a man, to go for morning walks, jogging, swimming, to keep his body fit because now there is a woman. For himself he was not caring about his body, but the woman....

And the woman is going to care about her body at least twenty times more. It will be a beautiful place because then in those old people's houses, people will paint their rooms in lighter colors, not dark and sad, gloomy. They will bring flowers, they will start gardening, may go for a world tour, may go for a long trip in a boat. Life can be joy. They can meditate, they can study. Much that they always wanted to do and had no time to do... now they have time, they have money. They can paint, they can sculpt.

My own idea is that special classes should be opened in every university for these old people who want to learn painting, who want to learn sculpture, who want to learn music, who want to learn dancing. They should enter the university again, a second phase of education. I have always had the idea that the first phase of education is the preparation for life and the second phase of education should be the preparation for death.

You don't have any preparation for death, no education for death. This is a lopsided situation. A person has lived half his life, and you trained him, educated him. Now the other half should not be left barren like a desert. He should begin again, with the second part of his education. He meditates, he learns creative arts, he dances. He writes poetry, novels.

Whatever he wanted to do in life... now life has respectfully given him time to do everything that has been just a desire in his mind, just a dream. Now it can be turned into a reality. And he should be freed from all old bondage – marriage, or any other kind of bondages – so he can start new adventures in every direction.

We can make the second part so beautiful that people who are still in the first part will feel jealous, will feel, "How long will it take for me to be retired? – because those old guys are really enjoying it. We are working, earning; they are simply relaxing, taking sunbaths on different beaches around the world, with different women."

The old people have to defeat the young – there is no need to be defeated. Right now they have taken a very defeatist attitude. They should take it as a challenge: "Now we will prove that old age is not a misery, that it can become a tremendously beautiful experience." In fact, it has to be more beautiful than the first phase, because the first phase was only a preparation for the second. And the second is the preparation for the eternal.

BELOVED OSHO,
WHEN YOU TALK ABOUT THE "ART" OF SOMETHING,
AND THE "SCIENCE" OF SOMETHING ELSE, WHAT IS
THE ESSENTIAL DIFFERENCE? IS IT THAT AN ART CAN
ONLY BE APPROACHED AND APPRECIATED
INTUITIVELY, SUBJECTIVELY, WHILE A SCIENCE IS
APPROACHED AND APPRECIATED WITH THE HELP OF
THE MIND AND OBJECTIVELY?

The scientific approach and the approach of art certainly have that difference. Art is intuitive, more of the heart, more subjective, more intimate. Science is objective, not intimate at all; it has nothing to do with your intuition or your feeling, nothing to do with your heart. In fact, it has nothing to do with *you* at all.

If you heat water, it will evaporate at one hundred degrees. Who heats the water does not matter – whether it is a man or a woman, whether it is a boy or an old man, a Tibetan lama or a Catholic monk. Water simply follows an objective rule; it is not concerned with the person who is boiling it. There may not be any person at all; it can be boiled just by pressing a button, a machine can do it. So that is certainly one of the differences. Art is a totally different matter.

First, it is not objective; it is something that is born within you. Then you project it onto something outside – it may be a painting. Vincent Van Gogh painted a single painting for one year continuously. He rejected it hundreds of times. He was painting the sun, and every day he would reject it. And his friends were tired; they said, "Nobody has painted the sun so much – and you have painted so many paintings so beautifully but you go on rejecting them." I am bringing him in because I want to tell you that he had a certain inner criterion, he had a certain inner painting of the sun. And it was not being projected exactly as he had it in him – that was the rejection; otherwise, there was no question.

That is the difference between a painting and photograph. A photograph is part of science, a painting is not.

One very rich woman asked Picasso how much he would take to make a portrait of her.

He said, "What do you want – a photograph or a painting?"

She said, "I don't understand the difference. What do you mean?"

He said, "A photograph is a simple thing. You will be sitting there, and I will make a drawing of your face, of your body, on the canvas. I will be simply functioning like a camera. It will be a photograph – although everybody will say it is a painting.

"But if you want a painting then you have to be ready, because in the painting I will not be a camera; in the painting I will be subjectively involved. So the outcome will not be just your picture; it will be a picture processed through my subjectivity. It may not even look similar to you."

The woman said, "I would like a painting because photographs can be done by cameras very easily and cheaply. You are asking one million dollars, so let it be a painting." It was a painting.

And when the woman looked at it she could not believe what it was.... She said, "Just one thing I want to ask: just tell me where my nose is?"

Picasso said, "I don't know anything about it. Do you ever ask a camera? You just look at the picture and find out. I have processed you through my subjectivity and this is what happens. I will try to find out where your nose has gone, where other things are – they must be somewhere. But I refuse to sell it." The woman was shocked. She said, "Why?"

He said, "You cannot appreciate a painting. Your question was so stupid. And I have worked so hard on your painting, I have put my whole soul into it, and you are worried about your nose! I am not going to sell it. You need only a photograph, which you can recognize." A photograph is prose.

A painting is poetry. It becomes mysterious because it passes through man's innermost feelings. It takes a new birth. It is not a reproduction. Another incident....

A man purchased a Picasso painting, and paid a million dollars. But when you pay a million dollars, you want to be certain that it is an authentic Picasso. One critic said, "Don't be worried, it is an authentic Picasso because I was staying with him when he painted this. I am a witness. You can purchase it without any fear."

He purchased it, but he said, "You will have to come with me to see Picasso because I want to hear it from him that it is an original, authentic." The critic said, "There is no problem." They went.

The critic was a friend of Picasso, and he said, "You must remember, I was staying with you when you did this painting."

He said, "I remember it perfectly well, but this is not authentic, this is not original. I have done it."

The critic said, "Are you going mad? On one hand you say you have done it, and on the other hand you say it is not authentic, not original. What do you mean?"

Picasso said, "I have painted the same painting before, and it is hanging in a museum. You can go and see — *that* was authentic, *that* was original. This painting... I was not getting any new ideas, and there was a customer who wanted a painting. So I simply copied my own painting — but it is a copy. It does not matter who copies it, whether Picasso copies it or somebody else does, it is a copy. It is not authentic, it is not original. I am not involved in it at all, it is not part of my subjectivity. The first painting is. They are exactly alike, you cannot find any difference — but I made the difference, and the difference is significant."

The scientific approach is about objects, which are common. Because art is personal, subjective, it can never be common. You may not agree on one painting — two persons may not agree at all that it is beautiful. To somebody it may be ugly, to somebody else it may be beautiful. It is a personal phenomenon.

But I was talking about more fundamental differences. When I say the science of hypnosis is not the art of hypnosis, my meaning is that the art is always invented, it has no reality in existence. It is invented by the artist.

You can find statues of horses with flying wings. Nowhere in reality are there horses with flying wings — there are wings and there are horses, you can combine them. But that is your invention, not a discovery. Art is invention. Science is discovery. Science only discovers that which is already there, and art creates. Science is never creative; it only finds out whatever is the case. Art creates out of nothing.

Hypnosis is not an art. It is a science; you can discover the principles – they are exactly the same anywhere on the earth. In any age, at any time, in any culture, in any society; those principles are there to be discovered. They are already there; you only have to discover them.

A painting by Picasso or the poetry of Rabindranath or a musical composition by Yehudi Menuhin are not already there. It is Yehudi Menuhin who creates it, it is Rabindranath who composes it – because it is subjective, personal and invented. You can have different opinions about art, but you cannot have different opinions about science. Opinions don't matter; science is factual.

Art is fictional. Art has beauty, and tremendous genius is needed to create it. The artist is almost like a god creating the world. If the story is true that God created the world, then it is an art, then God is an artist, not a scientist – because to be a scientist he will have to discover the world... the world is already there, and then he discovers it.

I want hypnosis to be understood as a science and not as an art for this basic reason: discovery and invention.

BELOVED OSHO,
THIS IS AN EXCERPT FROM A CONVERSATION WITH
GURDJIEFF; THESE ARE HIS WORDS: WITH ORDINARY
LOVE GOES HATE: I LOVE THIS, I HATE THAT. TODAY I
LOVE YOU; NEXT WEEK, OR NEXT HOUR, OR NEXT
MINUTE, I HATE YOU. HE WHO CAN REALLY LOVE,
CAN BE; HE WHO CAN BE, CAN DO; HE WHO CAN DO,
IS. TO KNOW ABOUT REAL LOVE, ONE MUST FORGET
ALL ABOUT LOVE AND MUST LOOK FOR DIRECTION.
AS WE ARE, WE CANNOT LOVE. WE LOVE SOMETHING
BECAUSE SOMETHING IN OURSELVES COMBINES
WITH ANOTHER'S EMANATIONS. WE ALLOW
OURSELVES TO BE INFLUENCED. WE PROJECT OUR
FEELINGS UPON OTHERS. ANGER BEGETS ANGER. WE
RECEIVE WHAT WE GIVE. EVERYTHING ATTRACTS OR
REPELS. THERE IS THE LOVE OF SEX, WHICH IS
ORDINARILY KNOWN AS 'LOVE' BETWEEN MAN AND

WOMAN – WHEN SEX DISAPPEARS A MAN AND A
WOMAN NO LONGER 'LOVE' EACH OTHER. THERE IS
LOVE OF FEELING, WHICH EVOKES THE OPPOSITE,
AND MAKES PEOPLE SUFFER. LATER WE WILL TALK
ABOUT CONSCIOUS LOVE. BELOVED OSHO, CAN YOU
PLEASE TALK ABOUT CONSCIOUS LOVE, BOTH IN A
MAN-WOMAN RELATIONSHIP AND IN THE MASTER-
DISCIPLE RELATIONSHIP?

The question is not only about conscious love. The basic thing
is consciousness. A conscious person does everything consciously –
love or painting or dancing or making a cup of tea; it does not
matter what. Consciousness prevails over all your actions, just as
unconsciousness prevails over all your actions. You love unconsciously, you hate unconsciously, you do everything unconsciously.

So the whole problem has to be reduced to these two words:
consciousness and unconsciousness. Love can be a good example.
People say they love, but they don't know what they are saying,
they don't know what they mean – because they love a car, they
love a woman, they love a certain brand of cigarette, they love the
football matches. It is difficult to figure out what they mean by
love.

Unconscious love is simply a magnetic pull towards something,
irresistible. But you are not going towards the object of love, you
are being pulled. You are fast asleep. In your whole life, you are
behaving like a somnambulist. There are many people who wake
up in the night without waking up; they get up, not wake up. And
they will do things, and they will go back to sleep and in the
morning they will not remember what they have done.

Many times when people think that their houses are haunted
by ghosts, it is just that somebody in the house is a somnambulist
who does things in sleep – sets fire to things, throws things away,
and goes to his bed and sleeps well. And in the morning he is as
puzzled as everybody else – not that he is deceiving anybody, just
he has no remembrance.

Your life – which one minute is full of love, the next minute all
the love disappears.... Not only that, it can turn into hate; you

were ready to die for the person and the next moment you can kill the person.

According to Gurdjieff, and according to those who have awakened, the whole of humanity is asleep, sleepwalkers. Things are happening but you are not the doers because you are not conscious enough to do something.

You fall in love. You cannot say that it is a conscious decision on your part. Perhaps the woman's hair is just like your mother's hair. Every male child loves his mother, that is his first love object. The baby girl loves her father, that is her first love object. And slowly, slowly the father and mother become imprints – the mother becomes imprinted on the boy, the father becomes imprinted on the girl.

And when the boy falls in love with a woman, his unconscious mind signals him, "Here comes your mother." You don't hear it. And nobody can be exactly like your mother, so there can only be some similarity – the way the woman walks, the face of the woman, the eyes of the woman, the way she talks. Anything can trigger in you the old figure waiting in your unconscious, deep in the well inside you.

The same happens to the girl – the way the man walks, just the sound of his boots, may remind her of her father. Any small thing can trigger it, and suddenly you feel a great love arising in you. But because it is only fragmentary, it cannot be very lasting. It can be lasting if you don't ever meet – then you will never come to know about the other fragments. So the most successful lovers in the world are those who never meet. They make the most romantic, beautiful stories – no quarrel, no nagging, no fighting. And they never come to find out that "This is not the woman made for me and I am not the man made for this woman" – they never come close enough to know this. But unfortunately, most lovers get married. That is the most unfortunate accident in life.

That destroys the whole beauty; otherwise they would have been Laila and Majnu, Shiri and Farhad, Soni and Mahival – great lovers of history. But all those great lovers never met, never lived in a one-room apartment in Bombay.

Once two persons are together, then other fragments of their lives are bound to surface. You have to become acquainted with the whole woman you have got; the woman has to become acquainted with the whole man she has got – and there is the trouble, because then slowly you find that the fragment you love is very small in comparison to the fragments you hate. Now just the color of the hair does not help, nor the face nor the eyes nor the nose – nothing helps.

In the West, women have been asking me – -because their love lives are not going well.... Nobody's love life is going well, it simply does not happen. So those poor women were asking if they should get their nose fixed by a plastic surgeon – because the husband is continuously talking about her nose, that it looks Jewish. And he is so much against Jews – the moment he sees the nose, all love disappears. The poor woman is ready to fix her nose.

I said, "Don't unnecessarily torture your nose. He will find something else, this is just an excuse. Right now he may become accustomed to this nose, but if you fix it then every time he sees you he will see that this woman has a fixed nose, she is really a Jew behind the nose. It will be very difficult for him to forget this. And the money is going from *his* pocket to fix *your* nose. You just leave it as it is."

In fact, for centuries a wrong concept has been prevalent: that lovers should like each other in every possible way. That is absurd. Lovers should make it clear – "These are the things I don't like." Both should make it clear, that "These are the things I don't like, and these are the things I love." And there is no need to quarrel about it every day because that quarrel is not going to change anything. They have to learn to accept that which they don't like – a kind of co-existence, a tolerance. This is for the lovers who are not awake.

A conscious love is a totally different thing. It has nothing to do with love as such, it has something to do with meditation, which makes you conscious. And as you become more and more conscious, you become aware of many things. One: that it is not the object of love that is important. It is your loving quality, your lovingness that is important, because you are so full of love you would like to share it. And the sharing has to be unconditional.

You cannot say, "I will not share if your nose is Jewish" – what has sharing to do with noses? Conscious love changes the whole situation. Unconscious love is centered on the object of love. Conscious love is centered in oneself, it is your lovingness.

Unconscious love is always addressed to one person; hence there is always jealousy – because the other person also knows that unconscious love is always centered on one person, that it cannot be shared. If you start loving somebody else, that means you have stopped loving the first person. That's the jealousy, the continuous fear that your lover may start loving somebody else – as if love is a quantity. Conscious love is a quality, not quantity.

It is more like friendliness – deeper, higher, with more fragrance, but similar to friendliness. You can be friendly to many people, there is no question of jealousy. It does not matter that you are friendly to five persons or ten persons or ten thousand persons; nobody will feel deprived because you love so many people and his share is going to be less and less. On the contrary, as you are able to love more people, your quality of love becomes mountainous. So whoever you love gets *more* love if your love is shared by many people. It dies if it is narrowed. It becomes livelier if it is spread over a vast area – the bigger the area, the deeper are its roots.

Consciousness gives everything a transformation. Your love is no more addressed to anybody in particular. It does not mean that you stop loving. It simply means you become love, you are love, your very being is love, your breathing is love, your heartbeats are love. Awake you are love, asleep you are love.

And the same is true about everything else – your understanding, your intelligence, everything goes through the same change. You become the center of the whole existence, the center of the cyclone, and everything radiates from you and reaches anybody who is able to receive it.

It is not a question of loving someone for certain reasons; it is love simply out of abundance – you have so much that you have to share it, you have to radiate it. And whoever receives it, you are grateful to the person. Conscious love makes you a doer, a being, a soul.

In unconscious love, you are just an emptiness – dark and dismal, hungry and thirsty. In unconscious love, you are a beggar. You are begging for love, because love is nourishment.

And this is hilarious: You are begging for love, the other person, whom you are in love with is also begging for love – two beggars holding their begging bowls before each other, and both begging bowls are empty.

Conscious love makes you an emperor. You don't beg; you simply give. And you give because now you see that the more you give the more you have. So whoever accepts your love, you are grateful to the person. The whole earth can become full of love, an ocean of love, but only with conscious people.

With unconscious people, it is just a disgusting place, nauseating... everybody pretending to be loving, and nobody is loving. Everybody is trying to exploit the other, and the other is doing the same to him. And because both are empty, sooner or later they are going to start quarreling: that "You deceived me," that "You cheated me," that "You betrayed me," that "You are not the woman you pretended to be," that "You are not the man you were showing yourself to be." But with beggars this is going to be the problem.

I have heard about a beggar who used to sit by the side of a bridge. One day he asked, "Give something to a blind, helpless old man."

So they gave him one rupee. He looked at the rupee and he said, "This is not real, this is false." They said, "But you are blind!"

He said, "I am not blind. The man who usually sits here is blind. Today he has gone to see a film. He is my friend, I am just sitting in his place."

But everybody in this whole world of unconsciousness is a beggar, trying in every possible way to snatch some love, some attention, some sympathy – because love is a necessary nourishment. Without love, you cannot live; just as food is necessary for the body, love is necessary for the soul. And everybody is suffering without love, because without love your souls are dying. But what we are doing is not right.

The right way is to bring consciousness to yourself. And from consciousness there will be many revolutions in many dimensions. Love will be one of the most important dimensions, and you will find the golden key of how to get love from the whole existence. The secret is: whatever you have, give it, share it. Once the universe knows that you have become a sharer, then all the sources of the universe become available to you. They are inexhaustible. Okay, Maneesha.

4 The mystery of the knack

BELOVED OSHO,

SOME TIME AGO, IN ANSWER TO MY QUESTION AS
TO WHETHER ENLIGHTENMENT IS THE ONLY WAY A
DISCIPLE CAN EXPRESS GRATITUDE TO HER MASTER, I
HEARD YOU SAY THAT NOTHING COULD EXPRESS
THE GRATITUDE. I REALIZED THEN THAT GRATITUDE
IS SOMETHING THAT WE USUALLY FEEL ALMOST
BURDENED WITH, AND SO WE SEEK TO FIND AN
OUTLET FOR IT SO THAT WE ARE RELIEVED OF A DEBT.
AS THE DISCIPLE CAN'T EXPRESS HER GRATITUDE –
AND WHAT WOULD THE MASTER DO WITH IT
ANYWAY? – IT SEEMS TO ME THAT IT COULD BECOME
A KIND OF QUALITY IN SOMEONE THAT COULD
TRANSFORM THEM. WOULD YOU PLEASE COMMENT?

Maneesha, the path of the mystic is the path of growing qualities, of transforming the quantitative into the qualitative. For
example, love can be a quantity – and as love is understood in the
world of sleeping people, it is a quantity; hence, it is followed by
jealousy.

If I love you, you are in continuous fear that I may start loving
somebody else too. And with the love divided, you will not be
getting the same quantity you were getting before. Jealousy is
nothing but an expression that love is still a quantity in your mind:
shared, it becomes less; shared with many people, you are getting
less and less. Hence a monopoly is needed, so that you can have
the whole lot of it.

And both of the lovers – because of this stupid idea – are suspicious, are always spying on each other. If your husband sees you
laughing with somebody else, even that is enough to create a
quarrel, a conflict, a fight. Your laughter is his monopoly. You cannot smile anywhere else, you cannot be joyful with somebody
else; you are confined to an imprisonment. And the same way you
are confined, you are jailed, in return you are creating a jail for
your jailer. All lovers are functioning as jailers to each other.
Hence, love promises so many roses but brings only thorns,
promises stars but brings only wounds.

The awakened person, the person who is conscious of his acts, of himself, transforms every quantity into quality. His love becomes lovingness. He is a loving person.

Now, lovingness is not a quantity, it is a quality. It is not confined to somebody, it has nothing to do with the other, it has something to do with yourself. Your heart is overflowing with a loving energy; everybody is invited ... whoever is receptive. The same is true about other ingredients of your consciousness.

Gratitude is also one of the most important things in the interior world of man. But always remember the distinction: if gratitude is a quantity, then you are going to become burdened with it because quantity is material, and matter has weight; you need to be unburdened. And when I said there is no way to show your gratitude to the master, naturally a problem arises: what you are going to do with this burden? You will be crushed under it. It may turn sour.

But gratitude can be transformed into gratefulness. Gratefulness has nothing to do with quantity; it is a quality. You are simply grateful – not only to the master, because the idea of being grateful only to the master is again a hangover of your old ideas of monopoly. The master is to free you; the master is to destroy all limits that confine you, imprison you. If you are grateful, you are grateful to the earth, you are grateful to the sky, you are grateful to the stars, you are grateful to the ocean, you are grateful to the whole of existence. This is the only way not to feel burdened.

Gratitude is transformed from matter into energy. Matter is like stone – heavy and hard. The moment it is transformed into quality, it becomes just an energy, a radiant energy. And energy can never be kept confined – its life is in the flow from one end of eternity to the other end; this whole universe is its space.

A single man can fill the whole universe with his gratefulness, with his lovingness, with his friendliness, and there will be no burden on him. In fact, the greater the transformation from quantity to quality, the lighter you will feel. A moment comes when you have transformed all that is material in you. In the immaterial you are freed of weight – then gravitation does not work on you.

Then you have wings and the whole sky is yours. And there are skies beyond skies, and they are all yours.

Love for the master, gratitude to the master should bring freedom to you. And that is possible only if you start changing nouns into verbs. Existence really consists of verbs. Nouns are fictions created by man. In existence, there is nothing which is a noun. You say this is a tree, but have you ever thought? – while you are saying this is a tree, the tree is bringing new leaves, old leaves are falling; new flowers are blossoming, old flowers are disappearing. It is not a dead thing; hence, it cannot be a noun. It is a living entity, it is changing constantly.

The word 'tree' gives a false idea, as if there is something unchanging. It will be better to call it a 'treeing' – because the tree is continuously moving. The river is 'rivering' – it is a movement, it is not stale, it is not dead. In other words, the existence does not consist of dead matter, it consists of living energy.

There is nothing permanent except change. If you can, with awareness, change your burdens into wings, your treasures into fragrances, you will be unburdened and the whole of existence will be more beautiful, will be more graceful, will be more blissful and a benediction to you. It will go on showering flowers on you. You have fulfilled your destiny – the whole existence rejoices.

There are beautiful stories.... I will call them stories because there is no way to prove that they are facts. I would love to think of them as facts. It is said that wherever Gautam Buddha moved, even if trees were out of season they suddenly became green, full of flowers, foliage. People used to know that Buddha had passed this way just by looking at the trees on the side of the road – because the whole forest would be naked, barren, no leaves, no flowers; it was not the season.

It looks like a fiction. But in a deeper sense, it is a reality. Perhaps visibly the trees had not become green with flowers and foliage, but invisibly the trees felt as if the spring had come. When a man has reached the highest peak of consciousness, it is not an individual achievement. In him, the whole universe has achieved its deepest longing. It is natural that the whole existence should rejoice and dance and sing.

Just remember: even things which are beautiful and good can become a burden, and the moment they become a burden you can even start taking revenge on the person.

Great masters have been betrayed, and they have been betrayed by their great disciples – not by their ordinary disciples, but by those who were very close to them. It is tremendously interesting to go into the psychology of it. What happened to Judas? He was very close to Jesus. He was the most intelligent of Jesus' disciples, he was the only one who was educated, and the only one with a very sharp intellect. What happened to him?

On the surface, the facts are very simple: He betrayed; he betrayed because Jesus' enemies offered him thirty pieces of silver. This is sheer nonsense. A man with the qualities of Judas cannot betray a master of the quality of Jesus just for thirty pieces of silver. There must be much more to it. Perhaps Jesus was becoming a burden.

Jesus was giving him so much love, and there was no way to return it. Jesus was giving him so much insight into existence, and there was no way to show his gratitude. Jesus was doing everything that a master should do for his spiritual growth.

But one should always remember that the person who is being benefited is also an individual. He cannot go on taking because deep down it is humiliating, it is a spiritual insult. And there is only so much one can tolerate. The same thing which was so sweet and so beautiful can turn into its very opposite, can become a poison. It was just to unburden himself that Judas betrayed Jesus.

And I say it with certain authority: When he saw what he had done to a man who has always been nothing but love, nothing but compassion, who was always ready to give everything; when he saw the crucifixion and the torture and he realized what he had done, within twenty-four hours he hanged himself from a tree and killed himself.

Christians don't talk about the suicide of Judas. But the whole secret is in the suicide of Judas – not in the crucifixion of Jesus. Judas crucifying himself – and all those thirty silver pieces, he had thrown on the ground – indicates something deeper than historical fact, something concerned more with the inner world. At a certain point, he became so burdened that he became angry at Jesus.

He was a disciple: he had loved Jesus his whole life and he was grateful to Jesus. But neither did Jesus tell him nor did he inquire how to transform love when it becomes a burden, gratefulness when it becomes a burden, how to avoid the danger of all those beautiful feelings turning into poison. But when he saw Jesus being crucified, suddenly all anger disappeared. Instead of anger there was only repentance – and not ordinary repentance; he threw down those thirty silver pieces and committed suicide. His suicide is so significant.

And the Christians' silence about his suicide is also significant: they don't want to bring it in because to bring it in they will have to go deeper than the superficial facts of history. History consists only of daily newspapers, collected, just superficial. It does not give insight. And if it was only the case with Jesus one could think that it may have been an exception. It is not so. It has been happening with almost every great master. Seeing that it happened with Mahavira, it happened with Gautam Buddha, I started thinking that there seems to be something much more than the mere fact that some important disciple betrays the master – but why?

My understanding is that it is because the science of the relationship between the master and the disciple has not yet been completely discovered. This is one of the basic contributions that I would like to make to the science: that a master has to be aware not to burden the disciple to such an extent that what was beautiful starts becoming humiliating, insulting. I am reminded....

I had a friend who was a great politician. He was the education minister, with great longings to one day go even higher, to the highest post in the country. He was also a very rich man. Once in a while, whenever I was not traveling, he would come to me to ask about peace, silence, relaxation. And I told him, "Unless you drop your ambitions, you cannot be at peace and you cannot be silent and you cannot relax – because in a competitive world where you are not the only one who is trying to become the prime minister of the country, if you are relaxing and others are not relaxing, you have lost the game. Those who are able to remain tense and go on rushing, speeding, who are almost mad, will not even stop to rest unless they have reached to the very peak." He said, "This is very difficult. I cannot drop the ambition, I have come so far – now the goal is only two steps away. Once I have reached the goal, I will renounce politics and I will sit with you and meditate, and do whatsoever you say. But before that, if I can have a little peace of mind, a little silence in the heart, a little relaxation, I can compete more efficiently." I said, "That is a contradiction.

" Again and again it was the same thing. I told him, "I will never change my position, and I think you are not going to change your position – why waste time? Don't you have any other problem?" He said, "I have so many problems. One problem particularly I came today to ask you about... " And his problem was that he was a very generous man, but very proud. He was not born into the family which he had become the head of – he was adopted. He was born a poor man, and suddenly he became one of the richest men in the country. All his relatives were poor. He made all those relatives rich – gave them factories, gave them shops, gave them as much money as possible because he had so much.

He said to me, "The problem is nobody loves me. I have been giving to everybody – my friends, my family, even strangers have come to me and I have never said no to anything. But nobody loves me. I don't see in their eyes any respect towards me and I am puzzled. I have done everything – nobody would have done what I have done.

" I said, "I want to ask you one question: Have you allowed those people to do something for you?"

He said, "I am a very proud man. I would rather die, but I will not beg. And in fact there is no need; I have everything. They cannot do anything for me, I don't need it.

" I said, "The problem is very clear: they are disrespectful, they are unloving, unfriendly, because you have burdened them; you have in a very subtle way humiliated them. You are the man who can help, who can give millions of rupees to people and who does not need anything in return.

" I said, "That is hurting their pride. I know your friends, I know the relatives you have supported and you have made rich. And I know that they are full of anger, rage and hatred for you. You have done everything good for them, but you don't understand human psychology. You do a few small things ... you need not ask them for big things, but you can ask them for something: 'I love your roses. One day can you send a few roses to me?' And all their anger will disappear. You have many cars. Those people have cars because you have given them money. There is no need for you, but once in a while you can just phone them and say, 'I need your car; can you send the car?' You have your own guest houses, you don't need any help from anybody, but once in while you can ask a friend: 'If your guest house is available, one of my friends is coming and I would like *you* to take care of him – just do this much kindness for me.'

And you can change the whole atmosphere around you; then they are equal to you. Right now you have reduced them to such a state – you are so high, so beyond their reach – they are just like insects crawling on the earth.

" He said, "I never thought about it in this way." And after ten years, he met me in a train and he told me, "You were right. I started asking for small things, which don't mean anything, and they have all changed. Now there is no anger, no hatred, no humiliation; they feel equal to me because they know they have also done something for me. It is not only me who is always doing things for them; they have also been doing things for me. It may be just bringing me a few roses from their garden."

The relationship between the master and the disciple is a very subtle one. And in the past, it has not been understood why great masters have been betrayed. If this understanding becomes part of the relationship in the future, no master will be betrayed; there will be no reason. But the master has to understand that the disciple is also a human being – and this game should not be a one-way traffic where the master goes on giving and the disciple has just to receive it. The master should be capable – whether he needs it or not; perhaps he does not need it – just to give the disciple an idea that he can do something for the master. If Judas could have done something for Jesus, there would have been no crucifixion.

So your question is significant. Transform your gratitude in gratefulness – and not towards the master only; the master is only a door. Beyond the door is the whole existence. Don't cling to the master – because the master is only the frame of the door; he allows you an opening into existence, he is not a wall. But remember that you are not to become attached to the frame; you have to go beyond the frame. There is no need to betray. Just go beyond. And let every experience in you become an expanding energy phenomenon, a resonance – not like a stone, solid and heavy, but with no weight ... just spreading all over space, with no limits.

BELOVED OSHO,
THE STRANGE THING IS THAT ALL DISCOVERIES COME
OUT OF THE BLUE; THE SCIENTIFIC EXPLANATION IS
ALWAYS MADE AFTERWARDS, AND THEN IN THE
LECTURE THE SCIENTIST USUALLY PRESENTS HIS
DISCOVERY, WHICH IS NOT HIS, AS IF IT FOLLOWED
FROM HIS THEORY – WHICH WAS INVENTED
AFTERWARDS; HENCE, THE LIE. THIS DRIVE TO FRAME
EVERYTHING, BEING TRAINED AS A SCIENTIST, IS
PRETTY STRONG IN ME. BUT STILL, THE MIRACLE CAN
NEVER BE EXPLAINED AWAY. IT HAPPENED – WHAT
MORE PROOF? HOW TO ALLOW TO BE MORE AND
MORE IN THE MIRACULOUS, TO BE IN THE MIRACLE
ALL THE TIME?

It is true that all scientific discoveries come to the scientist out of the blue. It is not his effort, but on the contrary his no-effort, allowing existence to reveal its secrets to him. This is not new. The East has known it for at least five thousand years. Lao Tzu has even given it a name: 'effortless effort', 'action without action'. And he was trying to explain that whatever man has come to know is not through effort, although there is much effort in-volved; hence there is great misunderstanding. I will give you an example that will help.

For six years Gautam Buddha continuously did everything that was supposed to make him enlightened, and he was such a sincere seeker....He lived with many masters. With ordinary people – insincere seekers, halfhearted seekers – even the bogus masters can go on pretending that they are authentic. But it was not possible with Gautam Buddha.

The masters themselves confessed to him, "Forgive me, you are such a sincere seeker. I can always say to others that, 'You are not doing it wholeheartedly,' but you are doing it so wholeheartedly that it simply proves that I don't know how one achieves enlightenment – I am not enlightened. With others it is okay, because they never do anything wholeheartedly, and I can always tell them that it is because they are not working that they are not achieving – and the question of my enlightenment does not arise, I remain enlightened. But with you it is impossible. To lie to you is inhuman. You simply go to some other master." He went to all the known famous masters, and the result was the same.

The last master said to him, "You have worked enough, you have done everything that is possible for human beings, nothing more can be done. Now you just retire into the forest. You have renounced the world, now renounce this spiritual effort. Forget all about enlightenment. And I know you are capable – if you can forget all about your kingdom, you can forget all about this enlightenment. Just relax, deep in the forest." He moved to the forest.

And the first night, relaxing under a bodhi tree near Bodhgaya by the side of a small river, Niranjana, on a full-moon night, he became enlightened. He was not doing anything for enlightenment. The enlightenment came out of the blue.

But don't think that you can go and catch the train to Bodhgaya, on a full-moon night lie down by the side of the tree near the Niranjana river and wait for enlightenment. Nothing will happen. Those six years of tremendous effort did not produce enlightenment, but those six years produced so much relaxation that enlightenment became possible.

Enlightenment is not caused by effort. By effort, relaxation is caused. You have done so much that you simply give up. But without doing it you cannot give up. So in the Buddhist religion there is a problem. There are sects who think that Buddha's enlightened happened because of six years of effort: those six years preceded, enlightenment followed. To the ordinary logic it seems so.

Only one school, Zen, has been very extraordinary in its insight. It says it was not caused by six years of effort; but six years of effort have caused relaxation – and relaxation simply opens you up to the unknown, to the unknowable. Enlightenment is not an effect of six years' effort, but without those six years' effort there would have been no enlightenment either. You have to understand the subtlety of it.

The whole day you work, and then you have a good sleep in the night. Emperors cannot sleep. And it is very illogical, because the whole day long they are resting – it is logical that the person who is practicing rest the whole day long should rest deeper in the night than you, who have been working the whole day, tiring yourself ... your practice is not for relaxation, your practice is against it.

But life is not logic, fortunately. Otherwise the person who has been working hard the whole day will have to work hard the whole night too. In his whole life he will not get any rest, because his training and his discipline will become more and more mature and more and more ripened. It is good that life has a dynamic, a dialectics. All day you have been making great effort – you have earned relaxation. You need relaxation, you have worked hard. Nature is compassionate. The emperor has been resting the whole day, he does not need any sleep at night. Nature does not care whether he is an emperor or a beggar.

The dialectics of life is that the people who make great effort for enlightenment will not achieve by their effort. One day they will have to give it all up, and in that moment of relaxation something opens up – you are not the doer, something happens to you.

And the same is true about scientific discoveries – the law is the same. A scientist works for years on a certain project, and then one day he has done everything that he could possibly think of;

he drops the whole idea. And suddenly a window opens, and what he was searching for with such great effort is made available to him without any effort at all.

In fact, there are deep reasons in it: whenever you are making effort you become tense; when you are tense, your mind becomes narrow. And you are so ambitious, so desirous, so much in a hurry to get something, that you are almost a chaos. And to know anything – either scientific or religious – you need to be a silent, peaceful awareness, not doing anything, not even desiring anything, not even looking for anything.

But all the time before, when you have been looking and not finding, has created a certain seed in you. In this relaxed moment, that seed starts becoming a sprout. It happened in Madame Curie's case – which is the most famous example. She was the first woman to achieve the Nobel prize. She had been working for three years on a particular mathematical problem. She tried from every direction, from every angle, but nothing happened – the problem seemed to be insoluble.

And one night she was working late, up to two o'clock, and finally gave up the whole thing, thinking "I have wasted three years, I could have discovered many other things. This idiotic problem is stubborn – just like me. I am stubborn too, but now I drop out of this fight." She closed the notebook in which she was working, went to sleep, and in the morning... She was alone in the room, and the room was locked from inside. And anyway, even if it was not locked, nobody could have done it ... if Madame Curie was not able to do it in three years. She went to her table and she found a piece of paper just on top of her notebook, under the paperweight, with the solution to the problem. She could not believe it.

Her husband was not at home; he had gone for a weekend with his friends. No servant would have been capable of doing it. Moreover, the room was locked from inside. Then she looked more minutely; the handwriting was her own. Then slowly she remembered that she had had a dream that she was working on the problem and she had solved it. Perhaps in sleep she got up and wrote down the answer which had come in her dream – not to forget it in the morning. This has been happening to almost all great scientists.

So you are right that the scientist has no right to say, "This is my discovery." In a way, it is not his discovery; in a way, it is existence that has chosen him to be a vehicle. Existence has not chosen anybody else to be a vehicle; he has been chosen because he has been working so hard that he had come to the point where relaxation is possible – complete and total relaxation. In that total relaxation, existence opens its secrets. Understanding this, you can see many implications: that in this way science and religion are exactly the same.

Their objects may be different – science may be looking outward, religion may be looking inward – but the discovery either of science or of religion happens in the same kind of state, the totally relaxed mind. Or to use the mystic word, a state of no-mind – because when the mind is completely relaxed there is no mind, the window opens. Mind is the block. And once the mind is no more, you start seeing things that were always there in front of you but your eyes were covered with thick layers of thought. You were not able to see. You are asking how one can live in this miraculous, in this unknowable continuously.

The moment you ask how, you are asking for a technique, and no technique is possible – all techniques are efforts. So any technique will do, just do it so wholeheartedly that you come to a point where you drop it – because the real thing is to drop it. There are one hundred and twelve methods of meditation.

But the real thing is not the meditation; the real thing is that after all those one hundred and twelve methods the same thing happens. You have done it exhaustively. You have staked everything and now – seeing that you don't have any more energy, any more desire – you relax. All efforts are dropped, all techniques forgotten. In this innocence, the miraculous is yours.

You are part of it; you have been always part of it. The unknowable is not something separate from you, it is your heartbeat. Your heartbeat has a synchronicity with the heartbeat of the whole universe.

But let me remind you again: first you have to do everything that is possible for you – not holding anything back, not thinking that anyway finally you are going to drop it so why put so much energy into it? No, you have to be madly in it, as if effort is going to give you the truth. Only then one day – tired, exhausted, finished with effort – you relax. You don't know ... that depth of relaxation will depend on the depth of your effort. If the effort was a hundred percent total, then the relaxation will be a hundred percent total; and with the total relaxation you have moved into the miraculous, into the unknowable. Then it is your world. Then you breathe in it, you live in it. This is what we have called the ultimate realization – enlightenment.

BELOVED OSHO,
WHEN I CAME TO YOU YEARS AGO, YOU TOLD ME TO
TELL YOU WHEN I FELT SOMETHING – I WASN'T SURE
WHAT – IN MY ENERGY, BECAUSE YOU HAD WORK
FOR ME TO DO. YOU SAID I WOULD KNOW IT WHEN
IT WAS RIGHT. NOW I FEEL SO FULL OF YOU. THESE
PAST MONTHS WORKING IN THE WORLD, NOTHING
HAS MEANT ANYTHING TO ME EXCEPT THE TIMES
I'VE BEEN ABLE TO TELL PEOPLE ABOUT YOU. AND IN
THOSE TIMES I WAS SO FULL AND CLEAR I DIDN'T
KNOW IT WAS ME. NOW I'M JUST HERE FOR TWO
WEEKS – BUT I FEEL LIKE THE ONLY THING I CAN DO
WITH MY LIFE IS YOUR WORK. I JUST DON'T KNOW
WHAT IT IS.
CAN YOU GIVE ME SOME IDEA BEFORE I GO?

The way things are happening to you is so beautiful and natural that it is better you should not interfere in it. If I give you any idea, you will start interfering in it. It is happening on its own. Just go with it, with the stream – never against the stream.

The watercourse way is my whole philosophy. Just go with the stream in a deep let-go, with all my blessings. I will not give you any idea. Existence will take care of it.

BELOVED OSHO,
ACCORDING TO GEORGE GURDJIEFF, NEARLY ALL
HUMAN BEINGS ARE NUMBER ONE, NUMBER TWO,
OR NUMBER THREE. VERY FEW CAN BE CALLED MAN
NUMBER FOUR, AND ONLY A GAUTAM BUDDHA,
MAN NUMBER SEVEN. I SOMEHOW HAVE THE
SUSPICION THAT YOU DON'T FIT IN THESE
CATEGORIES, BUT BECAUSE OF THE LAW OF SEVEN,
MORE THAN NUMBER SEVEN IS NOT POSSIBLE.
BELOVED OSHO, WHAT IS YOUR NUMBER?

My number is zero. So whenever you want to channel with me, remember zero!

BELOVED OSHO,
I HAVE HEARD MEDITATION SOMETIMES DESCRIBED
AS A SCIENCE, AND OTHER TIMES AS AN ART; ON
OCCASION YOU HAVE EVEN CALLED IT A KNACK.
PLEASE EXPLAIN.

Meditation is such a mystery that it can be called a science, an art, a knack, without any contradiction. From one point of view it is a science because there is a clear-cut technique that has to be done. There are no exceptions to it, it is almost like a scientific law. But from a different point of view it can also be said to be an art.

Science is an extension of the mind – it is mathematics, it is logic, it is rational. Meditation belongs to the heart, not to the mind – it is not logic; it is closer to love. It is not like other scientific activities, but more like music, poetry, painting, dancing; hence, it can be called an art.

But meditation is such a great mystery that calling it 'science' and 'art' does not exhaust it. It is a knack – either you get it or you don't get it. A knack is not a science, it cannot be taught. A knack is not an art. A knack is the most mysterious thing in human understanding.

For example, you may have come across people.... Somebody

has the knack of becoming a friend immediately; just meeting him in the bus for a few moments and you suddenly feel as if you have known each other forever, perhaps for many lives. And you cannot pinpoint what is going on, because you have just seen the man for the first time.

I have a friend. He is a doctor in philosophy. He has never earned a single cent in his life, but he lives like a king. He has a certain knack that anybody becomes his friend; he just has to look at you and you are his friend – and you feel as if you have been his friend forever. He has lived on borrowed money – which he never returns because he cannot, there is no way to return it, but nobody feels hurt about it. Even though he has borrowed money from you and he has never returned it, he has the nerve to ask you again – and you will give it! The man is so lovely, so beautiful, that to ask money from him simply doesn't seem right. And he never feels embarrassed, he never avoids people he owes money to.

I have asked him many times, "How long will you continue in this way?"

He said, "How long? The population goes on growing – even if I live a million years, I will always have people to give me money."

And the beauty is that you give him money and you feel honored that he asked you, not anybody else. Now what will you call it? – art? science? It is simply a knack.

He travels without a ticket, he has never purchased a ticket. I have been traveling with him many times. And he will say, "Why are you wasting money on tickets? Let the ticket checker come; after all, he is a human being." And once the ticket checker comes, he is caught into this man's net. He offers him a cigarette, and they are chit-chatting, and they start playing cards, and the ticket checker completely forgets why he has come. And now it is too late to ask for the ticket – they have become so friendly to each other that the ticket checker asks him, "Can I help you in any way?"

He says, "You have to – because I have lost my ticket!"

He said, "Don't be worried. I will be there at the gate."

He lives in friends' houses. He has no house of his own. He moves from one city to another city, but he knows all kinds of tricks with playing cards, chess, tennis, all kinds of nonsense things in which people are interested. And he is a genius. In chess you cannot win against him, in cards you cannot win. And he is such a happy person that people like for him to come to them even if he is going to take their money, even if he is going to take their car and never return – still people like him, because he is simply likable. It is not on any conditions that he is liked, it is just his whole personality.

Once he was staying with me. And just next door used to live another professor who was Indian, married to an American woman. The American woman was also a professor at the university. I spent the day at the university, so he started making friendships in the neighborhood. The American woman got into his net, and her husband also became very friendly.

Things came to such point that the professor's wife wanted to leave with my friend. But he said, "It will be very difficult. I have no house, no shelter anywhere. I don't know where I will be tomorrow morning. You will be in difficulty with me, and I love you so much that I will not create such a difficulty for you. And I love your husband too; I cannot disturb his life."

But the professor was so enchanted by him that he said, "If you want, you can take my wife."

I told him, "Don't be stupid. You can take cars, that is okay; you can take people's tape recorders, that is okay; you can take their cameras, that is okay. But if you start taking people's wives, you will be in great trouble. So make it a point this is the limit. Don't go beyond this limit."

He said, "You are right. Rationally I also think that this is right. But isn't it worth trying once? When the husband is ready...."

I said, "Any husband will be ready! You are an idiot. It is not because of your charm, every husband will be ready. How many wives can you manage? You don't have any money. And remember, you cannot bring any woman into my house."

He said, "That's not right, because that's what I was thinking – I will leave this woman here. Another woman ... I will get caught and I will leave her here. You can have disciples!"

I said, "I – these kinds of disciples are of no use to me."

A knack is something mysterious, just a few people can do it.

I know a man who can make his ear lobes move. I have not found another who can move his ear lobes. Now what do you call it? – science or what? Because I have asked doctors, "What do you say about ear lobes?" They say, "It is impossible."

But I brought my friend to one doctor and, I told him, "Show this doctor...."

And the doctor said, "My God! He moves his ear lobes very easily, without any trouble."

In fact, ear lobes have no biological possibility of movement, you have no control over them – you try. You don't have any control. They are your ear lobes, but you don't have any control. But I know one man who manages. And I have asked him, "How do you manage?" He said, "I don't know. Just from the very beginning I have been doing it."

It is absolutely impossible, physically impossible – because to move those lobes you need a certain nervous system to control them, and the nerve system is not there. The lobe is just flesh. Meditation, in the last resort, is a knack too. That's why for thousands of years people have been meditating, teaching, but very few people have achieved heights in meditation, and very few people have even tried. And the vast majority of humanity has not even bothered to think about it. It is something ... a seed you are born with.

If you don't have the seed, a master can go on showering all his bliss on you, still nothing will happen in you. And if the seed is there, just the presence of the master, just the way he looks into your eyes, and something of tremendous importance happens in you – a revolution that you cannot explain to anybody.

It is one of the difficulties for all meditators that they cannot explain to their friends, their families, what they are doing. Because the majority of humanity is not interested in it at all. And those who are not interested in it at all simply think about people who are interested, that something is loose in their heads, something is wrong.

Sitting silently, doing nothing, the spring comes and the grass grows by itself – but in the first place, why should you bother about the grass? Basho's beautiful haiku will look absurd to them. Grass is going to grow by itself whether you sit silently or not, why waste your time? – grass is going to grow by itself. Let the spring come – spring comes by itself, grass grows by itself. Why are you wasting your time? – do something else meanwhile.

If a man has not something in his heart already – a small seed – then it is impossible for him. He can learn the technique, he can learn the art. But if the knack is missing he is not going to succeed. So thousands of people start meditation, but very few – so few that they can be counted on ten fingers – ever achieve to enlightenment. And unless meditation becomes enlightenment, you have simply wasted your time.

5

Laughter – As sacred as prayer

BELOVED OSHO,
I AM VERY ANGRY WITH WOMEN. I DON'T LIKE
WOMAN. WHY IS WOMAN SELFISH? WHY HAS
WOMAN NO INTELLIGENCE? WHY IS A WOMAN LIKE
A CAT? OSHO, WHY DO YOU PUT WOMAN ON THE
WAY OF TAO?

Woman is what man has made of her. It is a vicious circle. Man has deprived woman of education and other social institutions, of economic freedom. And then you ask why women are unintelligent? *You* are the cause. Women have as much intelligence as any man – because intelligence has no concern with sexual hormones. Do you think if you changed Albert Einstein into a woman with plastic surgery, he would lose his intelligence? He would still remain Albert Einstein, but in a woman's body. The difference is only of bodies; the difference is not of consciousness, not of intelligence. But unfortunately man decided to repress woman.

For centuries it has not been clear to historians why it had to happen in such a way. But the latest psychological research makes it very clear why it happened: it happened because man feels a deep inferiority complex in comparison to woman. And the basic root of that feeling comes from the woman's capacity to become a mother. She is the source of life, she creates life. Man is incapable of it. This became the reason to cut the wings of all women – of freedom, of education – and confine her to a prison-like home and reduce her to just a factory of reproduction so that he can forget that he is inferior.

The woman had to be made inferior so that man could feel at ease, so that his ego could feel that now there is no competition with women at all. The woman is not the cause of all her bitchiness. You have been torturing her for thousands of years. No society in the world has accepted her as equal to man. No culture of the past has given the woman the same respect as it gives to the man. On the contrary, they have all tried to force her into a subhuman existence. And the reason why the woman did not revolt against such things is simple: again, the same motherhood. For nine months when she is pregnant, she becomes absolutely dependent – particularly in a society which lived by hunting.

And by the way, I would like you to remember that the society in which you are living now – where houses exist, cities exist – is a contribution of women, not of men. The house is the woman's contribution. Man was hunting. The woman was confined to a small space; naturally she started decorating it, cleaning it, making it beautiful, liveable – and she became attached. In a hunting society, the nomads had to go on changing... because when hunting was not giving them enough food, they had to move to where the animals were. They could not have permanent cities; they could have only tents, not houses.

And you can see it: when a man lives alone, his house is almost like a tent, it is not like a house. Without a woman, it remains a tent, a temporary place – just a shelter with nothing sacred about it. As the woman enters, the tent starts transforming into a house and finally into a home.

In hunting societies, the woman's function was nothing but reproduction. She was continuously pregnant. This became her failure: she could not fight, she could not rebel, she had to submit, she had to surrender – of course unwillingly. Nobody becomes a slave willingly. When somebody becomes a slave willingly, there is no problem. But millions of women have been forced to become slaves unwillingly. Naturally they try to take revenge in indirect ways. All those ways combined make them cats, their behavior becomes bitchy.

But remember: a woman can be bitchy only with a dog, and a woman can be a cat only with a mouse – and that's why you are angry. Seeing a woman, you are reminded that you are a dog, you are a mouse. Your male chauvinist attitude hurts. It is simply an unconscious reaction, and you have to be watchful of the reaction so that it can disappear. It is undignified of you. It shows something about you – not about the woman. It is your anger, it is your hate. If you will look at the history....

In many villages, the women cannot enter the temples. In some religions she can enter, but she has a separate section – not the same as the men. In all religions, the woman is not accepted as a candidate for the ultimate growth of consciousness. She is unworthy, not for any other reason – just because she is a woman; her crime is that she is a woman. And she can evolve but she will have to fulfill a condition: first she will have to be born as a man.

So in religions like Jainism, there are methods, rituals, religious disciplines for women, specifically intended for them to enter a man's body in their next life.

Now the whole Jaina attitude and philosophy can be disturbed because with plastic surgery a woman can become a man with no difficulty. There is no need for all those disciplines and rituals and arduous hostilities. Just a very small amount of plastic surgery and you are capable of entering the ultimate state of consciousness. Strange, that plastic surgery is needed for spiritual growth! But this has been one way to condemn the woman.

Another reason why man has condemned the woman is the power of the woman over the man. You can never forgive someone who has so much power over you. The woman is beautiful, attractive... her beauty, her body, her attraction and you become just a beggar – and you are going to take revenge for that too. But everything is going on in an unconscious state. You are not aware of what you are doing and why.

Man is almost magnetically pulled by the woman. He can see that he is just a puppet. How can he forgive the woman who has forced him to be just a puppet? – whatever he can do, he tries to do.

Women everywhere are not allowed to read the holy scriptures. In many countries the woman is not even allowed to show her face in the society. It used to be so in India; it is still so in all the Mohammedan countries. I have heard, when Mulla Nasruddin got married according to the tradition, his wife asked him, "To whom am I allowed to show my face?"

Mulla Nasruddin said, "First let *me* have a look, only then can I say anything." So he looked at her face, closed his eyes and said, "Enough! Except for me, you are allowed to show your face to everybody."

These are subtle ways of humiliation, of cutting women off from the world of power, from the world where everything is happening. The woman is not part of it. She is not part of your wars, she is not part of your businesses, she is not part of your religions. And there are countries like China – not a small country....

A woman was reading in the newspaper that of every four men, one is Chinese. She came very much worried and concerned. She said to her husband, "This paper says that every fourth person is Chinese. Now you have to be careful; we already have three boys, and I don't want any Chinese in this house."

In this vast one-fourth of humanity, for ten thousand years it was believed that the woman had no soul, she was as soulless as your furniture. Hence, if a husband killed his wife, there was no crime, he had simply destroyed his property. It was nobody else's concern to come into it. Thousands of women were killed by their husbands, but the court, the law, did not accept it as killing, because how can you kill somebody who has no soul?

In India millions of women have been burned alive simply because of the male ego: "My wife is beautiful, young. If I am dead, she may get married again." This jealousy was the reason for deciding that every woman should jump into the burning funeral pyre with her husband. The husband is dead; the living woman has to jump into the fire. And we have practiced this for ten thousand years. It still happens once in a while, although now there is a law against it.

One feels as if we don't give any attention to our social mores, our behavior mores. In the whole of Indian literature I have not come across a single statement saying that if women are required to die with their husbands to show their faith, their love, then why are men not required to do the same? What kind of game is this in which the rule applies only to the woman, not the man? The society is made by men. Women are living in a society which is not made for them, not made by them; it has not considered them at all.

Your anger towards women is worth understanding. Perhaps it is really your anger against yourself, your anger against men – what men have done to women. Women have been victims. You cannot be angry at them. In the home, the husband is the victim; and it can be said without any doubt that every husband is henpecked. In fact, every intelligent husband has to be – only some idiot may not be. But this is the price that every man has to pay for what mankind has been doing to womankind for thousands of years.

If you want to get free from your anger against women, you will have to go through a very deep inner spring cleaning and see that the woman is the victim. And because she is the victim and has no positive way to resist, to fight, she finds indirect ways: of nagging, of screaming, of throwing tantrums. These are simply hopeless efforts. And naturally her rage against the whole of humanity becomes focused on one man, the husband.

The freedom of women is going to be the freedom of men too. The day the woman is accepted as equal, given equal opportunity to grow, man will find himself suddenly free from the bitchiness that he used to feel from the women. And he will be surprised that neither is she a cat nor is he a dog – both are human beings. It is time.

Man has come to a certain maturity. We can create a world together, with men and women sharing their insight, their visions, their dreams. Because they are different, their dreams are different, their contributions to the society will be different. And if a society can be created in which men and women have participated equally, that will be for the first time the richest society in the world – and without all this bitchiness and nagging and fighting.

This is a strange and stupid way of living. But just because your father used to live this way it is accepted almost as if it is something religious. Your forefathers did it, you have to do it, your children will learn it from you. Every generation goes on giving its diseases to the coming generation.

My people have to be aware and alert not to pass on any sickness which they may have received from the past generation. Let this be the dead end. Don't pass it to the new generation. Let the new people grow – the new earth, the new man. The old has failed so badly that there is no point in renovating it. It is all ruins. It simply needs to be written in the history books, pieces of it preserved in the museums – but from life it has to disappear.

BELOVED OSHO,
I, LIKE MANY OF YOUR DISCIPLES, TRIED MANY WAYS
TO CHANGE MYSELF, TO GIVE TO OTHERS AND SERVE
THE PLANET. I WAS A MISSIONARY IN AFRICA, A
PSYCHOTHERAPIST IN BEVERLY HILLS, MARCHED
AGAINST VIETNAM, DID GROUPS AND YOGA, JOINED
VARIOUS SAVE-THE-WORLD EFFORTS, AND IT WAS ALL
LIKE PISSING IN THE OCEAN. I HAD A GOOD TIME,
BUT IT WAS FAIRLY INSIGNIFICANT COMPARED TO
THE RAPIDLY ACCELERATING DANGERS OF NUCLEAR
WEAPONS, OVER-POPULATION AND WARRING
NATIONS. ONE DAY IT OCCURRED TO ME THAT YOU
WERE THE ONLY ONE WHO WAS OUTRAGEOUS AND
RADICAL ENOUGH TO PERHAPS MAKE A DIFFERENCE.
I HITCHED MY WAGON TO A STAR – YOU – AND THAT
WAS THE SMARTEST AND MOST LOVING THING I
EVER DID. BUT OSHO, AM I – ARE WE – SO MUCH
MORE BRILLIANT THAN OTHER PEOPLE? WHY ARE
PEOPLE SO THREATENED BY WHAT I SEE IS YOUR LOVE
AND COMPASSION? WHY ARE PEOPLE WILLING TO
REMAIN DINOSAURS, RISK EXTINCTION, PREFER
DYING AND DESTROYING EACH OTHER? WHY DO
THEY CLING TO OUTDATED NATIONS, RELIGIONS
AND ARMIES EVEN THOUGH IT'S OBVIOUSLY NOT
WORKING? IF RONALD REAGAN HAD REALLY PAID
ATTENTION AND REALLY CARED ABOUT PEACE, HE
WOULD HAVE INVITED YOU TO BE HIS SPECIAL
ADVISOR – NOT CONSPIRED TO HAVE YOU OUSTED
FROM AMERICA. WHY ARE MOST PEOPLE AFRAID TO
DROP THE PAST AND COME TO SOMETHING OR
SOMEONE WHO COULD HELP PEEL AWAY
CONDITIONING, SO THAT UNLEASHED ENERGY CAN
REALLY CHANGE US AND THE WORLD? AND WHY
DON'T MORE PEOPLE WHO SPOUT, "ONE PLANET, ONE
PEOPLE!" DROP THEIR INEFFECTUAL EFFORTS AND
ALIGN WITH YOU. IN MY OPINION, IF WE WERE TO
RALLY AROUND SOMETHING THAT COULD MAKE A

DIFFERENCE, IT WOULD NOT BE AN IDEA, BUT YOU,
WHO HAS THE VASTNESS TO CREATE REAL
TRANSFORMATION. IS THIS RIGHT? AND ARE YOU
ALSO WORKING THROUGH US, YOUR DISCIPLES?

Kahlil Gibran has a small story. One full moon night, a few people came to his small pub and drank and drank. He was very happy, earning great. And when they were leaving, he asked the man who was paying: "Will you be coming again? We will do everything better."

The man said, "We are happy as things are, you have done them as beautifully as possible. Just pray for my business to run well and we will be coming every night."

He said, "There is no problem in it. I will pray for you every morning, every evening, every night. But just out of curiosity, I want to ask, what is your business?"

He said, "It is better if you don't ask. But I can understand, it will be difficult for you to resist the temptation. My business is to sell wood for funeral pyres. So when more people die, my business goes well; when less people die, of course it is unfortunate and I have to suffer it. So if you want your business to go well, you have to pray for my business to go well – our interests are the same."

In this whole society, as an intelligent and alert person, you are bound to be surprised: Why do things go on happening the way they should not? Wars are not needed, riots are not needed, bloodshed is not needed, nuclear weapons are not needed. Half of the earth is dying from starvation and you are preparing more destructive weapons. It is simply insane. But the trouble is that all these insane people have the same interest. The presidents and the prime ministers of all the nations, all the countries have the same interest. If nations disappear, they will disappear – what about their power trip?

The head priests of all religions are worried that if all religions disappear and there is only a religiousness, priests will not be needed, churches will not be needed. They have the same interest, that this society should remain as it is – miserable, in anxiety, in continuous fear, in deep anguish... a meaningless existence, carrying one's own dead bodies on one's shoulders from cradle to grave. And it is all desert – flowers appear only in dreams; in reality it is burning sun and hot sand, nothing green grows.

If we see this, why don't we change? Why do we go on and on in the same rut for thousands of years? The same misery, the same anguish, the same war – nothing seems to change. It seems as if we are caught in a wheel and the wheel goes on moving, fast – again and again the same thing. Yes, history repeats. And that it repeats in such detail is possible only because man functions like a machine.

These people are not going to support any change because every change means a disappearance of the old structure in which they are important.

With a silent, sincere, loving, compassionate, human being appearing on the world stage – with joy, these few moments of being alive.... And you cannot purchase life; the gift is invaluable.

Alexander the Great threatened one Hindu sannyasin, "My master, Aristotle, wants to see a sannyasin. If you don't come with me to Athens I will kill you."

The sannyasin said, "There is no problem in it. You simply cut off my head. You will see it falling on the ground and I will see it falling on the ground, because I am not the body. And I am no longer interested in carrying this body to my grave. If you are ready to do it, I would be thankful to you."

"In fact," the sannyasin said, "if you understand, you should not only cut off my head, you should cut yours too – because it is just a meaningless existence. As far as I am concerned, it is meaningless because I have achieved that which is significant, which is a higher quality than meaning. I have known, seen, felt. I have been in that wonderland, nothing more can be added to it. So going on living in the body is meaningless for me. It is also meaningless to you, but for different reasons: to you it is meaningless because you have not found anything, and time is running out of your hands."

And just after thirteen days, Alexander died – and he was only thirty-three years of age. And that old saint who had offered his head with such grace, with such joy... with so much fearlessness that Alexander for the first time felt it would be difficult to cut off the head of this man. He had cut off millions of heads and had never bothered about it, but with this man he hesitated, he pushed his sword back into the sheath. And in thirteen days, he was dead. He wanted, after conquering the world, to rest, relax, and to know what this life is all about. But the condition that he had put on it was very idiotic – "after conquering the world."

We have a small time. The world is big, and its problems are such that all the powerful people would not like any kind of change. That's the reason why they are annoyed with me – not that I am wrong and they are right. They know perfectly well they are wrong.

Because my whole life I have been challenging them on every single point of significance. No answer – because they don't have the answer. But your misery and their power are interdependent.

If you want to get out of the misery, you will have to drop these vested interests and the people who are powerful because of them. And certainly because they have power, they will do everything to prevent any revolution from happening. And if it happens, then too they will try in every possible way to sabotage it. Up to now they have been successful. Either they don't let it happen, or if it happens in spite of them, they sabotage it so beautifully and they are again in power – only the names change.

In Russia, those people who were in power before the revolution were the capitalists – just a word. There are still people in power – more in power than the previous ones. They are not called capitalists, they are called communists. They are more dangerous, they have more power and they are more aware how revolutions can throw out people who are in power – because they have come by throwing out the powerful people. So they are protecting their power number with every scientific, psychological, para-psychological device.

Russia is certainly in a strange position in this. It is the only country where revolution cannot happen. All the possibilities of revolution have been destroyed by the revolutionaries who have come into power. They know perfectly well how they have come into power. So they have broken all the bridges, all the ladders have been burned. In Russia, the powerful group and the masses are absolutely without any bridge between them.

It is true that every sannyasin of mine is working in different ways – not as a missionary but as a living mission, not trying to convert people by teaching them but challenging people for transformation by presenting their own life, by presenting their own joy, their love, their song, their dance.

This is no ordinary conversion – like a Hindu becoming a Christian. It is true conversion: a fast asleep person becomes fully awake, and goes from darkness to light, from untruth to truth, from death to immortality.

But I don't want you to deliberately become my missions. I want you to be absolutely selfish so that you can blossom in your full glory. Your blossoming will trigger blossomings in others; your flame will bring light, life and fire to many. But this has not to be done directly, it is not your business. It is simply the impact of your transformed life.

BELOVED OSHO,
IN THE WEST, THE PORTRAYAL OF WOMAN'S BODY IS
USED IN FILMS, BOOKS AND MAGAZINES. THIS ART
FORM IS KNOWN AS 'EROTICISM'. THROUGH THE
SCULPTURES OF KHAJURAHO AND AJANTA I HAVE
SEEN THAT A SIMILAR ART FORM WAS THERE IN THE
EAST. CAN YOU TALK ABOUT THE DIFFERENCE
BETWEEN THESE TWO CULTURES IN REGARD TO THE
FEMALE BODY?

Sarjano, superficially there is no difference. Khajuraho, Konarak, Puri, Ajanta, Ellora, Elephanta – they are full of erotic art, just like the contemporary erotic culture where the repressed sexuality of thousands of years has become such a burden that it has to be dropped. And suddenly a great erotic revolution is taking place.

Pornography is nothing but erotic and obscene – in paintings, in films, in dances. They don't create in you a longing for the beyond; they simply create in you more sensuality, more sexuality. But on the surface they look alike. And in India and in the outside world, they are being misunderstood.

After the country became independent, Mahatma Gandhi proposed that all these sculptures, all these temples should be sunk into mud. They would not be destroyed, so if Ronald Reagan comes to see, then you can clean it and show him – just for special people.... But for ordinary people they would be closed. Because Mahatma Gandhi thought, in the same way as it is thought all over the world, that they are erotic, they are obscene.

But I want to declare emphatically that there is a vast difference between the Eastern art in Ajanta, Ellora, Puri, Konarak, Khajuraho, and the modern Western erotic, pornographic photography, painting, music. The difference is that all these temples....

For example, there are thirty temples in Khajuraho. There were one hundred temples originally – Mohammedans have destroyed seventy temples, which are now ruins. The city was a city only of temples; people just used to come to see the art. One hundred temples must have been built in thousands of years by thousands of artists continuously working on stone – generation after generation may have died working on it. And they have created the most beautiful bodies in stone. In Khajuraho stone speaks, sings, dances; it is not dead. You can see that the artist has succeeded in transforming the dead stone into a living form. It looks so alive that any moment the statue may walk towards you and say, "Hello." And hundreds of statues....

These statues were not to satisfy your repressed sexuality. On the contrary, they were used as a tantrika method to release the repressed sexuality just by meditating on these naked statues. The method was simply to sit there in silence – only a dim light reaches there, and hundreds of statues surround you. Just watching them, you will be surprised to find that many of those dreams have occurred to you, many are such that they have been condemned in every society – sexual orgies, but they have happened in your dreams; they are part of your unconscious. And these places like Khajuraho were kinds of universities where people were coming to release, to cathart repressed sexuality.

And all these statutes are outside the temple. Inside the temple there is no erotic sculpture. In fact, inside most of the temples there is nothing – just silence, a cool peaceful milieu, with the vibes of thousands of years of people meditating there. The rule was when you feel, or your master feels, that now the erotic sculpture outside the temple no longer affects you, it does not create any sexuality in you, any sensuality in you, that it has cleaned your whole repressed sex....

It is the greatest psychological method invented by the East. Nobody is told what is happening, and for years there is no need. Once the master sees, and once you see that you are sitting there and nothing happens, it is as if the walls are empty – when you are absolutely certain that they don't affect you – that is a signal: "Now it is time, you can go inside. Now the door for the inner, for the interior is open." All that was rubbish has been dropped – a cleanliness, a weightlessness, and a silence which is full of beauty and song....

Khajuraho or Konarak... these are not pornographic. They are devices for meditation.

What is happening in the West is simply pornography, obscene. It does not help man to get rid of it, but simply gives him a temporary relief. The pornographic literature, photography, are all helping you to stay normal; otherwise, you will go mad. So I don't think there is any harm when somebody reads *Playboy* hiding it inside the Bible. What he is seeing in a pornographic magazine brings up his own unconscious.

This was used as a meditation technique in Khajuraho. In the West it is used to create more thirst for the same sexuality which has been aroused by the pornographic magazine, by blue films, by naked dances and striptease.

The same method was used to transform your energy into spirituality. In the West it is used to provoke more sexuality, more sensuality. And then there is a kind of insatiability – almost all painting has gone pornographic, all the movies repeating almost the same stories, the same plot, the same triangle: two women, one man; or two men, one woman, a simple structure – the same story. What attracts people to it? It is not great appreciation for literature!

What attracts is that in the story – needed for the story or not needed – they go on putting your suppressed needs, desires. It is a kind of relief. But tomorrow you will be repressing again, and again you will need the same kind of photography, the same dance. This way you will never be able to enter into the temple. In fact, pornography in the West has no idea that it is the outer wall of the temple.

The East has used every fragment of human nature for a greater change, a mutation, to bring something higher in you of which you are capable but unconscious.

BELOVED OSHO,
ONE SIDE OF ME IS RECEPTIVE AND VULNERABLE. THE
OTHER SIDE IS STRONG AND POWERFUL. WHEN I
LEAVE MY ROOM, I PUT OUT MY STRONG AND
POWERFUL SIDE TO PROTECT MYSELF. BUT MY
RECEPTIVE SIDE LIKES TO DANCE AND ENJOY
EXISTENCE. I'M IN A MESS. PLEASE COMMENT.

There is no problem. Everybody has these two sides; that is the man and the woman syndrome – half of you is man, and the other half is woman. And it has to be that way because one half has come from your father and the other half has come from your mother. So you are the contribution of two different kinds of persons, two different psychologies. Naturally they create two sides in you: the vulnerable, loving, trusting – that is your woman. And the strong, competitive, efficient – that is your man.

And naturally when you go out of your home, you have to change your personality. You have to hide your vulnerable part, and you have to put on a harder, steel mask. You are going into a world of competition.

It becomes a problem when you start thinking that this dialectics should not be in you; that is the time when it becomes a problem. If you understand that this dialectics is very necessary... they are complementaries. They are both needed, just like day and night, life and death – they are both needed. So one need not be worried that there are two sides. They are your two doors, and you have to start witnessing yourself as the third. You are not this, you are not that – because you can change them, they are clothes. You put on the clothes of a woman, you put on the clothes of a warrior – they are clothes. Certainly they are not you.

Those two parts in you are really two parts of your mind, two hemispheres of your mind, and they are as absolutely necessary as two wings or two hands. The bird cannot rise into the sky with one wing. Those two wings are absolutely necessary; they are not against each other. Even though their movements are against each other, they are supporting each other, they are helping each other. And more fundamentally, they are helping the bird, which is the third.

It is perfectly good: outside be a Don Quixote, always keep a sword. Even if it is a false sword, no harm, because a real one could be dangerous – how to hold it? – and you may harm yourself. Have a big mustache and find some good German glue to make the mustache stand out like Ranak Pratap's. But when you come back home, put this whole makeup aside – with care, because tomorrow you will need it again. And this has to be done without any seriousness. It is simply the ordinary business of life – different things are needed at different places.

There is a story that in Rajasthan... Rajasthan is the province of the warriors. The *Rana* of the town, the head of the town, the chief of the warriors... there was something crazy about him: he would not allow anybody to have his mustache grow upwards, it should grow downwards – that was the rule.

He was a very dangerous man. He would cut your head off immediately if you didn't appear with your mustache growing downwards.

So the whole town by and by had started growing their mustaches downwards, because it was dangerous – you might forget and come across that man and your life would be at risk, because he was just crazy, he simply cut people's heads. Only *his* mustache could be turned upwards – of course he was the chief.

A young businessman came to settle in the town. He also had a big mustache turning upwards. People said, "You are settling in this town? Then remember, either cut your mustache or turn it downwards; otherwise, you will soon be in unnecessary danger."

The young man said, "Don't be worried. I will see about that...."

And the next day he went with his mustache turned up to see the warrior. But as he was coming out of his house, the warrior was there. Somebody had told him that one person in the city had his mustache turned upwards. So he came to see who the man was: "Finish him, because there is no need to make unnecessary long stories when a shortcut is possible." Seeing him, he immediately took out his sword.

The young man said, "Wait! I cannot turn down my mustache. And it is not easy to cut off my head because I challenge you to a fight. But before that, I would like you to go and tell your friends – meet with your friends, your family, your children – because although I do the work of a businessman, I am up to now an unconquered warrior. Bring your sword and I will be waiting for you here.

"And while you are gone, I will go and cut off my wife's head and my children's heads, because after I am gone who will take care of them? – unnecessary trouble. After you are gone, who will take care of your children? – unnecessary trouble. Finish them! So we go from the world without any burden."

The warrior said, "It sounds logical." He went back, he finished off his wife, his children.

Everybody said, "What are you doing? Have you gone really mad? Just about the mustache was okay, we have accepted it – it is not much, just eccentric. But you have killed your wife, your children – what are you doing?"

He said, "Not only have I killed mine, another man has also killed his. It is a question of prestige; in this town only one man can live with his mustache turned upwards, not everybody. So this was the condition: that I can meet with my people, he can meet with his people, and he will be coming and I am going. We will face each other on the crossroad. The rumor is that he is a great warrior, but that is not a problem – being a warrior is in our *blood*."

He arrived at the crossroads and could not believe what he saw: the young man had turned his mustache downwards, just glued it down. You just need good glue – don't use Indian glue; otherwise, somebody may cut off your head unnecessarily. The warrior said, "What have you done?"

The young man said, "I just thought... why kill your wife, your children? Those poor people have not done anything to me, and I should become a cause of their death? Of course *my* wife and children are mine, I can kill them, but not *yours*. So I thought, just because of the mustache...? And it is not a big job; in two minutes I just turned it downwards."

The warrior said, "This is dangerous! What did you do with your wife, your children?"

The young man said, "There was no need to do anything, because when I'd turned my mustache down, why should I cut off my wife and children's heads?"

The warrior said, "You are dangerous. I have finished off my whole family!"

There are these people with different names, in different cultures, whose function is to fight and to destroy. And naturally when you come out of your house, you are coming into a battlefield, where everybody is competing with others – a thousand and one types of fight are going on which you cannot see. They are all invisibly joined in fighting each other; over small things these fights are going on.

One couple were just signing in the registrar's office – they were getting married. And as the man signed, the woman said to the registrar, "I want a divorce immediately, right now!"

He said, "Are you mad? You are just signing for marriage, and immediately you want a divorce?"

She said, "Seeing my signature, he has signed *his* signature three times – in big letters. It is better to have this fight here and now and say good-bye to this fellow. Everything three times for our whole life?"

Over small things, people are continuously fighting. Naturally you come with no love, no trust, a defense, hardness, doubt, suspicion, skepticism, taking everybody as your competitor, everybody as your enemy. But it is the game. Don't become too much attached to this part of the play. When you go home, just put it aside completely and be the other part which has been denied.

And once you start moving from one part to another easily, the more and more clearly it starts coming to you that you are separate, you are just a witness, a watcher; this is your mind, but this is not your being. The one who is aware of this whole game is the being. And to realize the being is to realize all that is worth realizing.

BELOVED OSHO,
IN A WORLD RIDDEN WITH HATE AND HOSTILITY,
SADNESS AND SORROW, YOU SEEM TO BE THE
LONELY BARD OF LOVE AND LAUGHTER. IS THIS NOT
HILARIOUS?

It is. Maitreya, it is hilarious but somebody has to begin it. We want the world to be less serious and more sensitive. Sincere of course, but serious never. We want the world to learn that the sense of humor is one of the most fundamental qualities of a religious man. If you cannot laugh, you will miss many things in life, you will miss many mysteries.

Your laughter makes you a small innocent child, your laughter joins you with existence – with the roaring ocean, with the stars and their silence.

Your laughter makes you the lonely part of the world which has become intelligent, because only intelligent people can laugh. That's why animals cannot afford to laugh – they don't have that much intelligence. You can try – you can tell a joke to your buffalo and see what happens.

And because seriousness has always been taught to be almost necessary for respectability, it has made everybody serious. It is not that they are serious for any reason, but it has now become their second nature; they have forgotten completely that seriousness is a sickness, it means the sense of humor is dead in you. Otherwise the whole of life all around is so full of hilarious things. If you have a sense of humor, you will be surprised that there is no time to be sad – every moment something or other is happening everywhere.

My mission certainly is to bring laughter to the whole of humanity – which has forgotten it. And when you forget laughter, you always forget songs, you forget love, you forget dance – it is not that you only forget laughter. Laughter has its own combination of qualities, just as seriousness has its own combination of qualities. Forget laughter and you will forget love. With a sad face, how to say to a woman "I love you"? You will have to smile a little bit. With a serious face you cannot say even the smallest thing. People are taking everything so seriously that it becomes a burden on them. Learn to laugh more. To me, laughter is as sacred as prayer.

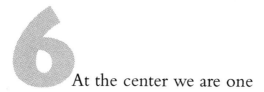 At the center we are one

BELOVED OSHO,

I LEFT MY MOTHER TWENTY YEARS, AND MY WIFE
OVER FOUR YEARS AGO. WHY CAN'T I LET THEM GO?

One of the mysteries of life is the law of reverse returns. There
are things which you cannot do. Although people have done
them, although it is possible they may happen to you too, they are
always *happenings*, they are never *doings*.

In fact the doer, the ego, is the barrier to the happening. Happening needs the innocent mind of a child who can still dream of
fairies, who can still find treasures in colored stones, whose eyes
are still not covered with the dust that we call knowledge. His
ignorance is far more beautiful than the knowledge of a great
scholar. Because ignorance is at least natural. At least it is yours; it
does not make you a hypocrite, it is never insincere.

I have been wondering and looking in thousands of scriptures
and commentaries on scriptures but I have not found a single
statement in five thousand years' literature which shows some
understanding about ignorance. In fact, they are all interested in
knowledgeability; ignorance they want to destroy. They want to
gain knowledge because knowledge will give them power –
knowledge is power. Knowledge will give you prestige, money,
respectability. Knowledge will fulfill many of your ambitions and
desires.

Ignorance cannot do anything for you, but it can allow something which is far more precious than knowledge can ever give to
you. But its whole secret is in allowing, in patiently waiting – with
a question mark in the heart, with a quest all over your being, a
quest which is not partial, a total inquiry.

Ignorance is the beginning of wisdom. Rightly understood, it
is not something negative. It is simply a tabula rasa – a clean slate.
Nothing is written on it. You have to write your own holy Bible,
holy Koran, holy Gita; you have to give birth. Ignorance is a
womb. It contains the quest for truth – and if you don't fall victim
to knowledgeability, ignorance is the right beginning. To know
absolutely that "I do not know," is the first step of wisdom. You
have known something of tremendous value: you have known

your innocence, and in this innocence, the ego dies. The ego can live only with the false – it is the accumulation of the false. The ego is interested in knowledge – borrowed, third-hand, rotten ... but knowledge is cheap.

To know by experience is a risk. You may burn your fingers in the experiment. In the experiment, you are dropping out of the crowd and moving alone in this vast universe and you don't have any guide, any maps, any instructions. All that you have is a thirst. But in the desert people say, and it is derived from thousands of years of experience, that when a man becomes so thirsty that he forgets everything.... The fiery sun on his head, the fire in the sand, and he is all thirst; now it is not even a verbal thing in him. It is not that he is thinking, "I am feeling thirsty." He *is* thirst. Not that he is thinking about it, he *is* it.

The desert people all over the world have experienced a very strange phenomenon. Whenever somebody comes to such a state of thirst – and many times it happens in the desert – he suddenly becomes intuitive. He starts moving towards the place where he will find water. He has no map, he has no instructions. He has no way to move logically in any direction because in the desert all directions are the same, and there is no reason to choose one direction and not another. But now there is no question of choice. There is no question of thinking, he is just thirst. And that thirst moves existentially towards the place where it can be quenched.

When I came to know about this, I was surprised that no other mystic has taken note of the fact that the same is the situation of the seeker. Of course his desert is bigger, and his thirst is bigger too. The ordinary thirst is momentary; his thirst is eternal – but the basic principle is the same. When a man becomes so aflame, he starts moving ... I will not say he starts going in that direction; he *finds himself going* towards a certain direction, having no other alternative. There is no reason to stop. And that's how those who have reached, have reached.

Remember one thing: that to get rid of the doer is the most essential thing if you want to taste another world – the world of happenings, where you are just a witness.

The law of reverse effect is: there are things which you can have but because you are trying to get them, you will not be able to get them. It is like when you want to fall asleep in the night. You try all kinds of tricks but you find that you cannot befool yourself – sleep is not coming. On the contrary, because of your tricks and because of all the things people have told you to do if you do not find sleep coming to you naturally – all those things keep you awake. Because to do them you have to be awake!

Somebody is repeating a mantra – but to repeat a mantra, you have to be awake. Somebody is doing some breathing exercises from Yoga – but breath is so deeply involved in life that if you are using breathing in a certain way, with a certain rhythm, it will keep you alert, awake, fresh.

Sleep needs totally different things. If you want sleep to come, forget all about sleep; that is the first rule. Do something else. Get involved in something so deeply that you are not at all concerned with sleep and it will start coming. You will hear small footsteps, you will feel it is coming, but don't pay any attention.

Sleep is a feminine energy. If you look at it – and here you come to a very significant point – the feminine energy functions in a totally different way than the male energy. The woman wants you to chase her. She does not want you simply to sit and wait for her to come. Even though the woman wants you, loves you, wants to be yours, first she will run away. She will not run very fast. She will run in such a way that you can catch her; she will give you every chance to catch hold of her. Every feminine energy has the same quality. Sleep is feminine, you cannot catch hold of her. You have just to close your eyes and lie down and wait. She will come ... she is just in the other room. In the same category are all great values: friendship, love, peace, silence, and ultimately the realization of your godliness – they all *happen*. You are not the doer.

So first, let this be settled in you: that there is a world of doings that is the outside world, the worldly world; and there is a world of happenings – the inner world, the otherworldly world. Certainly their principles are going to be diametrically opposite.

I have seen people trying to relax. I have seen a book with the title, *You Must Relax*! "Must" will not allow you to relax! Relaxation is not something that you do, it is simply the absence of all your doings. In that absence is the greatest experience of life, and all great values will grow on their own accord.

Of course, your ego will not be fulfilled. In fact, it will be dead by the time you have experienced a few things which only *happen*. You have to choose between the ego and the world of happenings. The ego can give you many things: misery, anger, sadness, despair, anguish ... and the line is long. It has its own treasures, if you are interested.

The absence of ego has also its own treasures. And the world of the ego and the world of egolessness are not very far away. They are neighbors. Just a very thin fence of thoughts divides them.

It is simply a question of understanding that there are things which cannot be done — so don't do them, let them happen. You just be a watcher. And once you have learned the knack of watching you will start growing up higher every moment towards the ultimate experience — of knowing oneself, realizing the nature of your consciousness ... because that opens the door of immortality.

A meditator slowly slips from the world of mortality into the world of immortality. On this side, the world of doings, there is death. On the other side, in the dimension of happenings, there is no death. And unless you experience a clear vision of deathlessness, you will remain miserable, you will remain in despair. And because you live in the world of doings, that is the only art you know — and that art is preventing you from entering into a different dimension.

So you have to learn sometimes just to be a child, playing, jumping, dancing, singing, for no purpose at all. Once in a while just lying down on the lawn, or on the beach — doing nothing, lying down in such a way ... as if you are in your mother's womb. In fact, the scientists say that people feel good near the ocean because the child in the mother's womb floats in a liquid which has the same proportion of chemicals, salts, as the ocean. And we are made eighty percent of water. It is a miracle! You just think once again ... you are eighty percent water — walking, running, going home! Just twenty percent, the skin, is functioning like a bag. You feel fresh near the ocean — the same salty air, some forgotten memory....

Scientists are now coming closer to the Eastern insight about human evolution. Now the latest researchers say that Charles Darwin is not right, man has not come as a growth from the monkeys. They are proposing that man was born as a fish, not as a monkey; in the very beginning he was born in the ocean. And because life needed all that the ocean contains, the mother's womb has to contain everything just like the ocean. A pregnant woman becomes very much interested in salty things, because the child is asking for more and more salt. Salt is a necessity....

But for nine months floating in the mother's womb the child knows the eternity of relaxation – no tension, no business, no worries, no taxation. The child simply is, just a pure isness – that is relaxation.

By the side of the ocean, lying in the sand, just move as if you are back in your mother's womb. You are not to do anything. Just lie down and enjoy the wind, the roaring ocean ... and you will be surprised that the meditation that you have been trying to do for years and has not happened, is happening. Once you know that there are things which need your support – not as a doer but just as a loving gardener looking at his rosebushes, waiting and trusting in existence ... the spring always comes and it will bring flowers.

The spring of your consciousness will also come, but you have to learn a simple secret – that of let-go. And the learning simply comes by trying to understand the nature of doing and the nature of non-doing.

I was taken to a theological college to talk about Jesus, and after I had talked with the students, the vice-chancellor took me around ... it is the biggest Christian college in the whole of Asia which prepares missionaries. He took me around, and I could not believe what I saw. If Jesus had seen it the Jews would have been saved from crucifying him – he would have committed suicide himself!

The missionaries are being prepared ... on what sentence what kind of emphasis has to be given, what sentence has to be spoken loudly and what sentence has to be almost whispered, at what point you should beat the table....

I told the vice-chancellor, "You are destroying these people. Jesus never went to any theological college; he was not trained in the art of oratory. He is certainly one of the greatest orators the world has produced, and he does not know any art; he is uneducated. His power and the fire that his words carry are not coming out of a training, they are coming from his heart. In fact, he is not doing them, they are happening."

The difference is very delicate and very difficult ... whether the person is *making* a gesture or the gesture has blossomed just like a flower. If you have to say something your hands will follow, because your hands are extensions of your mind. When the mind is trying to express something and finding it difficult, the hands add whatever they can contribute. And sometimes what words cannot say, the movement of the hand, the grace of the hand may say. The word may not reach its target but the heart may touch the hand extended towards you. Your eyes may catch the depth of the master.

I told that vice-chancellor, "You are spoiling three thousand students every year – and you think you are preparing missionaries who are going to convert others into religion. You are not even able to convert these people! Because if their hearts are with you, then their gestures will automatically follow, then their emphasis on certain words, phrases or sometimes just silence..."

A moment, a gap, one never knows ... what the moment is going to bring is absolutely unknown. Whatever you want to do, remember: Doing is material, worldly, mundane. There is nothing which can be called 'spiritual doing'.

Spirituality is a happening, it is bigger than you, you cannot do it. You can make a shelter of your house, but you cannot make the sky with all the stars. All great values are like the sky – so vast and with so many stars and with so many mysteries. You can enter into this world of the miraculous if you drop yourself, leave yourself out of the temple. I am reminded of a very ancient story....

There was a great sculptor in Rome. His statues were so highly praised that for the first time unanimously the critics said, "There is no more possibility of improvement." He has said the last word; his statues look almost alive, as if just any moment the statue will come out of its place to greet you, to shake hands with you or give you a hug" – although I don't think you will be ready! The hug may prove dangerous. But that was the appraisal from all over the world, that the man had come to the peak, and now there was nothing that could be added to the art.

Then the man became old, as everybody has to become old, and he became afraid of death. As oldness started settling he started thinking what to do about death. Being a sculptor this idea came to his mind easily: "I can make a statue of myself." And he had a beautiful round hall where hundreds of statues were standing and sitting. So he thought, "When death comes I will be standing somewhere inside the crowd of my statues; only I have to keep my breathing as slow as possible." And that was possible, because people used to say that his statues seemed as if they were breathing. They were so alive that they would do something, they could not remain standing forever in that way.

Death came and was puzzled. The sculptor had made a few statues of himself and placed them among other statues. Death could not believe that ... she went around watching, looking, trying to find some sign but she failed. She said, "My God! He has done only one thing wrong..."

And the artist forgot completely the situation and the scene and said, "What?"

Death said, "You cannot forget yourself. And that I could see even by your nose, but I did not disturb you. I simply went on looking around. I wanted to see whether you could remain silent. That would have been *really* going beyond death – but you could not forget your ego and you were feeling more and more satisfied. The more I was going ahead, looking like a failure ... I was seeing from the corner of my eye that you were looking more and more successful, certain that you had defeated death. I can be defeated but not by the ego."

The egoless has no death to encounter. You are born – have you done anything? can you take any credit for being born? for having two eyes and not three? for having eyes at all? Otherwise the world would be dark – no colors, no light, no beauty. But all these things have happened to you. Birth happens to you, youth happens to you, love happens to you, old age happens to you, death happens to you – whatever is essential happens to you and whatever is non-essential is left for you to do. So don't waste your whole life in the non-essential. That non-essential is also needed but remember that the essential has not to be forgotten. And you have not to do anything for it. You have just to be receptive, open, vulnerable, available ... so that if the call comes from the beyond you will be ready to say with your full heart, "Yes. I am coming."

BELOVED OSHO,
I LISTENED TO THE TENDER SOUND OF A COOL WELL,
BUBBLING WATER JUST FLOWING WITHOUT ANY
EFFORT AND YET BUSY ... SUNRAYS DANCING TO THE
MELODY, ETERNALLY FRESH. BUT THE 'I' FORGOT. ALL
THAT REMAINS IS THE THIRST TO COME BACK AND
BE THE WELL, SOMETIMES RECOGNIZED, SOMETIMES
NOT. OSHO, IS THERE ANYTHING TO BE DONE? IS
THE THIRST ENOUGH?

The thirst is enough. So the question is not whether the thirst is enough or not, the question is whether the thirst is *there* or not. Because there can be a false thirst – and you know about the false thirst: you are not feeling thirsty and suddenly you see a bottle of Coca-Cola. Strangely enough you start feeling thirsty, and just a moment before you were not thinking of thirst at all.

I used to live in one place ... just next door was the richest man's house; it was a beautiful palace. And in India nobody bothers about it; it is taken for granted that people will urinate anywhere. The whole of mother earth is a toilet. So by the side of this man's house there was a small street, very lonely and once in a while somebody would urinate there and he was very mad about it. In the morning he would be in the garden and if he saw somebody urinating there was going to be murder! So much trouble he would create for the man, and the police will come and....

One day I was by the side of his fence and I said, "Why don't you put small signboards around the house saying that urinating is prohibited?"

He said, "That's a good idea."

So he made beautiful wooden signs – beautiful because they have to go with the beautiful marble – all around the house. And by the evening he came....

I said, "You must have come about those signboards that you have put up."

He said, "Yes, I have come about those. Where is your father?"

"But," I said, "my father has nothing to do with them. It was my suggestion, the whole credit goes to me." He said, "You keep quiet, just call your father." So I called my father.

He said, "This boy is dangerous. He tricked me! Now my whole house is stinking of urine; all around the house you can find nothing but urine."

Just the human mind ... when you see a board: "You cannot urinate here" such a great desire arises! One can risk anything, but one cannot leave that place, it is hypnotic. The functioning of the mind is such that no prohibition can ever be successful. Prohibition becomes provocation, it becomes a challenge and suddenly ... you were going on your way, thinking your thoughts, and suddenly this board makes you aware that you too have a bladder. And somebody telling you not to do something makes it attractive. It can become an obsession. Don't create obsessions in your life. Live more playfully, less seriously.

Don't be rigid; these are the qualities of the dead. Be flexible. Grow a sense of humor so that you can remain protected from all kinds of dark nights, dark holes. Your sense of humor will protect you. And if once in a while you can have a deep laughter, from your very roots, it will give you a freshness, a new vitality, a new energy to move mountains.

Ten thousand years we have lived without understanding the subtle workings of the mind. Hence every religion says, "Don't do this," and creates the world that you see. This is the world created by people who have been telling you, "Don't do this, don't do that." And those are the things which are being done!

And the more emphasis there is on denial.... Life reacts with a tremendous force against any denial, and you are caught in a very difficult crisis. If you follow life you cannot follow your holy scriptures, and that will create guilt in you – and to go on collecting guilt is like growing a spiritual cancer within yourself. If you follow these commandments in the scriptures you are going against your nature, against life itself. So there is not going to be any fulfillment, there is not going to be any joy; there is going to be only darkness, misery.

Slowly, slowly you start feeling a kind of death happening to you, because life is not being allowed to live in its totality. Death is bound to fill the gaps where life has not been allowed to blossom.

And every man is carrying within himself so many poisonous, life-negative ideas that everybody is in a limbo, just hanging in between. Neither can he do what life wants him to do – fully, completely, not holding anything back – nor he can repress. Because you *are* nature; and who is going to repress? You will have to divide yourself into two parts. You will have to create classes within yourself. There are people who are thinking of creating a classless society – without knowing at all that inside, man as an individual is divided into classes.

In India, the brahmin is synonymous with the head and the *sudra*, the shoemakers and the poor manual laborers, are symbolized by the feet; the warriors are symbolized by the arms. And they have a hierarchy – the feet cannot become the head. So whatever you are, you cannot change, you cannot transform yourself. You have to accept your fate – this has been the teaching for thousands of years. And the result is this miserable humanity. This is the conclusion of all your religions and all your prophets and all your saviors. This is what they have done, this is how they have saved you.

They don't seem around too much nowadays – perhaps they have saved you completely! They may have gone to save somebody else on some other planet, some other star. These saviors existed because we wanted somebody else to do this work of spiritual growth for us: "Somebody else should do it." Nobody else can do it. It is your freedom to be miserable or to be blissful, to remain in darkness or to live a life of light. This is the prerogative of human beings. The saviors are cheating you. To say to somebody, "I am going to save you," means that the person stops his search and becomes only a shadow. He follows you. And remember, existence does not accept carbon copies; it needs the original. You have to take the whole responsibility for your life.

And it is not a burden. In fact, freedom can never be a burden. The moment you accept total responsibility, you become free to be whatever your nature demands, to be whatever your nature deserves. And only when you fulfill your destiny – alone – finding your path, risking everything for the search, then life is no more just vegetating. Then life is a song, a dance, a deep ecstasy.

But you have to drop the idea that anybody else can do it for you. You have to drop the idea that knowledge gathered from scriptures can do it. You have to be mature, you have to accept that "This is my life and only I can do something for it." In this way you become an individual. In this way you become free from organizational religions, in this way you become free from any political, philosophical ideologies. In this way you become innocent again. Your eyes are clean, have depth; your heart is ready to dance.

And if you can forget yourself and start the dancing, start the singing.... And when I say forget yourself, don't misunderstand me. Don't start emphasizing the fact of forgetting yourself – that will spoil the whole thing. When I say forget yourself, I simply mean that when you are dancing, let the dance be there and the dancer dissolved into it. When you are singing then what is the need of the singer? Let the singer melt into the song, and each moment of life starts taking on the qualities of truth, of beauty, of blissfulness. You don't have to go anywhere. And you don't have to be anybody else, either. Wherever you are, whatever you are, exactly there – in silence, in peace – you can discover the very center of the universe. That center exists in everyone. We are different only on the periphery; at the center we are one.

That's why a person who has reached to his innermost core becomes a magnetic force – because he is now at the center and you are at the periphery. He has all the gravitation. If you just relax a little bit ... because you are clinging with the periphery. A little relaxation and you will be pulled in.

And while you are slipping into the presence of the master, you will find that a dark shadow of your own, which we call the ego, is

7
Love and centering: One phenomenon

BELOVED OSHO,
IS IT POSSIBLE FOR A WOMAN TO BE IN LOVE AND
STILL CENTERED?

The question has many implications. First, you do not understand what being centered means. Second, you also have no experience of the phenomenon of love. I can say this with absolute authority, because your question supplies all the evidence for what I am saying.

Love and centering are one phenomenon, they are not two. If you have known love, you cannot be anything but centered. Love means coming to be at ease with existence. It may be through a lover, it may be through a master, it may be through a friend. Or it may be simply direct and immediate – to the sunrise, to the sunset. The very experience of love will make you centered. This has been the whole philosophy of devotees down the ages. Love is their science; centering is the result.

But there are people – and there are only two kinds of people – who have a dominant reasoning, logic. Their heart is undeveloped. And there are people whose heart is blossoming and now reason, rationality, only function as servants to the heart. Man's misery is that he is trying to do the impossible: he is trying to force the heart to serve the mind, which is impossible. This is your chaos, this is your mess.

The question has arisen out of the ordinary experience called love. It is not love, it is only *called* love – just a glimpse, just a small taste, which is not going to be a nourishment. On the contrary it is going to become a pathological state, because one moment you are high and everything is just far out and the next moment all is dark, you cannot believe that there has been anything significant in your life. All those moments of love appear to have happened in dreams, or perhaps you have imagined them. And these dark moments are absolutely joined with the beautiful moments.

This is the dialectics of human mind. It functions through opposites. You will love a man and you will love the man for absolutely wrong reasons. You will love the man or the woman because you are carrying within you an image of the other. The boy has got it from the mother and the girl has got it from the father. All lovers are searching for their mothers, their fathers – and in the final analysis they are all searching for the womb and its beautiful, relaxed state.

Psychologically, the eternal quest for *moksha*, ultimate liberation, enlightenment, can be reduced to the basic psychological fact that man has already known the most beautiful, the most peaceful state before he was born. Now if something greater does not happen in his life, some exposure to the divine, to the universal, he is going to remain miserable. Because unconsciously, every moment, there is judgment.

He knows he has lived for nine months... and remember, for a child in the mother's womb, nine months are almost eternity because he does not know how to count, he does not have any clock. Each moment is enough unto itself. He does not know there is going to be another moment afterwards, so each moment is a surprise. And with no worry, with no tension about food, about clothes, about shelter, he is absolutely at ease, relaxed, centered. There is nothing to distract him from the center. There is nobody there even to say hello.

This experience of nine months of being centered, of immense joy, peace, aloneness... the other is no more there; you are the world, you are the whole. Nothing is missing, everything is supplied by nature without any effort on your part. But life confronts you in a totally different way – antagonistically, competitively. Everybody is your enemy, because everybody is in the same market; everybody is your enemy because everybody has the same desires, the same ambition. You are bound to come into conflict with millions of people.

It is because of this inner antagonism that all the cultures of the world have created a certain system of etiquette, familiarity, formality, and they have emphasized it continuously to the child: "You have to respect your father." All the cultures all over the world throughout the whole of history – why are they all insisting to the child, "You should respect your father"? There is some suspicion that if he is left alone, the child is not going to respect the father – that much is certain, simple logic. In fact, the child is going to hate. Every girl hates her mother. To hide it – because it will be very difficult to live in a society where all your wounds are uncovered and everybody is walking around with uncovered wounds – a certain ethos, a morality, a certain style of life has to cover it and to show just the opposite – that you love your mother, that you love and respect your father.

Deep down just the opposite is the case. You have been divided into two parts by the society. The false part has been given all respect, because the false is created by the society. The real is denied any respectability, because the real comes from nature – which is beyond the control of any society, culture or civilization. Each child has to be trained in lies, has to be programmed in such a way that he will be subservient to the society, a docile slave.

All societies are breaking the very spine of every child so he becomes spineless. He cannot raise his voice, he cannot question anything. His life is just not his own. He loves, but his love is false. From the very beginning he was told to love his mother "because she is your mother" – as if being a mother has some intrinsic quality or some obligation that you should love her. But it has been accepted that the mother should be loved.

My emphasis is that the mother should be loving, and no child should ever be told to love somebody unless it happens on its own. Yes, the mother, the father, the family can create a milieu without saying anything; the whole energy can generate, can trigger your own forces of love.

But never say to anybody that love is a duty. It is not. Duty is a false substitute for love. When you cannot love, society goes on supplying duties. They may appear to be love, but inside there is nothing loving in it; on the contrary, it is only social formality. And you become so accustomed to social formalities that you forget completely that there are things which are waiting to happen in your life but you are so occupied that you don't give space, you don't allow love to blossom in you. Hence you don't know that centering and love are one thing. Centering is more appealing to the intellectual. Nothing has to be believed; there is nobody else to whom you have to surrender. It is because of the other that every love affair becomes a tragedy.

In Indian literature there are no tragedies. In my student days I was asking my professors, "Why are tragedies missing in Indian literature?" And not a single teacher or professor was able to say something significant about it. They simply shrugged their shoulders and they said, "You are strange; you find such questions... I have been in this university for thirty years and nobody has asked."

I said, "To me it seems very obvious that the question has deep roots in the culture. In all other countries except India there are tragedies – beautiful stories, novels, fiction – but in India they are missing. And the reason is... India is a more ancient land than any other land. It has learned many things from experience, and one of them is: that which should not be, should not be talked about; hence there should be no tragedy."

Their logic can be understood. If man feels that life is everywhere a comedy, then there is a possibility he might continue deceiving himself. He might never tell anybody his problems – because he thinks nobody has problems; why become a laughing-stock? Something is wrong with you – just keep quiet. There is no point in exposing yourself to a cruel society which will simply laugh at you and prove that you are an idiot and you don't know how to live. But it is not so simple. It is not a question just of knowing how to live. It is a question first of dropping all that is false in you. The false comes from the outside. And when all that is false is dropped and you are utterly naked before existence, the real will start growing in you. This is the situation which has to be fulfilled for the real to grow, to blossom, and to bring you to the ultimate meaning and truth of life.

It has to be remembered: You can start either from centering – and the moment you are centered you will suddenly find immense love overflowing – or you can start from love. And the moment your love is without any jealousy, without any conditionings, but just a sharing of the dance of the heart, you will experience centering. They are two sides of the same coin. Centering is a more intellectual, scientific method. Love has a different source in you – your heart. It is more poetic, it is more aesthetic, it is more sensitive, it is more feminine, it is more beautiful. And it is easier than centering.

My suggestion is, first drop all false ideas about love. Let something real grow in you, and centering will be coming, enlightenment will be coming. But if you find it very difficult to start with love, then don't feel in despair. You can move directly through centering. You can call it meditation, you can call it awareness. But in each case, the ultimate result is the same: You are centered and overflowing with love.

BELOVED OSHO,

YOU USUALLY SAY THAT WOMEN HELP MEN TO

BECOME ENLIGHTENED. HOW IS IT VICE-VERSA?

Latifa, I usually say that women help men in attaining enlightenment, and you must have been wondering what the situation is vice versa. To help somebody towards enlightenment needs immense patience, needs great love. The woman has a few higher qualities.

In the first place, the man more or less becomes interested in enlightenment because his wife is interested. Not to be interested in something in which the wife is interested is to keep a cold war going twenty-four hours a day in the house; it is wiser to go with the woman. The vice-versa will be very difficult. The vice-versa means the man pushing the woman towards enlightenment.

In the first place, who is going to look after the house? And a dozen nasty children... just your great contributions to the world. Afraid that one day you will have to die, you are leaving so many examples that whether your name is mentioned in history books or not, it does not matter – the real history will be made by your children. They will rape and they will murder and they will commit suicide and they will do all kinds of great things.

The husband is continuously worried about the financial situation; his whole life is devoted to earning money. He cannot persuade the wife because that will be the end of the family. Then both will have gone towards enlightenment, leaving those nasty children to destroy the neighborhood – just making places for more meditators.

Man is more ambitious. His ambition is mundane. The woman is not ambitious – and to move towards enlightenment you have to drop all your ambitions, all your desires.

Man is more in his head. He goes on continuously thinking, arguing. And there are things – and those are the only significant things – which first you have to experience and only then you can think about. Otherwise, what can you think about? You have heard only an empty word – "love." You have no experience; your word 'love' is only a container, empty, with no content inside it.

Man has not been helpful. He would like his children to fulfill all the desires that he has not been able to fulfill. He wants his children to become prime ministers, presidents, the richest people in the world. Those were his desires, those were his father's desires, those were his grandfather's desires and in heritage he will give those desires – which are maddening – to his children. He cannot talk about enlightenment.

Latifa is German. Even a German husband cannot manage to force a woman to become enlightened – what to say of other races? – because even the German husband is as henpecked as any husband. In that, there is no difference between the German and the Chinese and the Indian and the Japanese; it does not matter. There is only one kind of husband: henpecked. Whatever you do, you cannot change the situation. And it will be hilarious: a henpecked husband leading a wife towards enlightenment, and that too, in Germany! No Latifa, don't wait for a husband. You will have to do it yourself. Yes, once you have done it for yourself, you can drive one or many husbands towards enlightenment, like cattle!

People have been asking me, "Why, in the long history of man, have so very few people become enlightened?"

I said, "What to do? There was nobody to chase them!"

If women decide, you will see husbands in every house standing on their heads meditating, crying, that the time is wasted and the customers must be there and the shop.... But in enlightenment you are not supposed to think about such things as shops and customers. Women can help, but that much understanding has not come to men yet.

Even the smallest girl has qualities of a grown-up mother; a kind of motherliness surrounds her. That is not true about a boy. You will not find any vibe of fatherliness around him. To be a father is a social institution and to be a mother is a natural phenomenon. Husband and wife are faraway categories.

In India, although we have participated in the crime, the universal crime against women.... There have been people in the East – few, but at least there have been a few people – of great insight, and their insight can be seen in many ways.

In India, you can go and see temples of Sita and Rama, or Radha and Krishna – but have you observed that you always put the name of the woman first and the man second? It is always Sita first, Radha first... and the companion is no ordinary human being; it is a Krishna, it is a Rama. But still the woman is placed first because to her, enlightenment is far easier than a pregnancy. It is also a kind of pregnancy.

The woman knows the language. The man cannot understand it – pregnancy? He can make a woman pregnant but he remains an outsider. His work in giving birth to children is negligible; any syringe can do it. And nature has no preference for men over syringes – they are better used once and disposed of. With man, the difficulty is that once you get caught, it is very difficult to get rid of him. Then the syringe goes on hanging around you for your whole life and the syringe thinks itself very important.

Enlightenment is life's ultimate fulfillment. The woman is closer, her love is more sincere, her readiness to risk is great. You may be thinking otherwise, but because man thinks, he cannot take a risk. First, he will think and be *sure* that "success is going to be mine." Only then will he enter into any challenge. The woman jumps first and then there is the whole of eternity to think about it.

Latifa, whatever I have said is the best part of the story. It has rarely happened. It *has* happened, women have helped their husbands, sacrificed their whole lives, never thought about themselves. Their surrender, their devotion to their lovers has been total. In this totality, they have achieved before their lover has.

Man is fragmented; his mind is going in all the ways, in every direction. Nothing is complete because you have only a certain amount of energy and you are running in so many directions that you will end up just like a mad dog. You will not reach anywhere. Hearing about enlightenment, man becomes interested in becoming enlightened too, but that is only one of the items on his laundry list – and this is the *last* item. When everything is dry-cleaned, then finally he will come to me. And here we just do dry-cleaning of your brain, of your mind.

A man goes on thinking about enlightenment, *nirvana*, truth, but they never seem to become life and death problems. They remain questions – philosophical, theological – and you can go on living the way you are living and you can go on thinking and reading and writing but the world of truth has nothing to do with reading and writing.

When a woman becomes interested in enlightenment, her interest has a totally different quality. It becomes her whole life – not just one item on the laundry list but the *only* item. The woman is naturally capable of being one-pointed. That is not true about the man. Both are necessary, both help each other to create a rich life. But they can be great friends about the beyond also. They can help, discuss, meditate together, start changing their loving towards more and more a meditative state.

Men have been helped by women in another way also. The woman has been such a nuisance that because of her, the man started thinking of enlightenment. It is an escape – from the woman! He calls it the world but the *woman* is the world. And for thousands of years, man has been escaping from the woman, from the children, from the world – but these escapists have not attained anything worthwhile. Through escape, through fear, you cannot attain truth or love. So in this ugly manner also women have helped men – forced them, rather – towards enlightenment. Men cannot do even this to women.

In a small school, a teacher was asking the students – small boys and girls, "Can any one of you describe a strange animal that nobody else has seen?"

One small boy raised his hand. Even the teacher was surprised – "Where has he found a strange animal?" The whole class could not believe it, because this was the first time.... That small guy was a very silent boy. He used to stay at the back of the class, never creating any nuisance, never asking anything. And he was so certain of his answer that he was raising his hand. Finally the teacher said, "What is your answer?" He said, "The animal lives with me."

The woman said, "What? You *are* a strange fellow! First, you shocked everybody that you have seen a strange animal that nobody has seen and now you say the animal lives with you?" He said, "Yes. It is nobody else but my daddy."

The woman said, "Your daddy? But I am talking about animals!"

And the boy said, "You yourself have said that *anima* means life, and animals mean 'those who are living.' And certainly my father *is* living. And I call him a strange animal because when he goes from the house, he goes like a lion and when he comes back to the house, he enters like a mouse. He is... outside you should see him! And you would not believe it if will saw him inside the house."

Man cannot help in that way. He cannot create so much trouble for the woman that she starts thinking of renouncing the world. The man has certainly been helped, rightly or wrongly – rightly, very few times; wrongly, most of the time, he is driven towards enlightenment.

But the ugliest thing man has done is that he has not shown any gratefulness towards women. Whether their means were right or wrong, he has reached enlightenment; at least the woman deserves to be thanked for it. But perhaps they never thought about it in this way. They thought it was because of their understanding of the life of the world that they were going to the Himalayas. It was not understanding, it was really weakness in facing and encountering situations which are on every step in life and remaining silent, peaceful, blissful.

So man has chosen to drop the world and move to the mountains. It has not helped anybody. Those who have moved to the mountains have fallen into a kind of retardedness. Mind is a mechanism, it needs use. It needs situations where either it has to react or to respond or just to remain neutral, a witness, not bothering about it at all. But in the mountains where life is not around you, with just the rocks and with the trees, you will not come to a fight. They will not provoke your anger, your hatred; they will not provoke your ambition, because nobody is trying to be the president there.

A great emperor came to see a Zen master. He brought a beautiful robe, studded with diamonds. He wanted to be initiated into meditation and this was just a small gift.

The Zen master took the gift with great respect, but he said, "You are putting me in an embarrassing situation. It will be very kind of you, if you don't feel hurt, to please take this robe. It is perfectly suitable in your court. If I use it here, monkeys will giggle, wolves will laugh and the whole mountain will whisper wherever I will go: 'Look at this idiot! We used to think he was a saint.' Don't put me in this embarrassing situation. You take the robe away, it is enough that you brought it."

Men and women have to live together on the earth but they have not learned yet *how* to be together and yet not lose their individuality, how to be together so much so that they are almost one, without disturbing this oneness in mundane affairs.

Man and woman both can help – and if the right kind of help is available, there will be no need for man to escape to the mountains, to the caves, to the monasteries. There is no need, because you cannot find a better place than your home. A loving atmosphere, people who understand you, people who understand your silence and your meditation, will go hand-in-hand with your love. Even if you get into meditation in the mountains, you will have only one wing. You will not be able to fly to the sun. The other wing you have left in the world, which could have been a tremendous help to you, and you could have been a great help in return.

If a couple gets initiated into meditation together, they are really getting married for the first time. As for your other registration certificates for marriage – they are not valid for me. To me, there is only one certificate that existence gives you – where love and meditation have been helping each other, supporting each other and opening the doors of the sky for your flight, the flight of the alone to the alone.

BELOVED OSHO,
THE GERMAN PSYCHOLOGIST, WILHELM REICH,
STUMBLED UPON SOME INNER SECRETS OF BIO-
ENERGY. HE ALSO STARTED PRACTICING THESE ON
HIS PATIENTS BUT HE WAS DECLARED ANTI-SOCIAL,
WAS IMPRISONED AND PRONOUNCED MAD. OSHO,
WHAT IS IT THAT REICH WAS WORKING ON AND
WHERE DID HE GO WRONG. WHAT WAS HE MISSING?

Wilhelm Reich is one of the most important names in the world of psychology. Perhaps he was second only to Sigmund Freud – but he was the youngest disciple of Sigmund Freud and before I answer your question, I have remembered something which is the only incident in the long life of Sigmund Freud which shows something of Zen. It is something which was always present around the great masters but you can't expect it in Sigmund Freud's life. I want to tell you about it for the important reason that even a man like Sigmund Freud has the potential of being a mystic. If he missed it, that is another thing.

Wilhelm Reich was continually writing letters to Sigmund Freud. He was young – perhaps thirty-five, half the age of Sigmund Freud – and Sigmund Freud was not interested in such a young person. His work was long and he had old colleagues with whom he was working and his movement had become almost international. Now he was unable to go on taking new students and new responsibilities, so he refused. And he refused his best student.

But Wilhelm Reich was a German, stubborn; you could not just reject him and then things are finished. He went anyway to an appointment that had been canceled. He knocked on the door and Sigmund Freud himself opened the door. They looked at each other. There was a moment of silence.

Sigmund Freud said, "But I have canceled the meeting."

Wilhelm Reich said, "But I have not – and certainly a meeting means a meeting of two persons, so it is only you who has canceled it. From my side, I am still available and I thought that I should present myself because I have not canceled it."

Sigmund Freud again looked at Wilhelm Reich as if hesitating or weighing…"What to do with this man?" He said to him, "I am old. You are too young; I will not be able to finish my teaching. And you may not agree with me because there is a generation gap. So why waste your time? Start on your own, you have my blessings."

With tears in his eyes, Wilhelm Reich thanked Sigmund Freud and returned home. He learned about human energies, about the functioning of the mind, about levels of consciousness – and it was good that he was refused, because he opened a totally new door and he went on thanking Sigmund Freud his whole life; "If he had not refused me, I would have been just a Freudian. At that moment I was hurt but I am immensely obliged to him that he left me alone. I had to start from scratch but I went in a totally different direction and now I can see that all of Sigmund Freud's work is dream analysis and has nothing to do with reality."

Dreams are only shadows. At the most, psychoanalysis can give you normal dreams, can help you to avoid nightmares. But more than that has not happened.

Wilhelm Reich started working on human energy. Naturally, if you work on human energy you are going to come to the source of all – that is sexual energy. The moment he touched upon sexual energy, all the religions were against him. The government was against him, the psychologists were against him, and his situation was a very strange one.

He had come to experience that when two lovers are approaching closer to each other, there is a magnetic force – if there is love. If there is no love, then only two bodies meet, but not two energies.

He had a scientific mind. He made a box in which two persons would make love. His idea was that the energy love creates can be caught and can be used. Now this was a troublesome thing. He could not show anything – the box was empty. There was no way to materialize the biological energy, but he gathered every possible evidence.

Somebody was suffering from impotence. Wilhelm Reich would put him in the box and his impotence would disappear, at least for a few days, as if his battery had been recharged. It was an indirect proof but something had happened. In the box, something *had* happened, the box was not empty.

He told lovers, "Even without loving, you can simply lie down, cuddling, melting into each other." His work was strange, hard... and it was made more difficult by the society because they started immediately condemning him, saying that he was in conspiracy with the devil – just like me! – saying that sex had to be renounced and he was teaching people some strange exercises.

Those strange exercises show his genius. He had no idea of Tantra, he had never been to the East. But the exercises that he found are ten thousand years old. He discovered them and thousands of witnesses who were healed by him... because soon he started healing other patients, not only the sexual ones. Because sex energy is pure energy, it can be converted into many forms. It can become your intelligence, it can become your silence. He started treating people.

The treatment was simple: he would just put them in the box. They would remain for fifteen minutes or twenty minutes, a few sessions – and they were cured. But medical science was against him because "this man cannot practice medicine."

This is how law is blind. This man cured thousands of people of strange diseases which were not curable by ordinary, official medicine but that couldn't be counted. The question was whether he had a registration: "Is he licensed to practice?"

Wilhelm Reich said, "I don't use medicine, I don't prescribe anything. My whole medicine is the box. If you accept it as medicine, then the medical faculties of your universities have to prove what kind of medicine is there. When I tell you to look into what I have found, you think I am crazy and when I cure people, then I am criminal. I have not harmed anybody."

But medical science, the Christian Church, the government – all started many cases against him. You can start any case – it may be absolutely false, unfounded, but you can harass the person for years. So many cases... and the man became so tense and there was nobody to support him, not even the people of his own profession. They were against him because their psychoanalysis would die if his energy box succeeded.

Medicine is not ready to accept somebody who has no medical certificates. His friends left him. He was in great agony because he knew he had found something of great value for humanity and he also saw that he could not convince anybody. He was only convincing people that he was crazy. People were simply laughing, making cartoons, bringing court cases against him.

Finally he was jailed because he was practicing medicine without a license. Now you see the tricky world. He was not practicing medicine, he was practicing healing – that you can say, but you cannot say he was practicing medicine. He had not harmed anybody, and he was ready to cooperate with any research group. He was available to talk about everything he had discovered. But his discoveries were going against Christianity, his discoveries were going against your so-called morality. His discoveries were going against your whole social structure, educational structure, political structure.

He was one of the greatest revolutionaries ever and he has remained unknown, unrespected, unremembered. And in jail, they must have tortured him immensely. He was not a man who can fall apart easily; he was a very integrated person and the people who knew him testified that it is very difficult to find such a strong, well-rooted and grounded person – but he went mad in jail.

I suspect he was forced to go into madness. It is very easy to drive anybody mad when all the powers are in your hands and the person is made absolutely helpless. When he became mad....This is the world: when he was at the peak of his fame, there were friends, there were colleagues, there was a beautiful woman who loved him. But when he came out of jail, the woman divorced him, the friends disappeared, the colleagues made it clear to him that they didn't want any more connection with him because even to be connected with him created suspicion.

It is sad that he died, but I will say he was forced to die. If you boycott a person in such a way that he becomes an island in the great ocean of humanity – separate, isolated, cannot communicate with anybody, everybody thinks he is mad – naturally, his will to live will disappear. He shrank and died. And it is strange that after his death his work has remained where he left it. It has immense potentiality. It needs to be developed and it needs to be developed in collaboration with Tantra. I call Wilhelm Reich a modern Tantra master, although he was not aware of it. Perhaps in his past lives he may have known the secrets of Tantra – because his work contained the secrets of Tantra.

You will not believe that in India there were at one time, two thousand years ago, two hundred thousand followers of a special group of tantrikas. They lived naked. Couples used one gown, just one loose gown around both, made of a special silk which prevented the radiation of any kind of energy from going out or in. They would go for begging or anything but they would remain together, naked, in their gown.

They were doing a great experiment, of melting and mixing the female and the male bio-electricity. Because the very meeting of this bio-electricity can help you to go into deep meditation without much effort in fighting with your thoughts. There were one hundred thousand couples and Raja Bhoj, the king in those days, was so furious – "This is destroying our whole morality, this is corrupting our children. Children will see and they will ask, what kind of people are these? – naked in one gown.... These people will corrupt our whole religion and tradition."

Bhoj decided to kill all of them. One hundred thousand couples – that means two hundred thousand people – were killed all over the country, burned alive. Not a single couple was left alive; their literature was burned, their temples were burned. Never before or after has any tradition been so brutally destroyed, so inhumanely destroyed.

But when you bring up the subject of sex, immediately you annoy all the people who are in power because nobody who is in power wants people to live to their optimum sexually. They want you to live your *minimum* sexually because at the minimum you can be enslaved. At the maximum, you are so powerful, you are so intelligent – you are a rock and you cannot be destroyed. Whoever tries to destroy you will be destroyed.

Wilhelm Reich will have a revival because what he was doing was absolutely scientific. No Christianity can prevent it, no

government can prevent it. And perhaps.... I have so many sannyasins educated in psychology, in psychoanalysis, in analytical
psychology and different schools – perhaps a few of my sannyasins
will start working on Wilhelm Reich. He belongs to us. I give him
posthumous sannyas.

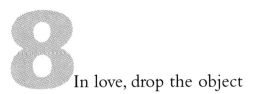

8 In love, drop the object

BELOVED OSHO,

WAITING FOR YOU TO GET WELL, THERE CAME A
POINT WHERE I WASN'T WAITING ANYMORE FOR
SOMETHING – IT SIMPLY BECAME JUST WAITING.
DISCOVERING THE BEAUTY AND SWEETNESS OF IT
WAS SO PRECIOUS. WAITING NEEDS NO PATIENCE. IT
IS LIKE LIVING IN MOONLIGHT – A MYSTERIOUS
QUIET JOY, SO NOURISHING AND RESTFUL,
BECOMING A WOMB CONNECTED WITH YOU IN A
CIRCULAR FLOW OF ENERGY. AND JUST WHEN I FELT I
COULD GO ON WAITING FOREVER AND EVER –
WONDERING IF I WAS BECOMING TOO MUCH OF AN
INDIAN! – YOU SHOWER ON US AGAIN THE GIFT OF
YOUR PHYSICAL PRESENCE, THE GOLDEN BRIGHT
SUNSHINE SETTING ME AFLAME AGAIN. BELOVED,
BELOVED MASTER, CAN YOU EVER BE AS HAPPY WITH
US AS WE ARE WITH YOU?

Purna, the experience has been immensely valuable. On the path of mystery, all objects are nothing but excuses – because you cannot wait without an object, without it being *for* something. The moment waiting is for something, it is desire; it is not waiting. And by its very nature, desire goes on becoming narrower.

You love – the beginning of love is a wider experience, because love has not become desire yet. You have not started to take your beloved for granted. The calamity of marriage has not happened yet, you are still free to move in any direction. The other is not yet binding. The other is not yet a hell because there is no relationship yet. No promises are yet given, no decisions for tomorrow are yet taken. You are entirely satisfied with the moment.

When you are in love, who cares about the future, about a life beyond death? When you are in love, life is *here* at the very center of your love, but only before you commit the common fallacy of humanity. You love somebody but the love is not defined yet, is not reduced to law – you have not been to the marriage registrar's office, you have not been to any priest to destroy your love and give you a guarantee.

You have not asked for the guarantee yet – that's why you are free. You have not asked the other person to be a certain way and only then you will love. Your love is still unconditional, you love the person as he or she is. Your love is not yet possessive. But soon that moment will come, and out of this beautiful experience of expansion of consciousness you will start being afraid to lose it. Who knows about tomorrow? The woman may turn away, the man may not recognize you.

Basically, we are strangers. And all that we know about each other is arbitrary – the name, the address, the face, the beauty – because all these will be changing. Your beloved may have the most beautiful eyes and tomorrow, blindness is possible. Unless you have learned to love *as the other is*, the beautiful beginning, the beautiful sunrise in your consciousness, will turn soon into a dark night of the soul. The same things that you used to love now create anger, now create hatred. The same things that you used to appreciate are now nothing but nagging.... The reception room was beautiful, and because of the beauty of the reception room you have entered a jail.

But this is not the only possibility, of lovingness turning into a narrow, ugly desire to dominate, to possess, to be jealous of. If this were all, no intelligent person would have tolerated life for a single moment. For the intelligent person, suicide would have been the only way out. But it is not so – because there is an alternative. Love can become too much concentrated on the object, the beloved. And this is the misery; then you become dependent and nobody loves dependence.

The alternative is that love does not become addressed to a single person or a single object, but takes a diametrically opposite dimension – not towards the object but towards one's own subjectivity. One becomes love. It is not a question of loving someone, of being in love with someone. It is simply a transformation of your consciousness: love is your fragrance. It has nothing to do with anybody else in the world. That's what happened, Purna, when you were waiting and waiting for me.

A moment is bound to come – if you are silent, joyous, trusting

– when waiting can become a depth in your soul. And because you are not waiting *for* something or someone, you *are* the waiting – a silent watchfulness. And because you are not concerned with anything particular, objective, then everything that happens feels as if you were waiting for *this*. All the flowers bloom for you and all the stars shine for you. Because you have not attached yourself to a particular flower, you have simply become an opening, a loving, a waiting consciousness.

This is not only true about waiting; it is true about all spiritual qualities. Either the quality can move towards an object or it can move towards one's own being. When there is no object, the energy is bound to move inwards – energy cannot remain without movement. Energy is movement. When there is nothing outside, your own life forces turn inwards to the very source of your being. And this is what I call enlightenment. You cannot desire enlightenment; you can only wait.

You are asking me if I love you in the same way, with the same intensity, with the same totality as you love me. It will be difficult for you to understand: there is a love which is not the love that you have known.

Your love, howsoever pure, carries something of biological unconsciousness in it. You are not totally free to love *anybody*. Suddenly one day you fall in love with a person. It is not your action. It is something unconscious in you – your chemistry, your biology, your physiology. They are all conspiring and giving you the idea of love. I cannot love you in that sense. My love cannot become a bondage to you in any way.

And my love is qualitatively different: I love not because you are lovable; I love because I cannot help it. And it is not a question of loving *someone*. Just the way I breathe in and out, and my heart beats, love radiates on its own accord.

It is possible that you will see that I love someone more, someone less.... Because you always think in terms of quantity: more or less. And your conclusion has a certain validity, too. But you are not looking at things right side up; you are looking at things upside down.

My love is just like the light – it is neither more for somebody nor less for somebody. But still, for the blind man it will not exist. For the one who cannot see properly, it will be dim. And for one who can see with a clarity it will have a different intensity. It is the same light, but it will depend how much you can receive. If you are totally open, you can receive it all.

And because it is not a quantity – it is pure quality; hence indivisible – I can give you my whole heart without having any trouble in giving my whole heart to many other people. Because it is not mathematics, such that I have given the whole heart to one person and now what am I doing? – I am finished! That is not my experience. I have always given my whole heart, because I am lazy. Who bothers to cut one's own heart into pieces? And then to give in a miserly way, pieces… and those pieces will be dead. The heart is alive only in its totality, in its organic unity. But the trouble is in your wrong conditioning.

I can give to the whole world, to each single individual, my whole heart – and still my whole heart remains with me to be given to any newcomer. Because newcomers are always coming!

You may not be able to understand many things about what the situation is when you *are* love. For example, when you are love, your love cannot be hot. And in this world, people want hot love. Hot dogs to eat and hot love to enjoy, and their paradise is complete! My love is neither hot nor cold. It is cool. Unless you become very calm and cool, you will not be able to understand it. You have known only the hot love – and remember, the danger with the hot love is that sooner or later it is going to become cool. Everything hot is bound to become cool sooner or later, and the final end is that it will become cold. You cannot prevent it, it is a natural process.

So each hot love turns into hot hate. But you are accustomed to hot – either friendship or enmity, but it has to be hot. You are so insensitive that unless something is very hot you cannot feel it. Hence, your question. My love is cool. To understand it, you will have come to the same temperature.

And cool love is not only love, it is much more. Because of its coolness, it is meditation, it is silence, it is serenity, it is tranquillity, it is centering. It is not a small phenomenon. I love you more than you can ever be loved.

But my love and your experience of love are so different that you will have to change gear. This is what happened while you were waiting. You waited one day, two days, three days.... And I was sending messages: "Within one or two days I will be starting...." You know I am crazy, I have my own ways of working.

I would not have started speaking. It is because of Darshan, Bhadra and Hansa. I was not seeing people for the simple reason that I find it impossible to say no to anything. And when Hansa recited a small piece of Urdu poetry, which means "I don't have any complaint. As it is, I am happy; I don't have any complaint. But life without you is not life at all...." It was impossible to say no.

So I said to them, "Inform my people that I will start speaking today. Rather than saying no to you, I can stop again!" I have my ways – and this time I will not allow Bhadra, Hansa and Darshan to see me!

But this is significant to understand: whether I am speaking or not speaking, whether I am seeing you or not seeing you, if you can be here feeling the invisible presence, that is more than can be expected of human beings. And that is the golden key.

And in what situation you will wake up nobody knows. Everybody is asleep for different reasons and needs different situations to wake up. Perhaps it helped Purna greatly. She was waiting one day, the next day.... Naturally when you have to wait too long, waiting becomes not an excitement but a settled state. She settled with waiting. She forgot even what she was waiting for. This is the moment when energy starts turning inwards. And to shower in your own energy is the greatest ecstatic experience available to man.

But the second part of her question... she will have to learn a little more, to experience a little more about love – object-less love; love not as a relationship but as a state of being. Then she will be surprised: it is cool, not hot. It is non-possessive, it is non-jealous, it has no conscious or unconscious desire to dominate the other.

True love is not a beggar; it does not ask you to "love me." True love shares its whole being, its whole joy, all the songs, all the flowers, all the stars. It is a celebration. And you are not obliged – true love is always obliged that you participated in the celebration, that "You allowed my love an entry into your being," that "You trusted me so much that I am grateful." I know you love me.

But I would like you to rise higher, because right now you are just walking on the ground, the lowest rung of the ladder. And you have the capacity to take off into the sky – sky beyond skies. You can reach to the very climax of existence and its beauty, its truth, its eternity, its deathlessness.

What has happened to you, Purna, continue it in other realms, in other directions. In love, drop the object. In meditation, don't meditate upon somebody or something – drop the object.

All over the world, whenever you tell people to meditate, they immediately ask, "On what?" because verbally, meditation is action, activity. On what has one to meditate? Meditation begins only when there is nothing to meditate upon, when there is simply consciousness – you are aware – but you are not concentrating on anything. Concentration is a kind of imprisonment. And all our educational programs around the world are teaching people to concentrate.

A man like Adolf Hitler creates concentration camps to kill people – his concentration camps are crude and primitive. All the religions have created concentration camps for you, but they are psychological. They have created a certain prison inside your mind. You cannot go out of it because wherever you go, it is always within you. You cannot run; howsoever fast you run, it is always with you. A Sufi story is....

A man was very much afraid of darkness; he had a paranoia. He was also afraid of aloneness – these two things are always found together. The man who is afraid of darkness will necessarily be afraid of aloneness, and vice-versa. Because darkness gives you a feeling of aloneness in a vast universe. It may be populated with nine hundred billion people, but in darkness you are alone.

As you start a revolution in you, transforming love from objects and pouring it into your own source, you will be absolutely mysti-fied – coming to know that you have so much love that you can bless the whole world.

But your love will be more like compassion, cool, more like friendliness. Your love will be free from its biological, hormonal, chemical past. For the first time it will be beyond matter. For the first time you will not be forced by some blind forces in nature – you will decide.

And when you have so much to give, and when you discover that the more you give, the more you have it, then love is no longer a relationship but a pure sharing, with no desire of gaining anything in return. Love has gone beyond the world of the marketplace; it is no longer business. It is for the first time pure play, *leela*.

But about the second part of your question: your love is certainly hotter. And you know, I don't like heat! You can see... two air conditioners!

You will have to experience a higher and more refined, more purified energy. Only then you can understand whether I love you more or you love me more. Right now it can be said that you love me more. My love is simply love – neither more nor less. I cannot figure out how to love less. I have tried! – but I am ashamed to say to you that I have failed continuously for my whole life. I have not been able to love less and neither can I love more. 'More' and 'less' are words that don't belong to the spiritual realm. They belong to the world of matter.

The English word 'matter' is from a Sanskrit root, *matra*. It means "that which can be measured." From the same root, *matra* comes the French word *metre*. That which can be measured is not my love. That which cannot be measured, that which cannot be more or less, that which is just for you to share.... Because this whole existence is made of the stuff called love. As you understand your reality, you have understood in miniature the reality of the whole existence – it is made of the matter called love. We are living in an ocean of love, unaware.

But there are ways to grow and become aware of the tremendous ecstasies that are possible to you. Just loving a single person you feel so happy... just think of yourself *becoming* love. The whole existence becomes your beloved – the trees dancing in the wind and the sun, the clouds moving in the sky, a beautiful sunset.... Once you understand that you are part, an intrinsic part of this loving existence, this constantly rejoicing existence, you will drop all boundaries and all limitations on your love, on your intelligence. You will be reborn – reborn as a Gautam Buddha, a fully awakened consciousness. Your experience has directed you towards a right source. Just follow it – with ease, with relaxedness. And much more, so much more that you cannot imagine, is going to shower on you... roses and roses and roses.

BELOVED OSHO,
YOU HAVE SAID RECENTLY THAT A SANNYASIN HAS
NO NATIONALITY ANYMORE. DO YOU SAY THE SAME
THING ABOUT AGE? SINCE I HAVE BEEN A
SANNYASIN, I HAVE FELT AGELESS. I AM SIXTY-TWO
AND YOUNG PEOPLE ACCEPT ME AS ONE OF THEM.
HOW IS THIS POSSIBLE?

Meditation is a transformation of your whole being. You are no more part of a crowd, no more a cog in the wheel. You have taken your responsibility on your own shoulders; you have become a free individual.

Nationality will disappear, because these are all arbitrary lines, man-made – and their existence is ugly, because their existence shows that man is not mature yet. Otherwise, what is the need to have so many nations, and every nation having great armies.... People are dying in poverty and seventy percent of the national income all over the world goes to the military. Humanity is living on only thirty percent, and the army gets everything better – naturally, because they have sold their lives and they are being prepared for death, either to kill or to be killed.

This seems so useless. Why should there be wars? Why should there be violence? And why should nations continue after five thousand years of experience shows that they are cancerous, destructive?

The man of meditation is bound to be a citizen of the world.

He is not going to be a Christian or a Hindu or a Mohammedan. Because he can contact existence himself; there is no need of any mediator, no need of any priest, holy book, church. All these religions have been creating nothing but bloodshed, burning living human beings and doing all kinds of ugly acts against innocent humanity.

As you become more silent, as your eyes become more clear, as the smoke that surrounds you disappears, then religions, nations, discriminations between black and white, discriminations between men and women – all are going to disappear.

And it is right that you are feeling ageless. Meditation starts taking you beyond time because it is going to take you beyond death. You will be surprised that in Sanskrit there is only one word for both death and time. It is *kal*. Kal also means tomorrow – tomorrow there is only death and nothing else; life is today.

As you become peaceful.... Your tensions are your weight. When the tensions are not there, you become weightless. And the consciousness which is your reality has no time-space limitation. Your body grows from childhood to youth to old age to death – these changes are happening only to the body. These are the changes of the furniture in the house... painting the house, changing its architecture. But the man who lives in the house – the master of the house – is unaffected by all these things. Consciousness is the master. Your body is only the house.

So the moment you enter meditation you have touched within yourself something of the universal – which has no age, which has no limitation either of time or space. This is not only happening to you. I receive many letters from older sannyasins saying that they are feeling so young, and they don't see any generation gap. They mix with sannyasins and not for a moment does the idea come that they are eighty years old and these are twenty year-old kids. But they communicate and nobody thinks that it is a little strange.

One woman sannyasin from Scotland wrote to me, "Now, Osho it is going too far!" She is seventy-eight, and now she is running after butterflies! And the whole village thinks she has gone mad because she is continuously laughing and enjoying and the village cannot believe it. Because they have seen her, always miserable... they cannot believe what has happened to her. She is behaving like a small child.

She asked me, "What to do? Should I try to behave in the old way?"

I said, "You can try, but you cannot succeed. So don't waste your time, just go after the butterflies. And why bother about the idiots of the village? You enjoy yourself." Meditation is not something mental. Meditation is something concerned with your being.

Just plugging into it a little... and suddenly everything is different. The body will go in its own way, but you will know that you are not the body. People will die, but you will know that death is impossible. Your own death will come — but meditation prepares you for death so that you can go dancing and singing into the ultimate silence, leaving the form behind and disappearing into the formless.

BELOVED OSHO,
MANY PEOPLE ARE EXPERIMENTING WITH THE DRUG
ECSTASY. I HEARD YOU SAY ONCE THAT A LIE IS
SWEET IN THE BEGINNING AND BITTER IN THE END.
AND TRUTH IS BITTER IN THE BEGINNING AND
SWEET IN THE END. I HAVE BEEN MEDITATING, BUT I
DON'T HAVE THE EXPERIENCES PEOPLE REPORT FROM
THE DRUG ECSTASY. IS THE DRUG LIKE THE LIE AND
MEDITATION, THE TRUTH? – OR AM I MISSING
SOMETHING THAT COULD REALLY HELP ME?

Ecstasy can create a chemical change for the time being. It can make you feel a great well-being, more intensity in life, more color in the world. But this is only going to last for few hours and then you will again be back with a thump on the ground, and now life will look even more miserable, because now you have something to compare it with. Drugs like Ecstasy cannot reach your consciousness. They can only reach your mind. They have nothing parallel to meditation.

Meditation reaches your consciousness. It is a state of no-mind. And drugs like Ecstasy reach only to the mind, and give you a euphoria, beautiful dreams, fantasies which appear to be real. So when people tell you that they have experienced so many beautiful things, you feel sad. You have been meditating and you have not felt anything and these people are feeling things through an ordinary, chemical drug. Their experiences will not happen to you. The path of the drug and the path of meditation are totally different.

On the path of meditation, you will experience silence; you will experience a joy without any reason; you will experience immense light, a luminosity arising from your very center – as if you have become a star. But these things only happen in the beginning part of meditation. As meditation grows, all experiences start going. The ultimate in meditation is a state of no experience. Just pure nothingness – because that is the source of existence and that is the place where existence goes again and again to renew itself.

Now we have on experimental grounds the conclusion that has been reached in the East by many mystics, that just as everything in existence moves in a circle – stars, sun, the moon, the earth, everything moves in a circle – everything that is born, dies. Earths are born and then they die. Of course, they have a long life. This earth has been here for four million years. But this is not a long life; it is still a child. Four million years means nothing because the sun is almost ten million years old and our sun is not very old; it is one of the youngest in the universe.

There are suns which are so old and so far away that when I came to know about it, it was really shocking. There are suns so far away that they will never know that the earth existed – for the simple reason that when the earth was born four million years ago, the rays that started moving towards the earth from those faraway suns have not yet reached. The distance is so great. By the time they reach, the earth will be finished. So if somebody from that star were trying to find about the earth, he would miss it completely because it would be lost between two rays. If he were taking a photograph, no image would appear on his film – just emptiness.

In this vast universe, the Eastern mystics have come to realize that even the whole universe goes into death once in a while. Planets die, suns die, stars die – every day new stars are born, new planets are born. Whole solar systems have disappeared, not leaving even a trace behind, and new solar systems have appeared. They say, and I agree with them, that the whole universe dies. Then there is darkness; everything has gone to sleep. And again there will be dawn; again planets will be born, stars will be born – a new cycle of creation. Millions of cycles of creation have happened and they will go on happening. Your consciousness belongs to the eternal which never dies. At the most, it goes into sleep when the whole universe dies, and comes back in the morning awake, fresh – a new world is beginning.

Just remember one thing: that for all the secrets of life, meditation is the only key. So go deeper into meditation and don't be bothered about experiences. Just look at those people who are taking Ecstasy. I don't think it is a dangerous drug, but look at those people. Do you see the light of the eyes of Gautam Buddha? Do you see in their gestures the grace of a Krishna? Do you see something in their life that has changed because of their experiences? Nothing has changed. They have become more sad, more miserable. Now the only hankering is to get the drug – they can remain hungry, but the drug is needed. They are deceiving themselves.

The only criterion for a right method is that it should transform your life. You will become more peaceful, more loving, more intelligent, more aware. Your life should show it – only then is what you are doing right. If by taking a drug you enjoy dreams, I will not say don't enjoy dreams because I am always for totality – enjoy totally! But you don't know anything about meditation. At least, don't disturb the meditators. You are disturbed.... Soon you will get fed up. Those same scenes which were psychedelic in the beginning will start becoming ordinary. And what are you going to gain? Your ignorance remains the same, your cruelty remains the same, your anger, your violence, your jealousies remain the same.

Meditation is a science of transforming the qualities of life. It is not just to give you a little consolation or a little entertainment. It is to transform you so that you can become part of the universal circus. It is so hilarious; you just have to be clear enough to see it. Just watch any man and you will be surprised: the world is full of hilarious people, but nobody is taking note. Otherwise you need not go and waste your money – just sit by the side of the road and watch the show.

Don't be bothered by any experiences that people who are taking drugs will tell you about. Meditation is not concerned with experiences but with the experiencer. Experiences are outside things. Meditation is concerned with you, not what happens to you, not what you see.... A beautiful rose – certainly under the influence of a drug it will look more beautiful, more radiant but still, what is the use? You remain the same person. Your heart does not open its petals, you are as dead as before. Except for meditation there is no way. Drugs can give you hallucinations, illusory experiences....

I am not in any way against anything. My whole approach is to use everything in such a way that it can become a nourishment to life, an evolution to consciousness. I am not against drugs either. It is such a foolishness on the part of governments all over the world that alcohol is not condemned, although alcohol is more dangerous than any of the drugs.

This is how you can see that you are being dominated by fools. Alcohol is allowed, and drugs.... Many of them are harmless, but thousands of people and particularly young men and women are in jails because they were taking drugs that the governments decided should not be taken.

It is strange that the government does not ask the medical colleges to investigate whether they are harmful or not, and if some drug is harmful, but gives a beautiful experience – illusory, hallucinatory, but at least something in this world which is just like a desert... If some drug has some harmful effects, medical science is advanced enough to remove those harmful effects. Drugs can be purified to such an extent that anybody can take them and have the experience. Because no government has the right to prevent anybody from having any experience. He is not harming anybody....

The function of the government should be to take care of people. There are so many medical colleges around the world – do research, find something which gives beautiful experiences to people, nourishment to the body, health to the mind. And you will be surprised at why I am saying this. I am saying this because if good, harmless drugs are made available and people are allowed to take them, these people are soon going to be fed up with the drugs and their experiences. Sooner or later they are going to move towards meditation – there is no other way.

We will have used the drugs. Without harming the person we will have managed it so that the drug has given him some experience and now he wants something more which the drug cannot give. And in fact, as you take a drug every day its impact goes on declining. Every day you have to add more quantity. But finally, every drug becomes useless, your body becomes immune to it.

I have been with people who have taken all sorts of drugs but they are not drug-addicted people; they are following an ancient path which has used drugs. And then the moment comes when drugs don't affect them at all. You can give them as much quantity as possible, and nothing happens to them.

In their monasteries they have dangerous serpents, particularly cobras. If you are bitten by a cobra you are finished. And these people allow the cobra to bite on their tongues! In the beginning they have psychedelic experiences, and now the cobra poison cannot kill them... they are full of poison.

The strangest thing is that the cobra dies because the poor cobra has never come across such a man – so full of poisons! The cobra has a small gland in his mouth, that is all – the rest of his body is without any poison. In China, the cobra is a delicacy – just cut the head and you have a beautiful vegetable.

The people I was talking about soon get immune to cobra poison too, and that is their test. Then their master allows them initiation. Now nothing can create hallucination in them.

So drugs have been used in the East for centuries as a help to meditation. Now they have destroyed all possibility in the man that any poison, any drug can create illusion. His consciousness is far stronger now. No poison can kill him, no poison can make him even unconscious – he remains alert and conscious.

As far as I am concerned these people were doing the right thing and it will be good if rather than behaving fascistically, we allow our people to have the experience if they want – but give it in such a way that soon it can indicate to them the path leading towards some meditation.

I am not against drugs. I am not against anything, because everything can be used in the right way and everything can be used in a wrong way. Poison can be medicine and medicine can be poison, it all depends.

9

Mind as a master is a disaster

BELOVED OSHO,

WHEN I LISTEN TO YOUR DISCOURSES, YOU TAKE ME
ON AN INDESCRIBABLE JOURNEY. IF AFTERWARDS
SOMEONE ASKS ME ABOUT WHAT YOU HAVE SAID, I
HARDLY REMEMBER. BUT WHEN PEOPLE ASK ME
PERSONAL QUESTIONS, ANSWERS ARE COMING OUT
OF MY MOUTH WHICH ASTONISH ME THE MOST.
OSHO, AM I BECOMING A PARROT OF YOUR WORDS?

Listening to me is less like listening and more like drinking. Although it is a verbal communication, that is only the superficial part of it. Hidden beneath it is the real communion where meanings are absorbed and words are forgotten.

You cannot become my parrot – at least while I am alive. It is impossible to become my parrot. You will go crazy! My words are so full of contradictions that the poor parrot will be crushed under those contradictions. And it is a sure signal that you are not becoming a parrot because you don't remember my words. The parrot only remembers words, but whatever is being communicated to you is absorbed.

It has to become part of your blood, your bones, your marrow – not part of your memory. Unless it becomes your blood, your bones and your marrow, it cannot transform you. And the transformation is happening. You are aware of it, that in answering a personal question or responding to a situation, something comes out of you that is not yours. You are surprised even by your own words – because listening silently, not paying attention to the words but to the wordless message contained in them, you are slowly, slowly moving your very consciousness.

You will not become more knowledgeable here. You will become a new man, a man who knows the meaning of life, a man who has experienced the great benediction of silence and serenity. His actions are bound to reflect his consciousness.

And if you cannot remember my words, don't be worried about it. You are nourished by the meaning, and it is the meaning that will change you, your actions, your responses. It is not the power of the words that transforms anybody. There is no need to be afraid, you are on the right track.

One thing has to be understood: you remember only things which you have not understood. Things that you have understood need not be remembered – they will act, they will be in your eyes. They will be in your gestures, they will be in your life, they will be in your love, they will be in everything that you do; but they will not be part of your memory system. They are far higher than the memory because they don't belong to the mind.

Mind is the lowest part of your consciousness. It is good enough as far as the world is concerned, but it is not of any use if you are thinking to go on an inner pilgrimage. You will have to leave that mind behind. Its whole training is for the outside world. It will create all kinds of hindrances if you start moving inwards. It is a trained outsider.

So it is good that words are not being caught by your memory system. Your listening is so total that the words go directly to your very being, to your consciousness – they don't need the mechanism of the mind.

The mechanism of the mind is good as far as the objective world is concerned but in the inner, in the interior of your being, mind has no entry. Mind has never entered into the innermost core of any human being in the whole of history; the very nature of its functioning prohibits it. It is by nature, extrovert. The moment you start moving inwards, you are separating from your mind system, you are leaving it behind. Now you are moving on the wings of consciousness.

If what I am saying to you is becoming a reality in your life, who cares whether you remember my words or not? It is perfectly right not to remember them; any remembrance of the words will be an obstruction. Let only pure meaning spread to the deepest core of your being where words have no access, where only wordless meaning is able to enter.

A bishop, thinking to convert a Zen master – because he saw thousands of disciples, he thought it better if this old man were converted; then naturally all these disciples would be converted too. With great respect he approached the master. He had brought with him the Holy Bible. He opened the chapter containing the

Sermon on the Mount. He wanted to show the Zen master the best of Jesus and if he agrees... and it is very difficult to disagree with the Sermon on the Mount. The argument inside his mind was that it is very difficult, almost impossible, to disagree with the Sermon on the Mount unless you have a superb, logical mind, something parallel to the genius of Friedrich Nietzsche – then perhaps you may be able to disagree.

Nietzsche is the only man in the whole of history who has disagreed with Jesus, and not on weak points but on the strongest. The ordinary way is to find loopholes, weaknesses, and hammer on them. If you cannot find them, create them – nobody is so much interested in going to the original sources to look. The world lives on newspapers.

Jesus says "Man cannot live by bread alone." I say to you, a man *can* live without bread but not without the newspaper. The newspaper is his whole wisdom. These are people who cannot argue against Jesus, Zarathustra or Lao Tzu. For example, Jesus says, that God is love, God is just, always fair, always compassionate. The Old Testament's God is a very angry God – never forgiving, never forgetting; nobody is going to avoid the punishment for his evil acts. The concept of Jesus' God seems to be far more refined.

Loving, just, fair, compassionate... it seems to be closer to the human heart. But Friedrich Nietzsche criticizes it and his criticism is foundational and crucial. He says, "You cannot say God is love because wherever love is, hate is and if your God knows no hate, he cannot know love. How will he find it out that this is love? To define love, a certain experience of hate is needed. To define silence, noise is needed. To define beauty, ugliness is needed. You are alive because every day many people are dying and you can see the distinction. If nobody was dying, you would not even be able to imagine what life is."

His criticism is very psychological. He is saying that you are taking one part, one side of a coin, and leaving the other side. This is impossible. You cannot have a coin with only one side. You can go on making it thinner but the other side will remain – either both or none.

Nietzsche says Jesus' God is nothing but the completion of the

Jewish concept of God. He was anger, he was hate, he was rage. Jesus has taken the other side of the coin, but both are halves and God is whole. If there is any God, he can only be whole.

Jesus says, "If somebody slaps you don't be angry, but with humbleness give him the other cheek also." It is such a beautiful idea, but a man like Friedrich Nietzsche has an insight and maturity which the common masses cannot have. His criticism is one of the examples of the highest reaches of logic.

Nietzsche says, "If somebody hits me on one of my cheeks, I am not so inhumane as to give him my other cheek. That is egoistic. It is trying to prove that 'you are just an ordinary human being – I am a messiah, a messenger of God. I forgive you and if you enjoy hitting me, you can hit me more.' Nietzsche's point is that you are reducing the other person to utter humiliation. Nobody in two thousand years' history has raised this question.

Nietzsche says, "If somebody hits me, I will hit him as hard as I can because I am just as human as you are. I don't want to prove myself holier than you, higher than you, superior to you. I respect your humanity and I accept your challenge. You have slapped my face. You have given the challenge to me."

He is saying that Jesus' idea is disrespectful. And certainly if you look deep into its psychology, you will find it *is* insulting. You are not accepting the other man as a man equal to you. He is an ignorant man, unenlightened. You are awakened. You are creating a distance between yourself and the person who has slapped you.

Nietzsche says, "I cannot create that distance. That distance is nothing but fulfillment of a very subtle kind – and fulfillment not of your being but only of your ego."

But this bishop thought that by reading from the Sermon on the Mount, the old man was bound to be convinced that Jesus was as enlightened as Gautam Buddha. He read two lines and the old man said, "That's enough. Whoever has written these will become enlightened in some future life but as far as this life is concerned, forget all about it."

The bishop said, "But the lines are so beautiful – each word a diamond unto itself."

The Zen master said, "It is not a question of words. While you were reading, I was also listening to the gaps. The man was articulate as far as words are concerned but the gaps expose him completely. What he is saying is only mind stuff, it is not his experience. But the man is good. Don't be worried; in some future life he will become an enlightened person."

Look – life is not a difficult matter. It becomes a problem when your life wants to go one way and your mind drags you in another and you are in a conflict, torn apart. You can go to neither side... because half of you is trying to go in another direction.

Life becomes absolutely simple once you start functioning from something that is higher than your mind. In the beginning for any seeker the whole search is to find a space above the mind.

Once you have found a small space above the mind, all dualism disappears, all tensions, all anxieties disappear. And strangely enough, the mind which was never in your control, suddenly surrenders itself to you. Mind as a master is a disaster. Mind as a servant is a beautiful gift of nature. You just have to find the master – and it is not far away. It is just above the mind. Only one step.

BELOVED OSHO,
YOU RECENTLY TALKED ABOUT HOW BOGUS
CHANNELING IS. AS A RAJNEESH GROUP LEADER, I
FEEL THAT MY WORK IS MOST SUCCESSFUL WHEN I
MANAGE TO GET OUT OF THE WAY AND BECOME A
VEHICLE FOR YOU. AT THESE TIMES, WHATEVER I'M
SAYING OR DOING, I FEEL YOUR LOVE AND SILENCE
POURING THROUGH ME. AM I IN A DELUSION, LIKE
ALL THE OTHER PEOPLE WHO THINK THEY
CHANNEL? COULD YOU PLEASE SAY WHAT MY
FUNCTION IS AS A GROUP LEADER, AS YOUR
DISCIPLE?

The people who have been proposing for thousands of years that they are the mediums of God – in other religions of "gods" – or of those masters who are no more in the body, *are* becoming vehicles to them, mediums to them. The possibility is there. If you have loved me, even when I am not in the body there can be still a contact. For love it makes no difference. But the whole thing depends on the medium – his purity, his silence, the absolute stillness of his mind. The silence has to be so great that it is as if he is no longer present – only silence is there. He has become just a hollow bamboo.

I criticized those Californian pretenders who are talking about channeling themselves with dead masters, with the people who have gone beyond and cannot come back to the earth because their work on the earth is complete. These people in California have not gone into any discipline which makes them mediums. They know nothing of meditation. They know nothing of the state of no-mind – because only in the state of no-mind is there a possibility of contacting some unembodied soul.

These people who have become channels are not in any meditative state, one thing. The second thing is that whatever messages they are bringing are such crap that it is disrespectful towards the dead. Those poor fellows cannot say anything now, that "this is not my message."

When a message comes from a master it has to be something so absolutely needed that the masters who are no more in their bodies feel that a message should be sent to all unconscious, sleeping, blind people. But it is only when there is something urgent; otherwise, there is no need.

I have looked into a few of the books which these channels have produced – they are absolutely rubbish! They can be valued only by weighing them – that much paper has been wasted. I have not come across a single mediumistic book which shows the greatness or the grandeur of a Gautam Buddha. And strangely enough, all these mediums are not mentioning the names of the real masters because then, compared to their statements, the rubbish message that they bring will look too poor.

If somebody says, "This is a message from Gautam Buddha," then it has to be of his quality. So they are talking about masters who have never happened, they are talking about masters who happened on the continent of Atlantis which has drowned. Fortunately there is no proof now, no document, no evidence left about whether there was such a master, ever. But I can say that these statements are not coming from any master. The statements themselves are not luminous. There is nothing that gives them the authority of experience. It is all gibberish.

And you should also see that these people who have been chosen for this great work of becoming vehicles... their lives don't prove it. They are just as greedy, as angry, as jealous as anybody else. Their mediumship would have transformed them. In fact, unless they were transformed, they could not become mediums.

My sannyasins working around the world in therapy groups have felt that sometimes they are open to me, available to me, and sometimes they are closed. It is human nature, ups and downs; they are not enlightened yet.

Sometimes they see the eternal snows, far away in the Himalayas; but they are far away and just once in a while, when there are not clouds and the sun is shining, you can see them. But you are not there.

When a sannyasin is closed, his first work should be not on the group participants, his first work should be upon himself. He has to open, he has to be available to me. This is simply an excuse – because if he is open to me, he is open to the whole existence.

The moment you open your door, immediately the fragrance of the flowers enters without making any noise. The sun rays enter. A cool breeze comes in. You have opened the door to the whole universe.

To be available to the master is just an excuse. You will be afraid to be open to the whole universe – it will be too much. The master convinces you that there is no need to open all the doors and all the windows: "You just open a small window – a special window for me." But once you open even a small window, the whole sky enters in. And the joy, the peace, the beauty that you feel will make you open all the windows and all the doors.

My therapists have been seeing the difference in their work. When they are open and available they can see and feel so decisively, so indubitably, that something from beyond is pouring through them. They have just become a hollow bamboo, playing the song, allowing the song to flow. The song is not of the flute.

The greatness of the flute is that it does not hinder the song in any way but helps it, allows it to reach into the world.

There is no question of channeling – although I have given you my number. It is a difficult number. Zero is my number and unless you are zero, you cannot find it. You have to be zero to be in tune with me. But then you will see a tremendous change in the quality of your work. You can do miracles to the participants.

If you are closed, you may be able to conduct a group because you know the technical side.... Do you know the difference between the scientist and the technician? The technician is not a scientist, and the scientist is not a technician. The scientist discovers the hidden treasures of existence and also discovers the techniques and methods to use those treasures. The technician is only concerned with the technique. He is not a discoverer, but he knows exactly what has to be done. There will be a great difference of quality but it may not be felt by the people who have never known anything higher.

A therapist who is not in deep meditation, is not open, is not merging into the universe, will not be able to become a real help to the participants. Perhaps a consolation... perhaps those participants will feel the euphoria for a few days and then it will fade out. Then again they need another group. They become addicts.

Group addicts are in the same category as drug addicts. The group has not helped them to be free and independent; the group has made them slaves. Now they will be continuously searching – this group, that group. But no group is going to give them an insight into themselves because the therapists themselves are not in a situation where all problems are solved, all questions dissolved, where they are simply relishing each breath. They have their problems just like you have. It happened....

One of the great psychologists, one of the founders of the movement of psychology, Alfred Adler – he is one of the trinity: Sigmund Freud, Carl Gustav Jung and Alfred Adler, these are the three pillars. He was talking to his students and a very embarrassing situation arose. One statement he made, that "My experience..." and it was a lifelong experience of the thousands of patients he had studied. He said, "My experience with people is that it is not just an accident that a person becomes a teacher in a school. He wants domination. He is not strong enough to become a terrorist, but he can become a teacher and can torture thirty small boys and girls." It seems there is some truth in what he is saying.

Everybody chooses a particular profession; there must be a psychology behind it. It has been found in many surveys that the people who study medicine are the people who are most afraid of death. Your doctors are more afraid of death than anybody else. They have come to medicine in search, unconsciously, of finding a way that leads beyond death. It is not a deliberate decision but if they are hypnotized and asked, the answer comes clear: they are afraid of death and they have joined the profession out of that fear.

In the life of one of the emperors of India, Aurangzeb, there is an incident. He had revolted against his father, kept him in jail, and taken over the empire. He writes in his autobiography: "My father requested of me from jail, 'I would like to have at least thirty students to whom I can teach religion, literature, poetry. In this way I will remain engaged, and engaged in an activity which is very close to my heart. I love children, I love poetry, and now there is no work for me.'"

The comment of his son is, "He still wants to dominate. The desire for having thirty students has nothing to do with education because in his whole life he was never interested in education; he never opened great universities or colleges or anything. He never did anything for poetry or literature. Now, in jail, he wants thirty students so that he can dominate. He can still remain an emperor although the empire will be very small – only thirty students." But people are even satisfied with one person – one woman, one man. Just a small empire confined in a small flat.

Adler was saying that politicians are all suffering from an inferiority complex. They feel inferior for any stupid reason. For example, Lenin, the man who created the Soviet revolution and the Soviet Union was very much worried and concerned and always was conscious of the fact that his legs were small. His upper body was bigger and his lower body was very small. His legs could not reach to the floor. Sitting on the chair, his legs were just dangling there and he was trying to hide them in every possible way so that nobody would see them hanging there in the air.

That was Lenin's problem. That created the Russian revolution. That made him the greatest revolutionary in the world. That made him the greatest, most powerful man on one-sixth of the land of the earth – the Soviet Union is one-sixth of the land of the whole earth. It is almost two continents. It starts in Europe and it ends in Asia, it covers the whole of Europe and Asia.

All politicians are in search of power. It is a will to power. But why? You must be feeling somehow powerless. You want to prove to yourself and to the world that you are not powerless because you know that if you don't do anything, you will suffer your whole life from inferiority and everybody else will look at you as inferior. This situation has to be changed.

In this way, Adler was going to describe every profession possible, and what is the psychological reason behind it. Just then, a student stood up and asked, "What about the psychologists? Is there something loose in their heads? Why does anybody choose psychology? According to the philosophy you have expounded there must be something wrong with his mind, and I agree totally with it."

Adler was very much shocked – that meant he was mentally retarded, sick, something was wrong in his mind. He never mentioned that theory again! He mentioned it only once in his whole life. That is rare, because the theory is very significant and very true.

Why does a man want to be a therapist? Has he done his own therapy? Is he finished with his homework? If not, then what right has he got to interfere in other people's lives, their minds, their unconscious, their superconscious? He has only read these words, and he is trying these words on poor people – poor because they are being treated as guinea pigs, poor because they have paid two hundred and fifty dollars to be treated as a guinea pig!

And there is a human tendency which is not taken note of.... When somebody pays two hundred and fifty dollars for a therapy session, if he says after the session, "Nothing happened," then everybody will say, "You are an idiot! They cheated you – two hundred and fifty dollars gone. And we have been telling you that you were hanging around wrong people, but you never listened."

Now two hundred and fifty dollars are gone, the whole week is destroyed, and to be treated by people as an idiot... this can be avoided. They come out and before they get out of the therapy premises, they start smiling. They start walking as they have never done before, so light! Now, let the people ask.

And people will say, "We were wrong, something has happened. Look at that man – singing a song, unafraid of the world. He has never been like that. It is worth two hundred and fifty dollars." And when they ask him, he tells them what great things have happened, great experiences. This way he saves face. This is an old phenomenon, and the psychology is simple. I must have told you a story....

A man was caught in the middle of the night, in the bed of somebody else's wife. The man was not supposed to come home that night but his work was finished so he came home earlier. He could not believe it. His wife was very devoted – that's how he had known her – and this man was also well known to him. He was certainly a nice gentleman, but what was happening was not nice. He became so furious that he took out a knife and cut off the man's nose.

The man was well respected in the society... now everybody would be asking tomorrow: "What happened? How come you were found in that house? Why did you go there in the middle of the night?" – a thousand and one questions, and he had no answer. And this nose, absent, will be seen more than when it was present and nobody bothered about it. There was not much time. He escaped in the night.

On the way, reaching the other town, he met another traveler who was going in the same direction. The traveler asked, "What happened to your nose?" He smiled, he danced.... The traveler said, "What is the matter?"

He said, "It is so simple. My master used to say, 'It is very simple but unless you experience it yourself, there is no way.'" He asked, "What do you mean by all these things?"

He said, "I have experienced God. Only the nose has to be

sacrificed, the nose symbolizes the ego."

The man said, "That's right! I am also a seeker. It will be a blessing if you accept me as your first disciple."

So he took the man by the side of the road, behind a bush and cut off his nose. The nose was gone. The man looked all around and he said, "But I don't see any God."

The master said, "Neither do I. But what to do? When your nose is gone some reasonable, rational and acceptable explanation is needed. Now you go into town, smile, dance and whoever asks, 'What is the matter?' just tell him that, 'It was such a simple thing and religions have made it so complicated just to exploit people. You have only to cut off your nose. Except for the nose, there is nothing between you and God.'"

People said, "We never heard this philosophy before. We have seen all kinds of scriptures and all kinds of religious preachers have been in the town. Nobody has told us that the nose is the problem."

He said, "You come to my master. He does not go inside the town, he remains outside. I am his chief disciple. Those who are interested in seeing God, I can give them appointments."

A few people were interested. In the evening, a few more noses disappeared and everybody looked all around and said, "But where is God?"

The master said, "Don't be foolish, there is no God. Now there is no nose either! But you will have to say something to people; otherwise, they will call you an idiot. It is up to you – to be intelligent, wise, enlightened or to be idiots."

Within two weeks, almost half of the town was without noses. And everybody was talking about God and the beautiful experiences. Even the king became interested. He said, "Just for a nose, losing God is stupidity. So many people cannot be wrong... and they are my people." He called them and asked them, "Tell us exactly what happened."

They told the king, "We met this great master and he said that there is not much of a problem. If you are just ready to remove your nose, the curtain is opened; God is available, and everything that saints have been talking about for centuries. And he was right.

Now for the first time we are alive." And they started dancing....

The king said, "These are all intelligent people, so make an appointment for me."

The prime minister to the king was an old man. He said, "Just wait a little. Let me try to find out exactly what the situation is because nobody has ever heard that cutting off the nose is the shortest way to God. You just give me three days and let me look into the whole thing.

In the night, he came with a group of army people and caught hold of the man, who had now become a great master. They took him to the palace, gave him a good beating and told him, "Unless you tell the truth, the beating will continue."

He said, "You know the truth, I know the truth, everybody knows the truth. I have been caught in the bed of somebody else's wife and that madman has cut off my nose. Now what do you suppose I should do? – go around town telling everybody what happened? So I thought this was a good chance. I have been thinking many times to renounce the world and this is the best chance. Even if I don't want to, I have to renounce at least this town where people know me and go to another town. Then I talked with this man on the road who was a fellow traveler. I was not certain that he would be convinced – because it is so stupid. But people *are* stupid, and the man agreed!

"I was feeling sad for the poor guy. It was at least relevant in my case because I was caught with somebody else's wife and he was angry. Now this poor guy has not even been caught with somebody's wife but he was so convinced... I tried to tell him, 'You are too young. First live your life – and this is a simple method, you can come any time.' But he wouldn't leave me so I had to cut off his nose.

"He could not find any God and I told him that I had also not found any God, but now this is the only way to protect our respectability. 'You go into the town and dance and sing and declare that, "Whoever wants to see God need not wait a single moment. My master is there, I will give you the appointment."

The prime minister brought the man to the king and said, "Listen to the story – and you were going to get your nose removed! Then *you* would have started seeing God – that seems to be very logical. And perhaps all of us in your court would have been forced to remove our noses because it does not look right that the king has achieved God-realization and you are living with a God-realized person, still in ignorance."

They told the man, "You go back to your home town. Otherwise, you will have to remain in jail." This man certainly seems to be criminal. But all your religions are doing almost exactly the same in different ways.

The therapist has to remember that the moment *he* comes in he should, if he is honest, tell the participants that "I am no longer open to existence and in this state of closedness, I can only do harm to you. I will work only when I am open, vulnerable." And the master is only an excuse. It is easier to be open towards me because you love me and you trust me. But while you are becoming open to me, you are becoming open to everything.

So it is not really being open to me – that is only a strategy, a device. The reality is to be open to the whole existence. With that vastness, clouds wandering inside your chest, you will be able to help many people to understand their situation, to accept whatever they are, to learn methods of becoming more conscious.

And the therapist has to remind people continually that he is not the master. The moment the therapist starts playing the role of the master, then he is going to do much harm to people. I have known hundreds of therapists. They have the same problems as you have, perhaps more, and they are trying to help you. They are drowning and they are trying to save somebody who is drowning – perhaps drowning together is better than drowning alone.

The therapist knows nothing beyond mind. His only work is to bring people to a normal, peaceful mind. This is not a great achievement but you will make the person able to function in life in a normal way. The madman is nothing but one who is behaving abnormally. The therapist simply pulls down the abnormal man to the normal state. His whole work is confined within the mind.

He cannot be a master and if he wants his therapy to be of significance, he has to function as a vehicle, as a channel to a master he loves. Then therapy goes through a transformation. Then you are not just trying to work out how these people should be brought to normality; that is only a preparation. You have prepared the ground, but don't think you have prepared a garden. After preparing the ground you will need seeds, plants and much care and much love to make a beautiful garden.

A man can be normally mad – that's what the whole of humanity is. A man can be abnormally mad – psychoanalysts, psychologists, psychiatrists are trying to somehow bring him back. And the third category is the man who has gone beyond mind. The function of the master is to take you beyond the mind.

The therapist can be helpful, he can prepare the ground, he can take out the weeds, but that does not mean that he becomes a master, that does not mean he becomes a gardener. That is a totally different affair.

Therapy in itself can be used as a step, but if you know only therapy and nothing more beyond it, that which was going to become a step, becomes a block. It is the same stone. Either you use it as a stepping stone or it becomes a block preventing you from moving further, higher, closer to your sources.

Right now, all over the world there are many therapists. But my therapist is unique in the sense that he is not only working according to the findings of psychology – he is working according to the findings of Yoga, of Tantra, of Sufism, of Zen, of Tao, of Hassidism. He's a spiritual guide. But for that, knowledge acquired only from books will not help. You will have to go through a transformation.

And the participants in your groups can also be helpful to you, just as you can be helpful to them; because their problems are your problems, your problems are their problems. And remember one thing: it is easier to solve somebody else's problem because you are not involved. You are detached, you can see more clearly because you are not in the mess. You can help that man to come out and you can learn something for yourself because many times, you will be in the same situation. I allowed therapists in my communes to work on the participants and to work on themselves. The real work is upon yourself. Only when you have a light within you, you may be able to share it with others.

BELOVED OSHO,
IT'S HARD TO IMAGINE MY EVER BEING VERY
COURAGEOUS. IN FACT, MOST OF THE TIME, I FEEL
LIKE A MOUSE. CAN THE QUALITIES OF LOVE AND
MEDITATION TURN EVEN A MOUSE INTO A
BUDDHA? PS I'VE BEEN SO MOUSY THAT THIS IS MY
FIRST DISCOURSE QUESTION IN EIGHT YEARS.

A mouse can become a Gautam Buddha. He just needs a bottle of alcohol; as he becomes drunk, he starts forgetting that he is a mouse. Who says he is a mouse? Under the impact of alcohol, he may start roaring like a lion. But as the alcohol goes, with its influence on your mind and body, you will be a mouse again.

And it is very painful. To be a mouse is okay but to be a mouse *again* – that hurts! But the mouse has his own qualities, he has his own intelligence. Millions of human beings have many potentialities, many talents, and they remain unused. So if other animals who are deeper in darkness, deeper in unconscious, cannot achieve to higher states of consciousness, you should not laugh at them.

You must have heard the ancient story, which is almost universal – in every language, in every country, something like that story exists....

For centuries it has been going on: that the mice are always tortured by the cats and they are always having conferences, discussion groups – how to get rid of the cats?

Finally, one old mouse said, "I have heard from the ancients... there is a way. You have to tie a bell round the neck of the cat, and all problems will be solved – because wherever she is, we will know. It is only when we do not know that we are caught."

But the whole crowd laughed, giggled. They said, "We have been hearing this type of thing in every conference, but the question remains the same: who is going to tie a bell around the neck of a cat?"

The old man said, "The solution is in our hands, but the person who can manage to transform it into a reality has not happened." A young boy said, "I can do it. This is nothing."

They said, "You must be mad. You are not even adult, you don't have any voting rights."

But the young boy said, "The problem confronting us has nothing to do with citizenship, old age. It has nothing to do with these things, it has something to do with intelligence. I have it."

They said, "Okay, give him a chance. We are afraid – because your father and mother have gone for a holy pilgrimage and surely you will be eaten by the cat. What answer will we give them?"

The boy said, "Don't be worried. I have figured it out completely scientifically." And he managed!

He used to go into the neighborhood medical store; that was his most-loved place. So he brought a few sleeping pills and dropped them in the cat's milk. Naturally, once the cat drank the milk, she fell unconscious for fifteen or twenty minutes. That was enough time – he tied the bell around her neck and the next day everybody was puzzled, the cats were puzzled because they could not get a single mouse. The mice were puzzled..."For centuries we knew that the only solution was a bell but nobody did anything. And now we can see that it was a simple thing."

If you look into the lives, the past lives of Mahavira – in many of his lives he was an animal. The same is the case with Gautam Buddha. Both have told hundreds of stories of their past lives. In many of their lives, they were plants, in many of their lives they were birds, in many of their lives they were other animals.

In one story, Buddha said he was an elephant and the forest caught fire and he was running – all the animals were running out of the forest. The fire was becoming more and more dangerous. The elephant was running and he came out of the circle of fire. Just for few minutes he wanted to rest under a tree, and as he was going to put his fourth foot on the ground, he was alerted by a small rabbit who was sitting there, under the protection of his foot.

The elephant was in trouble. If he put his foot down on the ground, the rabbit would be finished. If he did not put his foot down... the fire was coming. And the fire came but the elephant remained determined not to kill the rabbit. He died in the fire.

Gautam Buddha said, "I was born as a man because of my small act of compassion towards the rabbit."

No animal, no tree, nothing in existence is incapable of becoming enlightened. It may take a little time, or a little more time, but enlightenment is a destiny. It is a destiny of the whole existence. The whole existence has to become one day a festival of lights.

The idea of non-violence in the East arose because of this dis-covery: that each animal has the potential to become the highest peak of truth, consciousness, love. It is ugly to kill them for eating. The idea of not killing animals for eating came from the experi-ence that they all are capable of becoming gods in their own right. They are equal to you – maybe a little more unconscious, a little more in the dark, but they are not different. We are one fam-ily. And it is not only so about the animals; this whole existence is one family. To see and experience it as one family is what I mean by love. Love becomes the most important phenomenon in the transformation of man.

You have not asked a question for eight years. There is no need to be worried about it. You may not have asked, but I have been answering your questions too. It is only a question of waiting a lit-tle; if you are not going to ask, I am going to answer anyway.

And don't be worried that you have fear in your heart. Every-body has fear in the heart because everybody has death in the future. It cannot be said that you can enter into discipleship only when you have dropped fear – that will be closing the door. I say unto you: fear, greed, anger, everything is allowed. You just come a little closer, enter the temple. The very entry burns out all that is false in you. Only pure gold remains.

10 God is because you are full of fear

BELOVED OSHO,
RECENTLY I DEVELOPED EPILEPTIC FITS – APPARENTLY
DUE TO A TINY CYST IN MY BRAIN – WHICH THE
SPECIALISTS DON'T UNDERSTAND. BUT FOR ME IT
FEELS LIKE SOMETHING AMAZING IS HAPPENING.
THE FIRST FIT, IN JUNE, CAME TOTALLY AS A
SURPRISE, AND FELT LIKE A BIG HIT ON THE HEAD:
WAKE UP! SINCE LEAVING THE COMMUNE I HAVE
BEEN LIVING UNAWARE. AFTERWARDS I CHANGED;
WANTED TO BE ALONE, SILENT, TO MEDITATE AND
TO LISTEN TO YOU. GRADUALLY I'M MORE WITH
FRIENDS AGAIN, FEELING MORE MATURE, MORE
CENTERED. THEN, WHILE FEELING PHYSICALLY VERY
WELL AND CLEAR IN MYSELF, ANOTHER FIT
HAPPENED A FEW DAYS AGO. ALREADY I FEEL
SOMETHING DIFFERENT AGAIN, A GREATER
INTENSITY – SOMETIMES VERY AFRAID, SOMETIMES
SO ECSTATIC I FEEL I COULD EXPLODE! GENERALLY I
AM MORE PLAYFUL. FOR THE FIRST TIME I FEEL
BEAUTIFUL, SAFER, MORE LOVING. LIFE IS VERY
BEAUTIFUL AND JOYFUL. I ENJOY THE PRELUDE TO
THE FITS; MY 'LEARNED' KNOWLEDGE DISAPPEARS
AND I'M LEFT WITH A SENSE OF ME – VERY EASY, NO
EFFORT. BUT FEAR COMES TOO: I'M AFRAID OF WHAT
MIGHT HAPPEN, AND DURING THE FITS I SENSE A
HUGE "NO" IN ME. I FEEL THAT IF I COULD SAY YES
INSTEAD, IT WOULD SOMEHOW BE BETTER. BELOVED,
BEAUTIFUL OSHO, PLEASE COULD YOU COMMENT?

There are a few things which are important for everybody, not only to the questioner. The most important thing is that medical science, physiology, psychology, are very immature in the sense that they are only doing their work on the surface of human beings. They are not finding a way to man's center. And because they do not accept the existence of some consciousness beyond mind, of some consciousness beyond death, they are completely closed, prejudiced against the whole tremendous effort mystics have made in finding the center of consciousness.

Many times the diagnosis of a physiologist or a physician may be absolutely wrong for the simple reason that his vision is not comprehensive enough. He understands man only as matter, and mind as just a by-product of matter, a shadow phenomenon with nothing beyond it, nothing eternal, nothing that is going to remain forever.

They have created a picture of human beings which creates despair in intelligent people. And because of their outright rejection, their approach is not scientific; it is as superstitious as any other fanatic religious or political person's. Science has no right to deny consciousness unless it has explored the inner sky of human consciousness and found that it is dream stuff, not a reality but only a shadow. They have *not* explored – they have simply assumed.

Materialism is the assumption, the superstition of the world of science, just as God, heaven and hell are superstitions of the religious world. Science is not yet pure science and it cannot be, because the scientist is not yet innocent, unprejudiced, ready to go with the truth in spite of himself and his conditioning.

The fits that are happening to you are not a disease. I am not a physician but I am not looking from the physician's side of the phenomenon, I am looking from the other shore. Your fit is really a rushing, overwhelming consciousness that your mind cannot contain, and because it cannot contain it, it goes unconscious. I will not call it a disease. I will say you are blessed. And the reason I am so certain that it is not a disease is because after the fit you feel blissful, ecstatic as you have never felt. After a disease you cannot feel ecstatic – you will feel exhausted. After a disease you will feel weak, shaken, wobbly... but you are feeling ecstatic, you are feeling more blissful than you have ever imagined you could feel.

The fruit is the evidence of the tree it has come from. If it is juicy, sweet, tasteful, it is saying something about the tree because whatever it has is a gift from the tree. The tree must be young, the tree must be full of juice. Just looking at the fruit or the flower you can infer much about the tree.

What happens after your fits proves that your fits are not those of a sick man – and I want you to understand something which is missing from medical science. Your fit is because of an abundant release of energy. The mind is capable only of a certain amount: the day-to-day energy which is exhausted very easily. From your center, floods of energy are approaching the brain system. The brain system, the mind, is not able to absorb that much energy; it goes into a state of coma. The doctor will look at the coma, he will wonder about the fit, he will try to find the cause.... And your doctors have not been able to find the cause; they will never be able to find the cause because they are looking in the wrong direction. They are looking in the mind itself, as if something is wrong in the mind; hence the fit. Nothing is wrong in the mind – but the energy beyond the mind is becoming available to the mind.

Mind is a beggar. You will have to learn to live as an emperor, and the fits will disappear. The fits are symbolic that great changes are happening in you.

I am reminded of a few things which will be helpful to you. Five thousand years ago in China, acupuncture was discovered in an accident. A man had suffered his whole life from terrific migraines, and the Chinese medicine had not been helpful at all. They did everything but nothing worked. It seemed the case was hopeless. But they were in the same fallacy as your physicians are.

This man had gone to the forest to collect some wood and was hit by a hunter's arrow accidentally. The arrow hit his leg and his migraine evaporated instantly!

Now ordinarily you could not connect the two; this was a new revelation. He went back to his physicians and told them what had happened: "This arrow has done something: for the first time in my life I am feeling healthy in my head; otherwise it was always heavy." Even if it was not a severe migraine, something of the pain had become almost natural to him. But it had disappeared so miraculously that he was afraid to take the arrow out; it was better to live your whole life with this arrow stuck in your leg than to have that migraine again!

But the doctor said, "The arrow cannot be allowed to remain. It will create poison in the body; it may be poisonous already. It has to be pulled out. But don't be worried, it has given us some clue."

This is how acupuncture was born. The physicians took out the arrow, but the migraine never returned. Over hundreds of years, slowly, slowly they discovered that there are seven hundred centers, interconnected in the body, and it is not necessary that your migraine has its source in your head. The source can be anywhere in the body. It can be at any of those seven hundred centers. The only thing that has to happen is that that center is vibrating your brain, sending waves of energy to your brain which are hitting other centers and creating the migraine.

Now because of that arrow a particular center in the leg was dead – it could not broadcast anymore. That was the cause, and they were trying everything but it was all off the wall! And they had no idea, nobody ever had any idea that the center might exist somewhere else and unless that center was cured, the effect that was showing somewhere else would continue to show.

This fit is something very similar to the fits of Ramakrishna. He is the only mystic in the East who used to go into unconsciousness with any slight provocation. Somebody would start singing a song of devotion to God and that was enough... in the middle of the road, in the traffic of Calcutta – which is the maddest in the whole world! What you see in Bombay is the best in India; if you want to see the real thing, go to Calcutta! It is simply crazy. It was so difficult to take Ramakrishna from one place to another place because even if somebody said "Jai Ramji" – that is a common greeting in India, "Victory to the God, Ram" – that would be enough, Ramakrishna would fall flat on the ground. Just the name of Rama... he was so sensitive, his system had developed to such a delicate vulnerability, that even a small triggering and he would be in samadhi.

Doctors were called and they were in the same difficulty, they could not figure it out: the man was perfectly healthy, there was no reason for him to become unconscious, and it remained a mystery to the physicians. But the reason why it remained a mystery to them was that they were not ready to look from a different perspective. It is not the kind of fit in which you become unconscious because the quantity of consciousness in you is so small. Some shock – your wife dies, your business goes bankrupt – just a slight shock is enough because there is not much energy, you are not very conscious. It is just a small amount of energy, it can be crushed by any accident. This is the nature of the ordinary fit: you lose your conscious energy and only unconsciousness remains.

As far as the questioner is concerned, it is happening totally differently. It was happening totally differently to Ramakrishna. It is not that your consciousness disappears and you become unconscious; on the contrary, so much consciousness descends that you are not able to cope with it. Your mind is simply in a state as if suddenly frozen... so much is showering and your mind has no experience, no discipline to manage it. It is too much, and because of too much consciousness, it will be felt on the outside that you are having a fit.

The symptoms are the same. Only one thing is different and that is what happens after the fit – that is decisive. If it is a fit where consciousness has disappeared the man will find himself utterly weak, sad, feeling as if he has died and is coming back to life again. He will not have any memory that he has been unconscious for two hours, but his whole body will show symptoms that he has passed through a trauma, a painful trauma.

If it is not a fit but a glimpse of samadhi, the person will wake up rejuvenated, young again, fresh as he has never been – absolutely silent, peaceful, with a clarity to things. Even your question has that clarity. The question has not come out of your confusion but out of your clarity.

Rejoice, and allow those fits. Don't try to control them, don't even make an effort to control. Rather, try to be awake while the fit is there. Slowly, slowly you will become capable of being awake while the fit is there, and then there is no fit because you are no longer unconscious and there is no discontinuity in your consciousness. It is a continuous flow... growing, flowering, becoming wider and bigger.

You need not be worried about it, but you should not be going to the physicians and doctors because they will stigmatize you, convince you that something is wrong. They will make you afraid that you are losing control of your mind. They can make you so much afraid of the disease that you will start to unconsciously prevent the fit and that will be a disaster. Even now, although after the fit you are feeling beautiful, still – in the fit you feel a great "NO," you don't want to go into it. You have already accepted the idea of the doctors that it is a disease, that if you go deeper into it you will be mad.

I say to you: if you can go deeper into it you will be certainly mad in the same sense that Gautam Buddha is mad, Socrates is mad. These people are not really mad, they alone are sane but they are in a mad world.

And they are in such a minority that only after millions of people does there come a point when somebody becomes enlightened. He is so alone. And the whole world is not ready to accept anything that has not been happening to them... and naturally they are in a majority. And this man – Gautam Buddha or Mahavira or Bodhidharma – is trying to say that he has achieved something which you have not achieved. It hurts your ego, it annoys people, it irritates people because it brings the question clearly into their focus: "Is there life, a sane life?" They know life is not sane, but where to find the sanity?

All the religions have been saying that to find it is a very difficult job, it takes lives and lives to attain. So they are discouraging people... all the religions have been a tremendous disadvantage to humanity because they have all discouraged you. An authentic religion should encourage you.

You are asking me, because you must be feeling inside that if you can say yes totally to this strange space that overwhelms you.... Why do you want to say yes to it? And why does there come only a big no? The no is coming because everybody you talk to about it is going to tell you that this is a dangerous disease: "Pull yourself together, pull out of it." It is the world around you that is making you afraid.

I would like to say to you that there is nothing to fear. You can say yes. You can allow existence whatever it wants to do with you. You can simply leave yourself in the hands of the unknown, and a miracle is waiting for you.

BELOVED OSHO,
MY DAUGHTER, MA SHANTI MARA, WHO IS SEVEN
YEARS OLD, ASKED ME TO TRANSLATE HER QUESTION
TO YOU BECAUSE SHE DOES NOT SPEAK ENGLISH. HER
QUESTION IS: "WARUM GIBT ES GOTT?" – WHY IS GOD?
SHE IS NOW AT SCHOOL AND CONFRONTED WITH
"RELIGION," AND MORE AND MORE THE QUESTION
WAS FORMING IN HER HEART AND HEAD. NOW SHE
IS BEGINNING TO REALIZE THAT AT HOME, SANNYAS
IS HAPPENING, AND OUTSIDE, SOMETHING ELSE.
WOULD YOU PLEASE COMMENT?

The question is significant. Children always – almost always – ask, "What is God? Where is God? How does he look?" These are simple curiosities. But Shanti has asked a rare question, very rarely asked: *why* is God? There is no question of what God is, there is no question of where he is, there is no question of how he looks. Her question is more fundamental – "Why?" Why is the hypothesis of God needed?

It is not a simple curiosity. She has pinpointed the weakest point of all the religions – why God? No religion has been able to answer the question, no philosopher has been able to figure it out. Because whatever reason you give – "God is because of this reason," – God becomes secondary. And no religion can put God second to anyone, so they go on round and round giving answers and knowing perfectly well that none of their answers is going to answer the question. But I can answer the question because I do not belong to any established religion. God is because you are full of fear.

It has nothing to do with religion, nothing to do with philosophy. It has something to do with your psychology. God is your fear, projected, magnified unto the skies, made bigger....

The Indian God has one thousand hands. He must look like a centipede! So if you meet some big centipede, be respectful! – who knows.... The Indian God has three faces – obviously he needs them so that he can look all around; otherwise he is looking to one side and on the other side the world goes mad, which is always possible. So he has to be continuously on watch. The idea looks very good but it is basically your fear.

The fear is whether God knows you or not. So big a crowd on this small planet... and there are estimated to be fifty thousand planets in the world where there is life. And this is only about the world that we have come to know through science; it is not the whole world, it is only a small part. Every day new territory is revealed, and Albert Einstein said in one of his letters that it seems the world has no limits.

Logically it cannot have, because to make a limit you need two things. You cannot make a limit with one thing. You have a fence around your garden because the gardens of your neighbors are there. You can make a fence – but can you create a fence where the world ends, and there is nothing beyond it? And even *nothing* beyond it is something beyond it. Who knows what that nothing contains? And it will be infinite, the exploration has to continue.

Man's science is very undeveloped and you will be surprised; if you look backwards then you can understand. Whatever you are doing in the hospitals and the medical colleges seems to be right, but if you look at the history of fifty years ago, you will be surprised – everything that has looked right has proved wrong in fifty years' time.

Just fifty years ago the treatment for a madman was bleeding – his blood had to be taken out. Naturally, he became weak – if he was a violent type of madman, destructive, attacking people, naturally he will not do such a thing now. He cannot do it, he is so weak. Do you think this is treatment? You have simply made the madman weak. Soon, within a month or two, he will be back again. Once the blood that was taken out is replaced by fresh food, air, sun rays, he will prove that what you have done was simply stupid. And now they recognize that it was stupid, it had nothing to do with madness. But for three hundred years it continued to be the authoritative medical treatment for mad people.

Now whatever you are doing you cannot be very certain about it. Tomorrow it may be proved wrong. But experts have a tendency to be authoritative. They will not listen to what I am saying, because to listen to me means to change their whole vision of life.

For example, I was saying that the first questioner's fits have nothing to do with mind, that it has to do something with spiritual energy that is flooding the mind – and it has been happening to mystics, it is not a new phenomenon. They should not treat the person as insane. They should not try to prevent the fits because if the fits are prevented then the person can really go wrong, can go mad. Now, through fits the overflow of energy is released. If the fit is prevented you have closed the only outlet for it.

But they will not understand what I am saying, that you have to help the person to center his spiritual energy, to crystallize it.... And there are methods. Once it is crystallized and centered and rooted, it will not overflow the small mind and the fits will disappear, and without any harm to the person.

But to accept this small approach they will have to change their whole prejudiced mind and that seems to be one of the most difficult things for people to do. On the contrary, what they will do is to put a case in court against me saying that I am not a doctor and I should not tell people what is a disease and what is not a disease.

I am not prescribing medicines to anyone. I am simply making it clear that what you are thinking is a disease is not a disease but a blessing. If you can say yes, then the conflict between you and the overflooding energy will disappear, and for the first time you will know who you are, what the meaning of life is. For the first time you will know that there is no death – only forms change; the formless spirit continues. And you *are* the formless.

This is my way of deciding: If after the fit you were going into a bad state of mind – bitter, sad, frustrated, angry – then I would have said to continue the treatment because something is wrong with the mind. But because your experience after the fit is so grand, has such beauty... you should forget all about disease and the doctors. You are absolutely on the right path. Start saying yes to it and don't go into it with fear because fear causes a shrinking. Go with joy, dancing.

It is an invitation from the beyond. Accept it gracefully, and there is much in store for you to be surprised.

BELOVED OSHO,

IN RAJNEESHPURAM I USED TO WORSHIP FOR LONG
HOURS EVERY DAY. THIS WOULD STILL THE STATE OF
MIND IN GENERAL; AND THE PEAKS OF MEDITATION
I EXPERIENCED CONTINUOUSLY WERE GREAT. THAT
KIND OF THING DOES NOT SEEM TO BE HAPPENING
HERE IN BOMBAY, EVEN AFTER SO MUCH
RELAXATION AND NOT MUCH WORK TO DO. PLEASE
EXPLAIN WHETHER THIS IS DUE TO THE
SURROUNDINGS AND SITUATIONS HERE, OR FOR
SOME OTHER REASONS.

Suraj Prakash, the method that was being used in Rajneeshpuram comes from Gurdjieff. He himself got it from ancient Sufi
sources. You will have to understand a few things before you can
understand the answer to the question.

According to Gurdjieff – and I agree with him – your life
energy has four layers. The topmost layer of your energy is very
thin, it is only for day-to-day work. By the evening you are tired
and you want to go to sleep. That day-to-day energy needs
recharging every night. In the morning you are again fresh, ready
to work.

The second layer is the emergency layer. It is bigger because it
is a question of emergency. You come home tired, the whole day...
and it has not been one of those great days when whatever you
touch becomes gold; it has been a very ugly day. Tired, frustrated,
you just want to go and drop dead into bed, but as you are dropping into bed – unfortunately you are still alive – the house
catches fire! You forget all your tiredness, you are running for
hours to put the fire out. You have forgotten that you are hungry,
you have forgotten that you had come just to go to sleep. You are
so full of energy, so vibrant, that even when the fire is put out it
will take hours for you to go to sleep because you became so
excited. It was not only that the house was on fire, you were on
fire too! It will take a little time for the fire to cool down. All the
thoughts that have been moving so fast in you will take a little
time to settle. This is the emergency level.

When somebody fasts for many days he has to live on the emergency level. When somebody forgets his way in the forest for days together, he has to live on the emergency level. Ordinarily, we have made life so secure, comfortable and safe that millions of people never come to know their emergency layer of energy.

Then there is a third layer which is even bigger. That connects you with the whole life of the universe. And below that is the fourth which has no boundaries, it is unlimited. When you reach to the fourth you are one with existence. Then the whole energy of existence is your energy.

In the commune... and this was misunderstood all over the world; this is how everything is misunderstood. People understand only that for which they have been conditioned. They think that is all, while in fact the whole has no boundaries and you can go on exploring in any dimension, to any depth, without coming to the end.

People were working twelve hours a day and sometimes fourteen hours a day. To outsiders this looked like they had been hypnotized – otherwise who is going to work fourteen hours continuously? But the reality was that these people were under a certain program of evolving consciousness. It is somewhere from twelve to fifteen hours that the first layer disappears, is finished. If you have been working hard for twelve hours, the first layer will be burned out. Ordinarily you stop, it is time to take your supper and go to bed.

This is where Gurdjieff comes in. He says, "If you can continue *now*, when there is no energy, you are completely empty of energy as far as you know – those hidden layers are not known to you – continue!" A moment comes when suddenly all day-to-day energy is exhausted, and immediately the second layer becomes available to you. You are flooded with an energy so powerful that people who have come to that energy have felt that now they can do anything. Nothing is impossible, the energy seems to be so great.

But before you can reach the second level the first has to be exhausted. And there is no way of giving you any proof, argument or evidence. You have to do it and experience it.

Anybody who has done it has never come back empty handed. Once you have tasted the second layer of energy – which is purer, unpolluted – naturally your desire to go deeper becomes a thirst, an intense longing....

If you go on working for thirty-six hours, non-stop, you can open a passage to the third layer of your energies. And to be in the third layer of energies is to know things that you always wanted to know. It is in this layer of energy that one experiences love without attachment, one experiences love as sharing, not as relationship. It is in this part of energy that you experience yourself separate from body, from mind, from everything. You are just a witness – and that is the fourth.

Between the third and the fourth there is a very thin Japanese paper curtain. From the third you can even see things moving into the fourth, behind the paper curtain. And it is only a question of removing the curtain, because if it was for you to work and exhaust the third layer it would be impossible. You cannot exhaust it, it is far bigger than you. You are connected with the whole life system. The fourth brings you home, brings you back to the crystal-clear nature of your being.

Suraj Prakash, here in Bombay you are relaxed, there is not much work for you to do; that's why your meditation is not going deeper. That work part was an essential part. If the whole day long you are relaxed, your relaxation will remain superficial – it will be spread over a long period but it will be thin. If you have been working intensely for twelve or fourteen hours you deserve the same intensity, the same depth of relaxation – that is a natural phe- nomenon, a nature that is continuously looking after you. But even nature cannot go against its laws. The law is: if you want the experience of deep relaxation then you will have to go into deep exertion.

There is no need to go anywhere else. Here you can do jog- ging, running, swimming. Exert yourself so the first layer, which is never fresh.... It has to be used every day. It is just pocket money, you need not carry it forever. As you start some kind of work with totality you will find your meditation coming back – and it will be deeper this time, because in the commune whether you were consciously aware of it or not, unconsciously you felt that you were being *forced* to work. The very idea that you are being forced to work destroys the beauty. Your work remains half-hearted and your meditation will remain half-hearted too.

I know that working twelve hours or fourteen hours is difficult – and particularly if you have not worked so much in your life it is painful. The whole body hurts, sleep becomes difficult. Because you don't understand why this much work is being given to you, there is resistance... you do it, but not with a dance.

Here nobody will be forcing you. You will be doing your jogging or swimming or running on your own accord. This will bring you closer to totality and a total act brings its reward in a total silence.

Suraj Prakash, from tomorrow morning start... a few other sannyasins may be ready to come and join you, and it will be good on Juhu Beach. So first jog and dance and sing and then rest there on the beach for a few seconds or a few minutes just listening to the sound of the waves, feeling the sun, the wind. Fall in a kind of synchronicity, become one with it.

It is not that you are separate from the ocean and the earth and the sun. You are not. We are all connected. And to remember all those connections makes you a member of this vast universe. The trees and the rocks and the stars all turn into a great brotherhood.

Life starts giving you its secrets as you become more and more available to it. It is very just and very fair. You get only that which you deserve.

BELOVED OSHO,
I HAVE HEARD THAT SOME PEOPLE CLAIM TO BE
DOING THE SAME WORK THAT YOU DO. IS IT NOT
TRUE THAT WHILE OTHERS ARE TRYING TO ALTER
THE MAJOR DISTURBANCES IN PEOPLE'S PROGRAMS,
YOUR ONLY REASON FOR LIVING IS TO ENSURE THE
ELIMINATION OF THE PROGRAMS ALTOGETHER? IN
ANY CASE, COULD ONE PROGRAM ELIMINATE
ANOTHER, EVEN IF IT WANTED TO? ARE THEY NOT

LEFT BEHIND ON THE SHORES OF WESTERN
MAINTENANCE-MAN PSYCHOLOGY? – TEPID
REFORMERS, NOT REVOLUTIONARIES?

No program can replace another program. Every program can repress the older program in you. The older program goes deeper into the unconscious and the new program becomes your personality. And psychologists are deceiving the whole world by saying that they are deprogramming people. It is not deprogramming, it is only reprogramming.

Your insight is true, that the therapists, psychoanalysts and others of the same kind, are claiming that they are doing the same work as I am doing. In the first place, I am not doing any work. In the second place, their work and my approach are totally different. You have got the point, that they are simply adjusting people's normal behavior. All the psychologists are doing only one thing and it is the best paying profession in the world: they are just keeping you mediocre, normal.

It is good that these people did not appear a little earlier; otherwise Jesus Christ would not have been crucified but psychoanalyzed. All the mystics of the world would have been put into psychiatric hospitals – they have to be made normal, they are behaving abnormally. Mahavira walking naked – naturally it will look like something has gone wrong in this man's head.

The psychologists are just maintaining the society as it is. Hence the society pays them more than any other profession, although their work is nil. But the society pays them highly for the simple reason that the status quo should not be changed. If people remain normal then they cannot gather courage enough to change the structure of the society, to change the future of man. Normal people do normal things. Revolutionary action is not a normal thing. The very idea to change humanity completely, to change the human world so deeply that it becomes disconnected with the past is not within the hands of normal people. It needs geniuses, and all geniuses are abnormal.

The word 'abnormal' can be used for both: those who have fallen below the mind and those who have gone above the mind.

Both have become abnormal. That's why there is sometimes a similarity between a madman and a mystic, some kind of similarity. You may not be able to figure out what is similar but there is some kind of similarity, and the similarity is that both are out of the mind. One has fallen below the mind and one has gone above the mind. Both are no longer living in the mind – that is the similarity. But it is such an invisible phenomenon that to figure it out is difficult.

In the west there are many people of the quality of Ramakrishna who are in madhouses, because in the west going above the mind is simply not acceptable – there is no 'beyond', so Ramakrishna is simply mad.

In the east just the opposite has been happening for centuries. There are many mad people who are thought to be saints because their behavior has some similarity. You may not be able to grab hold of it but there is some similarity. I have been in touch with a few people who have been worshipped like incarnations of god but really they were just mad. But once you have accepted something, you start interpreting accordingly.

Near Jabalpur where I lived for twenty years, there was a man – Tuntun Pal Baba. no relation to Tintin! He was very old, ancient. He never said anything. I went many times and remained there for a few days just to watch him. He started becoming afraid of me because he certainly understood that I was not his follower or worshipper, that I was looking for something else.

He had a paralysis of the left side so he could not even hold a cup of tea with his own hands. His left hand was almost dead and his right hand was also trembling; he was old and weak so somebody would have to hold his cup. Even drinking the tea was difficult because half of his face was paralyzed. So tea would be flowing all over his robe and just in the middle... he lived only on tea. He would give the cup to somebody. half the tea he had taken himself, and half he would give to somebody – whoever was present there. That was his prasad.

Such a disgusting scene... because his saliva was going into it and people would drink that tea as if they had found nectar. And these were the people who had gone there for some desire to be fulfilled, some sickness to be cured. Somebody is childless... a child to be given; somebody's son is lost and he wants to find him... all kinds of people, but not a single spiritual seeker.

And there was no answer – the only answer was the cup of tea. So you would drink the tea, go home, and with the miracle of Tuntun Pal Baba have a child immediately! Hundreds of people were going, just a queue the whole day. If one hundred people come, fifty are going to be cured – they were going to be cured even if they had not come, because everybody who becomes sick does not die. So the business is perfectly good: at least fifty percent are going to be cured and these fifty percent will spread the news, they will exaggerate it – which is just human nature – and more people will be coming.

Because of the Indian conditioning, the other fifty who failed thought they must have done some evil act, so evil that even a paramhansa's blessing is not able to remove it. Or perhaps they would have to find another source of divine grace; perhaps Tuntun Pal Baba is not the right person for them. They will never come back to tell the story that the prasad, The present from Baba has not worked. Only the people for whom it has worked will come back again, and with new people... the crowd will go on growing.

I used to sit there and watch the crowd, the faces – what kind of people come and what does that man have? One afternoon in the hot summer there was nobody else, I was alone with the baba. He asked me, "Why are you unnecessarily torturing yourself in the heat in this village? I don't know how this idea entered people's minds that I am an incarnation of god. The more I denied it, the more they became convinced – because that is one of the symbols of the incarnation of god, that he will deny it.

"I am a humble man, I am not a reincarnation of god," he said. "I am a poor man, uneducated. I had no idea that I was creating trouble for myself. The more I denied, the more people were coming. And because of this paralysis I cannot talk much. And this tea! – I have not started it, people just started it themselves, because there is nothing else with me – I only drink tea. People just started it. The cup might be half full and somebody would take it out of my hand and give it to somebody else, and the whole day.... so the whole day I have to drink tea!"

I said, "You should have told them that this was nonsense. I can take you out of this place."

He said, "What is the point? Because they are being helped, although I am not helping them." He was a sincere, simple man.... "They are being helped so what is the harm? Even if fifty percent of people are helped... poor people, they cannot pay for medical treatment, they cannot go to big cities and big hospitals. If they are being cured, let them believe that I am a god. But sometimes even I start giggling in the night – what kind of a god? Half paralyzed, cannot eat anything, only liquid... and now that liquid has become only tea."

The last time I visited him he was dying. He whispered in my ear, "Try to explain to these people that you create these illusions yourself and you don't even give me a chance to refute it. I am saying I am not a reincarnation but you are not ready to listen to it."

I have seen a few more people. This man was not mad at least, he was only sick, old. But I have seen mad people. Their madness is thought to be something divine. In their madness they may do anything, they may dance on the street....

I was passing through Kanpur; I had a meeting in Kanpur and after the meeting, as I reached the railway station I saw a crowd. Somebody told me that there was a godman, and that's why the crowd was there. So I went inside the crowd and I could not believe... this man used to be a servant in the hostel where I had lived. He felt a little ashamed.

I said, "Don't be ashamed. in this country you can be ashamed of anything but not of being a reincarnation of god – enjoy! Because in your job what were you getting?"

He said, "That much is being collected by my followers now."

He had six followers who were continuously collecting money from people. If you gave money you could go close to him, touch his feet, have his blessings. He had nothing to say. I asked him, "When can I see you alone?"

He gave me a time in the night and he met me. I said, "You were a simple person, what happened?"

He said, "I also cannot figure out, what happened. I had gone to a marriage party and there, in the sweets, they had mixed some drugs so I started doing strange things. I threw my clothes off, went naked into the market... and a crowd followed me, and the same people who had given me the sweet started saying, 'He is a reincarnation!' I was half conscious, half unconscious. I could hear somebody saying, 'He is a reincarnation of god!' and I was not in a state to argue. In fact, I thought perhaps I was a reincarnation of God!

"I started dancing more madly and since that day, I am enjoying it. It is a good business. No qualification is needed."

In the West, they are making one mistake. Here we are making another mistake. But the mistake is possible....

The man who has gone beyond mind and the man who has fallen below mind – both are out of the mind, so there is some similarity. That similarity should not deceive anybody – because the person who has fallen below mind will be sad, tense, searching for the lost home, nervous, feeling unworthy. You have to look into the qualities and the feelings of the man.

The man who has gone beyond the mind will be feeling like a child, innocent, will be relishing existence and its beauty, will be creative. He cannot be destructive. He may paint, he may sculpt, he may sing, he may dance, but a man who is moving above mind is bound to pour a little more beauty into the world , a little more music, a little more poetry – that is his contribution.

Only your contribution proves where you are – whether you are mad or you have gone beyond mind to authentic sanity. What is happening is perfectly beautiful. Just say yes – not a verbal yes but an existential yes, in which every fiber of your being is involved. You are very close to the opening of a new world, of a new consciousness for you. It is for this consciousness that you are here with me.

11

I have to be offensive to wake you up!

BELOVED OSHO,
YOU CAN'T REALLY MEAN IT WHEN YOU SAY YOU
HAVE LOST ALL HOPES AND ILLUSIONS, BECAUSE YOU
KNOW PERFECTLY WELL WHERE HUMANITY STANDS
TODAY AND YOU KNOW HOW SLOW EVOLUTION IS. I
OFTEN WONDERED IF YOU HAD NOT COME A BIT
TOO SOON: HUMANITY WAS NOT READY TO
UNDERSTAND YOUR LIBERATING MESSAGE, AND
SIMPLY MISBEHAVED WITH YOU. AND THIS WAS THE
EXPLANATION THAT I FOUND WITHIN: YES, YOU
HAD COME TOO SOON – ALL GREAT MASTERS COME
TOO SOON (POOR JESUS' MESSAGE HAS BEEN
UNDERSTOOD BY ONLY A VERY FEW AFTER NINETEEN
CENTURIES, SO YOU'LL HAVE TO BE PATIENT!) BUT
THE SHOCK WAS NECESSARY – THE SPIRITUAL
EARTHQUAKE. YET SOME EGO-SKYSCRAPERS ARE SO
TECHNICALLY PERFECT THAT THEY CAN RESIST
PROBABLY EVEN THE DESTRUCTION OF THE ENTIRE
PLANET. ANOTHER THING I ASK MYSELF IS WHY YOU
ARE SO BRUTAL, SO VIOLENT, SO OFFENSIVE. I CAN
UNDERSTAND THIS BEHAVIOR WITH DISCIPLES IN
THE HOPE OF FRACTURING THEIR EGOS, BUT WITH
POLITICIANS...? THEY JUST CAN'T BE ANYTHING ELSE
THAN OFFENDED – BUT THEY WON'T LEARN WHAT
YOU WANT TO TEACH THEM (AT LEAST NOT IN THIS
INCARNATION) AND YOU KNOW IT, SO WHAT IS THE
SENSE? PLEASE EXPLAIN. COULDN'T YOU BE JUST AS
OUTSPOKEN (THAT IS WHAT I SO LOVE IN YOU) YET
LESS PROVOKING? IT WOULD HAVE SAVED YOU SO
MUCH TROUBLE, I'M SURE, AND WOULD NOT HAVE
CAUSED THIS RIDICULOUS ALLIANCE OF ALL
GOVERNMENTS AGAINST YOU.

I understand your love, and I understand your love for my work. But you do not understand the ways the masters use to work on the sleeping humanity. Jesus was offensive – deliberately, because there was no other way to wake up his contemporary humanity. His crucifixion has perhaps been understood by only one man up to now in the whole of history, and that man is not a Christian.

That man is George Gurdjieff. Because he is not a Christian he can stand aloof, with no prejudice at all. His insight into the crucifixion of Jesus is that it was planned by Jesus himself. On the one hand he was very offensive, very rude – that provoked the blind masses. On the other hand he was mercilessly hammering on the priesthood – and the priests in those days were very much more powerful than they are today. Today they are nothing but the Queen of England; it means nothing. The Queen of England or the queen of playing cards – they are synonymous.

Jesus sacrificed his life because in those primitive days there was no way to spread a message unless it thrilled the very heart of the merciless humanity. The struggle was not with the heart, the struggle was with the stones – or perhaps worse, because even stones are not as stony as a human being can be.

Everybody who has tried to understand Jesus has thought it: "Why was he offensive? He could have been a very respectable rabbi; people would have worshipped him, loved him. Instead of crucifying him they would have wanted to crown him."

But that was not the work Jesus was doing. The question was not the cross or the crown, the question was the awakened man or the sleepy, unconscious humanity. When you are deeply asleep you have to be shaken, your name has to be shouted, cold water has to be thrown into your eyes. But this is all done out of compassion. I have been offensive and I will remain offensive. I will go on growing more and more offensive, for the simple reason that you are so deep in a coma that perhaps only a scream might reach you – or might not reach you.

Perhaps you will look at me for the first time only when I am on the cross. Right now you take me for granted – only the cross will destroy your state of taking me for granted. Perhaps only the cross can shake you enough so that you can wake up.

You have said I may be hard with my disciples because they are committed to a certain work of evolution – it is not being done against them, they have come and they have joined me. The question is relevant: Why do I go on hammering on the politicians? Again, the questioner is innocent and ignorant. She does not understand the structure of human consciousness.

When I criticize the politician, it is not the politician outside you, it is the politician within you. The outer politician is only a manifestation, a collective manifestation of your inner politicians. You are all searching – in some way or other – to have more, to possess more, to be powerful, to be dominant, to be special: V.V.I.P. ... a V.I.P. is no longer enough.

When I criticize the politicians I am criticizing the political structure of your mind. Aristotle is right only on this point, according to me, when he calls man a political animal. Your politician is still in a latent state. It has not been possible for it to have an opportunity to come into its true colors. That's why power corrupts – in fact, power has nothing to do with corruption. It appears that power corrupts because power gives you the opportunity to bring out all your fantasies, dreams, and change them into reality. You have the power to do it. And Acton is right that absolute power corrupts absolutely.

I have to criticize the politicians because they are what you would like to be. Presidents, prime ministers, governors, ambassadors – that's what you would like to be, but it is only a seed in you. And in the seed you cannot see all the flowers and all the colors. When I criticize the politicians I am criticizing you as if your politician had come into power.

And in a certain way... you may not be very powerful, but everybody has a certain power over certain people. The parents have power over their children, the husband has power over his wife – at least he believes that. The real power is with the woman, she has all the keys. And husbands and wives are constantly fighting to prove who is higher, who is more intelligent, who is always right. So everybody has his own small area, his own small territory where he is powerful. The teacher in the classroom is almost a king.

In India, physical punishment is against the constitution. Children cannot be tortured in any physical way. But that is only in the constitution, not in reality. All over India children are beaten.

When I entered my high school.... One man was very notorious for beating children – he was our mathematics teacher. His subject was difficult and he had no compassion at all. He thought that by beating children you could raise their intelligence! By beating children you can destroy their intelligence, but you cannot raise it. Beating is destructive.

I had decided the very first day that in the very beginning I had to come to terms with this man. As he entered in the class, I did not stand up to greet him as every other student did. He looked very angry... a little surprised, too. For a moment there was silence and then he said, "It seems you don't know me."

I said, "It is true. I don't know you, but something more important is true." He said, "What is that?" I said, "You don't know yourself."

He said, "I don't want to go into philosophy – don't change the subject! You have to tell me why you remained sitting."

I said, "Because I have not seen anything honorable in you. Now, I am helpless – I cannot honor a person if I cannot find anything honorable in him. I cannot be a hypocrite."

He said, "You don't understand. I will bring you to your senses with just one good beating." And he took his cane out of his desk.

I said, "You can beat me, but just look outside the window." He said, "What is there?"

I said, "Just look...." because outside the window, far away, was the police station. He said, "What do you mean?"

I said, "You beat me first – then accompany me to the police station, because physical punishment is a crime."

His cane slipped from his hand. He had never thought about it, that a student could report against him. He said, "But this will become a precedent for others; nobody will stand up...."

I said, "There is no need. In what way does our standing help you? Just so you can feel powerful? These poor boys are standing out of fear, not in love, in trust; not in real gratitude."

Something happened to that man. He threw away the cane. And now because he was not beating them, for the first time he started encountering the beauties of small children. In violence, all those beauties shrink. In fact, the violence prevents their growth in all directions: in intelligence, in love, in friendliness, in sharing, in rejoicing.... The whole day long, from one class to another they are humiliated, insulted, beaten. Still you expect respect from them.

I made it clear to him: "I will give you respect – and only on that day can you decide that something has happened in your life. All the respect that has been shown up to now was out of fear. Unless I feel love for you and gratitude for you, you will have to wait. And you will have to be patient. It rarely happens that people change so quickly."

But perhaps he was just on the verge, and only a slight push was needed. He turned a complete circle, one hundred and eighty degrees. He came to be one of the most lovable, respectable teachers in the whole school. He was not senior enough, but because of his tremendous change he was chosen to be the principal of the school the next year when the old principal retired, although it was not his turn.

And he wept in front of me, holding my hands, and said, "The whole credit for making me the principal goes to you. Not only have you changed my relationship with the students, strangely, once I started changing, the change has affected every relationship. I have loved my wife for the first time, I have loved my own children for the first time. Now I am teaching not just to earn money, I love it. I enjoy it.

"When someone commits a mistake it does not make me angry. And now I can see that before I was angry twenty-four hours a day, so any slight excuse was enough. I was fighting with my father, with my mother, with my wife, with my brothers... I was carrying all that mountainous burden and these small children were simply victims. You were right: it was because I could not show my domination towards anybody else – I am just an ordinary school teacher – but I could show my domination and my power and my greatness and my superiority, and deep down fulfill a certain ego. Since the day I dropped the idea of being violent with the students, slowly, slowly my eyes have become clean and clear, and I can see that to err is human."

I said to him... and he has remembered it; the last time I saw him in 1970, he reminded me. He said, "To err is human and to forgive is divine – that is the old proverb."

I said, "That proverb is dangerous because it makes forgiving so far away. Gods forgive, and you are not a god. To err is human. To forgive is more human, it is not divine – just more human."

In fact, the moment you have achieved your own humanity, you have achieved your divinity. They are not two things. Your humanity at its climax is the beginning of your divineness, of your godliness.

My criticism of the politicians, first, is the criticism of the hidden politician inside you – as a husband, as a wife, as a mother, as a father. You are expecting obedience, you are thinking that your child is not only born out of you but has to be just a carbon copy of you. Children are born of you, but they don't belong to you. They belong to the future, of which you know nothing. You are the sunset, your children are the sunrise – and the gap of the whole night is there.

Secondly, I don't see men as islands, separate from each other. And I don't see their activities as separate from each other either. They are all part of a network. If I want a revolution in human consciousness I will have to hammer on the heads of politicians as hard as possible, because politicians are the ones who are always standing and they have the power to prevent any kind of revolution, any kind of change. They want a society with a status quo, because any revolution is going to throw them from their power positions. A conscious humanity cannot tolerate idiot politicians guiding it.

I have had to criticize the so-called leaders of religion, high priests, popes, *shankaracharyas*, because they are making every effort that man's mind remains retarded. Only a retarded mind can be exploited. And you ask me not to be offensive, not to be violent. Your idea must be that if I am not offensive, if I am not outrageous in my statements, if I don't criticize those who are in power – politically or economically – then my message will spread more easily. You are wrong.

The whole of the world's media is interested in something sensational. They are not interested in the softer values of life. It is said that a good man has no life – as far as reporting about the good man is concerned, he has no life. At the most you can say he is a good man, but life? Where will you find it in a good man?

It is a very ancient part of wisdom that you cannot write a novel or a drama around the life of a good man, and even if you write it you will have to print it yourself. And it is not going to be a best seller, it will be a no-seller! It will have its uniqueness... but you will be in constant trouble – what to write? A good man is just good man, tastes good. It is the bad man who has a life. He is colorful, he is not monotonous. You can enter into his life and you will find surprises upon surprises; a great story is possible.

If I speak softly, very lovingly, it will be impossible to reach within just few years to every nook and corner of the world. I have my own method, and I know how to turn the tide at any moment. It is just a question of turning the switch. First let me create a good number of enemies – which I am successfully doing! – and you will see for yourself: these same enemies will turn into friends. I just have to go on creating enemies for a few days more. Once I have touched your heart – right or wrong, it does not matter – then it is a very simple phenomenon to change anything.

Those who are behaving as enemies have already become emotionally attached to me. Just the other day I received a message from Oregon that Oregon is missing me very much... because who has ever heard the name of Oregon? But for five years Oregon was international news.

I was a tourist in America and my visa had expired long before, so I was illegally there – kept by the government! The illegality goes to the government, because I was asking them: "Either you extend my visa or you say no. If you say no I am going to court – on what grounds can you deny me?"

So they were in a puzzle: they could not say no, because once they have said no their power would be gone. Now the power would be in the hands of a court where they would be a party, and they would have to prove why they had been harassing me for two years continuously. And they could not say yes because the president wanted me and my commune to be destroyed. The attorney general of America wanted my commune to be completely destroyed. America's richest man, Rockefeller, wanted me to leave America. The archbishop of America was certainly after the president continuously.

They wanted me to leave the country but for that they needed to say no to extending my visa. And they were afraid to say no because once it went to court then it could take twenty years... from one court to another court....

These people were trying hard that the newspapers, radio, television, cable television should not report me, for one thing. Every pressure was put on all kinds of media: "Either report negatively or don't report at all." And in the world of the news media freedom of expression exists only in the ideas, in the great human rights and human values of the constitution; but basically it does not exist. And this is simply because to have a big daily newspaper you have to be either a political organization, a religious organization or a rich man to invest money.

And all the newspapers survive on the advertisements given by the government. The moment they don't listen to the government the advertisements stop – and no newspaper can exist without government advertisements. The situation is such that freedom is just an empty word.

Coming in contact with the news media people, I was surprised: these people were beautiful, they tried to do their best. And later on they informed me – "We are sorry. The bosses are editing things out, adding things, changing the whole flavor. And we are poor people; we cannot risk our jobs." When their news reports came out on television, it was totally the opposite of what was felt in the direct encounter with the person.

I inquired of a few journalists: "What happens? You write, you listen... I have seen tears in journalists' eyes. I have seen them dancing with sannyasins. What happens to you when you report to your newspaper, your radio, the television?"

They said, "We are ashamed. Our work is to give the reports and then it goes to the editorial department. Then – particularly because of you – it goes to the boss for a second check. Unless they have destroyed it to utter negativity they are not satisfied."

It is because once it becomes negative, people enjoy it. People are living in negative minds, so whenever a negative report is given they fall in rapport with it. They say inside themselves, "Right! We knew it already."

One journalist told me, "If we write exactly what we feel, the whole staff thinks we have become hypnotized. If we don't put something against you.... And it does not matter whether it is right or wrong; something against you is a protection: They will not say, 'You are hypnotized.'"

Perhaps Satyananda is here. He came as a journalist from *Stern* magazine in Germany. He was one of their topmost journalists, but he wanted to *feel* it – the meditations, the groups, silent sittings with me, discourses... he remained there for a few weeks. He wanted an inside story, not just a story from an outsider. He collected so much material and he was so happy when he went... before leaving he became a sannyasin, too. But as he reached the *Stern* office they started laughing. They said, "He is completely hypnotized! Look at his red clothes, mala... he is not the man we sent."

When they saw his report they simply said, "Not a single word from this report can be published. You have been brainwashed, you don't know what you are writing. You are under hypnosis, you are being used as a medium; you don't know what you are doing."

He said, "What nonsense are you talking? I have not been hypnotized."

But what can he do? The report belongs to *Stern*, not to the writer. The writer is paid for it.

He went on struggling, negotiating – "This much you can cut... this much you can cut...." And finally only one sixth remained. They distorted his whole beautiful article.

But he was disillusioned completely – this freedom of expression, all these democratic values are just words. He resigned his position on the grounds that they had been printing things which were not true, and because they had inserted whatever they wanted into his article.

He told them, "I cannot serve here like a slave anymore. You have not purchased my mind."

He wrote a book, which became a best seller in Germany. He came back to live in India, and then he was in America with me. And soon – once I settle somewhere – he will be coming.

So the problem for me is that if I simply talk about meditations, about ecstasies, spiritual experiences, then the message cannot reach those who are in immense need of it, and I will feel guilty. I should make every effort that the message reaches.

To provoke people, you have to be offensive. To create a new ground for a new humanity, you have to destroy much of the past – and you cannot be other than hard. If I simply talk about abstract concepts which are not any danger to the existing society, to the vested interests, I will be respected – the same people who are enemies will start talking about me as a great saint – but I will not be of any help to those who are really thirsty. So I am not worried about all of humanity.

My concern is that I must reach each door and knock at least once. If somebody can understand, he should not miss. If somebody cannot understand, there is no harm – he was not going to understand anyway. So everything that is being done is well planned and deliberate. It is not accidental.

I can understand your love, but you have to grow into a little more clarity about the function of the master. And you cannot suggest to the master what he should do and what he should not do! With good intentions... but you are doing a stupid thing.

BELOVED OSHO,
IF THE EXPERIENCE OF GOD IS A SUBJECTIVE
EXPERIENCE, THEN WHAT ARE PRIESTS AND POPES
FOR? IF THE EXPERIENCE OF GOD IS AN OBJECTIVE
EXPERIENCE, THEN WHY DON'T THEY PRODUCE HIM?

God is neither subjective nor objective. God simply does not exist. Your question is that if God is an objective experience, then scientists should be able to produce it. If man can go to the moon, it is conceivable that scientists would be able to put on their table the experience of God or the presence of God. That's what Karl

Marx used to say: "Unless God is proved in a scientific lab I am not going to accept it."

One communist friend used to stay with me once in a while. He wrote this passage to me.... I said, "Marx's statement is self-contradictory. First you say, 'If God is an object...' Your statement begins with *if*. It is not your experience. If you have the experience then there is no possibility of ifs and buts. It is purely an intellectual question. If God is an object, then certainly scientists will be able to produce it. They have not been able to produce it; hence Karl Marx says there is no God."

That's why I say that even our so-called great thinkers go on committing very small mistakes, but their impact can be tremendous. Karl Marx is saying that scientists have not been able to bring God into the lab, dissect him, find out what is inside him, turn him inside out, just to have a look all around. Because this has not happened, he says God does not exist.

I told my communist friend, "Marx was eligible only to say that God does not exist *as an object*. It is simple logic. You have given the objective to the scientist and the scientist has not been able to produce it, so only one thing has become certain: that God is not an object. Not that there is no God – because you yourself say that there is another side, the subjective side. What about it? And Marx remains silent about the other side, which has simply been dropped!" God is an experience.

It is not right to say "the experience of God." That creates difficulty, it makes God an object. There are three things: God the object, you the experiencer, and the experience between you two, as a bridge. God is not a subjective experience, God is just the experience of the inner.

There is no God as a person. God is your subjectivity – it is another name for your inner being. It is you, asleep. You can be awake. Then too you will not be able to see God, because God is not a person at all.

God is our inability to experience the inner reality and give it an expression. When we try to express it, trouble arises. Any name is good. Mohammedans have one thousand names for God. Hindus have *vishnu sahasranam* – one thousand names for God. And I say to you, the reason God can have one thousand names is because he does not exist. If you exist, then one name or maybe two – at the most three.... But one thousand is just meaningless.

It is almost impossible to find any name among Mohammedan names which is not the name of God. Arabic is not a very great language; its scope is very small. It is the language of nomads wandering in the desert – very primitive. Even to find one thousand names in it is a little bit of a difficult job. All the Mohammedan names that you come across are names for God.

Something has to be said – the experience is valid; it has been validated by thousands of mystics around the world. There is something more than you know, than you feel, within you. Your consciousness, your existence..."God" is only a symbol. You can use it, but it has fallen into wrong company. Being with Mohammedans and Hindus and Christians, it has lost its beauty and grandeur. It has become too ordinary, too mundane.

And its associations are not good – because in the name of God, thousands of people have been killed. In the name of God, conflict continues around the world; thousands of undercurrents of fighting, efforts to convert people to your fold – because numbers are very decisive as far as politics is concerned.

You have to understand the politics of numbers. Why do Mohammedans go on insisting that they will continue to marry at least four women? Although they cannot rationally support their idea, the question of reason does not arise. They say their holy book says, the holy Koran says you can have four wives, or even more – Mohammed himself had nine wives. So it is not a question of argument or discussion. You are interfering in their religion – it is a question of religion.

Marrying nine women and depriving eight men – for their whole lives they will not get any women. Naturally, you are creating the institution of prostitution – what are those eight persons going to do? Religions have created prostitution, they are the sources.

Just forty years ago, the Nizam of Hyderabad died. When he died he had five hundred wives! This is superficial reasoning, that their religion is being interfered with.

The real thing is if you allow a man to marry many women, many children are possible; your population will increase. It cannot happen vice-versa. You can have one woman with five husbands and still she will produce just one child. Nature is not going to bother that she has five husbands so just be a little kind and give her five children, numbered according to the husbands. So it is pointless to have one wife with many husbands.

To have one husband and many wives is political – it has nothing to do with religion. Now, if I say it is political, it is not religious.... Because what has religion to do with numbers? Religion is basically individual. You alone can be religious, there is no need for anyone else to be with you for you to be religious. It is not a social phenomenon. Its whole growth is individual, purely individual.

I have to criticize religions which are obstructing human progress, in many ways. Right now all the Christian priests, Hindu priests, Mohammedan priests all around the world are doing one thing: teaching poor people against birth control, because it is overpopulation that is going to give them numbers. And it is overpopulation that is going to keep half of the earth poor, starving – and the poor and the starving are easily vulnerable to being converted. You just give them education, food, a house to live in and you have brought gifts from God – they will be Christians. Poverty should continue; otherwise who is going to be in the churches, who is going to be converted?

I have to say categorically that all conversion is criminal. Nobody has the right to impose his own ideology on other people. You have the right to express your ideology and leave it for people to think about. If you have provoked thinking, that's enough. You have done a great job if you have triggered thinking.

A child was just asking, "Why is God there? What is the need?" The child must be very intelligent, he has asked a very significant question. It is because of fear. It is because of ignorance. It is because inside, you are full of darkness. Hence you are continuously afraid. Outside, you know there is going to be death, sooner or later. You know there is going to be old age, there is going to be sickness, all kinds of diseases, and you are going to suffer all these things. Humanity has to be somehow consoled: "Don't be worried, God is taking care of you. He is the creator – you may not be looking at him, but he is always looking at you."

Don't get afraid of the idea – because once you are alone in your room and you start feeling that he is looking from the roof.... And man is so imaginative, he can manage it that behind those two eyes there is a head, and of course you will be in a panic! You may have been talking about God but you don't know... if you meet him, what are you going to say?

For the part of humanity that is not going to try and experience its own light, society has to give substitutes. God is a substitute, a name – just a lollipop... nothing of much use, no nourishment, but sounds good: "lollipop." Because of the concept of God, man has been able to live – not very joyously, because his whole living is based on wrong principles. But still, somehow he has been able to drag through his life.

Without God you suddenly feel a cold wave around you, a dark night surrounding you. God was the great father – protection, security, hope... all are gone. This makes one mature – if you can get rid of God you are mature. According to me, twenty-one years of age does not make you mature, adult. Only one thing makes man mature, and that is getting rid of God – because God is a bundle of all kinds of fears, greeds, hopes. It is opium; it keeps you drugged. But while you are drugged your life is slipping by, and soon death will knock on the door and then it will be too late.

To find the real answer to the question you have to sit silently, alert, not falling asleep, and just going inwards, slowly, slowly.... First it will start becoming darker and darker and darker, and then suddenly there is dawn, and the birds are singing and the sun is rising and you are free. Your wings are open for the first time. Now you can claim the whole sky with all its stars.

A man without God is an authentic man. A man with God is just a shadow, he has not entered into the world of reality yet. You have millions of priests and none of them has the courage to say that he has encountered God. Not even the representatives – the pope, the shankaracharyas, Ayatollah Khomeini – not even these people are courageous enough to say that they have encountered God. They are as afraid as you are; there are doubts in their minds as there are doubts in your mind, because doubts disappear only when you have experienced something.

God is not a question of belief, it is an experience of inner light. Then you can give it any name. You can call it God, you can call it truth, you can call it love, you can call it peace. You can call it life – it does not matter what word is used, but it should be based on experience. Once you have experienced your light, you know there is no need of any other God. The whole existence is godly.

BELOVED OSHO,

I GUESS I HAVE TWO QUESTIONS. WHY DO WE ALL
WANT TO BE THERAPISTS (MYSELF INCLUDED)? IS
GOSSIPING AMONGST YOUR SANNYASINS HARMFUL
TO YOUR WORK, OR AM I TOO SERIOUS?

First, you are too serious. Gossiping amongst sannyasins is like gospels amongst the Christians. If I have to choose between gossips and gospels, my preference is for gossips. They are juicier, more alive. Gospels look sad, dead, heavy. If you have to listen you can manage to listen, but it is not a dance of your heart.

So I am in support of my sannyasins completely. Gossip as aesthetically as possible, as religiously as possible! And gossip something beautiful, something ecstatic. Your gossiping should not be mundane and ordinary: that somebody has escaped with somebody's wife... this kind of gossiping is third-rate; it is nobody's business. In the first place, no woman is anybody's wife; every woman is a woman. Husband and wife... these are social institutions, and to live in an institution either you have to be mad or you will *become* mad!

Institutions are not places to live, but they say that marriage is a "divine institution." It is nothing divine; it is simple, mundane business. It is a convenience; it is making a lifelong contract. Otherwise, a few people prefer temporary contracts, a few people prefer lifelong contracts – these are preferences.

And nobody possesses anybody. So if somebody's wife has escaped – great! Great for the man because he is free, and great for the woman because for a few days at least the man will not want to kill her! It is freeing and beautiful for the other man also, because somebody else's wife is always beautiful....   .

It is a strange thing. I have been looking into the chemistry of it. As one relationship changes – particularly if it is a marriage, which is the center of our civilization and must be a very rotten center, because the civilization is rotten....   .

You can be serious but your seriousness shows a sickness of the soul. The healthy soul is smiling, is ready to burst into laughter. So please don't be worried about sannyasins gossiping. In no scripture of any religion has gossiping been condemned as sin.

But your instinct to condemn it comes from religions. They have been condemning everything that is pleasant to human beings; no pleasure has to be left uncondemned. This is the most ancient strategy: catching hold of people and getting them into particular religions, sects, theologies – and before you can be caught in a church you have to be miserable. Only miserable people go to religious institutions, only miserable people read holy scriptures. If you are rejoicing in the gifts of existence, it is enough to feel grateful – and gratefulness is religiousness.

Secondly, you must be a new sannyasin. It will take a little time to live with my people – who are basically misfits. They cannot adjust with the society. They are so sensitive they cannot tolerate a futile, meaningless life; hence they have fallen out of the folds and they are trying to live alone, contacting existence directly.

And existence is hilarious! If you just have eyes to see the hilarious points you will be surprised: in life there is no place to be serious. Everybody is slipping on banana peels – you just need an insight to see.

I have heard that Sigmund Freud, the founder of modern psychotherapy, was following a lady elephant into the forest. Finally he introduced himself: "I am Sigmund Freud. You must have heard my name; I am the founder of psychoanalysis."

The elephant could hardly hear what he was saying. She said,

"But what do you want from me?"

He said, "I have a strange problem which I cannot tell to anybody – and my whole philosophy is not to repress, but I have been repressing it."

The elephant said, "Don't be sad, just tell me – what is the problem?"

He said, "I feel so ashamed. I have solved all other problems, but this problem simply goes on persisting in my head. The problem is that I want to make love to an elephant."

The lady elephant said, "Love? Are you mad? Because no elephant ever wants to make love to a human being. They are not interested at all. Beautiful women go on passing – they don't whistle, they don't sing a film song; they simply don't care. This is strange – and you are a great psychoanalyst and you could not solve this problem?"

He said, "I have tried hard but without a lady elephant, what can I do? I have been watching many ladies, and you look very loving, kind and very beautiful."

The lady elephant said, "Okay. It is absolutely crazy... have you brought some ladder or... because how are you going to make love to me?"

He said, "Yes, I have brought a ladder. Before I had this ladder, I used to carry a couch for the patients to lie down on during psychoanalysis. For a few days, I have been carrying this ladder, because who knows where you can meet the lady of your heart? And today, the day has come."

So he climbed the ladder, and while he was making love, his disciple Carl Gustav Jung was sitting on a tree just above them. He had heard the gossip that Sigmund Freud had been seen with a ladder, going towards the forest.

He had said, "What will he do with the ladder? Because a ladder does not fit with a psychoanalyst... a couch is okay." So he had come ahead and was sitting on top of the tree and when Sigmund Freud started making love, it was so hilarious and Carl Gustav Jung himself became so excited that the branch that he was holding started moving and a coconut fell and hit the lady elephant's head. She said, "Ah!"

Sigmund Freud, who was deeply involved in making love, looked up and said, "Darling, am I hurting you?

The elephant said, "I don't know where you are – so are you finished or not? And who is this fellow in the tree?"

Sigmund Freud said, "He is my disciple, and he got so excited seeing such a beautiful scene that he started shaking the tree, doing his own thing."

One just needs a little alertness to see and find out: Life is really a great cosmic laughter. Those who become silent and happy join in the laughter. Laughter is my message. I do not ask you to do prayer. I ask you to find moments, situations, in which you can laugh wholeheartedly. Your laughter will open a thousand and one roses within you.

12
Love is the greatest alchemy

BELOVED OSHO,
YOU HAVE TALKED ABOUT THE
SUPERIORITY/INFERIORITY DIALECTIC AS THE BASIS
OF AUTHORITARIAN AND FASCIST RELATIONSHIPS. IT
IS ONE OF THE MIRACLES OF BEING WITH YOU THAT
IN SPITE OF HAVING BEEN CONSTANTLY PERSUADED
OF OUR UNWORTHINESS BY OUR PARENTS, TEACHERS
AND PRIESTS, YOU ARE ABLE TO SHED LIGHT ON ALL
OUR UNCONSCIOUS HABITS WITHOUT EVER MAKING
US FEEL BAD ABOUT IT. YOU ALLOW US TO BE AWARE
OF OUR POTENTIAL FOR ENLIGHTENMENT IN A WAY
THAT DOES NOT MAKE US FEEL SUPERIOR, AND YET
SIMULTANEOUSLY YOU NEVER MAKE US FEEL
INFERIOR BECAUSE WE ARE NOT ENLIGHTENED. IN
GROUPS, TOO, WHILE YOU ARE PRESENT, WE CAN
REVEAL OUR NOTIONS OF INFERIORITY BUT BECAUSE
YOU ARE THERE AND SIMPLY NOT PART OF THE
EGOTISTIC INFERIORITY/SUPERIORITY GAME,
DEPENDENCY AND SPIRITUAL SLAVERY CANNOT
HAPPEN. BUT WHAT HAPPENS IN GROUPS WHERE
YOU ARE ABSENT? SURELY, IF THE THERAPIST HAS A
TRACE OF EGO, THEN DOESN'T THIS KIND OF
PSYCHOLOGICAL FASCISM INEVITABLY EMERGE?

Amrito, you have seen something so significant that everybody must be made aware of it. There is only one possibility for sanity to exist in relationships so they don't turn into inferiority and superiority games, so they don't become sado-masochistic tortures. And that only possibility is in the presence of an unconditional love. Love is the greatest alchemy. It transforms base metals into gold. Your ingredients are the same – the murderer and the Gautam Buddha are not different as far as their ingredients, their intrinsic potentialities are concerned. It is just that man is not a one dimensional machine. Man is not one-dimensional; otherwise, his whole world would be sheer boredom. And man's search is basically to be one with existence – separation hurts. In our other loving relationships, in small measures we are searching for the same unity. In love with a woman, in love with a man, in love with a friend, in love with some creative activity – dance, music, poetry – we are trying to have a certain synchronicity with existence.

Our situation is that of a small child in the forest who has lost his mother and is searching in the forest, not knowing where to go. This situation allows many exploiters... this helplessness is used by those who are in power, by those who have money. The helplessness is used to convert you into a slave, into dependence.

Hence, all the religions have developed particular programs. They begin with God – and with God, your relationship cannot be anything else but that which exists between a puppet and a puppeteer, between the slave and the owner. With God, you cannot expect more than that, because he is the creator; he has made you – he can at any moment destroy you too. Neither did he ask you whether you wanted to enter into life, nor will he ask you whether you are in favor of destroying the world. All the gods of all the religions are dictatorial. They are fascist. I don't have any God; hence I don't have any program for you in which you will be transformed slowly into a slave.

I am fulfilled – nothing more can be added to my experience. That's why the people who are with me will not feel in any way inferior. Nobody *is* inferior. People may be in different spaces, but nobody is inferior and nobody is superior. They are all made of the same stuff you call God. How can somebody be superior and somebody be inferior? We belong to the same existence, our roots are nourished by the same existence. Existence makes no distinctions, no discriminations between the sinners and the saints. My approach is existential.

Hence, nobody is superior and nobody is inferior here. Naturally, by destroying this complex of inferiority and superiority, we are removing the very possibility of any kind of fascist mentality, fascist personality – because to me, it is inconceivable that a fascist can ever be religious.

And your so-called religious people are more or less all fascist fanatics. They are not in search of truth; they think they have found it already – in their scriptures which are dead, in the old superstitions which even they know have no basis in reality. Just a clarity of vision dispels all darkness out of which all the monsters are born.

Here with me, whether you are a man or a woman, whether you are white or black, it does not matter; nobody even takes note of it. It is enough that you are a human being. And it is your freedom to choose your own lifestyle; it is your basic right how you want to blossom. Those who love you can help in taking care of the garden in which you are growing – watering your roots, showering their warmth.

It has now been scientifically proved that even the plants know who are their friends and who are their enemies. They have developed something like a cardiogram which is attached to the tree, and if a man comes with the idea to cut a branch of the tree or to uproot the tree – he just has the idea – suddenly the graph that is being made by the cardiogram on the tree starts trembling. It loses the rhythm it had... now you can see how fear is felt by the tree.

And remember that the tree has telepathic sensitivity; otherwise she could not know the thought in the man's mind. He has not done anything – visibly, nothing has happened. And when the gardener comes – with his warmth, with his love – suddenly the graph becomes the most harmonious. Now the tree is no longer afraid, the tree is immensely blissful. Loving warmth is not only a poetic phenomenon. It is a reality of great importance.

Now the flowers will be bigger, the fruits will be juicier; the tree will respond. Except for man, perhaps there is no ingratitude in this whole existence. The tree cannot give anything more – she cannot give money, she cannot give gold – but she can give beautiful flowers, as big as possible, to a loving heart. She can give juicier fruits.

Love has never been thought of as food, but it is a very subtle kind of food. And now psychologists have concluded that if a child gets everything necessary – all chemicals, all hormones, food, exercise, fresh air, rest, everything that is necessary for life – still he will die in three to six months unless there is someone to pour love. He will not feel that life is worth living without love; he will simply shrink and die. And in thousands of labs around the world, many animals have died in these experiments.

Ordinarily, it is understood that these experiments are being done on animals first and that unless we have found safe principles we do not apply them to human beings – this has been the idea prevalent in the masses. Even the medical professionals – doctors, physicians – also believe in it. But the truth is something very different.

Just a few days ago.... For almost two years, a group of senators in America were investigating about a certain amount of money... not a small amount of money; two hundred million dollars is there in the books, but where has it been spent, where has it gone? The cabinet went on denying any knowledge of it, the president went on denying. The suspicion was that the government of America today is the greatest terrorist. And the money is going to the terrorists in a small country in the middle portion of the Americas, between South America and North America.

Just like Cuba, another small country has become communist. It is their right, whether they are right or wrong. Nobody else has to decide it. If they want to live a wrong kind of life, then too, they have the absolute freedom to live it; only they should not harm anybody else. They should not interfere in the lives of others.

Two hundred million dollars had been given to guerrillas, terrorists, to destroy that small Central American country because it had gone into the hands of the communists. And after two years of continuous struggle, only now has the president accepted that, "Yes, that money has gone to the terrorists."

And the whole world is silent, nobody has criticized it! Governments are to save people from terrorism, and here governments are supplying money and arms and food to terrorists. And then they go on lying....

I have looked into the scriptures of all the religions, I have looked into the ideological literature of all the political parties and I am amazed: they go on piling up lies upon lies. And the whole of humanity is asleep – not only does nobody object, but nobody even suspects.

Here with me, you are gathered for a special purpose: the search for the truth, the search for the purest kind of love, the search for a life which is a dance of sheer joy.

Nowhere else in the world are people gathering for the same reasons. They are gathering for the purpose of creating more hatred; they are gathering to create more wars; they are gathering to create more destructive activities in human life. Naturally, we have a sick world, an insane world.

Here, it is impossible to feel any superiority or inferiority. I have tried my best to convince you of only one thing: that enlightenment is your nature; that it is not something achieved, you bring it with your birth. All that you have to do is not to create it but just to open the hidden secret of your life.

The moment you start feeling your inner light, your whole perspective starts changing. You will feel compassionate towards human beings even if they are doing stupid things. And you will feel immensely joyous, celebrating, even though you don't have anything to celebrate. Nothing is needed to celebrate – only excuses... my birthday is just an excuse! But if you want to celebrate, you will find a thousand and one excuses.

It is your life, and whatever becomes of it is your creation. Remember, there are hidden signatures on it. You cannot disassociate yourself from what you create, from the way you live, the way you respond. Once you are overflowing with love and blissfulness, you cannot, even in your dreams, act in a way which is humiliating to another. Because the other is not really the other, it is just part of us. We are one consciousness filling the whole universe. But a little experience will help... and you will start seeing the same light in others. And to see light within yourself and light within others is to live the whole year round surrounded with a festival of lights.

In the outside world, there are people who want to dominate and there are people who want to be dominated. The responsibility is not one-sided. There are people who want to be enslaved, because slavery has one thing about it: it takes all responsibility away from you. Then the responsibility is of your owner. You are just instrumental – whatever he says, you do, but you don't feel any burden. So most human beings deep down want to remain slaves.

Slavery in religion means you remain a Hindu, a

Mohammedan, a Christian. And you are afraid also, because your slavery is based only on beliefs. So everybody is trying to protect his flock from coming in contact with others.

Just the other day I received a message from friends in Germany. The German parliament has passed a resolution that I cannot enter Germany. Sannyasins are protesting it because it is absolutely against the German constitution, against German law. There is not a single precedent! Not only in Germany but all over the world, there is not a single incident prohibiting a man who has never before entered your country. How can you judge that he is going to be dangerous?

So they asked five hundred world-famous, prominent intelligentsia from different fields – professors, scientists, poets, painters, dancers, actors. Up to now they have received one hundred and fifty letters of strong support, an absolute protest against the government.

They have also received a few letters which are in support of the government. A few points in those letters were so hilarious that they have sent me those few points. One point was: One Protestant high priest has supported the government because he thinks I am a Catholic, and Germany has to be saved from the Catholic religion. Such fear shows deep doubts. You are not certain about your Protestant theology; you are afraid somebody may make punctures in the balloon of your faith.

Here with me, there is a religious fragrance but no religion as such. That gives you total freedom. That makes you proud of yourself and grateful for all that existence has done for you. Remember, pride is not ego. Ego is something without content. For example, a man who cannot even draw a straight line thinks himself a great painter – that is ego, there is no content. But if Picasso thinks he is a great painter, that is simply a fact, and if he is proud of his genius there is nothing wrong in it. In fact, people should be helped to find some pride in their individuality because that pride will make their eyes shine, their faces luminous; that pride will make them unique individuals, with no more question of inferiority and superiority.

And secondly, anybody who is proud is always grateful. Because the genius of Picasso or Yehudi Menuhin is not their own; they are only vehicles. It is the beyond that comes through them – in music, in dance, in painting, in scientific research, in poetry, in thousands of ways, but the real genius will know it for sure, that it is coming from the beyond.

He is proud that he has been chosen, he is not proud *in comparison* to you. Ego is a comparison: you are higher, you are superior, but there is comparison. You cannot be superior living alone in a forest – superior to whom? You cannot even be inferior – inferior to whom?

The man of pride has a deep feeling of gratitude that existence has chosen him, although he is not worthy. It is a strange phenomenon. The more worthy you are, the more you feel you are not worthy enough. You have been given so much and you cannot do anything in return.

Here, there will be people with pride. I would like my sannyasins to be proud, even of the fact that they are sannyasins, that they have been courageous enough to move against all orthodoxies, traditions, conventions, all that is rotten, and come out into the fresh, into the young, into the new. You are blessed. But your blessedness will be full of gratitude. That is the distinction to be remembered between ego and pride. I destroy the ego and I create the pride. Ego is something like a cancer that simply eats you and eats others. Pride, self-respect is a creative phenomenon. It fulfills your own potential and it also shares with the world all the treasures that you have brought into the world. So here the situation is totally different.

I would like it to be so in the whole world, but they are so afraid. Their fear that I can destroy their morality, their religion, their past, is a clear-cut indication that they are already uprooted from the past. They are just hoping against hope that somehow all this old garbage can be carried. Because we have respected it as golden for centuries. Now, to suddenly drop it as garbage by the side of the road hurts the ego, because it means the ego has been wrong for centuries.

A sannyasin needs the courage to drop the fear – because unless he drops the fear, the ego cannot be dropped. And without dropping the ego, the whole load, the whole luggage, all rotten, has to be carried. Your whole energy is wasted in carrying the dead.

Just think of yourself carrying your father, your grandfather, your forefathers, all on your back and going towards Marine Drive. Do you think you will ever reach Marine Drive? Because the people lined up on your back is going to be endless; all your skyscrapers will look like pygmies. The load is going to be so tremendous that you will not be able to carry it without the help of Suraj Prakash – you will need trucks, transport vehicles. And your whole life will be simply wasted carrying these dead people.

And we are all carrying them. That's why life becomes serious, burdensome, heavy, juiceless, dry. Otherwise, there is no reason. You can be lush green with red flowers.

And there is no need for any comparison. Why not have all the people of the planet be emperors? What is the problem? It is a question of understanding the world – and if you understand yourself, to understand the world is not difficult, it is the simplest thing.

And once you have understood that to be an emperor or to be a slave is *your* decision, who is going to choose to be a slave? When you can put your whole energy into creating something that will give you satisfaction, that will give you a deep sense of fulfillment, a sense that you have not been here unnecessarily, you have contributed something; you have made the world a little more beautiful – a few more flowers you have added to it. If everybody is adding a few more flowers, this whole world can again become a garden.

There is no need to fight. There is no need for you to be superior to anybody, because I am giving you something which is far higher than superiority. I am making you unique individuals.

BELOVED OSHO,
AS FAR AS YOU ARE CONCERNED, IS YOUR BIRTHDAY
JUST LIKE ANY OTHER DAY IN THE YEAR? OR IS IT IN
SOME WAY SPECIAL FOR YOU?

Time exists no more for me. That's why I have to go on look-ing at my watch, because I don't have any sense of time. If I don't look at my watch, I may speak for the whole night!

To me, every day is the same, every moment is the same. But when I say every moment is the same, it means it has the same blissfulness, the same ecstasy, the same joy, the same silence, the same peace that passeth understanding.

I don't see any difference between two points, between two days. As far as I am concerned, all differences have disappeared. I live in absolute silence. Even while I am speaking to you, believe it or not, I am silent. Only the mechanism of the mind is being used, but my consciousness is centered in absolute beauty and silence.

BELOVED OSHO,
I IMAGINE THAT IF YOU HAVE THE FACULTY TO
PREDICT THE FUTURE, YOU WOULD NOT USE IT. YET,
YOU DO SEEM TO KNOW HOW EVENTS ARE GOING
TO UNFOLD. IS THIS BECAUSE THE ENLIGHTENED
MAN IS SO IN TUNE WITH EXISTENCE THAT HE CAN
SEE HOW ITS RHYTHM IS MOVING? OR IS IT THAT
BEING THOROUGHLY FAMILIAR WITH MAN'S
MECHANICAL MIND, HE CAN FAIRLY CONFIDENTLY
FORESEE HOW CERTAIN THOUGHTS AND ACTIONS
ARE GOING TO PRECIPITATE CERTAIN OTHER
THOUGHTS AND ACTIONS? OR IS IT A COMBINATION
OF THE TWO? IS THIS FACULTY INCREASINGLY
AVAILABLE AS ONE BECOMES MORE CLEAR, OR IS IT
AVAILABLE ONLY TO THE ENLIGHTENED
CONSCIOUSNESS?

Maneesha, spirituality is an explosion. With enlightenment, suddenly all the great qualities start blossoming in you. Before enlightenment, meditating... as your meditation goes deeper, new qualities start emerging. But it is something like a rehearsal. Or better to say, what emerges before enlightenment is like on a full moon night when you are sitting by the side of a silent lake and you see the full moon in the water. It is the full moon, and it is tremendously beautiful but it is only a reflection. Just throw a small pebble and the reflection is disturbed; the silver of the reflection is spread all over the lake. The moon disappears.

In meditation, you become acquainted with the reflected qualities. They are the same qualities, but they are only reflections – reflections of the qualities that you will have when enlightenment has happened. But for the seeker, even the reflected qualities are so great that they transform his whole character. They prepare him for the moment when he will look up into the sky to the real moon.

But before enlightenment, you cannot be in possession of the real qualities. It is more than enough that existence allows you even the qualities which are only reflections – but they give you the taste, the conviction. They bring you the real conversion; you remain in the world but your eyes start moving inwards. You remain in the world but the distance between you and the world starts becoming bigger. You are coming closer to home, but the real experience will be when you enter the home, when you enter your center.

Don't think that if meditation gives only reflected qualities then why bother about meditation? Those reflected qualities are going to become steps towards the real. If you don't have them, the temple of the real is so far away that even to conceive of any bridge is impossible.

With meditation – slowly, step by step, without any hurry – you go on coming closer and closer to home. And it is good, because you have time to absorb, you have time to get acquainted, and when you reach to the real it will not be absolutely unknown. You have seen it in the reflection, you are already in love with it. It is just like a photograph....

Once in a while it happens. I have received a few letters saying that somebody has seen my picture and has fallen in love. He had no money to come; it took ten years to reach here, but for ten years he has been a sannyasin. For ten years he has meditated and now he has come – a mature person. Even the photograph has helped; something in the photograph turned him on. And it must have made a great impression because for ten years he was earning money just to come here.

The way, the path, is very simple and can be made even more simple. But simplicity is against the priests, they want it to be complex – so complex that they are needed to interpret it; so complex that without a mediator it is impossible to grow in your understanding.

The reason why religion looks so complex is because religion became a business, and priests found that unless it is complex enough, it will not be attractive enough either. It has to be complex, it has to be challenging, it has to be far away, and then the priest becomes an absolute necessity. And they have been exploiting in every possible way.

Just recently, I was reading a joke. A beautiful woman is standing in the confession box of a Catholic church. The bishop has seen the woman – the woman is certainly rare, very beautiful, and the bishop is an ordinary human being as everybody is. And the woman starts saying that she has been raped. He asks a few questions and then he completely forgets all Catholicism, all Christianity, all religion.

He says to the woman, "Your thing is very complex. You come into the other room." And there in the other room, he puts his hand around the woman. She looks a little puzzled because she was always calling him "Father" and he was always calling her "my dear daughter" – but the way he has put his hands around her, does not feel like the hands of a father. The very vibe is disgusting.

The bishop asks, "Did that nasty fellow make some movement like this?"

And the woman says, "This is nothing; he did something worse."

He says, "Something worse?" So he kisses the woman and asks,

"Did that man do this too?"

The woman says, "Father, you don't understand. He was really the *worst* type of man."

By this time, the father was also sexually aroused. He forced the woman onto the bed, made love to her and then asked, "Did that evil man do this thing too?"

The woman said, "Father, you don't understand; he did even something worse."

The bishop said, "Something worse? Worse than this? My God! But I wonder what he could have done?" The woman said, "He gave me AIDS!"

These poor priests are just as ordinary as anybody. They have no training in meditation, no training in yoga, no training in Tantra – which are absolutely essential for the maturity of a man. All these bishops and cardinals and priests are all amateurish. They will be saying things and doing just the opposite – they have to! I'm not angry, I'm simply stating the fact.

All the religions have been telling people that anger is bad, greed is bad, sex is bad. And the list is long... almost everything that gives you pleasure is bad. Put it on the list without any fear; it will be found in all the scriptures of the religions – if it gives you pleasure, it must be counted as a sin by the religious scriptures.

So all that is pleasant has been poisoned, and all that is unpleasant has become your life. And these millions of priests of different religions are living on your wounds. They are simply parasites; they have been sucking your blood for centuries, saying stupid things without any evidence, without any reason. But they have destroyed such a beautiful world.

The only way is to take the world out of the hands of the priests. Man, free from priests, will have a beauty of his own. Priests have crushed and crippled him from every direction.

Just remember one thing: you have to remain one. Whatever divides you is against you; it makes you schizophrenic. And almost everybody is schizophrenic in different degrees. You cannot do anything wholeheartedly, something always remains uninvolved. The action remains partial; hence, unfulfilling.

Man need not be miserable unless he chooses it. He has the

possibility of living at the highest blissfulness possible, but that is a little arduous because it is an uphill task. But when you get to the peak, to the sunlit peak, all the arduousness of the journey is completely forgotten. Just the very idea that "I have arrived" relaxes you. You forget all the hell that you had to pass through.

In fact, you even feel grateful to all that hell because that helped you to find this sunlit peak.

BELOVED OSHO,
WHAT YOU TALK ABOUT CAN MEAN SO MUCH TO SO
MANY PEOPLE. YOUR MESSAGE HAS SPREAD. IT HAS
TO BRING ABOUT A SPIRITUAL EXPLOSION. THAT
SEEMS TO BE THE ONLY HOPE THERE IS FOR US
TODAY. HOW DO YOU INTEND TO LET YOUR IDEAS
GROW AND SPREAD AND BLOSSOM, TO FLOWER INTO
SOMETHING MORE UNIVERSAL, MORE ACCEPTED,
MORE USUAL?

You are asking the impossible. My ideas *are* universal. That is the reason they cannot be accepted. People's minds are not universal; they are very local. First, the nation, the religion, the language – perhaps a sect of the religion, perhaps a dialect of the local language. They are very much confined. Otherwise, Sikhs asking to have an independent country would not be possible.

On the contrary, there should be intelligent people around the world asking for one world. That is going to solve the problems. The world is already dissected into so many small parts that if you go on dissecting it more, your capacity to solve the problems becomes less and less.

So the first thing: my message is already universal – that is one of the problems. If it were Hindu, at least I would have been at ease with four hundred million Hindus. If it were Catholic, I would have been at ease with seven hundred million people. But my message is universal – neither Hindu, nor Mohammedan, nor Christian, but purely existential; not based on the past but based on my own experience.

Secondly, you are asking if I can speak, can bring my message to the people in such a way that it becomes more acceptable, that it becomes more usual. It cannot become – at least, as long as I am alive, it cannot become usual. You have so many usual doctrines, usual religions, usual ideologies. My approach is going to remain unusual, because the usual approaches have all failed. Something unusual has to be tried.

I know you love me and you want my message to reach people, but your love is blind. You don't see the implications of what you are saying. You are saying, "Can't your message be more acceptable?" That means I will have to compromise. I will have to think of the blind people all around me and adjust to their ideas. It is betraying the truth. Every compromise is a betrayal.

My message will remain universal even if I am the only person who trusts in it, because its universality does not mean *numbers* of followers. Its universality means that it is the foundational doctrine of existence. And I cannot conceive how it can be more acceptable.

The only way is to knock on as many doors as possible, to shout from rooftops hoping that somebody may not be deaf, somebody may not be blind. But I cannot compromise on any point, because it is not a business. Who am I to compromise on behalf of truth? And a truth compromised becomes untruth. A truth is absolutely uncompromising.

But that has been always the case. All the masters in the past had to face it. They are always ahead of their time. It seems to be something in the very nature of life, that the people who are going to be decisive about human consciousness will always come ahead of their time – because it takes one hundred years, two hundred years for people to understand them. If they come in their own time, then by the time people have understood them, they will be out of date. They *have* to be ahead of their time so that by the time human mind, human consciousness reaches the point where they can be understood, their message will be available.

So the greatest work for sannyasins is to keep the message pure, unpolluted by you or by others – and wait. The future is bound to be more receptive, more welcoming. We may not be here but we can manage to change the consciousness for centuries to come. And my interest is not only in *this* humanity; my interest is in humanity as such.

Keep the message pure, twenty-four carat gold. And soon those people will be coming for whom you have made a temple – although it is sad when you are making the temple; nobody comes. And when people start coming, you will not be here. But one has to understand one thing: we are part of a flowing river of consciousness.

You may not be here in this form, you may be here in another form, but keep it in mind never to ask such a question that I should be more acceptable, more respectable, more in agreement with the masses. I cannot be. And it is not stubbornness on my part. It is just that truth cannot compromise. It has never done it; it would be the greatest sin.

BELOVED OSHO,
ACCORDING TO GURDJIEFF, A NORMAL MAN NEEDS
LAUGHTER AS A MEANS TO DISCHARGE AN EXCESS OF
ENERGY. WHEREAS, FOR A MAN LIKE GAUTAM
BUDDHA, LAUGHTER IS SIMPLY NO LONGER POSSIBLE.
PLEASE COMMENT.

I don't agree with George Gurdjieff. I love the man, I agree with him on many points, but on many points he is uninformed. Particularly about Gautam Buddha, he has no in-depth connection with the sources that Buddha made available to the world.

He is saying that for the normal man, laughter is just a release of excessive energy. It is an absurd statement. Firstly, the normal man cannot have excessive energy. He is tired, he is somehow dragging himself; he does not have excessive energy. So why does he laugh? Gurdjieff's diagnosis about laughter is not right. The normal man has to laugh just to live. Life is so miserable... it is all sadness, frustration. The normal man is burdened with only negative feelings. He needs something positive to live, and he needs some way to get rid of the negative feelings. Laughter is a great medicine – it does both jobs. It helps you not to be unburdened of extra energy but to be unburdened of *negative* energy – your anger, your sadness, your frustration.

And because Gurdjieff is wrong about the normal man, he is certainly going to be wrong about Gautam Buddha. Gautam Buddha does not laugh, that is true. But the reason why he does not laugh is that he has seen everything, he has known everything. There is nothing more to know, there is nothing more to experience, there is nothing more to see. Life has come to a tranquillity... not even a ripple. It is so calm and quiet and collected... and because it is so peaceful, so silent, so blissful, laughter is absolutely unnecessary.

What Gurdjieff is saying about the normal man.... My suspicion is that he was acquainted with many mad people. He studied madness in order to evolve his psychology for the future man. Mad people certainly laugh because of excessive energy. They don't have anything to do. The energy accumulates, and it needs some way.... Mad people will talk to themselves, mad people will talk to walls, to trees. And mad people have their own arguments, their own rationality – you cannot defeat a madman; he follows a totally different system of logic.

Because he is not involved in life anymore – you have isolated him, put him in a mad asylum – his energy goes on accumulating. What is he supposed to do? If he is a violent type, he will express his excessive energy in destruction, but if he is not a violent type then he will find other sources. One of the sources is laughter, and a madman's laughter has a beauty, a purity, an innocence.

When you laugh, your laughter has a judgment in it. If somebody has slipped on a banana peel and you laugh, you are judging – and that man will feel embarrassed. His embarrassment shows your judgment.

In my high school days.... Every year in India there is a certain day for worshipping the serpent. On that day, all over India there are wrestling matches – Indian-style, not like boxing, but more human, more artful. Boxing looks just primitive, because you are hitting the other person just like an animal. Indian wrestling is far more refined and if you have seen a really beautiful wrestler, you will not forget the experience. I am reminding you.

There was a wrestling match. All the schools of the district had sent their wrestlers, but our wrestler had graduated the year before. We held the shield – that's why all the wrestlers had to come to our school. But there was nobody in our school who was ready. I just passed by a young man I loved very much for the simple reason that he was never serious.

I asked him, "Would you like to try? I can make you a famous wrestler within seconds. Because the principal has given me the task to find somebody, but nobody is ready. They know they are not wrestlers, and good wrestlers will be coming here from every school."

The boy said, "You know I'm not a wrestler. I have not even had a fight with anybody. In fact, I am a Christian. If somebody slaps one of my cheeks, I will give him the other and go home – I believe Christ is right. And I don't even know the ABC of Indian wrestling, and it is an art, an ancient art."

I said, "Nobody else is willing – but the difference between you and the others is, they are all serious so they cannot be persuaded. You are the only man who is not serious. You can even accept defeat with laughter."

He said, "That's true, because what is the harm? If I am defeated I don't see that there has been any harm to the world. So okay, I am ready."

I said, "Okay. Remember, you will be in the finals and you will get the toughest guy."

He said, "Don't be worried, you have given me the key – laughter."

And that was a match which was remembered for years. Because we had been winning the trophy for almost seven years; just one time more and the trophy would have become our possession – it had to be won eight times consecutively. We had won seven times, but the man who was the reason for our winning was not really a student. He was admitted into the school and he was given some scholarship, but the only reason to keep him was for the wrestling match. There was a possibility that he might have become champion of the whole state, but then suspicions began – because for seven years this man was in the same class, and people had seen him working with a doctor as a pharmacist. The whole day he was in the dispensary, so when did he study? Because questions had started, he had to be dropped.

But this gave such a beautiful opportunity. There were other wrestlers, they fought... then the finals. The other school had also brought a professional wrestler, because seeing the situation – and this was the eighth time, something had to be done; otherwise the shield would be gone. So they had brought a professional wrestler. Because of his age, his body and everything, he looked like he was a professional. This poor boy... and my principal was standing by my side.

The principal said, "What have you done? You don't even see that there are times to be serious. *This* is not the time to be humorous! You have put the wrong person there – he cannot do anything, he does not know anything."

I said, "Don't be worried. He will do something, and he will do something that will be remembered for years to come. Your trophy will be forgotten." And then the bell rang, and the student I had chosen – he was my friend – and the wrestler from the other school came, and they stood in the middle of the ring.

I had told my friend to have a dance first: "You are going to be defeated, so about that we are certain. Forget all about it. Enjoy, and help this crowd to enjoy. So first you go around dancing...." And he really went dancing! And people suddenly became silent. They could not believe it! – a very giant wrestler was standing there and this small boy is dancing! He has some nerve.

And then he came in front of the wrestler, fell on the ground, completely touching the ground with his whole body, and had a good laugh. The other wrestler could not understand what was happening. He had fought many times but this was a strange type... and the whole crowd could not understand. The referee went there and asked, "What are you doing?"

The boy said, "All that I *can* do I am doing! – I am doing my best. Now it is up to him to do something! He is standing there like an idiot." But there was nothing to do, because the boy had already done to himself what was to be done by the wrestler – he was lying down flat on the ground! The wrestler could not even touch him. When he is flat on the ground, he has accepted defeat. And now he is laughing and the whole crowd is laughing and the man who has become victorious is standing there sad, completely lost.

My principal whispered in my ear, "You are right. You chose the right person." His laughter was so out of context that nobody could have imagined… and the way he did it, lying down flat on the ground, leaving no chances for the other person – he could not even touch his body. And without fighting, he became the hero. The crowd took him up, the victor was forgotten. Everybody loved him. Nobody said anything like "You are defeated."

And when I met him, I said, "It has been a great victory because not a single person said that you were defeated. The other man has not even touched you. So don't be worried; now we will raise the legal question. The shield cannot go to the other side." The principal said, "What are you saying?"

I said, "The shield cannot go from this school. It can wait one year longer, because our wrestler has not been defeated. He has not been touched."

The principal said, "You are something. First you brought that boy, and now you are bringing this law!"

I said, "You have to stand by me and we have to fight it. The other wrestler has not done anything and even the crowd has not accepted it. We have photographs to show that he is standing completely defeated and our man is laughter – all laughter, and people are carrying him like a hero."

So the principal had to agree with me. He said, "What is your whole plan? You tell me, because this… you caught me unawares. It was wrong to ask you in the first place."

I said, "Now, I want to tell you that that man is a professional wrestler, he is not a student. But keep quiet – we also have professional wrestlers, so next time we will hire a professional wrestler. The shield has to remain once it has come to us." And we had won seven times and we had a very good group of wrestlers in our town; it was famous for wrestling. So I looked around all the gymnasiums and found a very strong man, almost steel. If you hit him, you would be harmed. His whole life was just preparing and preparing – he was hoping to become a national champion. He was already a state champion.

Seeing him – everybody knew him, he was state champion – the other wrestler started saying, "This man is not a student!" Their principal and all the staff had come this time; the whole school had come to support their wrestler because somehow the shield had to be taken. Now this great difficulty arose. They all started saying, "We will not accept this man. This man is a professional wrestler."

I said, "Yes, this man is a professional wrestler, because *your* man is a professional wrestler." And we had collected all the information about the other person: where he worked, what he did, how old he was, how educated he was – and he was not a student. When we put forward all the information, they felt so ashamed.

I said, "What do you want? If your wrestler is not ready to fight, you lose. Because now it is no longer a question that somebody is a professional wrestler – both are. So it is equal. So let us go into it, and whoever wins.... But the other wrestler stepped out and the shield stayed in the school, although it was not completely conquered because of that one time. Then that school dropped the idea, because it was exposed to the newspapers that they had been bringing in a professional wrestler and that because of them we had to bring in a professional wrestler, just to expose it.

But one thing I have always remembered about that young man: that he could laugh in such a situation, where everything was against the poor fellow. But laughter saved him.

Gurdjieff has a different system of changing the chemistry of man. So in his system, what he is saying may be perfectly right. But the way I am working, laughter is one of the most significant religious qualities. And if Gautam Buddha does not laugh that does not mean he cannot laugh. That simply means he has come into a space where all is joy.

For laughter to exist, the contrary to laughter is needed, just like white chalk is needed to write on blackboards. Laughter is visible if you are sad, and dark clouds in your heart give it a background.

But when all dark clouds have disappeared, laughter remains but it is no more the old form; it has taken a totally new shape.

Gautam Buddha himself has *become* laughter. He is so joyous, each of his movements, his silence or his sermons, are all nothing but his laughter resounding into our hearts. It is a resonance. You will feel it; perhaps you may laugh. Just being with Gautam Buddha, you may start laughing. He may trigger your energies. He himself is now complete, entire, a cosmic whole. His very being is laughter – that's why there is no question of him laughing the way we laugh. After enlightenment, every quality of life changes. We have all those qualities but in a very raw condition. Enlightenment refines them, purifies them, and it takes some intelligence to recognize that they are the same qualities.

13

Jealousy — The by-product of marriage

BELOVED OSHO,
MASTER OF MASTERS, I WANT TO TELL YOU THAT I
AM TOTALLY TURNED ON TO YOU, AND IT'S JUST FAR
OUT BEING WITH YOU. I HAVE JUST ONE QUESTION,
MAYBE IT'S NOTHING SPIRITUAL BUT FOR ME IT'S
QUITE SOMETHING – MY JEALOUSY. I HAVE BEEN
WITH MY BOYFRIEND FOR TWO YEARS AND WE STILL
ENJOY BEING TOGETHER, BUT IF HE GOES WITH
OTHER WOMEN I FREAK OUT. THIS EMOTION IS SO
STRONG THAT I'M AFRAID I WILL DESTROY THIS
BEAUTIFUL THING WHICH IS BETWEEN US. BELOVED
OSHO, WOULD YOU PLEASE TELL ME THE VERY ROOTS
OF JEALOUSY, HOW I CAN DEAL WITH IT, OR EVEN GO
THROUGH IT? AND I ALSO WANT TO SAY THANK
YOU FOR EVERYTHING BUT THE WORDS DON'T
EXPRESS WHAT I FEEL FOR YOU. MY HEART IS
BEATING WITH LOVE FOR YOU.

Jealousy is one of the most prevalent areas of psychological ignorance about yourself, about others and more particularly, about relationship. People think they know what love is – they do not know. And their misunderstanding about love creates jealousy. By 'love' people mean a certain kind of monopoly, some possessiveness – without understanding a simple fact of life: that the moment you possess a living being you have killed him. Life cannot be possessed. You cannot have it in your fist. If you want to have it, you have to keep your hands open.

But the thing has been going on a wrong path for centuries; it has become ingrained in us so much that we cannot separate love from jealousy. They have become almost one energy. For example, you feel jealous if your lover goes to another woman. You are disturbed by it now, but I would like to tell you that if you don't feel jealous you will be in much more trouble – then you will think you don't love him, because if you loved him you should have felt jealous. Jealousy and love have become so mixed up. In fact, they are poles apart. A mind that can be jealous cannot be loving, and vice-versa: a mind that is loving cannot be jealous.

What is the disturbance? You have to look it as if it is not your question – somebody else has asked, it is somebody else's problem – so that you can stand aside and see the whole fabric. The feeling of jealousy is a byproduct of marriage.

In the world of animals, birds, there is no jealousy. Once in a while there is a fight over a love object but a fight is far better than to be jealous, far more natural than to be caught up in jealousy and burn your heart with your own hands.

Marriage is an invented institution, it is not natural; hence nature has not provided a mind that can adjust to marriage. But man found it necessary that there should be some kind of legal contract between lovers, because love itself is dream-stuff, it is not reliable... it is there this moment and the next moment it is gone. You want to be secure for the coming moment, for your whole future. Right now you are young; soon you will be old and you would like your wife, your husband, to be with you in your old age, in your sickness. But for that, a few compromises have to be made, and whenever there is compromise there is always trouble.

This is the compromise that human beings have made: to be secure about the future, to be certain about the tomorrows, to have a guarantee that the woman who loves you is going to love you forever, that it is not a temporary affair....

That's why religious people say that marriages are "made in heaven" ... a strange kind of heaven, because if these marriages are made in heaven, then what can you make in hell? They don't show the signs, the fragrance, the freshness, the beauty of heaven. They are certainly disgusting, ugly... they show something of hell certainly. But man settled for marriage because that was the only way to have private property. Animals don't have private property – they are all communists, and far better communists than have appeared in human history. They don't have any dictatorship of the proletariat and they have not lost their freedom, but they don't have any private property. Man also lived for thousands of years without marriage, but those were the days when there was no private property. Those were the days of hunting; man was a hunter. And those people thousands of years ago had no cold-storage system, no technology – whatever food they got they had to finish as quickly as possible. They could only hope that tomorrow they will get some food again.

Because there was nothing to accumulate, there was no question of marriage. People lived in communes, tribes; people loved, people reproduced, but in the beginning there was no word for 'father'. The word 'mother' is far more ancient and far more natural. You will be surprised to know that the word 'uncle' is older than the word 'father' – because all the people who were the age of your father... you didn't know who your father was. Men and women were mixing joyously – without any compulsion, without any legal bondage, out of their free will. If they wanted to meet and be together there was no question of domination. The children never knew who their father was, they knew only their mother. And they knew many men in the tribe; someone amongst those men must have been their father, hence they were all uncles.

As private property came into existence with cultivation.... With hunting, man could not survive long. People have destroyed complete species of animals. Hundreds of species which once used to dance and sing on this earth... man has eaten them up. Something had to be done because hunting was not reliable. Today you may get food, tomorrow you may have to be hungry. And it was very arduous. The search for animals did not allow man to develop any of his other talents, his genius. But cultivation changed the whole life of man.

You must be reminded of the fact that cultivation is the discovery of women, not of men. The woman was confined – she was not able to go hunting. Most of the time she was pregnant, she was weak, she was carrying another soul within her. She needed care, protection... so she was living in the house. She started making the living space more beautiful – and this you can see even today, after thousands of years. If you enter into a bachelor's room you can immediately say that it is a bachelor's room. You may not be able to decide by seeing the bachelor whether he is bachelor or not, but his room certainly is a bachelor! The woman, her touch, is missing. The house of a bachelor is never a home, it is just a place where he sleeps. It is not something with which he feels a certain intimacy, a certain creative relationship.

The home, the village, the city and the whole civilization are because of the woman, because she was free from hunting and she had different values of the heart and of the mind – she was more aesthetic, more graceful, more earthly, not at all interested in hell and heaven and God and the devil and all that crap! No woman has written a single religious scripture. No woman has been a philosopher thinking about abstract, faraway things.

Woman's consciousness is interested only in the intimate surroundings – she would like a beautiful house, she would like a beautiful garden. She wants to create a small world of her own – cozy, comfortable. She imparts a certain quality to a dead house and it becomes a living home. It is a magical transformation.

Man continued to hunt, and the woman started looking around... the man had no time. He has always been busy without business, but the woman had all the time there is. The basic work of hunting was being done by the groups of men and the woman started looking around. She discovered cultivation because she saw wild fruits growing, she saw many other things growing and she also saw that every year the crop dies, the seeds fall back into the earth and when the rains come, again those seeds sprout in thousands of plants. She started experimenting to find what was edible and what was not edible. Soon, as hunting was becoming more and more difficult, men had to agree with women: "We have to shift our whole economic focus. We have to go for cultivation, for fruits, for vegetables. And these are in our hands – we can produce as much as we want, as we need it, and there is tremendous variety."

Slowly, slowly the nomads, the wandering tribes... because hunters cannot stay in one place. They have to go on moving as the animals escape. Once hunting was dropped and cultivation became our very measure of survival a new thing also happened alongside.

There were people who were powerful people and there were people who were weak people. The people who were physically powerful managed to claim much ground as their property. They earned much... slowly, slowly the barter system started, because when you have too much of one crop, what are you going to do with it? You have to exchange it; then you can have many more things. Life became more complex, with more excitement.

But a problem was felt: after a person dies, who is going to inherit his property? Nobody wanted their property to be inherited by any XYZ. They wanted their property to belong to their own blood. It is out of economics, not out of the understanding of love that marriage came into existence. Its very birth was wrong, under the wrong stars.

And because man had to agree for marriage.... The woman was very willing for the simple reason that for thousands of years in the hunting period she was not financially a part of the society; man was all. Man continued his power, although the whole social structure changed. The hunter's nomadic life became a peaceful life in a village but man's concern about his property.... He wanted a contract with the woman to be certain that the son she was giving birth to is not somebody else's, but his own. For this simple purpose all the woman's freedom had to be destroyed. She had to live almost like a prisoner, or worse.

Man agreed – under compulsion, he compromised. If the woman was losing a few things – her freedom of movement, her freedom in changing lovers – man was also ready to sacrifice his freedom. They would remain devoted to each other forever.

But it is against nature. Even if you want to do it nature is not going to support you. Nature is for freedom, not for any kind of bondage. So new problems started arising. Men started finding prostitutes who were no-one's wives, or as it was phrased in India, the prostitute was the wife of the whole town: *nagarvadhu*. She belongs to anybody, she is a commodity; you have to pay and buy her time and her body. Because of marriage it was very difficult to find married women because then there were more complexities: they had their husbands.... Prostitutes were good.

And you will be surprised to know that in India every city had its topmost prostitute – she was the most beautiful girl born in that city. Because she was so beautiful it was not right to let her get married to one person, she had to be shared. She was so beautiful that if she got married there would be trouble, there would be problems – people would go on falling in love with her. It was better to keep her free for anybody who would pay.

Marriage created suspicion. The husband was always suspicious about whether the child born to them was his own or not. And the problem is, the father had no way to determine that a child was his own. Only the mother knew. Because the father had no way of being certain, he created more and more walls around the woman – that was the only possibility, the only alternative – to disconnect her from the larger humanity. Not to educate her, because education gives wings to people, thoughts, makes people capable of revolt, so no education for women. No religious education for women, because religion makes you saints, holy people and it has been a male-dominated society for centuries and man cannot conceive a woman to be higher and holier than himself.

Man has been cutting from the very roots any possibility of woman's growth. She is just a factory to manufacture children. She has not been accepted by any culture in the world as equal to man. There are even cultures like the Chinese which have denied the soul to woman; woman is only a machine, without a soul. In China you could kill your wife, no law existed against it. The wife was your possession and if you wanted to destroy it, it was nobody's business to prevent it.

All over the world the woman has been suppressed. The more she has been suppressed, the more her whole energy has turned sour. And because she has no freedom and man has every freedom, all her repressed emotions, feelings, thoughts – her whole individuality turns into a jealous phenomenon. She is continuously afraid that her husband might leave her, might go to some other woman, might become interested in some other woman. He might abandon her, and she has problems: she is not educated, she is not financially capable of standing on her own feet. She has been brought up in such a way that she cannot go into the world; she has been told from the very beginning that she is weak....

Indian scriptures say that in childhood the father should protect the girl; in youth the husband should protect the girl; in old age the son should protect the woman. She has to be protected from the very childhood to the grave. She cannot revolt against this male chauvinist society. All she can do is go on finding faults, which are bound to be there. Mostly she is not wrong; she is mostly right.

Whenever a man falls in love with another woman something in him towards the first woman changes. Now they are again strangers, there is no bridge. She has been crippled, enslaved and now she has been abandoned. Her whole life is a life of agony. Out of this agony arises jealousy. Jealousy is the anger of the weak – one who cannot do anything but is boiling within, who would like to burn the whole world but cannot do anything except cry and scream and throw tantrums. This situation will continue until marriage becomes a museum piece.

Now there is no need for marriage. Perhaps it was useful. Perhaps it was not useful, but it was only an excuse to enslave the woman. Things could have been worked out in a different way, but there is no point in going into the past. Right or wrong, one thing is good about the past: it is no more.

As far as the present and the future are concerned, marriage is absolutely irrelevant, inconsistent with human evolution and contradictory to all the values we love – freedom, love, joy.

Because man wanted the woman to be completely imprisoned, he wrote religious scriptures making her afraid of hell, making her greedy for heaven... IF she follows the rules. Those rules exist only for women, not for men. Now it is so clear that to let women live any longer in this poisonous situation of jealousy is against their psychological health. And women's psychological health influences the pyschological health of the whole of humanity – man is also born of woman. The woman has to become an independent individual.

The dissolution of marriage will be a great, festive event on the earth – and nobody is preventing you: if you love your wife or your husband you can live for lives together, nobody is preventing you. Withdrawing marriage is simply giving you your individuality back. Now nobody possesses you.

You are not to make love to a man just because he is your husband and he has the right to demand it. In my vision, when a woman makes love to a man because she *has* to make love, it is prostitution – not retail, but wholesale!

Retail is better, you have a chance to change. This wholesale prostitution is dangerous, you don't have a chance to change. And you have married for the first time – you should be given chances because you are an amateur. A few marriages at least will help you to become mature; perhaps then you can find the right woman. And by right woman I don't mean the woman who is "made for you."

No woman is made for you and no man is made for any woman. By the right woman or the right man I mean that if you have understood a few relationships, if you have been in a few relationships, you will understand what things create miserable situations amongst you and what situations create a loving, peaceful, happy life. Living with different people is an absolutely necessary education for a right life as far as love is concerned.

You should first graduate from a few relationships. In your college, in your university you should pass through a few relationships. And you should not be in a hurry to decide – there is no need, the world is big, and each individual has some unique quality and beauty.

As you go through a few relationships you start becoming aware of what kind of woman, what kind of man is going to be a friend to you – not a master, not a slave. And friendship needs no marriage because friendship is far higher.

You are feeling jealous because that jealousy you have received as an inheritance. With me you will have to change many things – not because I say to change them but because you understand that a drastic change is needed.

For example, the idea has been spread all over the world that if a husband sometimes goes to some other woman then this is going to destroy the marriage. It is absolutely wrong. On the contrary, if every marriage has the weekend free it will cement your relationship more strongly, because your marriage is not disturbing your freedom, because your wife understands the need for variety. These are human needs.

The priests and the moralists and the puritans first decide on an ideal. They make beautiful ideals and then they force the idea on you, for you to become like the ideals. They want to make you all idealists. For ten thousand years we have lived under a very dark and dismal shadow of idealism. I am a realist. I don't have any ideal. To me, to understand reality and to go with reality is the only right way for any intelligent man or woman.

My understanding is – and it is based on thousands of experiments – that if marriage is not such a tight thing, rigid, but is flexible, just a friendship... so that a woman can tell you she has met a beautiful young man and she is going this weekend to be with him – "And if you are interested I can bring him back with me, you will also love the person." And if the husband can say, not as a hypocrite but as an authentic human being, that "Your joy, your happiness is my happiness. If you have found someone, forget about the house, I will take care. You enjoy, because I know whenever you come back, enjoying a fresh love will make you fresh also. A fresh love will bring fresh youth to you. You go this week, and next week I may have my own program."

This is friendship. And when they come home they can talk about what kind of man she met, how he turned out, that it was not that great.... You can tell her about the new woman you have met.... You have a shelter in the home. You can go once in a while into the sky, wild and free, and come back and always your wife is there waiting for you – not to fight but to share your adventures. It simply needs a little understanding. It has nothing to do with religion, but just a little more intelligent behavior. You know perfectly well that howsoever beautiful a man or woman might be, she starts becoming heavy on your nerves sooner or later. Because the same geography, the same topography, the same landscape....

Man's mind is not made for monotony; neither it is made for monogamy. It is absolutely natural to ask for variety. And it is not against your love. In fact, the more you know other women, the more you will praise your own woman – your understanding will deepen. Your experience will be enriching... the more you have known a few men, the more accurately you will be able to understand your own husband. The idea of jealousy will disappear – you both are free, and you are not hiding anything.

With friends we should share everything, particularly those moments which are beautiful – moments of love, moments of poetry, moments of music... they should be shared. In this way your life will become more and more rich. You may become so attuned to each other that you live your whole life together, but there is no marriage. Jealousy will persist as long as marriage remains the basic foundation of society.

Just give the man, with your full heart, absolute freedom. And tell him he need not hide anything: "To hide anything is insulting. That means you don't trust me." And the same has to happen to man, that he can say to his wife: "You are as independent as I am. We are together to be happy, we are together to grow into more blissfulness. And we will do everything for each other but we are not going to be jailers to each other." Giving freedom is a joy, having freedom is a joy. You can have so much joy, but you are turning that whole energy into misery, into jealousy, into fight, into a continuous effort to keep the other under your thumb.

I have heard about a man who was in utter rage and despair because of his wife's behavior. It was not her fault... she was a nymphomaniac. Now what can you do? Somebody has a headache, somebody is a nymphomaniac. She was continuously falling in love with anybody! He took her to the doctor.

She was a beautiful woman. The doctor asked her to go inside the examination room. He went with her and soon, after a few minutes, moans and groans... and the husband was sitting in the office listening – it was too much! He just entered the room and what he saw he could not believe – the doctor was making love to his wife. The husband said, "What is happening?"

The wife said, "You idiot, you will never understand. Now you are asking what is happening! Can't you see?"

But the husband was furious. He said, "I am not asking my wife, I am asking you, doc! What is happening?"

The doctor said, "Nothing is happening, John, *you* are doing everything. I am simply taking her temperature."

John was afire. He had suffered so much and even the doctor... and what nonsense is he talking, that he is taking her temperature? So he took out his switchblade knife and started rubbing the knife against the doctor's shoulder. The doctor said, "What do you mean? What are you doing?"

He said, "Nothing. Just be careful. When that thing comes out, remember – it had better have numbers on it!"

We have created this circus instead of a culture. It goes on and on in different ways. I hope that in your life you can drop being a part of this stupid game. And it is easy: if you understand yourself, you will be able to understand your wife too. Don't you have other women in your dreams? In fact, to see your own wife in a dream is a rare phenomenon. People never see their wives or their husbands in their dreams. They have seen enough of them! Now even in the night, even in the dream, no freedom....

In your dreams you have the wives of your neighbors, the husbands of your neighbors... you should understand that somehow we have made a wrong society, a society which is not according to human nature. The desire for variety is an essential quality in anyone who is intelligent. The more intelligent you are the more variety you would like – there is some relationship between intelligence and variety. A buffalo is satisfied with one kind of grass; for her whole life she will not touch another kind of grass. She does not have the mind to change, to know new things, to discover new territories, to adventure into new spaces.

The poets, the painters, the dancers, the musicians, the actors – you will find these people more loving but their love is not focused on individuals. They are more loving but to as many individuals as they come in contact with. They are the intelligent people, they are our creative part.

Idiots don't want to change anything. They are afraid of change because any change means you will have to learn something again. The idiot wants to learn something once and remain with it his whole life. It may be a machine, it may be a wife, it may be a husband – it does not matter. You have known one woman, you know her nagging, you have become accustomed... sometimes not only accustomed, you have become addicted too. If suddenly your woman does not nag you, you will not be able to sleep that night – what happened? What has gone wrong?

One of my friends was continually complaining to me about his wife; "She is always sad, long faced and I am so worried to enter the house... I try to waste my time in this club and that club but finally I have to go back home and there she is."

I said to him, "Do one thing just as an experiment. Because she has been serious and she has been nagging, I cannot imagine that you enter the house smiling."

He said, "Do you think I can manage that? The moment I see her something freezes inside me – smile?"

I said, "Just as an experiment. Today you do one thing: take beautiful roses – it is the season; and the best ice-cream available in the city – tutti frutti; and go smiling, singing a song!"

He said, "If you say so I will do it, but I don't think it is going to make any difference."

I said, "I will come behind you, and see whether there is any difference or not."

The poor fellow tried hard. Many times on the way he laughed. I said, "Why are you laughing?"

He said, "I am laughing at what I am doing! I wanted you to tell me to divorce her and you have suggested I act as if I am going on a honeymoon!"

I said, "Just imagine it is a honeymoon... but try your best."

He opened the door and his wife was standing there. He smiled and then he laughed at himself because to smile... And that woman was standing almost like a stone. He presented the flowers and the ice-cream, and then I entered.

The woman could not believe what was happening. When the man had gone to the bathroom she asked me, "What is the matter? He has never brought anything, he has never smiled, he has never taken me out, he has never made me feel that I am loved, that I am respected. What magic has happened?"

I said, "Nothing; both of you have just been doing wrong. Now when he comes out of the bathroom you give him a good hug." She said, "A hug?"

I said, "Give him one! You have given him so many things, now give him a good hug, kiss him...." She said, "My God...."

I said, "He is your husband, you have decided to live together. Either live joyously or say good-bye joyously. There is no reason... it is such a small life. Why waste two person's lives unnecessarily?"

At that very moment the man came from the bathroom. The

woman hesitated a little but I pushed her, so she hugged the man and the man became so afraid he fell on the floor! He had never imagined that she was going to hug him. I had to help him up. I said, "What happened?"

He said, "It's just that I have never imagined that this woman can hug and kiss – but she can! And when she smiled she looked so beautiful."

Two persons living together in love should make it a point that their relationship is continuously growing, bringing more flowers every season, creating more joys. Just sitting together silently is enough....

But all this is possible only if we drop the old idea of marriage. More than friendship is unnatural. And if marriage is stamped by the court, is killed under that stamp in the court.... You cannot bring love under the rule of law. Love is the ultimate law. You just have to discover its beauties, its treasures. You have not to repeat, parrot-like, all the great values which make man the highest expression of consciousness on this planet. You should exercise them in your relationship.

And this has been my strange experience: if one partner starts moving on the right lines, the other follows sooner or later. Because they both are hungry for love, but they don't know how to approach it. No university teaches that love is an art and that life is not already given to you; that you have to learn from scratch. And it is good that we have to discover by our own hands every treasure that is hidden in life... and love is one of the greatest treasures in existence. But instead of becoming fellow travelers in search of love, beauty and truth, people are wasting their time in fighting, in jealousy.

Just become a little alert and start the change from your side – don't expect it from the other side. It will begin from the other side too. And it costs nothing to smile, it costs nothing to love, it costs nothing to share your happiness with somebody you love.

BELOVED OSHO,
SITTING IN MY ROOM THOUSANDS OF KILOMETERS
AWAY FROM YOU, I CAN FEEL YOU. AND IF HAD
HAVE EYES TO SEE, I WOULD SEE YOU STANDING
RIGHT IN FRONT OF ME. I REMEMBER WHEN YOU
SAID TO US IN DISCOURSE 'IF YOU DON'T FEEL ME
WHEN YOU ARE NOT HERE, YOU HAVEN'T LET ME IN.'
IT'S SO TRUE – BUT WHAT A GIFT THAT YOU REALLY,
REALLY CAME WHEN I WAS OPEN, THAT YOU REALLY
FILLED MY BEING. IN SOME MOMENTS SITTING IN
FRONT OF YOU I GOT IT. IN OTHER MOMENTS IT
HAPPENED BUT I WASN'T AWARE OF IT AT THAT
MOMENT. PUTTING THIS OUT TO YOU MY HEART IS
BEATING FASTER AND MY HANDS ARE TREMBLING.
FOR THE FIRST TIME I FEEL TO SHOW SOMETHING OF
MYSELF. THIS IS A GIFT ALSO. IT MAKES ME
TREMENDOUSLY THANKFUL, MAKES ME CRY AND
LAUGH AT THE SAME TIME. OSHO, I LOVE... ONLY
LOVE COUNTS. THANK YOU FOR SHOWING ME THAT
DOOR.

Love is the only religion, the only God, the only mystery that has to be lived, understood. When love is understood, you have understood all the mystics of the world.

It is not anything difficult. It is as simple as your heartbeats or your breathing. It comes with you, it is not given to you by the society. And this is the point that I want to emphasize: love comes with your birth – but of course it is undeveloped as everything else is undeveloped. The child has to grow.

The society takes the advantage of the gap. The child's love will take time to grow; meanwhile the society goes on conditioning the mind of the child with ideas about love which are false. By the time you are ready to explore the world of love, you are filled with so much rubbish about love that there is not much hope for you to be able to find the authentic and discard the false.

For example, every child everywhere has been told in a thousand and one ways that love is eternal: once you love a person you love the person always. If you love a person and later on you feel that you don't love, it only means you never loved the person in the first place. Now this is a very dangerous idea. It is giving you an idea of a permanent love and in life nothing is permanent... the flowers blossom in the morning and by the evening they are gone.

Life is a continuous flux; everything is changing, moving. Nothing is static, nothing is permanent. You have been given the idea of a permanent love which is going to destroy your whole life. You will expect permanent love from the poor woman, and the woman will expect permanent love from you. Love becomes secondary, permanence becomes primary.

And love is such a delicate flower that you cannot force it to be permanent. You can have plastic flowers; that's what people have – marriage, their family, their children, their relatives, everything is plastic. Plastic has one very spiritual thing: it is permanent. Real love is as uncertain as your life is uncertain. You cannot say that you will be here tomorrow. You cannot even say that you are going to survive the next moment. Your life is continuously changing – from childhood to youth, to middle age, to old age, to death, it goes on changing. A real love will also change.

It is possible that if you are enlightened your love has gone beyond the ordinary laws of life. It is neither changing nor permanent, it simply is. It is no more a question of how to love – you have become love itself, so whatever you do is loving. It is not that you specifically do something which is love – whatever you do, your love starts pouring through it. But before enlightenment your love is going to be the same as everything else: it will change.

If you understand that it will change, that once in a while your wife may become interested in somebody and you have to be understanding and loving and caring and allowing her to go the way her being feels... this is a chance for you to prove to your wife that you love her. You love her – even if she is going to love somebody else, that is irrelevant. With understanding, it is possible that your love may become a lifelong affair, but remember it will not be permanent. It will have its ups and downs, it will have changes.

It is so simple to understand. When you started loving you were too young, with no experience; how can your love remain the same when you have become a mature person? Your love will also attain to some maturity.

And when you have become old your love will have a different flavor to it. Love will go on changing and once in a while love will need just an opportunity for change. In a healthy society it will be possible and yet your relationship with someone will not be broken.

But it is possible that you may have to change your lovers many times in life. There is no harm in it. In fact, by changing your lovers many times in life you will be enriched, and if the whole world follows what I am saying to you about love, the whole world will be enriched.

But a wrong idea has destroyed all possibility. The moment your partner looks at somebody – just looking, and his eyes show attraction and you freak out. You have to understand that if the man drops being interested in beautiful women on the road, in beautiful actresses in the movies... That's what you want; you want him not to be interested in anything except you. But you don't understand human psychology. If he is not interested in women on the road, in the movies, why will he be interested in you? His interest in women is a guarantee that he is interested in you, that there is still a possibility that your love can go on and on.

But we are doing just the opposite. Men are trying so that their women should not be interested in anybody other than them-selves; they should be the only focus, her total concentration. The woman is asking the same, and both are driving each other mad. Concentration on one person is bound to lead you into madness.

For a lighter life, for a more playful life, you need to be flexible. You have to remember that freedom is the highest value and if love is not giving you freedom then it is not love. Freedom is a criterion: Anything that gives you freedom is right, and anything that destroys your freedom is wrong. If you can remember this small criterion your life, slowly, slowly will start settling on the right path about everything – your relationships, your meditations, your creativity, whatever you are.

Dropping old concepts, ugly concepts.... For example, in this country, millions have died by jumping alive into the funeral pyre with their husbands. It shows that the possessiveness of the husband is so much that not only does he want to possess the woman while he is alive, he is afraid of what will happen when he is dead! He will not be able to do anything – it is better to take the woman with him.

And you can see that this was applicable only to women – not a single man has jumped into the funeral pyre of a woman in ten thousand years. What does it mean? Does it mean that only women love men and men do not love women? Does it mean that the woman has no life of her own? Only the husband's life is her life – when the husband is dead, she has to be dead.

Such nonsense ideas have settled in our heads. You have to do continuous cleaning – whenever you see some nonsense in your head, clean it, throw it away. If you are clear and clean in the mind you will be able to find solutions for every problem that arises in your life.

BELOVED OSHO,
I WAS 56 YEARS OLD WHEN I FIRST CAME TO YOU
AND REALIZED WHAT A WASTAGE MY LIFE HAD BEEN
UP TILL THEN, AN INCREASING UNREALITY. NOW I
AM 67, AND ALTHOUGH I STILL FEEL YOUTHFUL, I
HAVE TO KEEP REMINDING MYSELF THAT I AM OLD
SO THAT I CAN IT ACCEPT GRACEFULLY. SO MUCH OF
ME STILL FEELS LIKE A LOST, LITTLE GIRL AND WHEN I
LOOK AT YOUR GRACE AND BEAUTY – AGELESS,
YOUNG AND OLD BOTH TOGETHER – I DO NOT FEEL
SO SAD. WILL YOU SAY SOMETHING TO ME ABOUT
OLD AGE?

It is one of the significant problems because the way we have lived up to now has been unnatural, unpsychological, unspiritual. It has created so many problems. For example, oldness – a person can either grow old or grow up. The person who grows old only has not lived at all. He has passed time, but he has not lived. All his life is nothing but repression. I teach you not to grow old. That does not mean you will not become old, it means I give you another dimension: growing up. Certainly you will grow old but that will only be as far as the body is concerned. But your consciousness, *you*, will not grow old; you will only grow up. You will go on growing in maturity.

But all the religions of the world have been committing such crimes that they cannot be forgiven. They have not been teaching you how to live, they have been teaching you how not to live – how to renounce life, how to renounce the world. This world, according to the religions, is a punishment. You are in jail. So the only thing is to try to escape from the jail as quickly as possible. This is not true.

Life is not a punishment. Life is so valuable that it cannot be a punishment, it is a reward. And you should be thankful to existence that it has chosen you – to breathe through you, to love through you, to sing through you, to dance through you. If one keeps growing up in maturity and understanding, one never becomes old; one is always young because one is always learning. Learning keeps you young. One is always young because one is not burdened with repressions. And because one is weightless, one feels as if one is just a child – a newcomer to this beautiful earth.

I have heard that three priests were going to Pittsburg. They reached the window to purchase their tickets and the woman at the window who was selling the tickets was extraordinarily beautiful. Her clothes were almost negligible – she had beautiful breasts – and with a V-cut.

The youngest of the priests went up to the window... but he had forgotten all about the journey. He was only seeing those beautiful breasts. The woman asked, "What I can do for you?"

He said, "Three tickets for Titsburg."

The woman freaked out. She said, "You are a priest!"

The second one pushed him aside and told the woman, "Don't get angry, he's just new, immature. You just give us three tickets for Titsburg."

The woman looked..."Are all these men mad or something?"

"And remember one thing: I would like to have the change in nipples and dimes."

Now the woman started shouting and screaming, "This is too much!"

The oldest priest came in and he said, "My daughter, don't be angry. These fellows stay in the monastery, they don't come out, they don't see anything. You should have a little understanding about their life. They have renounced life. Just sit down... three tickets for Titsburg."

The woman could not believe them – all three seemed to be idiots! And the old priest said, "Remember one thing, I admonish you: use better clothes to cover your beautiful body. Otherwise remember, on judgment day Saint Finger will point his Peter at you!"

This is the situation of the obsessed person. The more you deny life, the more you become obsessed with the same life. Up to now, we have not allowed man to live a non-obsessional life. All the religions and the governments are angry with me for the simple reason that I am in favor of you, your freedom and a non-obsessional life – a pure, natural flow, joyous, making the whole of life a paradise.

We are not searching for any paradise in the clouds. If it is there, we will get hold of it, but first we have to make a paradise here on the earth; that will be our preparation. If we can live in a paradise on the earth, then wherever paradise is, it is ours; nobody else can claim it – at least not these priests and monks and nuns! All these people are bound towards hell, because on the surface they are one thing and inside it is just the opposite. Try to be natural. Risk everything to be natural and you will not be at a loss.

14

The psychology of the buddhas

BELOVED OSHO,
WHAT DO YOU MEAN BY "THE PSYCHOLOGY OF THE
BUDDHAS?" HOW IS IT DIFFERENT FROM THE
PRESENT PSYCHOLOGY THAT PREVAILS IN THE
WORLD?

The present psychology is not yet comprehensive enough, it touches only the periphery of human individuality. It remains confined to the mind. It is not right to call it "psychology." Psychology means "the science of the soul" and the present psychology is not only *not* the science of the soul, it denies even the existence of the soul. The moment you deny the soul, consciousness, something which is beyond the mind but within you... This denial is not an ordinary denial because it destroys the whole dignity of man. It takes away his very center. He becomes centerless, soul-less, just a robot.

The right name for modern psychology is "robotology" because it studies only the mechanical behavior of man and the mechanics of mind. Its studies cannot go very deep for the simple reason that if mind is all and there is nothing more to life than mind, you cannot ever become one, undivided. To be divided is the nature of the mind; to be always balanced between opposites – love and hate, courage and fear, yes and no, atheism and theism. Mind does not feel at ease unless it has divided a thing in two. It cannot conceive of light unless it is contrasted with darkness, it cannot conceive of life unless it is defined by death.

And because psychology remains within the boundaries of the mind it cannot help man to grow to his potential heights. Psychology will discourage you: spiritual search is nothing but a mirage, the seeking of truth is hallucinatory.

It is not a coincidence that we are the most intelligent generation, because ten thousand years of growth is within us. So on the one hand it is the most intelligent generation that has ever existed and on the other hand, because of psychology spreading these poisonous ideas – that there is no consciousness, no soul, no life beyond death, and man is just matter; that mind is also nothing but a certain combination of material elements – this has created a very strange situation. Intelligence is pulling man towards more growth and the people who deal with growth are pulling man backwards, telling him, "There is no beyond, just be normal – that is more than you can dream of." "Just to be normal" is the goal of psychology. A great goal: just to be normal.

People have lived for thousands of years without any psychology – and normally. In fact, as you go backwards you will not find so many murders, you will not find so many suicides, you will not find so many rapes, you will not find so many sexual perversions. As you go back they start becoming less. Primitive man was more innocent than you are. He was not as intelligent as you are, but he was more innocent. You inherit his innocence but you are keeping it repressed.

The combination of intelligence and innocence is meditation. The moment innocence and intelligence start growing within you... it is not that you become capable of solving all the problems of the mind, but a totally new thing happens: you start going beyond mind. The problems of the mind are left far behind, as if they never belonged to you – in fact they never belonged to you.

And once you know how to slip out of your mind, a totally different psychology will be founded on the art of slipping out of the mind. A person who can get out of his mind helps the mind to cool down. The mind is getting no more energy – it cools, calms down on its own accord. That's why I have said meditation is a medicine too – and both words come from the same root.

Once your intelligence and your innocence are available to you, just like two wings, the whole sky is yours. There are no more boundaries for you.

I have called the psychology that is based on meditation the psychology of the buddhas. Modern psychology is the psychology of people who are asleep.

It has to be understood; the people who came to Sigmund Freud, the founder of modern psychology, were all sick people – obviously, otherwise why should they come to the psychoanalyst? They were seriously sick, their minds were falling apart. Sigmund Freud came in contact only with sick people – that gave him the impression that man himself is sick. In a way he is logical because everybody he examined, everybody he analyzed, everybody he treated was sick. And these were high-class people, bourgeois – professors, scientists, very rich people – because a psychoanalyst's time is the costliest thing in the world today. All these people were basically living an insane life, but because everybody else is also living the same insane life you don't become aware of it.

If Sigmund Freud denied that there is any possibility of a soul in man he cannot be blamed. He never came across a Gautam Buddha, he never came across a man who had gone beyond mind.

The trouble was these people who have gone beyond mind have no reason to go to Sigmund Freud. And Sigmund Freud is afraid to go to such people because they are against the very foundation upon which he has raised a whole empire – certainly there was a great vested interest. If just a simple method of meditation can help a person... not only to be normal, because to be normal can never be accepted as the goal. That means you remain a mediocre person for your whole life; you never go beyond the boundaries of the society. In everything you remain half-hearted, there is no intensity, there is no totality. A normal person is wishy-washy, just in a limbo, neither here nor there... hanging in between.

It is unfortunate that the great psychologists of the West had no opportunity to know the mystic and to become acquainted with his world – which is absolutely extraordinary. He lives twenty-four hours among you, but not with you; his kingdom is far away. He has tasted love, of which you have been only dreaming. He has experienced truth, of which you have been only thinking and philosophizing. He has encountered existence directly without any mediation of a priest, a prophet, a savior. He has seen existence in its freshness. He is not a Christian, he is not a Hindu – because these are so old, so full of dust and borrowed, they cannot give you a transformation.

Remember one thing: unless the truth is your own experience, whatever you believe about truth is only a belief. And all beliefs are lies, and all believers are blind.

The psychology of the buddhas means that we accept man as a three-storied building. There are a few who remain only on the ground floor, only in their bodies; all their interests are centered in the body – this is the lowest life for someone to choose, as if you are living on the porch when the whole building is yours.

The second level of life is that of a well-understood mind – but who is going to understand the mind? You can see the difficulty of the psychologist: he studies the mind but if you ask who is studying the mind.... Mind cannot study itself.

There must be something beyond – a witness, a watcher who studies the mind. The scientist is studying only from the outside. He is studying the behavior of other people and from their behavior he is deducting principles upon which human behavior is based. But his observation is of the behavior, not of the real being inside. He can be deceived.

You can be sad but you can smile, you can hold back the tears. Or if you are a little artful, you can manage to bring crocodile tears. Your behavior is not reliable. We don't know what is happening inside you, whether your behavior is an expression of your inside or it is a camouflage, hiding you in beautiful garbage.

Buddha accepts three steps: the body, the mind, the consciousness. Even the consciousness is only a step. These three steps lead to the temple of the divine, of the immortal, of beauty, of celestial music.... You start touching heights, Himalayan heights where you can find virgin snow which has never melted. In your inner being also you are carrying greater peaks than Everest, with eternal beauty.

The psychology of the buddhas is comprehensive of the whole individuality of man – and it does not end there. By studying, by experiencing the body, the mind, the consciousness, and the beyond, Buddha is preparing you to dissolve into the universal. Just like a dewdrop slipping from a lotus leaf into the lake.... On a beautiful morning the sun is rising and the whole sky is so colorful... just a cool breeze is there, but it is enough for the rosepetals, for other flowers... for the lotus....

In the early morning sun the dewdrops on the lotus petals look like pearls – or it will be better to say that pearls look like the dewdrops. They are slipping slowly, slowly towards the vast ocean, in which they will be lost and yet not lost. As dewdrops they will be lost, but they will emerge as the whole ocean.

Unless psychology can bring human beings to this oceanic experience it is immature, it has just started its ABC's. And in the West it is going around in a circle – because you do not accept higher realities; where can you go? You are stuck with the mind – analyze it, analyze its dreams, analyze its repressions. But it should be taken as a very significant question that there is not a single man in the whole world who is completely analyzed. This is a failure of the whole system of psychoanalysis – twelve years, fifteen years people have been in psychoanalysis and they have not moved anywhere. Yes, they have learned psychological jargon, it has become more difficult to talk with them! But they are the same persons with all the weaknesses, with all the frailties. Twelve or fifteen years of psychoanalysis has not been able to a make even a single dent in their personality. It is a rich man's game. Just as poor people have their games, rich people have their own games. Psychology is still a game, guesswork, with no foundation in reality.

The mystics in the East have never bothered too much about the mind; they have only developed methods to bypass the mind. Those methods are the techniques of meditation – they are just to bypass the mind. Once you have bypassed the mind, once you can have a bird's-eye view of your own mind, things start settling.

It is your energy that disturbs the mind, that gives it the power to be violent, to be sad, to be angry, to be hateful, to be jealous. Now you are no longer giving it any energy. It won't take a long time. The mind withers almost like a cloud – it was there and it is no more.

The moment mind disperses, your meditation has come to maturity. Now your meditation will be the medium, not the mind. The mind will be used as a mechanism by your meditative forces, but mind is put aside; it is no longer the master. And it is one of the strangest stories that for ten thousand years in the East we have worked on meditation and we have been absolutely successful, not only in becoming meditative, but also in dissolving all the problems of the mind. There is only one way to solve the mind and its problems, and that is to get out of it.

But modern psychology has no idea of where to go, so they go on around and around but they remain just ordinary beings. Now Sigmund Freud and Alfred Adler and Assagioli have devoted their whole lives... but you don't see the eyes of Gautam Buddha, you don't see the gestures of Mahavira, you don't see the insight of the seers of Upanishads. You don't see the transforming presence which all the mystics in all the countries have always radiated.

In my way of looking at things, mind itself is sick. Unless you get out of it, you cannot help the poor mind to become healthy. You are too much identified. Not being identified with the mind is the shortest way to your own being. And your being is always healthy, it does not know what sickness is. It cannot know, it is not in its nature. Just as mind cannot know peace, your being cannot know tensions, anxieties, anguish. The question is not of curing the mind, the question is shifting your whole energy, your whole focus, from mind to being. Meditation helps you to shift.

This great shift of your attention, of your awareness, is what I call the psychology of the buddhas. And any other psychology is going to be wrong, because only a man of eyes knows what light is. There may be millions of people who are blind – there are millions, but it is not a question of democracy. They cannot vote, they cannot assert a single word about light. That one man is right and those millions of people are wrong. The question is not of numbers. The only question that is significant is the transformation of your being from mind to no-mind.

Modern psychology thinks it is the science of the mind. The psychology of the buddhas will be the science of no-mind.

BELOVED OSHO,
I THINK I AM GROWING TO LOVE AND ACCEPT
MYSELF, AND THEN I RECOGNIZE HOW MUCH I HOLD
BACK AND KEEP SEPARATE FROM OTHER PEOPLE TO
HIDE MYSELF, AND I AM ASHAMED. I TRY TO SHOW
OTHERS HOW STRONG I AM. WHY CAN'T I BE
STRONG, WHY CAN'T I ACCEPT THAT I AM WEAK?
WHY CAN'T I EVEN ACCEPT THAT I AM NOT WILLING
TO SHOW MY WEAKNESS?

It is the society, the culture, the civilization in which you are born which gives you wrong ideas. Those wrong ideas go on haunting you from the cradle to the grave. There is nothing wrong in being weak. But this society trains every child to be strong.

Just across from my house in my village there was a gymnasium. My uncles and my father were all going to the gymnasium – it was the best in the town. They tried to persuade me. I said to them, "The idea of the strong man is primitive. It comes from the days when people were hunting. I am not going to be a hunter!"

And I don't think that you can ever be so strong that the need for being stronger disappears. Even the strongest people have found weakness, disease, old age, death... There was one man in India, Gama, who was the world champion in the Indian type of wrestling. But he died at the age of forty, and the diagnosis of the doctors was that he died because he exerted himself too much, exercised too much. The body is not made of steel – he killed himself. He became the world champion but he lost his life. And even if he had lived, he would have lived in utter misery, pain, because all his inner body functions were out of control. The simple reason was that he tried something against nature.

I refused to go to the gymnasium. I told them, "To be healthy – or to be more accurate, not to be sick – is enough."

Weakness has a wrong connotation, and through that wrong connotation half of humanity, the world of women, has been condemned to weakness because they don't have muscular bodies. But for what are muscular bodies needed? Those who need them will get them. But a poet does not need a muscular body – in fact it will look very ugly, a muscular man writing poetry. In fact, no muscular man, no great wrestler, boxer, has ever written any poetry or painted, or played on musical instruments. They exercise too much, to make the body almost steel; they also have to eat too much, and it is now a proved fact that the people who eat too much don't live long.

In experiments on mice, it has been found... one group of mice were getting as much as they wanted to eat – the American way, five times a day – and another group was kept on one meal a day, saintly, religious. It was thought that they would not be able to last long. But the mice who were getting one meal a day lived to be *twice* the age of the group that was eating American style. Then many other experiments proved it conclusively. And the reason is simple: the stronger you are, the more food the body needs – more nourishment, more water; your digestive system needs to work more, and work hard. They all start failing – they are not meant to work too hard.

There are still tribes alive who eat one meal a day, and they live the longest. There are even a few people who are one hundred and eighty years old. They live longer and they live younger – mostly, even at the age of one hundred and eighty, in the provinces of the Soviet Union near the Caucasus these people are still working on the farms. One of my friends from the Soviet Union has sent me a photo. He thought it would be hilarious in India, and it does look hilarious: a man who was one hundred and eighty was going to marry a woman who was one hundred and seventy two – but she looks great!

The idea of being strong is based on continuous fight, war, struggle... in life too it is a cut-throat competition, every day, continuously. If you are not strong, you will be thrown out of the traffic that is going to New Delhi!

I have heard a story about a dog. He used to live in Varanasi – he was a very religious dog. But everybody was going to New Delhi, everybody was wearing hand-spun clothes, carrying spinning wheels which they never spun upon, but symbolic – that they belonged to the ruling party – and wearing Gandhi caps. A strange thing... have you ever seen any picture of Gandhi with a cap? This cap can be anybody else's, but NOT Mahatma Gandhi's. He never wore it.

The dog became curious. Everybody was dying to go to Delhi, so he thought he should have a look – perhaps something was cooking. He figured out that it would take almost twenty-one days. He was a strong dog, and he went towards Delhi.

Rumors reach faster than anything, and in every village there was some difficulty. Dogs are, after all, dogs. They would catch hold of that dog – the whole village full of dogs would bark at him – and they would not allow him to rest. The question of food or anything was just irrelevant.

Dogs in Delhi were waiting because they thought this dog must be a mahatma, a saint, coming from the holy city, the most ancient city in the world. They were waiting... and they could not believe it, because they were also thinking that it would take three or four weeks at least. This dog reached Delhi in three days! They said, "You have done a miracle! In the whole history of dogs, you are the greatest."

He said, "First let me explain to you what happened. I am not the greatest dog, but our country's dogs are *really* great. One bunch of dogs from one village chased me to the boundary of the next village. Then the next bunch took over. They did not allow me to rest anywhere, so I have been running continuously, without food without rest. And in this way, the journey that was going to be fulfilled in twenty-one days is finished in three days. And I am finished too!" Saying this, he died.

We are still living under barbarous ideologies. Our education is still poisonous. Our whole approach – calling Alexander "the great," Genghis Khan "the great," Peter "the terrible"... these are the strong people who have overruled the world. And every child is being prepared to be the richest, to be respectable, to reach to the highest pinnacle of glory. Certainly strength is needed and weakness has to be condemned.

Weakness can be seen from a different angle – that is *my* angle. Weakness is beauty. Weakness is a delicate structure. Women are not weak, they are more beautiful, they have a more symmetrical, more proportionate body. Why look at weakness as something bad?

The rose is going to be weak; you cannot make a rose as strong as a stone. If the rose and the rock clash together, the rose is going to suffer, to die, not the rock. But it is not weakness. It is a delicate structure, a beautiful phenomenon that looks to be not of this world.

I am not saying anything against those who are strong; that has a beauty of its own. But its days are gone. What you are going to do with physical strength in a world of nuclear weapons? Just don't be foolish – are you going to do push-ups when nuclear weapons are exploding? The days of that kind of strength are gone.

But whenever two persons fight, the old mind supports the stronger, the winner. This is very inhuman. The one who is weak should be praised, because in spite of all the struggles he has been able to keep his delicate body, just like a child. The strong one should be condemned because he is behaving like an animal.

But it is an insane world, where Muhammad Ali can declare himself three times great, because now one time does not matter. Alexander was great, but only one time; and nobody thought of being great two times, double the amount of Alexander the Great. But Muhammad Ali has figured it out. He is not even talking about a second time, he is talking about a third time. He is saying, "Muhammad Ali thrice great." And what is creative about him? This man has broken many people's noses, has fractured many people. He is awarded, he is thought to be a hero. He should be kept in a cage in a circus – that is the only place where he belongs.

Our values govern people and their behavior. If you are by nature strong, use your strength for your deeper inquiry; use your strength for higher flights in your consciousness. It is not right to destroy this strength in wrestling, in boxing, in being idiots. And if you are weak, unless you are sick and ill there is no problem. Your weakness should be the weakness of a flower; it should be loved, respected. And the days of strength are gone anyway. The days of beauty and the days of more delicate human beings are going to come.

I have been looking into all your great heroes. None of them has been creative, none of them has increased the beauty of life, none of them has been a stepping stone for future progress. They have all been cruel, ugly, violent – murderers, butchers. The history that you are teaching to your children in your schools, colleges and universities, should be banned. You are teaching small students things in your history which are ugly.

Gautam Buddha appears only in footnotes, not to mention other mystics who are not so well known. Sarmad you may not find in your history books at all; Kabir, Farid, Meera you will not find in your history books. These people don't belong to the mainstream humanity. These people are a kind of rebellious category in themselves, rebellious spirits who have left the crowd and have moved alone.

Gautam Buddha's body was weak and delicate and beautiful, but no strong man has been able to reach higher than Gautam Buddha. That is real strength – not that you have the body of a bull. Just drop the whole idea. If you are not sick as you are, then accept yourself; don't compare. Love yourself, because if you cannot love yourself how can you think of somebody else loving you? If you cannot accept yourself, who is going to accept you?

If you are continuously feeling an inferiority complex because you are weaker, you are this, you are that... and there are a thousand and one things, it is not a question of one thing. Somebody has a more beautiful face, somebody has a sharper intelligence, somebody is taller – if you are going to look all around and compare yourself you will commit suicide because there seems to be no way....

The competition is not one-dimensional, it is multi-dimensional. And wherever you are, whatever you attain, you will forget about it – you will remember only that which you don't have. People remember only that which they don't have. Once you have it, for one or two days you can feel the euphoria and then things settle. You cannot remain in the excited state forever; it will kill you, it will give you a good heart attack.

Weakness should not be taken as weakness; it is the comparison that gives you the word. Call it a more delicate body. The moment you call it a more delicate body, your whole conception about it changes. Words become realities to people. Always remember to use words with right connotations.

So I don't see that there is any problem. Stop trying to be strong. Start to be what you are, pour all your energy into what you are. If you are a beautiful, delicate person, pour your energy into making yourself more delicate, more beautiful. There is no need for you to change places. Everybody, as he is, is needed – and he is needed *as he is* – that's why you are born in a certain way. Don't try to go astray from your nature.

Once or twice I went with my father to see the gymnasium and I told him, "I hate it."

He said, "Why? You can see so many beautiful bodies there."

I said, "I cannot call them beautiful. They are trying to force their bodies, to make them almost as they must have been thousands of years before, the bodies of animals. These people should not be made heroes." I asked my father, "Can you tell me that any of your wrestlers, any of your boxers in the world has been a genius, a great scientist, a great poet, a great painter? What have these people contributed? These are either mediocre and most probably idiotic people." Life is not to fight. Life is to live and life is to grow.

Life is to bring to the world all that is hidden in you to share. There is only one thing: you should discover your treasures and start sharing them with people. This is your only strength, because in this way you will be finding more and more roots – in people, in the earth, in the trees, in the stars. You will be finding more and more friends.

I used to sit by the side of a river in my village, under a small tree. It was the same kind of tree under which Gautam Buddha became enlightened, and because of Gautam Buddha's enlightenment, the tree's name has become the *bodhi* tree. In English it is the *bo* tree – that too is coming from Buddha, *bo*. 'Bodhi' means enlightenment.

And a few scientists have discovered that there is a certain chemical, without which mind cannot function. The more you have it, the better your intelligence will be – sharper, quicker. The bodhi tree has that chemical. And strangely, *only* the bodhi tree – of all the trees in the world – has that chemical in it. It may not be just a coincidence that Buddha became enlightened under a bodhi tree.

I used to sit under this bodhi tree by the riverside for hours. It must have been almost the middle of the night, a full moon night, and we had become such friends....

Just that day one of my teachers had told me, "I hear that you are saying to people that there is a possibility of communication between man and trees?" I said, "Yes."

He said, "Don't spread strange ideas for which you don't have any proof."

I took him with me on that full moon night and I told him, "You touch the tree and just tell me how you feel." He said, "It is cold."

And I said to the tree, in front of the teacher, "It is a question of your friend's word. I want you to respond in some way. And the easiest will be that when my teacher puts his hand on you, show your warmth, don't be cold."

The teacher said, "You must be mad, you are talking with the tree!"

But I said, "There is no harm in trying. The tree is willing – I feel the willingness all around. You put your hand there."

He said, "I don't believe that there is any possibility of communication." But he put his hand on the tree and was shocked – the tree was so warm, and it was a cold night. He said, "My God, now you have got me also into trouble! Everybody thinks you are a little bit crazy, now what about me?"

I said, "You are my disciple – first disciple! Just start spreading the news that...."

He said, "I have never done such a thing... but I will have to do it because I have experienced it myself."

He told others and everybody laughed. And I never wanted so many people to hear, because I was not certain how much the tree liked people, who she liked, who she did not like, whether she liked to be in a crowd or just to be alone, standing high in the sky – or perhaps just with a chosen few friends.

People started asking me: "That teacher is saying this phenomenon...." I said, "I don't know anything about it."

The teacher met me by the evening, he said, "The whole day I have been searching for you!"

I said, "I have been escaping! Because now you have become an idiot; can't you understand, trees and man cannot communicate!"

He said, "My God, you are saying that? The whole day long in school I have been spreading the news." I said, "Which news?" He said, "I never thought you were so dangerous."

I said, "Now you know... that full moon night we never met!"

All around your life it is the same life, the same consciousness in different forms. You don't need strength; the whole universe is yours, its strength and vitality is yours. All you need is more vulnerability, more softness, more openness, more receptivity. Perhaps all these things have been condemned as weakness – "become almost like a citadel, close your heart completely so nobody can harm you." It is true – if you close your heart nobody can harm you. I can even suggest better methods: if you commit suicide, after that nobody can harm you at all! Even if the third world war happens *you* are saved.

Naturally, to accept oneself and to love oneself are the foundations of the psychology of the Buddhas. It is only the beginning, but the whole meditative process reaches to the highest stars. Modern psychology has not even started its real work. What it is doing is just exploiting rich people.

BELOVED OSHO,
YOU HAVE SAID THAT THE SEEKER IS THE SOUGHT,
THAT WE ARE THE ANSWER TO OUR QUESTIONS.
HOW IS IT THAT THE ANSWER CAN ASK QUESTIONS?

Milarepa, you are the answer but you are fast asleep. The answer within you is just a seed. It needs the right soil, it needs a master gardener, it needs your cooperation, your willingness to die as a seed so that you can be born as a plant. Otherwise, you have the answer. Because it is in a seed form, questions arise. Those questions are really in search of the answer that is within you, so there is no contradiction.

BELOVED OSHO,

HOW CAN I COME OUT OF SELF-DESTRUCTION? ARE
ALL UNENLIGHTENED PEOPLE SELF-DESTRUCTIVE?

Yes. Unfortunately, all unenlightened people are self-destructive. They are self-destructive because they don't know why they are here, where they are going, what the meaning and purpose of their life is. Without knowing anything about themselves, whatever they do is going to be harmful.

It is going to be harmful to you, and through you, to others. You cannot do anything but harm because your eyes are closed, you don't have any inner sensitivity, you don't have any creative joy. And above all, for centuries you have worshipped self-destructive people.

There was a man in Alexandria who remained seated on a thirty-foot-long pole. It was a pole from an old, ancient temple which was now in ruins but the pole had remained intact. This man, Peter of Alexandria, remained for twelve years sitting on the pole. That was his only contribution to the world, but he was recognized by the Christians as a saint. The pope himself – and this has happened only once; otherwise whenever the pope declares somebody as a saint....

And by the way you should know that the word 'saint' in English is very ugly. It comes from 'sanction'. It means the pope has sanctioned that this man is holy – it is a certificate. The saint who is going to receive the reward as a certificate travels to the Vatican and receives it there, touching the feet of the pope. It is strange... the pope is not a saint and nobody has bothered about a simple matter: how can a man who is not a saint himself recognizes anybody as a saint? What authority does he have to declare somebody a saint? And what kinds of saints are these who travel thousands of miles just to receive a certificate? It does not look saintly.

But with Peter of Alexandria it was difficult. He could not come down, he had taken a vow to remain till death on the pillar. And he was doing all kinds of nasty things from the pillar, it was disgusting. For thirty years he had not taken a bath – in Alexandria, which was hot, burning hot. And he was urinating, he is doing everything while sitting on the pillar. He could not sleep – or perhaps slowly, slowly he became accustomed to sleeping while sitting on the pole, which is a very difficult thing but not impossible. If you can remain in your bed without falling out of the bed in the night, St. Peter can remain sitting. But except creating this nauseous spot he has not done anything and he has become a saint! You have always worshipped people who can do things which you feel you cannot do. Suddenly, if you cannot do it and somebody else can do it, he becomes higher, he has some superior power.

A real saint need not be dependent on any pope to give him a certificate. His certificate should come from his own experience. It will be a declaration, nobody else can do it on his behalf.

Take your delicacy and put your energy into creating beauty – in any direction, in any dimension. Remember one thing: that you should not leave this earth unless you have made it a little more beautiful, a little lovelier, a little more loving. To me, this is the only strength, the only power – that we can transform life, we can transform consciousness.

Accept it peacefully and joyously – wherever you are, whatever you are, however you can use your energies into some creativity. Your creativeness will help you to become enlightened, just as enlightenment brings an explosion of creativity. And unless you create, you are going to remain self-destructive – it is the same energy. You have the energy, you are creating the energy, you are a dynamo of energy continuously being created from the cosmos. What will you do with it? If you don't create you are going to be destructive, you are going to destroy.

All your so-called strong men have been destructive. And the people I call the mystics have not been strong men, but they have created. They have participated with God in creation, they have known power at its highest peak.

BELOVED OSHO,
DO YOU HEAR SERMONS IN STONES?

My God! Stones hear sermons when I pass them. People like me – who have been speaking continuously for decades – become deaf, because we only speak, we never listen.

Stones are giving sermons – that much I know. But when I am with them the poor stones have to sit down silently and listen to a long sermon.

BELOVED OSHO,
WHILE I WAS JOGGING ON JUHU BEACH YESTERDAY
MORNING, YOUR OLD FRIEND MULLA NASRUDDIN
MET ME AND, BY THE WAY, HAS SENT A LOT OF
SALAAMS TO YOU ON YOUR BIRTHDAY. FURTHER, HE
FEELS THAT YOU HAVE FORGOTTEN HIM NOWADAYS.
BEAUTIFUL OSHO, ANYTHING TO CONVEY TO HIM
ON THIS AUSPICIOUS OCCASION?

Suraj Prakash, do you see? Jogging brought results immediately! You have started meeting great mystics.

I have not forgotten Mulla Nasruddin. I heard that he died. He died in Iran – he had gone to see Ayatollah Khomeiniac – and as a proof they have made a marble memorial in Iran for Mulla Nasruddin. It has been made according to his will. His will was certainly unique, but not unexpected. His whole life is essentially concluded in his will. The will is simple. It says, "When you make a memorial, on the memorial put a door. Lock the door and throw the key in the ocean."

They were all puzzled because just a door without walls... what is the point of locking it? Anybody can go around the side. But they knew that that man was a strange type, and there must be some meaning in it.

So a marble statue with a marble plaque was made, with a door – just the frame of the door. On the door is a big lock and it makes everyone curious because there are no walls – you can go around this side or around that side and at the back there is nothing, just the same grave.

He used to talk with me about this will and he used to say, "I want humanity to remain puzzled about me even after my death."

So everybody who goes to his grave comes back puzzled: "Why did he do it?" It is impossible not to ask the question why he did it. There is nothing behind the door, there are no walls. Why did he ask for the door and the lock and leave special instructions that the keys should be thrown in the ocean, because the door is not to be opened again?

Now Suraj Prakash has met him on Juhu Beach. That either means somebody played a joke on Suraj Prakash or perhaps Mulla Nasruddin is back as a ghost. And if he is back as a ghost, he will stay somewhere close by my side. Many of you may have the chance of meeting him!

He loves me, and you are asking for something for him. I will tell you a joke, Suraj Prakash. Tell the joke to Mulla Nasruddin if you happen to meet him again.

In a circus it happened. By mistake the cage of the zebra was left open and in the night, the zebra escaped and ran away to a nearby farm. As it was getting to be morning, and he was enjoying the freedom and the fresh air... he approached an old hen, saying, "What do you do around here?"

She said, "My work here is to lay eggs for my master's breakfast."

The zebra then walked over to the cow, asking, "What do you do?"

The cow said, "I give milk for the farmer's breakfast."

The zebra then spied an enormous bull, and asked the same question. The bull looked at him with a quizzical smile on his face and he said, "Listen you queer ass, take off those faggy pajamas and I'll show you what I do around here!"

Just tell Mulla Nasruddin. He will enjoy it and he will tell other ghosts. Mulla Nasruddin cannot go to heaven, obviously, and hell is overcrowded. People are on a waiting list. Many people on the earth must have died before but there is no place for them to go, so they are living. And they think they are *living* – it is simply that there is no space in hell. Also, Mulla Nasruddin cannot be accepted in hell even if there is space someday, because he is a character of his own type. Neither God nor the devil can manage him, so he's going to remain in limbo – that limbo is called the world of ghosts. In the world of ghosts, you will find very rare people – people who are not allowed in heaven and people who cannot even be allowed in hell. For them, there is a special category so they don't create trouble anywhere.

It is good that Mulla has become a ghost. If you see him, Suraj Prakash, or if somebody else sees him, just tell him to come. And for ghosts, there are no passes!

15

Cancel your ticket, there's nowhere to go!

BELOVED OSHO,
WHEN I CAME TO PUNE TEN YEARS AGO I WAS A
FIFTEEN YEAR-OLD TEENAGE GIRL WITH A HEART
FULL OF TRUST AND A LONGING FOR TRUTH. DURING
THOSE FEW MONTHS THAT I COULD STAY WITH YOU
UNDISTURBED I EXPERIENCED THE MOST BEAUTIFUL
TIME OF MY LIFE. WHEN I WAS FORCED BACK TO
GERMANY BY THE LEGAL AUTHORITIES AND MY
PARENTS, WHO ARE NOT YOUR SANNYASINS,
SOMETHING BROKE INSIDE AND LEFT A WOUND
WHICH NEVER HEALED. NOW, BEING WITH YOU IN
INDIA AGAIN, THE MOMENT I WALKED THROUGH
THE ASHRAM GATE IN PUNE SOMETHING SLID INTO
PLACE, AND A DOOR OPENED. WALKING THROUGH
YOUR GARDEN, JUST SITTING SILENT, UNDER THE
TREES, YOUR FRAGRANCE IS STILL IN THE AIR. MY
BEING VIBRATES, MY HEART SINGS, "HOME, HOME,
THIS IS THE PLACE WHERE I WAS BORN." THERE IS SO
MUCH JOY THAT IT IS ALMOST PAINFUL, AND JUST
BEYOND THAT, THE SILENCE. BELOVED OSHO, WHAT
IS HAPPENING WITH ME? AND WHY COULDN'T IT
HAPPEN ANYWHERE ELSE?

The parents represent the establishment. They love you, they have no intention to harm you, but they are unconscious beings – with all good intentions. They have joined hands with the vested interests not to allow their children to become intelligent, to become courageous, to become self-respectful, to have a certain pride that existence has chosen *you* to be. They have done this to their children instead of making them feel at home in existence, helping them to be more and more in tune with the seasons, with the trees, with the clouds, so that by the time they are mature enough they can have a religion....

The word religion originates from a root which means 'that which joins you' – joins you with what? 'That which connects you' – connects you with what?

If you are not being conditioned, if your mind has not been

filled with superstitions of all kinds, if your search has not been killed, if your parents have really loved you – and the first requirement of real love is to allow absolute freedom, unconditional freedom to the other – then one day you will find *your* religion.

Religion is not a commodity. You cannot purchase it in the marketplace and you cannot have it just by believing in certain scriptures, rituals. You cannot get it so cheap – just by believing in Jesus Christ, in Gautam Buddha, in Mohammed, in Krishna. Religion has to be earned. It is the greatest learning on the earth; it needs tremendous awareness, so that you are not influenced by others. And this must be the duty of the parents, to see that their children are not influenced by others, because all influences create a spiritual slavery. If you remain fresh, clean, open, searching, you will find it.

There has never been any exception. Anybody who has been open to reality, available to existence, immediately gets connected with the whole. And to be connected with the whole is the greatest experience that life can provide to you.

When you are born, you are disconnected from the womb, from the mother. You had lived in the womb for nine months as one with the mother's body, mind, soul. There was no separation. You were not in any way different from your mother. Her heartbeats were your heartbeats, her breathing was your breathing, her blood was your blood.

The disconnection from the mother is the most traumatic experience in life, the most painful, the most agonizing. Just think of the small child who is being taken away from his home, who is being taken away from his very world, the only world he knows; he is being taken away from love and warmth. The shock is great.

Psychologically, the search for truth, for God, for home, is nothing but an effort to be again connected with the universe. It is a search for the mother's womb. Of course you cannot find your mother's womb, but you can find the existential womb. The whole existence can become the womb for you – nourishment, life, relaxation, silence. This is religion.

Christianity is not religion; Hinduism and Mohammedanism are not religions. In the whole history of man very few people have experienced religion, although everybody has been a member of some religion. The strange phenomenon is that those who experienced religion were the people who renounced the religion into which they were born – that was the barrier. Something false was given to you when you were so innocent and so trusting that you believed – "This is the truth." And when you think you have the truth, there is no question of inquiry, there is no question of searching.

This is how the whole of humanity is blocked, remains unevolved, remains blind, dark, in a kind of coma. And these people go on producing children; naturally, whatever they know they share with their children. If they are Christians they drag you to the church, if they are Hindus they drag you to the temple.

What happened with you – and this is not only your story, this is the story of most of the young sannyasins who are somehow dependent on their parents – was that you found something that felt as if "This is the path." And the feeling was so total, there was no doubt anywhere in your consciousness. To me, this is conversion. Not a Hindu becoming a Christian; that is stupidity. Not a Christian becoming a Hindu; that is simply changing your prisons, changing your superstitions. It is just moving from one darkness into another. Perhaps the newness may have a little appeal, but for how long? The new will become old tomorrow.

But you came here, and suddenly your heart fell in tune with the mysterious change that is happening here. Naturally, your parents at home forced you to drop sannyas, threatened you legally, and of course parents *can* threaten you. And it is a good experience; in this way you know your parents in their reality. They can take away all your legal rights to their property, they can disown you, and the whole society is with them – the government is with them, the school authorities are with them, and wherever you go you will be treated as an outsider.

Naturally a child is not in a position to fight. He has to agree, although what he is agreeing to is not from love of the parents but from fear. It is not because of intimacy with the parents, but because of their blackmail.

They have lived without religion, they don't know the real

taste. They have never been drunk with the divine. They are too much in the world, they know only the mundane. They have never raised their eyes upwards to see the stars. There is no challenge in their life and a man is dead if he has no challenge in his life. It is the challenge that proves that you are alive – just breathing and temperature and heartbeats do not prove that you are alive, they only prove that the body is still alive. Whether you are alive or not is a different question.

You are alive when faraway stars challenge you for a pilgrimage. Unknown realities, unheard-of truths, inexperienced beauties... when they become your real world you have a life with joy and with dance and with song. Out of this joy, this rejuvenation, arises the most delicate phenomenon in life: gratitude, gratitude to the whole. Gratitude is the only prayer, all other prayers are false. And gratitude need not be expressed in words. It is just a wordless fragrance arising out of you.

It is good you are back. In fact, anybody who has been a sannyasin, who has known individuality, has known freedom, has known playfulness... it is impossible that anything can prevent the person forever from going deeper into the experience of sannyas.

Your parents stopped you, they forced you not to be a sannyasin. That does not matter. In fact, their forcing you and taking away your sannyas has taken you away from them; they have created a gap unknowingly. Now there will not be any communion, everything has become formal. They have destroyed something which they cannot create; they have destroyed innocent trust, they have destroyed innocent love.

But it has not been in any way harmful to you. You are back – with better insight into human relationships, with better insight into the fact that even parents are trying to dominate, that it is a political relationship and there is no love. Their whole effort is... in the world they may not be able to be dominating, but at home they can dominate the children. As long as the lust for domination remains, love does not appear.

But to you, particularly... I would like you to remember that whatever they have done they have done almost in sleep, so don't be angry at them. They have done to you what their parents have done to them – so rather than being angry you should feel sad for them, you should feel pity for them. You are fortunate because you have found something which your parents, their parents, and for centuries the whole line of your family, have not been able to find.

Rejoice. Be silent and be as joyful as possible. Perhaps you can become a message to your parents and your family members, your neighbors. But the message cannot be delivered in words. In words, people know everything, they are all knowledgeable. And nobody wants to accept that he is ignorant.

The only way to break the ice is not through words but through your life, through your very being. They will still resist, because their whole life – not only theirs but their forefathers' – all their wisdom, all their philosophy, all their religion is at stake. You are proposing a new way of life. They cannot easily accept that all their parents since Adam and Eve have been ignorant and only you are no longer ignorant. So it will take a little time for them to come down from their egoistic attitude.

You can help them. Never try to show that you know more than their knowledge; that is something which hurts people very much, because knowledge is the most nourishing element for the ego. When you challenge somebody's knowledge, you have challenged his whole being; all that he knows himself to be is just his ego.

I have heard that a Catholic priest was watching Michael, and he saw that he pulled out two ten dollar bills from the collection plate and did not put anything in the plate. The priest said to himself, "I had better be watchful of Michael."

The next Sunday it happened again. Now, this was too much! Again, Michael pulled out two ten dollar bills. The priest went outside the church and waited there for him. As the mass finished, Michael came out and the priest accosted him, asking him, "Michael, why are you doing this? Instead of putting something in the collection plate, for two weeks you have been taking twenty dollars each time, and I have been waiting...."

Michael had tears in his eyes... he said, "Father, forgive me, but I was in such a situation that I had to do it. If you were in my situation even you would have done it." The father said, "What was the situation?" Michael said, "I so much wanted a blow job."

The priest had never heard the words "blow job," but nobody wants to recognize his ignorance, to admit, "I don't know what this is."

So he said, "Okay, okay – do whatsoever job you want to do, but don't pull money out of the plate! Otherwise I will have to expose you before the whole congregation."

But now... more than those dollars, the priest was worried about this blow job! What is it? He has read all the literature... theology, psychology – blow job? He could not do anything else, he was continuously thinking – what is it? But who to ask? because asking means you don't know, asking means recognizing your ignorance.

He couldn't sleep. That blow job continued in his mind. Finally he got up and phoned Mother Agatha. She was an old lady, experienced, and he thought she could be asked. Many times when there had been some theological problem he had asked her, and she had always given him good advice.

So he asked her, "Mother Agatha, you have always been such a help to me – whenever I am stuck with some problem you have always given me the right key. Today I again have a question for you: What is a blow job?" Mother Agatha said, "Oh, about twelve dollars."

For the poor priest nothing was solved. He knows the price, but he does not know what the job is! But it was better now to keep silent.

Never make anybody feel ignorant, never make anybody feel judged, never make anybody feel inferior. Be respectful, be loving, even to those who may not agree with you. Perhaps you can create an atmosphere, and you can become the bridge for your whole family, your friends, to sannyas. Sannyas has to be shared. It is the alchemy of inner transformation. You would like anybody you love to be a sannyasin.

BELOVED OSHO,

THANK YOU FOR TALKING ABOUT YOUR COOL LOVE.
I'VE WANTED SOMETHING FROM YOU WHICH IS
UGLY, AND NOT IN YOU TO GIVE. BUT IT IS WHAT I
HAVE KNOWN – THE ATTACHMENT AND POSSES-
SIVENESS OF HOT LOVE. I HAVE WANTED AND
WANTED FOR SO MANY YEARS FOR YOU TO LOVE ME
MY WAY. I HOPE I AM READY TO LEARN TO LOVE
YOUR WAY. OSHO, I FEEL SO GRATEFUL FOR YOU. CAN
YOU FORGIVE ME FOR BEING SUCH A RELENTLESS
BEGGAR?

Sudha, one thing – in fact, you will have to forgive *me*. I cannot forgive, for the simple reason that I have never been angry, I have never taken any offense. For what can I forgive you? I can only rejoice in your understanding. This has been your problem – like many other people, you love me and naturally you would like a response from me.

Your conception of love is very small. I cannot manage to love in such a small way. That does not mean I don't love you, that simply means you are not receptive and open and available to me so that I need not come down, rather I can take you upwards.

Love can do both miracles. It can bring you down – and in all the ancient literature of all religions, love has been portrayed as bringing people's consciousness downwards. Nobody has explored the psychology behind all those stories and parables, but it is a tremendously rewarding experience to look into the psychology of them.

For example, in the East there are hundreds of stories that whenever somebody is coming close to enlightenment... In Indian mythology the god Indra – who is the highest god in heaven – becomes troubled, because if somebody becomes enlightened there is a possibility that he may be chosen by existence to be Indra, and Indra may be demoted. There should not be any enlightenment anywhere; that is a protection of his power. Other-wise there will be a competitor who may be far superior.

So whenever somebody is coming close to enlightenment,

immediately Indra sends beautiful girls from heaven to drag that man down from enlightenment. Just a step or two and he would have been enlightened, but the beautiful girls, called *upsaras...* they are not just women. They are always young, they never grow old. They don't perspire, they don't need deodorant. They are always fragrant.

And naturally, a man who has been avoiding the world, escaping deeper into the Himalayas, who has been repressing all his natural instincts – particularly sex – is sitting almost on a volcano, the sexual energy can explode. It is the same energy that was taking him to enlightenment. Enlightenment is also an explosion, but creative. It gives you a new birth.

But these beautiful girls are sent to provoke the person sexually, dance sexual dances around him, create a whole pornographic atmosphere. In most cases the man falls down, thinking it is love, and love sent from heaven! But those women have come simply to destroy his meditation, to create lust in him, and once that work is done they disappear. Only when they disappear does the person become aware that he was reaching to the climax of consciousness and now he is standing in total darkness.

In all the languages of the world, strangely enough, people use the phrase "falling in love." Without any exception, in all the languages people say "I have fallen in love." But why should you fall? Why can't you rise in love?

Love up to now has been the condemned part of humanity. To me, love is the only divine quality in you. All other qualities are part and parcel of your godliness, but love is the center. You love me. I can accept your love. But you will receive *my* love only by rising a little higher towards enlightenment in your consciousness. It is just the opposite from the whole of history. I want you to say one day, "I have risen in love." Love should bring more light to you, more understanding, more maturity, more freedom, more creativity.

Sudha, you need not be sad about your past. You may have desired the same kind of love; it is natural. You know only one kind of love and you can desire only that love. My whole life is devoted to you, to making you aware of a higher love – a love which replaces God, a love beyond which nothing exists. But to understand my love you will have to climb higher in consciousness. You will start feeling me only when you are close to enlightenment. It will be the same moment as when the god Indra becomes troubled: you will feel my love.

And if you become enlightened you will see all the psychedelic colors of love. Only the enlightened person knows the very spirit of love. So it is not your fault but just your laziness in becoming enlightened!

And remember: I cannot forgive your laziness, because I am here today; tomorrow I may not be. I cannot be here with you forever; while I exist in the body, be a little quicker. If you can taste a little love while I am alive, then even after my death your connection with me, your trust, your love, will remain valid. It will go on for eternity. And a love that is not for eternity is just a biological strategy to produce more children.

Have you observed one fact, that while animals are making love, they don't seem to be happy? Just... you know I am a little crazy; I have been studying things nobody else bothers about. My father was very much ashamed, because two dogs would be making love and I would be following them for half a mile, and my father would say, "You are a strange person. People come to us...."

I said, "But that is none of their business, I am studying."

My father said, "My God, can't you find something else to study?"

I said, "This is the most essential thing."

I have watched all kinds of animals, birds... deep in the countryside near the villages it is so easy to see and watch. But nobody looks happy, that is the problem. They are making love... and just look at their faces! It seems they don't mean it, it seems that it is a kind of torture. They are unhappy, and there is a reason for it: they feel the biological slavery. They are more sensitive than you are. They can see that it is not *their* love, it is just something else forcing them. They are doing it in spite of themselves.

That's why all animals just have small seasons for reproduction; it seems biology has not been able to convince the animals to make love all year round. And once the season is over the animals completely forget all about love and sex and girlfriends and boyfriends. Looking at the animals I used to wonder: is "boyfriend and girlfriend" applicable to animals? Because they look so sad that it seems "boy-enemy and girl-enemy" would be a better description of the reality.

It is only man who makes love all year round, and it is only man who thinks that this love is all. This love is not all; otherwise the whole world would have been a beautiful place to live.

This world is created by your love, your relationships – and you have virtually created a better hell than the one described in the scriptures! And everybody is loving – the father is loving, the mother is loving, the husband is loving, the wife is loving, the children are loving, the teachers are loving. Everybody is loving and the total result is always a world war. This is a strange kind of logic. Everybody loving, and then finally... where does the war come from?

Our love is of the very lowest kind, it is animal love. This love is not going to help you. This love can only be part of your biological slavery. And you have accepted it, you have not even raised the question that it is slavery.

When you come to me and you love me, your love has shadows on it of your past experiences. I cannot meet you on that wavelength. That does not mean that I don't love you. I love you, but it just goes on above your heads. I try hard to hit your head at least, but it goes on above your heads.

If this understanding settles in you, Sudha, that you should try to raise your consciousness higher, then forget all about my love. One day suddenly you will be showered by it. You have been showered by it always. But your umbrella is open, so close your umbrella!

BELOVED OSHO,
I DON'T KNOW WHERE I'M GOING, AND I DON'T
KNOW WHAT THERE IS TO DO. DO I HAVE WHAT I
NEED FOR THIS ADVENTURE?

There is no need to know where you are going. There is no need to know why you are going. All that is needed to be known is that you are going joyously, because if you are going joyously you cannot go wrong. If you are going dancing, singing, celebrating, the direction does not matter, the road does not matter, the goal does not matter. Every moment becomes paradise.

Let me repeat it again to you: there is no goal in existence. There are only moments, and the art is to squeeze the moment, its whole juice, herenow. And as moments go on coming into your hands, go on squeezing all the juices that existence contains for you.

In fact, you are where you are supposed to be, so if you are going somewhere it is just a morning walk. Don't be worried. There is no goal, you can turn back from any point. You are not going anywhere! My whole teaching is just to be here and let all the blissfulnesses of existence shower on you.

Why should you go anywhere? And anyway, where will you go? Trains are there, buses are there, planes are there and you can go wherever you want – to the moon you can go. In just a few years you may be able to go to Mars; in a few more years you may be able to go to some star. But that is all stupidness – what are you going to do standing on the moon? Have you ever thought about it? You will look utterly weird to yourself: "What are you *doing* here?" Life is the way. Life has no goal.

That's why I love the word *Tao*. *Tao* means the way, with no goal. Simply *the way*. It was courageous of Lao Tzu, twenty-five centuries ago, to tell people that there is no goal and we are not going anywhere. We are just going to be here, so make the time as beautiful, as loving, as joyous as possible. He called his philosophy Tao, and Tao means simply 'the way.'

Many asked him, "Why have you chosen the name Tao? Because you don't have any goal in your philosophy...."

He said, "Specifically for that reason I have chosen to call it 'the way,' so that nobody forgets there is no goal, but only the way."

And the way is beautiful, the way is full of flowers. And the way goes on becoming more and more beautiful as your consciousness goes on becoming higher. The moment you have reached the peak, everything becomes so sweet, so ecstatic, that you suddenly realize that *this* is the place, this is home. You were unnecessarily running here and there. Never think of going somewhere.

Think in terms of transforming yourself *here*. "There" is a cunning strategy of the mind to deceive you. The mind always makes you interested in things far away, *there*, so that you can be led away from *here*. Or at least your attention is no longer here, it is there. And you will never *be* there. Going from here to there, slowly, slowly you acquire the habit of always looking *there*, so wherever you reach, that place is no longer in your focus – your goal has shifted somewhere else.

In India there is an ancient proverb – *diya tale andhera* – "there is darkness under the lamp." The lamp gives light all around, and just exactly underneath it there is darkness. This is the situation of man. You are capable of seeing everywhere, all around, but you are incapable of seeing where you are, who you are.

So cancel all the tickets you have booked! There is nowhere to go; just being here is so blissful. Close your eyes, so that you can see the reality of the *here*. There and then are only fictions. Here and now are the only realities.

BELOVED OSHO,
WOULD YOU PLEASE COMMENT ON WHAT HAS
ENABLED AND ALLOWED YOU TO GO INTO AND
CONTAIN SO MUCH OF EXISTENCE. THAT YOU HAVE
PENETRATED AND ABSORBED SUCH VAST REALMS
AND INEXHAUSTIBLE ENERGIES IS A BEAUTIFUL AND
MAJESTIC OPENING, AND YET SEEMINGLY SO FAR
AWAY, SO UNREACHABLE. WHAT CAN BE SAID OF
YOUR REALITY?

First: I am not far away, I am here. The difference between you and me is not of how far away I am. The difference is of depth. I am here, but at the deepest, most interior center of my being. You are also here, but just on the circumference. And the difference between the center and the circumference is not big, because they are related. The circumference belongs to the center and the center belongs to the circumference. They cannot exist separately, they are always together. Can you have a center without a circumference, or can you have a circumference without a center?

But you can choose one, become obsessed with it, and completely forget your own center. It is easy to forget it, because it is obvious. It is easy to forget it because you are born with it. You have not earned it, you have not traveled to it, it has not been arduous for you. It has been the sheer grace of existence to give you a center, a soul, a consciousness.

Secondly, it may seem to you and to thousands of people that I contain so much... what is my secret? There is no secret, because I am not containing anything. I am just an open space, alive, fully alert. So when you ask a question, it is not from some stored knowledge that the answer comes to you. When you raise a question, my whole being responds to it. It is not my memory. In this moment, this is my response. It is not an answer which was accumulated within me.

I have been living in my room for many years, and people are naturally curious because I don't do anything. I don't even look outside the window! So to me, whether I am in India or in America or in England or in France does not matter. I am always in a room. Living in my room for almost twenty, twenty-five years, I am simply sitting in emptiness. But it is such an exquisite experience that I don't want anything more... although every day something more goes on happening.

But basically, I remain empty. When you ask me a question I have to encounter the question as if it is my question, and what I would do if this were my question, and then I reply to you. But the reply, the answer, was not waiting there in my memory system. I am the most empty man on the earth today.

Yes, I am full only of one thing, and that is emptiness. But emptiness is not a negative state, emptiness is full of existence. The whole of existence has come out of emptiness, and whenever it becomes tired it goes back into emptiness. You are born out of emptiness and you die to again rejuvenate yourself in emptiness. You will be born again... thousands of times you have been coming and going.

Emptiness is the complete, total rest, where everything ceases. But in that rest and in that cessation of everything you are becoming again ready to go for another run, another existence... thousands of lives.

My answers are not confined to any religion, confined to any theology. My answers are confined only to this minute – and I am not committed. Tomorrow you cannot say to me, "You are contradicting yourself." What can I do? It was so yesterday, and this is how it is today. I cannot lie. I can answer only that which arises in my emptiness.

But to you it will seem... I must have answered at least fifty thousand questions. Anybody looking at those questions is bound to wonder how much knowledge I contain. The reality is, I don't contain any knowledge at all. I am just a mirror, an empty mirror. You bring your question – that is, you bring your face – and my mirror reflects. The moment you are gone, my mirror is empty again; your coming and going leave no marks on my mirror.

This should be understood clearly, because any wrong understanding about me and you will start following that line. You may start collecting more knowledge, more scriptures. I have done that dirty work, and I have wasted so much time on your holy scriptures and the commentaries, but they are all just words. In fact, to expect more from books is not logical; books are collections of dead words.

While I am here, you have the opportunity to listen to a living word. Once I am gone, you will read the same words in books, but they will be dead. My warmth, my love, my heartbeat will not be in them. And if you cannot understand while I am behind my words, it is absolutely impossible that you will be able to understand them from a book when I am no longer behind those words. So while listening to me you have to be aware of a few more things. It is not just a lecture. It is not imparting information to you, it is not something that you have to remember. It is a totally different phenomenon. Listening to me is not listening to my words. Of course, you will hear them. Hear my words, but listen to me. And while listening to me, remember: it has to be more like drinking something, eating something, digesting something; not accumulating something in the memory. While listening to me, just be as empty as I am. The answer is coming from emptiness. And this kind of answer can be understood only if it is heard in emptiness.

BELOVED OSHO,
WHEN I GOT INITIATED INTO SANNYAS, EXACTLY SIX
YEARS AGO, I DIDN'T KNOW HOW TO WALK, HOW TO
SING, HOW TO DANCE. TODAY I CAN DANCE UNDER
THE STARS, LAUGH, SING, PLAY, REJOICE. SO MUCH HAS
BEEN HAPPENING ON THE WAY. I DO NOT KNOW
WHAT IS GOING ON, OR WHERE I AM GOING. ALL I
KNOW IS THAT IN MY HEART THERE IS A BURNING
DESIRE TO GO WITH YOU ON THIS CRAZY JOURNEY.
BELOVED OSHO, WHERE ARE YOU TAKING US?

I am taking you to yourself. You have gone far away from yourself. Perhaps you have completely forgotten the way back. I am persuading you that unless you discover your home, you will remain miserable. Don't go anywhere – just stop going. If the energy is not moving towards objects and goals, the energy starts turning upon itself. That can be called enlightenment, *samadhi*, *sambodhi*, awakening.

You always want to go somewhere. People are running all over the world, from Kaaba to Manali, from Manali to Kathmandu, from Kathmandu to Goa, from Goa to Bombay. They are just running, hoping that somehow they will reach. Where they want to reach they don't know. Whether there is any need to reach anywhere they don't know. Whether there is any place they can reach, they don't know. I say to you, there is no place for you to reach.

You are already born in that place, in that space.

My whole effort is somehow to convince you – not with my words but with my silence and presence, with my love and with my joy – that you are at the very center of the universe, every one of you – because there is only one center. Only on the periphery are we separate; at the center we are one. And only at the center, the blossoming of your being happens.

But people are going in all directions, doing all kinds of things. It is really hilarious how much energy is spent. Even animals are wiser....A few days ago there was news of a bishop in Europe who was caught making love to animals. He admitted in the court that for twelve years he had seen making love to animals, and he said, "I am not the only one who does it."

The natural sexual energy has been prevented; now it will go into perversions. And it is easier to make love to an animal, because the poor animal cannot tell anybody what this priest, this bishop, this cardinal is doing. He cannot go to a police station. So the thing will remain unknown to people.

I have heard that one woman had a beautiful parrot. The woman was a prostitute, but a high-class prostitute. Being in the wrong company, the parrot was completely spoiled. And particularly, whenever that woman would bring a man with her into the house, the parrot would start using obscenities, four-letter words. And he would always end up with the sentence: "It is gonna happen to somebody tonight, it is gonna happen." It was very strange for the man who had come, and for the woman also, it was very awkward.

She went to a pet shop to inquire what to do. The man said, "There is no problem. It is so simple – and even a woman like you cannot see the problem – the parrot needs a lady parrot. Right now I don't have any lady parrots on hand. I will order one immediately, and within two weeks you will have her. And for two weeks you can take this beautiful owl. Just put it beside him. Perhaps... because he has remained a monk for years, and in a place of prostitutes! Perhaps he will get interested... and this owl is a beautiful lady."

So she took the owl and put the owl's cage next to the parrot.

But from the beginning the woman suspected that it was not going to work, because the parrot did not even look at the owl. But by the evening she had brought a gentleman home and this time she was not feeling her usual nervous self because of the parrot. She thought he must be engaged by now.

But as she opened the door and the man entered, the parrot said, "Ahah, so here it goes again," and he started all his obscenities. He ended up with the same, "It is gonna happen to somebody tonight." The lady owl asked, "Hoo, hoo?"

And the parrot said, "You sonofabitch, it is not gonna happen to you, that much is certain!"

Even animals can understand that a parrot will not be interested in an owl... but a priest can be.

The repressed mind is the ugliest thing in the world. And for thousands of years we have not been doing anything else – we have been only repressing and repressing, so you are full of repression. I am utterly empty. If there is any truth in my words, that truth comes out of my emptiness. It does not belong to me, I am just a passage. I allow existence to connect with you – and it is possible only if I am absolutely empty.

Waking up in the morning, I have to think whether it is morning or afternoon, because I sleep in the afternoon too. And sometimes things get puzzled. One day in the afternoon, I went to the bathroom without looking at the clock – thinking that it was morning – and prepared, took a bath, got ready, because you must be coming. Only when I got out of the bathroom did I ask Nirvano. She said, "It is not time to get ready for the meeting."

Then I looked at the clock and I said, "My God, now I will have to take a third bath!"

When I was in the American jails they would ask the names of my attorneys. I said, "Don't ask such great philosophical questions. If you want to ask, you can ask about God, about heaven and hell, but about attorneys.... In one jail I was really in difficulty, because the US Marshall in the jail was insisting – in the middle of the night – that I should sign not *my* name on the form, but the name of David Washington.

I said, "This is illegal and you will repent for it, because soon I will be out and the whole world will know what has been done to me. On what grounds do you want me to sign under the name of David Washington? And do you think that I am not able to understand a simple thing? It means that even if you kill me, nobody will be able to find out where I disappeared – because even in the register, in your files, on my form, there is no mention of my name. I never entered this jail according to your records. So I am not going to sign as David Washington. And if you want – because I can see you are tired in the middle of the night, you want to go home – *you* fill in the form in your own handwriting. I will simply sign it with my signature."

He could not figure out what the purpose was, so he filled out the form and I signed my signature, which is known all over the world. He looked at the signature and he said, "What have you written?"

I said, "How can I write anything other than David Washington?"

He said, "But I cannot see any sign of David Washington in it."

I said, "This is your problem, but this is my signature." I asked him, "Before you leave I want to contact my attorneys, because this paper shows your intentions."

He said, "You can phone."

I said, "My God, I have never phoned in my life! And I don't know the numbers of the attorneys, I don't exactly know how the phone operates, so you will have to find my attorney's phone number and get him on the phone." He said, "This is strange."

I said, "It is not strange because I have so many secretaries, and they are doing their work so well. And I hate the telephone; it is a nuisance."

He said, "That's right, it is certainly a nuisance. And there seems to be no way to get rid of it."

I said, "There is a way, I can throw it out right now."

He said, "Wait, don't do that."

I said, "Go and get into your bed because in the morning, on all the televisions and radio stations, in the newspapers, the news is going to be there: Osho has been forced to sign under the name of David Washington. You are going to be in trouble."

"But," he said, "how could you manage it? I know the press people are surrounding the jail" – at every jail where I was kept, the press was surrounding it twenty-four hours a day, so they could not take me somewhere else in the middle of the night or any other time – "but how can you send the message to them?"

I said, "I have sent the message."

One girl was going to be released, and she had filled out her forms and everything just before me. Then she came and sat by my side and she said, "We all feel so much for you. Although we don't know much, we have heard you on television, we have been reading your books in the jail library. I would like to do something for you, whatever you want."

I said, "Just do one thing, don't leave right now. Slip into the corner where it is darker and wait until my conversation with the Marshall is finished. Then go outside and tell all the newspapermen who are waiting there exactly what you have heard."

And she did well. She reported exactly every word. At five o'clock in the morning it was in the newspapers, on the radio. And the Marshall came running and perspiring and he said, "You are right. I could not sleep the whole night, I was turning and tossing. And it *was* in the newspapers – but how did you manage it?"

I said, "Truth always has a way of managing things."

He said, "You get up and get ready, because you have to leave this jail."

I said, "I am not in the mood. First let all the press come here and let them see the form. Once I leave this jail you are going to destroy that form with my signature. You cannot destroy it while I am here, so I will wait. And remember, you cannot do any violence to me. You cannot force me outside, because outside are the press, all the cameras are ready – then you will be in more difficulties. I had warned you last night, but you didn't listen."

He said, "Find some way... because I will be in trouble." I said, "Do you have a back door?"

He said, "Yes, there is a back door." So he went out the back door, but he was not aware that the press people were all over the place. They were at the back door too.

And they asked me only one thing: "What do you think about this incident? Is it true?"

I said, "It is more than true, but remember that these people will destroy the documents once I have left. That's why they are in such a hurry to take me out of this jail. Try to find the documents; their photographs should go on television."

And that man became very polite... I said, "Don't be deceived by his politeness, because he is the man who kept me waiting for three hours in the middle of the night because I was not ready to sign under David Washington's name. And this man's coat has writing on it saying the 'Department of Justice' – I asked him, 'Under what kind of justice or law can you ask me to change my name?' But he didn't listen. I even asked him to at least remove his coat, because it is embarrassing to me to see that people who are there to protect the law, to protect people's rights, are doing just the opposite. They are destroying the law. They are destroying the constitution and they are destroying the values upon which the constitution stands. They are destroying individuals, they are not protecting them."

This is the world in which we are living. It is almost insane. And the reason for its insanity is that nobody knows where he is going, why he is going, from where he is coming and what is the meaning of it all. Unless you know the meaning of life and the significance of existence, you cannot call yourself a sane person. I want my sannyasins to be the sanest people on the earth. The earth has been very thirsty for sanity.

16 Recognizing the master

BELOVED OSHO,
CAN YOU SAY SOMETHING ABOUT RECOGNITION?
WHY DO WE TAKE YOU FOR GRANTED? WHY WILL
WE, YOUR DISCIPLES, NOT RECOGNIZE YOU UNTIL
YOUR CRUCIFIXION? WHEN YOU SAID THAT, IT WAS
LIKE A SWORD THROUGH ME.

Sudha, the recognition of a master depends on your becoming more conscious, more aware, more alert. Coming out of your sleep, coming out of your dreams and thoughts, in an absolutely silent mind, the recognition happens – because the master is silence. The master is awareness. The master is love.

The master is not a person but a presence. The person died the day enlightenment happened. After enlightenment, there is no person as such but only a presence, a light. You can recognize it only if you have some of the qualities: love, awareness, compassion, consciousness – just a small window. Not that you have to be perfectly awakened – then, certainly you will recognize, but then recognition is of no use. Recognition is of use when you are on the path moving towards the unknown, not knowing exactly whether there is something ahead of you or you just have fallen victim to some fallacious philosophy.

The recognition of the master will help you in spite of your doubts, in spite of your uncertainties, in spite of your ups and downs. The recognition of the master will keep you on the path because you know – it happens, and if it can happen to somebody else, there is no reason why it cannot happen to you.

Every human being has an equal possibility of becoming enlightened. That is true communism. Only enlightened people can be really communist. The unenlightened is always thinking himself superior to somebody, inferior to somebody. He is always struggling to go forward, to be the first in the race, to reach the highest glory on this earth of money, of power, of prestige.

But if you are not aware and alert, if you have not yet experienced the love that is no longer part of biology, then there is only one way you can recognize the master and that is when he is crucified. His crucifixion is bound to wake you up, at least for a moment. And in that very moment will be the recognition – and a tremendous feeling of loss, because when the master was alive, you remained asleep. Now the master is no more, and because of his death... the shock is so much that it awakens you for a moment. But even that single moment is like when lightening suddenly happens on a dark night, and you see the whole scene.

I know it hurts to think that the master you have loved can be crucified. But remember one thing which has not been discussed in the past two thousand years; even Christians have not discussed it, although their master was crucified. Neither in the Greek tradition after Socrates have his disciples ever conceived of what I am going to tell you:

The crucifixion of Jesus was not only the responsibility of the Jews. The real responsibility for his crucifixion was his disciples'. It was very easy not to be caught by the Jews. Judea was such a small country; you could get out of Judea any moment. And Jews were not free people – they were in slavery under the Romans. They could not do anything directly. They had to persuade the Roman emperor, the Roman viceroy, and it was known almost all over Judea that if Jesus should go to Jerusalem for the Jewish holidays when people go on a holy pilgrimage, he would be crucified.

It was common knowledge. And there was no need for Jesus to go. Jews were not listening to him – what was the need? Jews were gathering and the rumor was that they would try to crucify him, they would put as much pressure as possible on the viceroy, Pontius Pilate. But if he is not there, nothing can be done. He insisted on going there.

And I suspect that George Gurdjieff is right – that Judas simply performed the function of a devoted disciple; he was not the enemy of Jesus and he did not betray. It was Jesus himself who sent Judas to inform the enemies where he was. It must have been very difficult for Judas, but to follow the master, he went against himself. And Jesus was caught because of the information given by Judas.

And I say that he must have done it against himself because as Jesus was crucified, suddenly he became aware of what he had done. Death is not a small matter. He had killed the man he loved, he had killed the man he worshipped. He was feeling so much repentance that within twenty-four hours he committed suicide.

Christians don't talk about why Judas committed suicide, why Jesus insisted against the will of his disciples to go on that ugly night to Jerusalem. As far as I am concerned, my feeling is that his disciples were fast asleep – and Jesus had tried *everything* to wake them up and they would not wake up. Hence, he had chosen the last resort of a master. Perhaps his life cannot help. There is no harm in taking the chance – maybe what life has not been able to do and perform, death succeeds in doing.

And it succeeded – the shock not only made an impact on the disciples but on sympathizers, on curiosity mongers, on people who were absolutely neutral, on people who had never thought about Jesus Christ. The crucifixion made everyone give a thought to this strange young man. Where do you think so many Christians have come from? Their basic number has come from the Jews.

While Jesus was alive, not even a single rabbi – and Jerusalem was full of learned rabbis; it had the Jewish university, all the scholars were there – not a single scholar, not a single rabbi recognized him. Not a single man of reputation... because everybody was afraid. Just to be associated with Jesus' name could be dangerous to you. But when he was crucified – and crucified in such a primitive and ugly way that it shocked the whole nation – even those who were in opposition felt that what had happened was not right. Because the man was innocent.

He may have been saying outrageous things but he had not done anything against any law, against any morality. And to reward him with crucifixion simply condemned the whole Judaic religion and tradition. Thousands of Jews who had never paid any attention to Jesus became Christians, and the basic number came from Judea. Perhaps the strategy of crucifixion worked. And for a man like Jesus, life and death don't matter. What matters is that he has found something and he wants to share it – but it is so difficult to find somebody willing to share life's greatest blessings and benedictions.

Sudha, it hurts but I have to tell you the truth. And you have to understand: It is not being told to somebody else, it is being told to *you*, to each person individually. If you are not awake, then perhaps it is worth my being crucified. If that helps you to be more conscious, to be more loving, to be more alert, to be more integrated.... My life and my death are both for you. For a single purpose, I go on continuing breathing. I hope... it is time that man should become more conscious on a worldwide scale, because except for that, nothing can save humanity from the destruction of the third world war that is looming darker and darker every day on the horizon.

BELOVED OSHO,
MEHER BABA SPEAKS ABOUT TWO DIFFERENT KINDS
OF ENLIGHTENED MASTERS. ONE HE CALLS "MAN
BECOMING GOD," THE OTHER HE CALLS "GOD
BECOMING MAN." GAUTAM BUDDHA BELONGS TO
THE FIRST – SLOWLY, THROUGH MANY LIVES, HE HAS
FLOWERED INTO THE STATE OF BUDDHAHOOD.
MEHER BABA ASSERTS THAT HE BELONGS TO THE
SECOND, "GOD BECOMING MAN." I HAVE NOT REALLY
UNDERSTOOD WHAT HE MEANS. CAN YOU SAY
SOMETHING ABOUT THIS?

The question is difficult because there is a misunderstanding on the part of Meher Baba. In India, there are two types of religions: Hinduism believes that God comes down and becomes man. They call it *avatar* – the very word *avatar* means descendence. Rama and Krishna, according to Hindu mythology, are gods in disguise. God is coming from above to be a man; that is the Hindu idea. In India, there are other religions – Jainism, Buddhism – which have a totally different standpoint. God does not come down because there is no God above; God is sleeping within you. It has to be awakened. So man, slowly, slowly becomes more and more conscious and finally becomes God. God is the transformed, purified consciousness of man.

Meher Baba must have been in difficulty – which one to choose? He tried to console both types of people in India by making this statement that "God happens in two ways: First he descends and becomes a man and second, he ascends through man and blossoms, manifests himself."

I am not, even for a single moment, in favor of consoling anybody because all consolations are lies. And this is a consolation. The truth is, there is no God above, so the very question of him descending does not arise. Secondly, just for the sake of argument – if we accept the hypothesis that God is – what could be the purpose for him, to come down and become man? According to the same scriptures, God is omnipotent, all-powerful; omnipresent, present everywhere; omniscient, knowing past, present, future, all that has happened and all that is going to happen.

God knows everything. Then what is the purpose of him descending in a human form? Can't he do something without becoming a man? Then his omnipotence is not omnipotence. That creates a great suspicion about his powers. Secondly, he has come in many reincarnations in Hinduism but humanity is living in a madhouse. What purpose has been served? God has not been able to change anything. The world goes on and on into darker realms, into more miserable hells, into more meaningless patterns of life. What have the reincarnations of God done?

Thirdly, the reincarnations of God – if seen without any prejudice – do not look divine in any sense. For example, Rama and his wife Sita, and his brother Laxmana, were sent to live beyond the boundaries of their kingdom for fourteen years. Because the father of Rama had four wives... and the youngest and the most beautiful wife certainly had power over the old man. She wanted *her* son... but her son was the youngest; there were four sons and her son was the youngest. But she wanted her son to be crowned and to succeed the old, dying father. She forced her husband to send Rama, at least for fourteen years, into the jungles.

Dasharatha, the father of Rama, must have been a very henpecked husband, a weakling. Rama was to succeed him; preparations were being made for his enthronement. But Dasharatha, almost dying, called Rama and said, "This is my last wish and I hope you are able to fulfill it."

Rama promised, not knowing what the wish was. And the wish was that he should go outside the kingdom for fourteen years into the jungles, into the mountains. Dasharatha was so weak in his last moments... and Rama's only quality was obedience, so he did not even ask why – "Why this punishment?"

But because he was going – and he was just ordered; I don't think gods can be so docile, so obedient to things which are absolutely wrong – his wife insisted that she would come with him. They had just got married, they had been coming home from their marriage. Now Rama could not deny her. He tried to persuade her that life would be difficult in the jungles: "You have lived as a princess of a very great king, you don't know the life.... Fourteen years will be too long. You live in the palace and wait."

But she refused. She said, "I am married to you, not to the palace. And if you can manage to live in the forest, don't be worried about me. I will manage."

And then the second brother, Laxmana, would not agree with Rama or Sita that he need not come. He had also married at the same time as Rama; he was married to Sita's younger sister. But he loved Rama so much, he said, "I cannot live without him, I am coming."

In the forest, as they woke up on the first day, Rama and Sita were standing outside the cottage and they saw a golden deer. Now, even an idiot knows deer are not made of gold. And Sita became very much interested in the deer and she asked Rama to go and hunt the deer: "Either living or dead, but you have to bring him to me."

And the strangest thing is that even Rama does not say to her that "Deer are not made of gold." There is no mention of the fact. I cannot see Gautam Buddha being befooled by a deer, but Rama is befooled. Being an incarnation of God, the mistake he is committing – it is perfectly good for human beings.... But even for intelligent human beings, it is not good; and God is behaving in the worst, most unintelligent way. If you look at the life of Rama and dissect it, you will not find anything godly in it. He may be a great king, he may be an obedient son, but these are ordinary human qualities – nothing to do with God.

One day a brahmin came with the dead body of his son and said, "It has never happened that a young son has died before the death of his father. So something very serious is involved in it, you have to find the reason." Rama asked, "Do you have any idea?"

The brahmin said, "I know perfectly well what happened. I will tell my story, and then you can search and find out who caused the death of my son." He said, "We were doing a Vedic ritual...."

And the *sudras*, the untouchables, the poorest in India — they are one-fourth of the whole population. They are not allowed to read the Vedas, the Hindu religious scriptures. They are not even allowed to *listen*. If somebody else is reading, they are not allowed to listen. And these brahmins were doing the ritual and a young, curious untouchable was hiding behind the bushes and listening to what was happening and he was caught red-handed. The brahmin's argument was that a sudra had heard the Veda, and that's why his son had died.

Do you see any kind of connection between the two? — logical, illogical, any connection? Animals are hearing, dogs are hearing, birds are hearing, trees are hearing. But a sudra — an untouchable, a poor man — cannot hear. And the brahmin proposed that his act of hearing the Vedas was the cause of the death of his son — this is absolutely unrelated. Why particularly *his* son? There were many brahmins in the ritual, but nobody else's son had died. And in fact, if there was to be any punishment, the young sudra should have died. If it is something as Hindus think, a book written by God, it would have looked logical that the sudra should die, because he broke God's law.

The son of the brahmin has not done anything at all. What is he being punished for? The father has also not done anything. The punishment should be pointing towards the sudra — if that is God's law, then there is no question.

But Rama does not say a single thing to this irrelevant, idiotic, conclusion. On the contrary, he orders that the sudra be brought to his court. That poor man was brought and he said "I was listening because I wanted to hear something about God. I am also human. There is a desire for search in me."

But the reincarnated God in Rama does not listen to the poor man. Instead of listening to his absolutely rational explanation, he orders that: "Such things should not happen in the country again."

To prevent it, this young man will have to suffer. Bring hot melted lead and pour it into his ears. That will be the punishment, because he heard with those ears the words prohibited to him." Melted lead was poured into the ears of the sudra and he became deaf for his whole life. Do you think these acts are divine?

I have been to many courts unnecessarily because whenever I would say anything about Rama, somebody's heart would start having attacks; their religious feelings would be hurt. Their religious feelings are not hurt by the act of Rama. Their religious feelings are hurt but in a wrong situation; I am simply saying what is written in their scriptures. I cannot believe that Rama is an incarnation of God. And the same is the case with other incarnations. Their life proves that they have nothing to do with God.

Gautam Buddha, or Mahavira, or Bodhidharma, or Nagarjuna – these are evolving consciousnesses. They don't believe there is a God. Their experience is that you have to create a god within you, you have to become a womb, and you have the potential to become a god. And looking at Gautam Buddha – just the way he sits, just the way he moves, just the way he speaks, or remains silent – gives valid evidence to anybody whose heart is open to understand that he has moved to the highest peak of consciousness. In his small acts you can see that.

Christians are very proud of the miracles of Jesus and they are most proud of one miracle: bringing Lazarus back to life. He had died. But nobody bothers that Lazarus died and remained dead for four days. Wherever he has been, in hell or in heaven, he must bring back some report. Four days is enough time – and seeing death, seeing beyond death, his consciousness must change. He cannot remain the same old person.

But he remains the same old person, nothing changes. So what is the miracle? And sooner or later, one day he has to die. So at the most his death is postponed a few years, but he will live these few years in unconsciousness, in violence, in hatred, in jealousy. And he will accumulate more sin. And you call it a miracle! No, a miracle needs a more refined perspective of understanding.

The same situation arises in Gautam Buddha's life; that's why I have taken Lazarus' case. One woman comes crying madly – her only son has died. Her husband has died, her other three children have died and now this child was the only hope of her life; she was living for him. Otherwise, there was nothing for her to live for. She was asking in the village, "Do you know of any physician who can help?"

They said, "No physician can do anything once a person is dead but Gautam Buddha has arrived in town today. Perhaps his presence may trigger life again, perhaps his touch.... You go directly to Gautam Buddha; don't waste time."

She took the corpse of her son, went to Buddha, laid down the corpse at his feet and said, "My only son has died. You have taken my husband – I didn't say anything, I did not complain. You have taken my three other children – I remained silent, I accepted it as my fate. But this is too much."

And for an Indian widow there is no life. She cannot go to celebrations, she cannot wear colored clothes, she has to shave her head. She has to live only in white clothes, doing all kinds of things the whole day long that nobody in the home is ready to do. Her life is simply the life of a slave.

That woman said to Gautam Buddha, "Either give life back to my son or kill me."

Buddha said, "Don't be worried. I will bring your son back to life, but you have to do a small thing." She said, "I will do anything, just tell me."

He said, "You go into the town, inquire at a few houses. We need a few mustard seeds, but we need those mustard seeds from a house where nobody has ever died."

She was in such misery, in such a mess. She could not see the point. She ran from house to house. They all said, "We are willing to give you as many mustard seeds as you want, because our whole village produces crops of mustard seed. We can bring bullock carts full of mustard seed if your son can be alive again, but our mustard seeds won't work. You have not heard the condition well. The condition is that nobody in the family should have died. We are sorry... so many people in our family have died."

By evening it was clear that mustard seeds from a family where nobody had died could not be found. And slowly, slowly it became clear to the woman that death is a natural phenomenon. It happens to everybody in every family.... "Even if my child again becomes alive, he will have to die again. Asking for his life is asking for another death, it is pointless. He cannot live forever."

She came back almost a different woman and she told Buddha, "I could not find the mustard seeds. I was in such misery that I could not understand your strategy. I could have got the idea when you told me, because I know it is impossible to find a family where people have not died. Your father must have died, your grandfather must have died... it is impossible to find a family which has had no encounter with death. But now, I come with an understanding – I don't want my son to be brought back to life, because he will have to die again. I want you to bless his future journey, so that he achieves what you have achieved.

"Life is not significant. Life is significant only when you have attained the eternal light, the eternal being, the immortal continuity from the very beginning, if there has been any beginning – to the end, if there is going to be any end.

"And for me," she said, "initiate me. Because before I die, I want to know that my essential being is not going to die."

Buddha said, "Now this seems to be reasonable. You are an intelligent woman." She was initiated and became one of the most important woman disciples of Gautam Buddha.

Now, both cases are almost the same, but the way Gautam Buddha transforms the whole thing.... From death, he turns the mind of the woman towards immortal life. He has used the opportunity for a great transformation.

Remember: God is the highest evolution of your consciousness. It is always man who becomes God. It is never God who becomes man. The idea of one God that is prevalent in Christianity, in Judaism, in Mohammedism, is childish. According to the Eastern mystics and seers, every being is potentially a god. And finally, when the whole garden comes to blossom, there will be millions of gods.

The very idea of one God is fascist, dictatorial, monopolistic. The idea of *everybody* being a god brings equality to existence; it is the finest democratic foundation. All other values are secondary.

This simple fact, that everybody is a hidden god and is capable of realizing it any moment he decides, makes the whole world godly – and gives you an opportunity not to wait for some God or Godot, not to wait for some savior, messiah or messenger. Because there is no God; all these messengers are lying. They are not courageous enough to say, "This is what I am saying." They are using the name of God – "It is God who is saying it." They are simply the messengers, the vehicles.

Gautam Buddha is not a vehicle of anybody, Mahavira is not a vehicle of anybody. What they are saying is their own experience. That's why they have a great authority. You will not find that authority in other theologians – their authority is borrowed from others. Nobody knows if those people had any experience or if they were also borrowing it.

Meher Baba is trying to console this country's mind, so he accepts both possibilities: either man can rise and become God, or God can come down and become man. But he is not aware of a simple fact: that man rising towards God has an evolutionary purpose, there is some meaning.

God descending and becoming a man – that is a fall! Why should this be done? And whatever your God wants to do, he can do without becoming a man. He could create the whole world without becoming a man; now, what is the need?

On the one hand, the religious people say, "Without God's will, not even a single leaf on a tree can waver." If this is the situation, then for all the sins and for all ugly things that go on happening – God is responsible. If even a leaf cannot move without his support, how can a man be murdered without his support? How can a woman be raped without his support? And what is the purpose for him to come here? Because he has not done anything. So many times, so many incarnations but humanity has not grown up, it has not been enhanced by their presence.

So Meher Baba is simply trying so that the Hindu masses will be satisfied with him. And in India, Jainas are very few – negligible, not even one-percent. The number of Buddhists is negligible; just forty years ago there was not a single Buddhist. Even in the temple of Bodhgaya where Gautam Buddha became enlightened, the priest is a brahmin, because there was no Buddhist even to be a priest in their holiest place. This is their holiest place, their Kaaba; Buddhists come from all over the world to worship there. And strangely enough, Buddha was continuously fighting against brahminism and the priest is a brahmin! And the priest is not only a brahmin today, he has been there for fifteen hundred years – the same family. Because for fifteen hundred years, Buddhism disappeared. So there is no problem about satisfying the Jainas and the Buddhists. This country is basically Hindu – and you must be made aware that Meher Baba was not a Hindu, he was a Parsi. And because he was a Parsi, he was condemned by the Parsis – just the natural law.... So the Parsis were not ready to accept him. Now who is going to accept this man?

Jainas and Buddhists are out of the question. They are such small minorities, even if they accept him it is not going to make much difference. Moreover, it is not easy for them to accept him for the simple reason that he was proclaiming, "Up to now, God has sent only his messengers, but I myself am God." Only Hindus might be persuaded to accept the idea that God has become man. Mohammedans cannot be persuaded, because even Hazrat Mohammed is not a reincarnation but only a messenger. Christians cannot be convinced; they have their God and they have the only begotten son of God, Jesus Christ. Whenever God needs, he sends his own son; that shows his concern.

Meher Baba was in difficulty. He had to fall on the side of the Hindus, that was the only possibility. Parsis had renounced him and nobody else would accept him; only Hindus could give him scope. So he says, "There are two types. First – man becoming God; Gautam Buddha comes in that category. And second – God becoming man." And he says, "I fall into the second category."

But I say to you, there is no possibility of two categories. Life knows only evolution; it never goes backwards. And a god becoming a man is simply stupid. For what should God become man? What will be the purpose? All that he wants to do he can do from wherever he is. But he is nowhere – and that gives the chance to a few charlatans to proclaim that they are God, reincarnations of God. Meher Baba is certainly an enlightened person.

But every enlightened person finds himself in different situations. Meher Baba's situation was very unique, because in the history of Parsis there is no such thing as enlightenment. The Parsis were very angry when he declared that he is God himself, because to Parsis, to Mohammedans, to Christians, this declaration that "I am God" hurts very much.

They want their God to remain as far away as possible, so they can go on doing whatsoever they are doing. God standing just there... and you were going to hit your husband with the pillow... it doesn't look right. But he is standing there – that's what millions of believers think, that he is everywhere present. So remember: when you are hitting, look around and hit some suspicious place where you think God might be, rather than hitting a poor husband!

Meher Baba lived in a strange situation. Parsis were denying him, Jainas and Buddhists would not accept him; Mohammedans, Christians, Jews would deny him because he was saying he is the whole *God*, what to say about the only begotten son? The only possibility was that a few Hindus may gather around him, and that's what happened. Finally, only a few Hindus were around him. And as he died, his movement died too. Because he could not manage to be a master. He remained a mystic. He tried, but as a master, he was a failure.

As a mystic, he succeeded. As far as *he* is concerned, he has arrived, but alone – no fellow travelers, no friends, no lovers. It has not been a celebrating procession of many enlightened people, moving with him into the universal life sources. He has moved alone.

BELOVED OSHO,
I'M CONSTANTLY AMAZED AT HOW YOU USE YOUR
MIND LIKE A COMPUTER – SUCH PURE AND SIMPLE
GENIUS, IN FACT, SUPER-GENIUS. LAO TZU SAID HE
WAS A MUDDLEHEAD, YET THE CLARITY OF GENIUS IS
THERE ALSO. BELOVED OSHO, WHEN A PERSON
BECOMES ENLIGHTENED, IS THE MIND SO FREE OF
EGO THAT ONLY GENIUS IS LEFT? OR ARE SOME
PEOPLE ACTUALLY ENLIGHTENED MUDDLEHEADS?

Enlightenment has nothing to do with mind. In meditation, you bypass the mind. Meditation reaches with you to the highest peak – with all its silence, with all its flowers, with all its beauty. As you become enlightened, your mind drops all the rubbish it has carried for hundreds of lives; it is an autonomous happening. As you become enlightened, the mind immediately drops all rubbish, that rubbish you were clinging to because you had no idea who you are. That rubbish had become your identity, and now you know your real identity; you don't need that false burden on you. It simply falls naturally, on its own accord.

Your mind becomes a simple, immensely powerful mechanism. But it remains now as a servant. Up to now it was the master; after enlightenment, it is a beautiful servant. And certainly, as you say, it is a computer. The people who work with computers say that we have not yet been able to make a computer of the size of the human brain which is capable of containing so much information. Your brain has seven million cells, and each cell can contain millions of bits of information. The experts say that one percent can memorize *all* the books from *all* the libraries of the world – this is the capacity of your mind.

But in jealousy, in anger, in hate, in possessiveness – who has the time? Once you are enlightened, you can use the mind the way it is meant to be used, as a beautiful computer. And because you are enlightened, it is no longer clouded with sentiments and emotions; it is clean, a sky without any clouds. Its clarity is its genius. And every mind is a genius, there are no other kinds of minds in the world.

So there is no possibility of an enlightened man having a muddled head, an enlightened man having the mind of an idiot – that is impossible. The enlightenment is such a transforming force, it changes everything in you; particularly in the mind.

BELOVED OSHO,
THE OTHER NIGHT, I WAS VERY TOUCHED BY THE SINGING OF THE INDIAN SWAMI WHO SINGS BEFORE DISCOURSE. I FELT AS IF HE WERE PLAYING ME LIKE A MUSICAL INSTRUMENT. I FELT LIKE A BIG EAR, JUST LISTENING. MOST OTHER MUSIC I HEAR BASICALLY AMOUNTS TO NOISE – IT'S ENTERTAINING, BUT IT DOESN'T TOUCH ME. WHAT IS IT ABOUT HIS MUSIC AND THE MUSIC OF ALL THOSE MUSICIANS WHO TOUCH SOMETHING INSIDE US, THAT HELPS US TO FLY?

Music is born out of deep experiences of meditation; it is a dimension of meditation. By meditating, you may be able to be touched by music, but the reverse is also true: If you are totally absorbed in music, your heart will be touched not only by music but by meditation too. Music is sound. Meditation is soundlessness.

The highest music is where the sound does not destroy the soundless moments in between. As the musician becomes more and more refined, he can manage to create sound, and between two sounds he can give you an experience of soundlessness. That soundlessness touches the heart. In the East, music has always been part of meditation. Temples have been full of music and dance.

Ashok Bharti loves me. His music is just a communication of his love. He pours himself totally into it. The same is happening with the other sannyasin musician who is present today. They are not just technicians, they are not singing because they are paid. They are singing out of love, out of gratitude. Their singing is just pure innocence. And their words are not just words – they mean it. And because they mean it, they can touch your heart, they can transform your heart.

BELOVED OSHO,
WHAT IS YOUR DEFINITION OF PERVERSION IN
REGARD TO SEX?

Sarjano, perversion means your energy is not going in the natural way; the natural way has been blocked, suppressed, condemned. But the energy is there and collecting, it is bound to find some outlet. That outlet will not be natural. That outlet will be perversion. And the whole past of man is nothing else – from different directions, for different excuses you have been told to cut off your natural paths for energy and expression.

Man is an intelligent being. Even unintelligent animals are bound to find some way. In the wild, no animals turn homosexual; there is no need because there is no priest. But man is so much conditioned against a few things – sex being the main one – that if he lives sex naturally, he feels guilty that he is going against God, against religion. If he prevents his natural expressions, then soon his energies start moving into perverted forms.

Just the other day, I received the information that by the end of this century, there will be one billion people suffering from AIDS. And this is the lowest estimate. I don't feel the number will be so low. The number, according to me, may be double.

AIDS is the ultimate expression of perverted sexual energy. And the wonder is that you are surrounded with such dangerous things.... AIDS can destroy the whole planet, because we don't have any medicine and the doctors and the scientists are openly saying that there seems to be no possibility, at least in the near future, to find a medicine. So once you have AIDS, your death is certain within six months to two years, and you cannot do anything except wait.

A disease like AIDS has come through homosexuality. It is the ultimate.... And the perversion is not condemned; on the contrary, in different ways it is supported because every religion believes in *brahmacharya*, in celibacy. Now those who believe in celibacy are standing in the queue – first they will be homosexuals, lesbians and sooner or later, they will receive the ultimate reward, the Nobel prize – AIDS. Now religions are responsible for it. But this is what I say, human insanity....

In Texas, they have made a law against homosexuality. Now it is a crime in Texas; you can get five to ten years in jail. Texas is a backward state in America. Even I was surprised that one million homosexuals demonstrated against the legislature and these may not be *all* the homosexuals in the state of Texas. But *one million* homosexuals! And they made it clear to the government that by making homosexuality illegal, you cannot prevent it. You have made many things illegal in the past, and what have you prevented? Has theft disappeared? Has murder disappeared? Is rape something of the past?

You cannot stop it with your laws because you have never stopped anything with your laws. You are just befooling the masses, making a law so people feel the government is doing something. But they don't see that what they are doing, they have been doing for ten thousand years, and things have gone from bad to worse.

When I read about it, I had two ideas: one, that to make homosexuality a crime and not to make celibacy a crime.... Because these homosexuals are products of your religion. Your religion condemns sex so much... your monks, your nuns, you have put them almost in prisons. Now these one million homosexuals in Texas will go underground. Just now, they had their clubs, their discos, their restaurants; they were openly homosexual. Now you have made it a crime. They will go underground. When they were open and known, there was a possibility to check them medically, to help them in some way. If somebody had AIDS already, he could be isolated. Places could be made where only AIDS people would be living, working.

Now, nobody is going to accept that he has AIDS – why should he go for an examination? This is the danger. A single person can spread the disease like wildfire because it not only transferred by sexual contact – that is something more than ordinary sexual diseases – it can be transferred by other means.

Blood transfusion... now you don't know whose blood is being transfused into you. And if the man whose blood is being transfused into you has AIDS, you will have it. It can be transferred even just by kissing because saliva carries the virus. Now for the first time, the Siberians have been proved right because they have never kissed in their whole history, and they always laughed when they came in contact with Christian missionaries, watching them kissing each other. They could not believe it. These people have come to teach religion to you and they don't even know hygiene. Mixing each other's saliva, playing with each other's tongues – and these idiots have come to preach religion!

In Siberia, they have never kissed. It is a dirty habit... you just think about it. Siberians rub noses with each other – that is pure hygiene. And as far as love is concerned, it can be expressed in many ways.... But repression is going to grow.

In one monastery in Europe, half of the monastery has just declared that they are homosexuals, so the monastery is now divided in two parts. They are fighting amongst themselves – the homosexuals and the non-homosexuals. I am saying non-homo-sexuals because I cannot say they are celibate. It is almost impossi-ble to be celibate unless something is wrong with your body.

I have heard that Stanley was a very healthy sperm and the whole day he used to do push-ups while all the other sperm were just relaxing. And they were puzzled: "What is wrong with this Stanley? The whole day, exercises, exercises."

Finally, one of these lazy people asked Stanley, "Please tell us what the secret is? Why are you exercising so much? The whole day, from the time you wake up till you go to sleep, you are exer-cising, doing this, doing that. What is the purpose?"

He said, "You don't know? You guys are fools. Only one sperm is going to reach the woman's egg. And next time when the release comes, I am Stanley, the one who is going to get to the egg. That is the purpose."

And one day suddenly they started feeling very hot and they all thought the time had come. Before they could have discussed among themselves what to do, they were released so suddenly... but they all saw Stanley far ahead. He was swimming so fast, they could not believe that one could swim so fast and then suddenly, Stanley turned back, screamed loudly, and said, "Go back, go back! It's a blow job!" Even poor sperm are laughing at humanity.

If man is allowed to be simply natural, his life can give him immense joy, peace, silence, and finally the truth – but if his energies are perverted, then he goes round and round wasting himself.

I have heard about an army officer who had been around the world, posted at different places – and naturally, the monks and the soldiers are in the same boat because you don't allow soldiers their wives, their girlfriends. This officer, Major Benson, was in Hong Kong and got into real trouble. He was going to prostitutes all over the world, but he was not aware of Chinese prostitutes. They are the most dangerous. He fell into the trap of a Chinese prostitute and seeing the situation, looking at the naked body of the prostitute, he felt that it was better to have a medical check-up: "This woman seems to be sick and one does not know what kind of sickness she is carrying."

So he went to the American section of the city and found a doctor. The doctor examined him and said, "Nothing can be done. You need an immediate operation; your cock has to be removed." The man was shocked. He said, "My God!"

The doctor said, "You have so many diseases that in this one life, they cannot be cured."

He came out dazed. He thought it would be better to have another opinion, so he went to another American doctor. He checked him thoroughly and said, "I'm sorry, the first doctor was right. It is too late. Nothing can be done and if you don't have the operation soon, even an operation may not help; the diseases may have spread all over your body. So don't waste time. I can do the operation tomorrow."

He said, "I will be coming tomorrow," but he was not satisfied with the idea that he would have to live his whole life without a cock.

Suddenly, he saw a Chinese doctor's signboard. He thought, "Perhaps a Chinese doctor might be helpful."

He went in. The doctor looked. The other doctors had spent hours in checking his whole body, this and that. The Chinese doctor just looked with a magnifying glass and said, "There is no need for any operation."

Benson was very happy. He said, "Really? Is there any hope?"

He said, "*Every* hope. First, you went to a Chinese woman – because these diseases you can get only from a Chinese prostitute. The second wrong thing you did was, you went to American doctors who are just after money, money, money – and money means you have to do something. Even if your cock disappears, they are not worried; they need money. An operation means money. You don't be worried, there is no need of any operation."

Benson was very happy. He said, "Thank you!" He gave much money to him and the old man said, "Whenever there is any trouble, come to me, don't go to American doctors. They are simply cheating people."

Just to have a final word from the doctor, he said, "So now I can go? There is no need?"

He said, "There is no need, I have told you. Just wait two or three weeks and the pecker will fall off by itself."

17

The poetry of the feminine

BELOVED OSHO,
WHY IS IT STILL SO DIFFICULT FOR ME TO SEE THE
WORTH OF MY FEMININE QUALITIES? THERE IS STILL
SOMETHING IN ME THAT JUDGES THEM AS WEAK
AND HAVING A FEELING OF NOT BEING ABLE TO
SURVIVE. CAN YOU PLEASE SAY SOMETHING ABOUT
THIS?

It is the long condemnation of feminine qualities that has gone deep into the blood and the bones of women. It is man's conspiracy to prove himself superior to women – which he is not. Man is deep down aware of the fact that the woman has something which he does not have. In the first place the woman is attractive to him, she looks beautiful. He falls in love with the woman, the woman becomes almost an addiction to him – and that's where the trouble arises.

The feeling of dependence on women which every man feels, makes him react in such a way that he tries to manage the woman as a slave – spiritually a slave. He's also afraid because she is beautiful; ... she is beautiful not only to him – she is beautiful to whomever looks at her, to whomever comes in contact with her. Great jealousy arises in the egoist, male chauvinist mind. He has done with women what Machiavelli suggests to the politicians – marriage is politics too. Machiavelli suggests that the best way of defense is offense, and man has used the idea for centuries – centuries before Machiavelli recognized it as a basic fact in all political spheres.

Wherever there is some kind of domination, offense is certainly the best way of defense. In defense, you are already losing ground; you have already accepted yourself as the defeated side. You are just protecting yourself.

In India, hundreds of invaders have come – small groups of invaders but they conquered this vast country, which is a subcontinent, it is a world in itself. By the end of this century, one man in every four will be Indian. It is one-fourth of humanity.

In this country, there are religious scriptures like *Manusmriti*, five-thousand years old, and they suggest that if you want to have peace in your house, giving a good beating to the woman once in a while is absolutely necessary. She should be kept almost imprisoned. And that's how she has lived – in different cultures, different countries, but her imprisonment has been almost the same. And because man wanted to prove himself superior.... Remember, whenever you want to prove something that means you are *not* that thing.

A real superiority needs no proof, no evidence, no witness, no argument. A real superiority is immediately recognized by anybody who has even a small amount of intelligence. The real superiority has its own magnetic force. Because men condemned woman – and they had to condemn her to keep her in control – they reduced her almost to a subhuman category. What fear must have led man to do this? – because it is sheer paranoia....

Man continuously compares and finds the woman superior. For example, in making love to a woman, a man is very inferior because he can have only one orgasm at a time while the woman can have at least half a dozen, a chain – multiple orgasm. Man simply feels utterly helpless. He cannot give those orgasms to the woman. And this has created one of the most miserable things in the world: because he cannot give a multiple orgasm, he has tried not to give her even the first orgasm. The taste of the orgasm can create danger for him.

If the woman knows what orgasm is, she is bound to become aware that one orgasm is not satisfying; on the contrary, she is more thirsty. But the man is spent. So the most cunning way is not to let the woman know that anything like orgasm exists in the world.

It is only in this century that we have given recognition to a certain orgasmic state while making love. No sex manual, no treatise written on sex in the East or in the West even mentions the word orgasm. It seems to be a conspiracy. Vatsyayana, the first man in the history to write about sex energy, to explore it in a scientific way, wrote the first treatise on sexology five-thousand years ago – *Kamasutras*, aphorisms on sex. He has gone into the subject as deeply as possible from all directions. He has not ignored the smallest detail. He describes eighty-four postures of lovemaking.

You cannot improve on it; you cannot find an eighty-fifth posture, he has done exhaustive work. But even Vatsyayana does not mention orgasm. That is simply unbelievable – that a man who inquired so deeply into sex did not come across the fact of orgasm.

No, my feeling is that he is hiding a fact – and to hide any fact is a crime, because that means you allow the false to continue as if it is the truth. And it is not an ordinary fact concerning chemistry or geography; it is something which is the most important in human life.

The experience of orgasm not only gives you the ultimate pleasure that the body is capable of, it also gives you the insight that this is not all. It opens a door. It makes you aware that you have been unnecessarily looking outside, your real treasure is within.

Meditation has been found by people who had deep orgasmic experiences. Meditation is a byproduct of orgasmic experience. There is no other way to find meditation. But orgasm brings you naturally into a state of meditation: time stops, thinking disappears, the ego is no more. You are pure energy. For the first time you understand: you are not the body and you are not the mind; you are something that transcends both – a conscious energy.

And once you enter into the realm of conscious energy, you start having the most beautiful experiences of life, the lightest, the most colorful, the most poetic, the most creative. They give you fulfillment and contentment on the one hand – as far as the body, the mind and the world are concerned.

On the other hand, they create a tremendous, divine discontentment. Because what you have experienced is great, but the very experience of it makes you certain, for no reason at all, that there must be greater experiences ahead. Before you knew anything about orgasm, you had never dreamed about it; now you *know* it. This is going to become an incentive to seek and search: Is there anything more juicy, more blissful, more psychedelic than any psychedelics can deliver to you? This search led man toward meditation. It was a simple insight into the orgasmic experience.

What happens? – time stops, thinking disappears. The feeling of

I is no more there. There is a feeling of *isness* – pure, existential – but there is no ego attached to it. I, me, mine – they have all been left far behind. This gives you the clue for meditation. If you can manage a transcendence of time, a transcendence of mind, you will be entering into a orgasmic space alone – without a woman, without a man.

To be *exactly* true, meditation is non-sexual orgasm. But half of humanity has not known orgasm for centuries. And because the woman has not known orgasm, you should not think that man has been in a better position. Not giving orgasm to the woman, he has to lose his own orgasm too.

Something significant has to be understood: Man's sexuality is local, it is confined to the genitals and a sex center in the brain. But with the woman, it is different. Her sexuality is all over her body. Her whole body is sensitive, is erotic. Because man's sexuality is local, it is tiny. The woman's sexuality is something very great. Man is finished within a few seconds; the woman is not even warmed up. Man is in such a hurry – as if he is doing some duty for which he is paid and wants to finish it quickly – making love is the same.

Why, in fact, does man bother to make love I wonder? – just two or three seconds and he is finished. The woman was warming up and the man is finished – not that he has attained orgasm; ejaculation is not orgasm. The man turns on his side and goes to sleep. And the woman – not one woman but millions of women are crying tears after men have made love to them because they have been left in a limbo. You have encouraged them and before they can come to a conclusion, you are out of the game.

But this fact of the man finishing quickly has a very significant background; that's what I have been bringing you to. In not allowing the woman the *first* orgasm, he has to learn to finish as quickly as possible. So the woman has lost something tremendously beautiful, something sacred on the earth – and the *man* has lost.

Orgasm is not the only thing in which the woman is powerful. Everywhere in the world the woman lives five years longer than the man; her average age is five years more than the man's. That means she has more resistance, more stamina. Women are sick less than men. Women, even if they are sick, heal themselves more quickly than men. These are scientific facts.

One hundred and fifteen boys are born while one hundred girls are born. One wonders: why one and hundred fifteen? But nature knows better. By the time they are marriageable, fifteen boys will have popped off! Only one hundred boys and one hundred girls will be left. Girls don't die easily.

Women don't commit suicide as much as men; men's suicide rate is double. Although women talk about suicide more than men – man ordinarily never talks – women make much fuss about suicide but they always choose to survive because they don't use any drastic methods to kill themselves.

They choose the most comfortable and most scientific and most contemporary – sleeping pills. And strangely enough, no woman takes so many pills that it becomes impossible for her to be revived. So her suicide is not suicide but a kind of protest, a threat, a blackmail to make the husband understand that this is a warning for the future. Everybody is condemning him – the doctors, the neighbors, the relatives, the police officers. He has unnecessarily become a criminal, and everybody's sympathy is for the woman – although *she* was going to commit suicide.

As far as murder is concerned, the difference is vast. Man commits murder almost twenty times more; a woman, very rarely.

Women go mad less than men. Again, the proportion is the same: men go mad twice as often as women. And still, after all these facts established by science, the superstition continues that man is stronger. Only in one thing is he stronger and that is that he has a muscular body. He is a good manual worker.

Otherwise, on every point he feels – and he has felt for centuries – a deep inferiority complex. To avoid that complex, the only way is to force the woman into an inferior position. And that is the only thing that is more powerful in man: he can force the woman. He is more cruel, he is more violent, and he has forced the woman to accept an idea which is absolutely false: that she is weak. And to prove that the woman is weak, he has to condemn all the feminine qualities. He has to say that they are all weak, and all those qualities together make the woman weak.

In fact, the woman has all the great qualities in her. And whenever a man becomes awakened, he attains to the same qualities which he has been condemning in women. The qualities that are thought to be weak are all the feminine qualities. And it is a strange fact that all the great qualities come into that category. What is left are only the brutal qualities, animal qualities.

The woman is more loving. The man has not shown greater love than the woman. Millions of women have died – they have jumped alive into the funeral pyre with their beloveds because they could not conceive of a life without their husband or friend. But don't you think it is a little weird that in ten-thousand years not a single man has dared to jump into a funeral pyre with his wife? Enough time, enough opportunity... and you are stronger. The delicate woman, the fragile woman, jumps into the funeral pyre and the stronger Mohammed Ali goes on doing his push-ups. And he is still stronger!

Strength has many dimensions. Love has its own strength. For example, to carry a child in the womb for nine months needs strength, stamina, love. No man could manage it. An artificial womb could be placed in man – now scientific technology has come to the point where man could have a plastic womb implanted but I don't think he could survive nine months! – they are both going to jump into the ocean.

It is difficult to give life to another soul, to give a body to another soul, to give a brain and mind to another soul. The woman shares wholeheartedly in giving to the child whatever she can manage. And even after the child is born, it is not easy to bring up children. To me, it seems to be the most difficult thing in the world.

Astronauts and Edmund Hillary... these people should first try to bring up children. Then only can we accept that they have done something by going to Everest; otherwise it is pointless. Even if you have reached the moon and walked on the moon, it does not matter. It doesn't show that you are stronger.

A living child – so volatile, such an energy overflowing that he will tire you within hours. Nine months in the womb and then a few years.... Just try one night to sleep with a small baby in your bed. During that night, in your house, something is going to happen. Either the child will kill you or you will kill the child. Most probably, you will kill the child, because children are the nastiest people in the world. They are so fresh and they want to do so many things and you are dead tired. You want to go to sleep, and the child is fully awake and he wants to do all kinds of things and he wants your advice, and questions, and if nothing works then he wants to go to the bathroom! He's feeling thirsty. He's feeling hungry in the middle of the night....

It happened... A great saint was delivering a religious discourse and one of the richest women in his congregation was sitting in front of him with her small child. But the child disturbed the whole discourse – because people started laughing... and the reason was the child.

The child asked, "Mom, I want to piss." In the middle, when he is talking about God, this idiot thinks about.... After the meeting, he took the woman aside and told her, "You should teach manners to the child. In a religious discourse, such words... and in the middle, and everybody starts laughing and I feel awkward. And you went on pushing him away and he went on again and again after two minutes – 'Mom....' And slowly there was no need for him to say the full sentence. Just 'Mom' and the whole hall was laughing. You should train him that there are situations where you cannot use such words." The woman said, "Then what should be done?"

He said, "Just tell him, for example, that if he wants to go to the toilet he can say, 'Mom, I want to sing.' You will understand... just a code word that nobody else will understand. Then you can simply take him out." The woman said, "I will try."

After six months, the saint was staying in the woman's house and suddenly one of her relatives died. In the middle of the night she and her husband had to go to the place of the person who had died. So they brought the child to the saint and asked him: "It will be a great kindness if you can let him sleep with you. It may take a few hours for us to get back."

The saint said, "There is no problem. Let him sleep here with me."

But there *was* a problem. After just half an hour, the child said to the saint, "Swamiji, I want to sing."

The old fellow was tired. The whole day long he was in religious meetings and he wanted to sleep. So he said, "This is stupid. This is no time to sing; keep quiet and go to sleep. You can sing as much as you want in the morning, but not now."

For a moment, the boy became afraid. He's alone, the father and mother are gone and this man seems... he used to look very loving, very compassionate. "But his behavior now that I am alone is very rude." But he could not contain it. He had to go to the bathroom. He said, "Swamiji...."

Swamiji said, "Again? Will you let me sleep or not?"

He said, "Unless you allow me to sing, I cannot allow you to sleep – because I cannot sleep without singing."

He said, "I have never in my life heard... you are a born singer. You cannot sleep without singing?" The boy said, "No."

The saint said, "But what will the neighbors think? In the middle of the night... please be understanding. And your father and mother will be coming, they can take care of you. Don't disturb my sleep. I am an old man, tired."

He said, "You may be tired, you may be old. I am neither old nor delivering spiritual discourses but what to do about singing? Everyday I sing at this time."

The saint decided that this is not going to be. He said, "Remain silent. No more a single word; otherwise I am going to give you a good beating. Singing and singing... just go to sleep."

But how can the boy go to sleep? For two minutes he closed his eyes, and then he said, "Swamiji, now if you don't allow me, it is going to sing on its own."

The saint could not understand what the boy was saying – "It is going to sing on its own?"

"Then don't tell me... I am warning you. Now I am at the last point of control."

The swami said, "If it is such a necessity, then you can sing slowly, just like whispering in my ear."

The boy said, "I have no problem, but it will be a little warm."

The saint said, "You are an idiot! How can singing be warm?"

The boy said, "I *know* because every day I am singing. Perhaps you are too old and it has gone cold, but mine is real hot. Don't say anything to me – that's why I am making things clear."

He said, "I am not going to say anything. You sing, hot or cold as you want; just finish so I can go to sleep."

And it was too late to do anything. The boy pissed all over the saint, his whole bed... and the saint jumped out of the bed, the old man fell on the ground and he said, "You idiot! This is singing? You call this singing?"

The boy said, "You have forgotten, it is your advice. Six months ago you advised my mother that 'pissing' is not a good word. Now you know – *this* is a good word!"

The child sleeps the whole day. In the mother's womb he sleeps twenty-four hours; then, slowly, slowly... twenty-three, twenty-two, twenty... but he is almost always asleep. And in the night, he wakes up. The whole day he will be asleep and in the night he will wake up to torture you.

I don't think there is any man who can have a pregnancy or who can bring up children. It is the strength of the woman. But it is a different strength. There is one strength which is destructive, there is another strength which is creative. There is one strength which is of hatred and there is another strength which is of love.

Love, trust, beauty, sincerity, truthfulness, authenticity – these are all feminine qualities, and they are far greater than any qualities that man has. But the whole past has been dominated by man and his qualities. Naturally in war, love is of no use, truth is of no use, beauty is of no use, aesthetic sensibility is no use. In war, you need a heart which is more stony than stones. In war, you need simply hate, anger, a madness to destroy.

In three thousand years, man has fought five thousand wars. Yes, this is also strength but not worthy of human beings. This is strength derived from our animal inheritance. It belongs to the past, which is gone, and the feminine qualities belong to the future, which is coming. There is no need to feel yourself weak because of your feminine qualities. You should feel grateful to existence that what man has to earn, you have been given by nature as a gift.

Man has to learn how to love. Man has to learn how to let the heart be the master and the mind be just an obedient servant. Man has to learn these things. The woman brings these things with her, but we condemn all these qualities as weaknesses. Even if you have chosen women as great individuals, you can see what you have chosen – you have chosen a man. Because you have chosen the qualities of man that were in the woman. For example, Joan of Arc had all the qualities of man. The Queen of Jhansi in India had all the qualities of man: she could fight with a naked sword, could kill people without any problem. Such women have been chosen in history and great tribute is paid to them by the historians. And they don't represent women. In fact, that is the reason why they have been chosen, because they are just carbon copies of men.

The women's liberation movement has to learn one fundamental thing: that is not to imitate man and not to listen what he says about feminine qualities, the feminine personality. The feminine qualities are clear.

Friedrich Nietzsche has a great insight into many areas of life, but he could not create a coherent, comprehensive system of philosophy. And the reason was not that he was not capable – he was the most capable of all Western philosophers. The problem was, he had so much to give that it was not possible for him to make a whole system; otherwise, much would not be part of it. Hence, he chose an aphoristic style of writing. Just as you can write in a very condensed form, many things which ordinarily you would write in an essay, Friedrich Nietzsche would write in four lines or at the most in a paragraph. But that has created great misunderstanding about the poor man. Because it is too condensed – unless you have the clarity to see into the density of his insight, into the far-reaching effects of his insights, into all the implications which are not said but are there... you will have to search for them and then you will be surprised.

Nietzsche is going to come back. Now is the time that he should be understood perfectly well. Adolf Hitler misunderstood him. His followers misunderstood him, his enemies misunderstood him. But to be misunderstood is a seal from human beings, that you had something really important. Otherwise, who cares to understand or misunderstand?

Nietzsche had this insight: that men have to suppress women. Otherwise, if things had gone naturally, it would be more possible that the woman would be the master and the man would be the servant, because his qualities are those of a servant – of a soldier at the most. And the feminine qualities are almost divine. They have a royalty about them.

Drop all the ideas of man that he has been putting in your heads. And also drop the ideas of the women's liberation movement, because they are also putting nonsense into your minds. Their nonsense is that they are trying to prove that men and women are equal. They are not – and when I say they are not, I don't mean that someone is superior and someone is inferior. I mean that they are unique. Women are women and men are men; there is no question of comparison. Equality is out of the question. They are not unequal and neither can they be equal. They are unique.

Rejoice in your feminine qualities, make a poetry of your feminine qualities. That is your great inheritance from nature. Don't throw it away, because the man does not have them. To be equal, you may start doing idiotic things.

And that's what is happening in the women's liberation movement. The women are smoking cigarettes or, if there is an opportunity, then a joint. Now in the East, the woman cannot even think – neither can the man think... if you go home and find your wife relaxing on the sofa with a cigarette, you will not be able to believe what has happened.

We have a deep respect for feminine qualities and those qualities prohibit many things, encourage many other things. The woman should not try to imitate man, because even if you succeed.... It is difficult to succeed. Imitation is always imitation, it is never equal. But for argument's sake, if we accept that you can become exactly like a man, you will lose all that you have and you will not gain anything. Because even in the eyes of man, you will not be beautiful anymore, and in your own eyes, you will be shattered. It was better to be unequal than to be equal, because now the man takes no interest.

A woman should keep her separateness, should save all her

feminine qualities and purify them. In this way she is going, according to her nature, towards enlightenment. Of course once you are enlightened, you have gone beyond the discrimination of sexes. Beyond enlightenment, you are simply human beings. But before that....

Nor should man try to imitate woman, which he has been doing.

I entered the university, and I entered the university without having any money with me, because my parents wanted me to become a doctor, an engineer, a scientist but they were all against the idea that I should go to study philosophy, religion, psychology. They said, "You will be a beggar on the streets, and we cannot support you to become a beggar. So either you choose something which will make you *somebody* – respectable, powerful – or we are not going to support you financially. Then you can study anything you want." I said, "This is very clear. Agreed."

They were simply threatening me. They were not the kind of people to refuse to give me financial help. They loved me. In fact, because they loved me, they wanted me to become somebody in the world. And because nothing was working, their arguments and persuasion were not working, they threatened me. So I had to go to the university on the train without a ticket.

It was eighty miles from my village. I went to the ticket collector and told him, "This is the situation. If you can help me... and I will remember. Whenever I have money, the ticket will be paid."

But he said, "Don't be worried. So many people are traveling without a ticket, but you are at least truthful. You yourself came to me, you have not been hiding." He said, "You rest and I will meet you at the station where you have to get down and help you to go out."

And he helped me; I reached the university. I had no money for the taxi that I picked up from the railway station so I went directly to the vice-chancellor's office. The pune at the gate tried to prevent me.

I said, "Forget it. As far as I am concerned, remember not to prevent me, because that will create chaos."

The vice-chancellor heard: "What kind of talk is going on?"

He was looking from the window and he saw this new, young man. He said, "Let him come in." He asked, "What do you want?"

I put before him all the applications for fellowships, for food, scholarship, for university fees.

He said, "But you have not graduated from this university. And this has been the convention: If somebody has graduated from this university, he will have the first preference."

I said, "Even though he does not have the same marks and the same qualifications?"

He said, "No, your case will be considered, but I'm becoming curious about something else... you sit down. Would you like to have some coffee or some tea?"

I said, "No, you just first tell me what your curiosity is."

He said, "My curiosity is about your small beard" – it was just starting to grow – "Why you are growing a beard and mustache and long hair?"

I said, "You are asking a wrong question. I'M not growing them, *they* are growing. In fact, I should ask you why you have been shaving your beard and your mustache, because that is a positive act, and you have to be responsible for it and answerable. Nature has not given beards to women – just think of a woman who starts growing beard and a mustache! And it is not impossible; she just needs a few injections, a few of the hormones that grow the hair of the beard and the mustache."

I said, "Just imagine – would that woman look like a woman? Could you fall in love with her if, by some magic, you can again be given your youth?" He said, "My God! A woman with a beard?"

"But," I said, "yours is a similar case; a man *without* a beard is no different. You have been imitating women."

And there is an unconscious reasoning, because the man feels women are beautiful – perhaps if he also takes away the beard and the mustache, he may look more beautiful. He's a hundred percent wrong. It is one thing that women go on tolerating, him because it is a man's society and he develops ideas and enforces them on everybody else who is in some way dependent on him. But if women are free to express their feelings, a beard is as natural, a mustache is as natural as your nose. You don't shave it. Be proud of your qualities. Increase them, refine them because they are the path towards godliness.

Man is not in a better position than woman as far as religious experience is concerned. But he has one quality and that is of the warrior. Once he gets a challenge, then he can grow any kind of qualities. Even the feminine qualities, he can grow better than any woman can. His fighting spirit balances things.

Women have qualities inborn. Man needs only to be provoked, given a challenge: these qualities have not been given to you – you have to earn them. And if men and women both can live these qualities, the day is not far away when we can transform this world into a paradise.

Again, I remember Friedrich Nietzsche. He said that Jesus Christ, Gautam Buddha... these were not real men, because their qualities are feminine. Nobody else has said that; no follower, no enemy. But Nietzsche certainly has a knack of finding absolutely fresh insights. He is against Jesus and against Gautam Buddha, because if people follow them, everybody will become feminine. He loves the qualities of man – particularly of the warrior. He says that in his life, the most remarkable, unforgettable experience happened in a strange way... and perhaps nobody will believe it.

He was sitting on the terrace of his house and a group of soldiers marched on the road by the side of the house with naked swords, their shining boots, walking in rhythm... a beautiful morning with the sun, no clouds.

Nietzsche said, "Those shining swords, that music of the soldiers' boots was the greatest aesthetic experience to me. I have never seen anything more beautiful, more musical."

He is for the qualities of man: the naked sword moving in the sun gives him the most beautiful experience. The sound of the boots gives him the greatest music. He is for the qualities of man.

I am for the qualities of women. Because of Nietzsche's insistence for man's qualities, Adolf Hitler was born. Adolf Hitler, Goebbels, and the whole bunch of criminals who surrounded him, are pygmies compared to Friedrich Nietzsche as far as intelligence is concerned. They misunderstood him completely. They took out portions that supported fascism, murder, invading innocent people, killing innocent people.

I am here to counter Nietzsche. I love the man, I love his insights, but that does not mean that I agree with him. I disagree with him. I would like the whole world to be full of feminine qualities. Then only can wars disappear. Then only can marriage disappear. Then only can nations disappear. Then only can we have one world: a loving, a peaceful, a silent and beautiful world.

So drop all the conditionings man has given to you. Find your own qualities and develop them. You are not to imitate the man; neither is the man to imitate you. When I say he has to grow feminine qualities, I don't mean that he has to imitate women.

Every person, whether man or woman, is born of a father and of a mother. Half of his being is contributed by man and half by woman, so everybody is both. If you are a man, then the man is on top and underneath it, hidden, are all the feminine qualities, the contribution from your mother. If you are a woman, then your feminine qualities are on top and your male qualities are underneath it; that is the contribution of your father. And there is no need of any conflict between you, because you are man and woman together, simultaneously.

Rather than creating a conflict, my whole work is to indicate to you the path, how you can create an orchestra of all your qualities together. That will be your wholeness as a human being.

BELOVED OSHO,
WHY AM I CONFUSED OVER DEVOTION AND
DEPENDENCE? IN RELATIONSHIPS I FEEL AN
OVERWHELMING DEVOTION TO THE OTHER BUT
THEN FEEL DEPENDENT AND UNHAPPY WITHOUT
THE OTHER. DO DEVOTION AND DEPENDENCE COME
TOGETHER LIKE TWO SIDES OF THE SAME COIN?
HAVING TASTED THE BEAUTY OF THE PEAK OF
DEVOTION I FEEL AN URGE TO ALWAYS LIVE THERE. IS
DEPENDENCE THE VALLEY TO THE PEAK OF
DEVOTION, AND TO BE ACCEPTED AS SUCH?

The question indicates one thing very clearly, and that is that you don't know what devotion is. Devotion and the feeling of dependence cannot exist together. The feeling of dependence arises in you when somebody enforces in a subtle slavery, particularly psychological and spiritual. Then it hurts, because these are the realms of freedom; nobody can force them upon another. Devotion is a flower of another world. It is not forced on you. Devotion is totally *your* act. You have responded to someone who has played on the guitar of your being.

It is a love affair, and love of the highest quality. It cannot feel dependence, because nobody is making you dependent. It can make you feel relaxed, because you have found a hand and the warmth of the hand and the love of the hand and the strength of the hand... although it is all dark all around.

Finding this hand, finding the master, you can relax. Now the journey is almost over. To have found the master – I repeat – the journey is almost over. And the master can only shower you with his love – there is no question of any power number; you cannot feel dependence.

And you are free at any moment to withdraw your devotion. Nobody is going to prevent you except the experience of devotion itself, because you have never known so many stars in your life. You have never known so many colors in your life, you have never danced, you have never been in such an ecstasy that the dance arises out of it; not out of technological knowledge, not because you know dancing. Ecstasy brings a dance which is fresh, beyond technique, beyond learning.

I have never heard that anybody who has reached the point of devotion has ever fallen back – it is impossible. For what will you fall back? What have you left behind, except misery and darkness? What was your life before devotion? – nothing but hell.

Your question is only intellectual. Intellectually, you thought that in devotion there must be dependence; you are devoted, you have to be obedient. But there is a great surprise for you....

The greatest master never gives orders. That belongs to the very lowest categories of teachers, not masters. A master simply creates a certain energy field in which you start changing, transforming. One day suddenly your old life is dropped, like a snake slipping out of its old skin. He does not even look back.

Devotion will transform you – from a thousand and one dependencies in your life towards an independent individual. Devotion can become the door for the highest liberation possible.

But people get into trouble because they're always thinking rather than experimenting. Experiment. Experience; then your question will have a reality about it. About such questions you can have a good conversation, but these questions are not going to help you in any way. That's why I told you from the very beginning that you don't have any experience of devotion. You know only the experience of dependence. In love, you have found dependence. In friendship, you have found dependence. In all your relationships, sooner or later you find you are caged.

In devotion you will find freedom – freedom not only from darkness, from death, but freedom from everything that you have known up to now – so that you can fly into the fresh sky, enjoying the exhilaration, the ecstasy of the new, of the novel, of the mysterious.

18
Totality: The foundation of freedom

BELOVED OSHO,
HERE AGAIN, I FIND MYSELF IN THE DISTRESS OF A
RELATIONSHIP FINISHING. IT'S STILL THE SAME
PATTERN. I FEEL THAT I CANNOT DEAL WITH IT ANY
DIFFERENTLY THAN BEFORE. IS THERE NO OTHER
WAY THAN PLAYING THE RECORD AGAIN AND
AGAIN AND AGAIN AND JUST WATCHING IT? EACH
TIME, I THINK, "WITH AWARENESS IT WILL BE
DIFFERENT THIS TIME." BUT NO – THE ANGER, THE
DISTRESS, THE HURT, THE ALONENESS, AND ALSO
THE UNDERSTANDING THAT LOVE COMES AND
FADES AWAY. I ALSO AM DOUBTING THAT THESE
MOMENTS OF LOVE WERE REAL. BUT WHEN THOSE
MOMENTS OF LOVE AND CONNECTING ARE THERE,
THEY DO FEEL REAL.

Life is a vicious circle. One things lead to another thing until the circle is complete. To go on moving in a circle is boring, is monotonous, is heavy on the heart. It destroys all playfulness, it destroys weightlessness; it takes away the charm, the magnetic pull towards life. You go again and again in the same routine, in the same circle, unwillingly. You do not want to repeat; nobody wants to repeat. Repetition is the function of a machine. Wherever there is a consciousness, there is a revolt against mechanical repetition.

So I can understand your tragedy. Moreover, it is the tragedy of millions of human beings. They are all caught in a circle and then they don't know how to jump out of it.

The problem can be reduced to very simple terms: You find it difficult to jump out of the routine because you have some vested interest in the routine. If it were a hundred percent boring, a hundred percent nothing but a nightmare, you would have jumped out of it without asking anybody.

You don't need a map, you don't need a guide – all you need is totality in whatever life you are living. Totality is the foundation of freedom. Whenever you live something totally, either it is nourishing to your being – then you start absorbing it; it is no longer routine, it becomes your love affair – or you find that it is nothing but complete boredom. To see something as a hundred percent boredom and to ask how to come out of it is just stupid. It is as if your house is on fire and you are asking people from the window, "How to come out?" Just jump out of the window!

When the house is on fire, there is no question of manners, that you have to go from the right door, that you cannot go from the back door, that you cannot jump from the window. All those manners are good when the house is not on fire. Your houses *are* on fire, and you go on asking how to get out of it.

Nobody is holding you in. There must be some subtle investments which are forbidding you from coming out of a life that you don't like, that you don't love, that you don't rejoice in. Perhaps to be miserable helps you to get sympathy from people – from your wife, from your children, from your parents, from your friends. And because you have not known love, even sympathy is more than you can hope for. Sympathy is not love. It is not even a poor substitute for love. And the mind which starts asking for sympathy is sick. So you have to go inside your mind and find out what it is that is holding you in a fixed style of life.

Three hundred years ago, there was, in Bengal, a very great logician. Indian logic differs from Western logic, totally – and Western logic will remain childish unless it absorbs the vast developments of Indian logic. It is a ten-thousand-year work of love and art.

In the Middle Ages, Indian logic went through a revolution; a new logic came into being, replacing the old. The new was even more complex, but more comprehensive too. The man who helped the science of logic to reach its peak was a unique personality. He was so physically beautiful too, that people have forgotten his original name; they simply call him Gaurang Prabhu, "a beautiful god."

As he was getting to a marriageable age, his family was worried, because he was continuously studying, arguing... he never showed any ordinary, mundane interests. He was in his own category.

They were afraid. If he said no, then it was no forever, so one had to be very diplomatic with such a person. To bring out the yes, you cannot be straightforward, just asking a question. But finally it had to be asked.

They tried in different ways to work it out, but anyway marriage had to be mentioned. And knowing Gaurang very well... if he says yes, then nothing can prevent him. The whole tradition of celibacy will not prevent him – but if he says no, then there is no hope at all.

They were very loving towards him, creating an atmosphere, waiting for the right moment, and Gaurang was watching the whole scene that was going on in the house.

One evening, he went to his father and he said, "Why this unnecessary drama? You just be sincere and honest. What do you want from me?"

The father said, "We never wanted to confront you or to put you in a position where you have to choose between yes and no – but since you are asking, the question is marriage. We have found a beautiful woman. Are you willing to marry?"

He said, "I have been marrying for many, many lives. And the only result has been misery and anguish and anxiety. In my past lives, twice I have committed suicide. Once I have killed a woman – my wife! I am not such an idiot, to go on repeating the same circle – I am jumping out of it. I am not saying no, I am not saying yes. I am simply out of it. Even a relationship of 'no' is dangerous because 'no' can be changed into 'yes'; they are not as separate as they appear. 'Yes' can become any time 'no.' So I am not saying yes or no because I am simply out of the vicious circle."

I don't know whether the father understood him or not, but what he is saying is of great importance. You cannot solve the problems of your life remaining in the same vicious rut. You have to jump out. And the miracle is, the moment you jump out, all those problems subside and disappear. The only problem is being in the mind. And the only solution is to get beyond mind. I call it *meditation*.

Western psychology tries to solve the problem *inside* the mind. It has not yet come to the understanding that the mind itself is the problem. Problems arise out of mind just as leaves grow out of trees. You can go on cutting those leaves, pruning those leaves, and they will come thicker and thicker; the foliage will become thicker than before. You cannot solve problems of the mind by getting answers to them, because they are not intellectual problems. The problems are existential.

For example: you are thirsty, the problem is existential, and somebody starts giving you a discourse on thirst, on water, on the components of water; explains to you how water quenches the thirst. You will say, "That is all right, but I am thirsty *right now*. I am not interested that water is composed of hydrogen and oxygen, and that is not my problem. I am not inquiring intellectually about thirst and water; my problem is a problem of life and death."

I have heard.... On one Saturday night in a pub, there was a great crowd and people were enjoying. Suddenly, a stranger came from the street and announced in the pub: "I challenge anybody! My expertise is to tell the make of the wine, the year it was made, the company by which it was made — blindfolded, just by tasting it, I can tell you about all kinds of wines."

There was great interest; they were all wine lovers. Immediately, a black cloth was put over his eyes. Wine after wine was produced.... "Lafitte Rothschild, 1938."

The pub was running out of its wines, and each time he was right, about the make, about the year — even about the year! He had developed that sensitivity for almost half a century. And in fact, that had been his family's business for centuries — they were famous for being able to taste a wine and determine its quality, to decide the year of the wine.

Then, somebody produced a glass — he sipped... looked bewildered. He sipped again. There was pindrop silence. He sipped a third time and he said, "My God, this is urine!" He pulled off the black cloth covering the glass and he said, "Hell, you men! This is pure urine, fresh — still lukewarm!"

And in the crowd, from the back came a small voice, "But *whose*?"

Mind is such — question after question, relevant, irrelevant. Now the poor man, how is he to... he is a wine expert! He's not Morarji Desai. Morarji Desai perhaps could manage to tell whose urine this is and what year.

But any question, and any answer... the question will produce more questions from the answer, and in this way you can go on thinking your whole life, never reaching anywhere, never finding anything. Try to solve existential problems by existential methods. Except for meditation, you cannot find a space within you which is questionless. And as questions disappear, what purpose do answers have?

Questions gone, answers are also gone. You have come to feel the peace that passeth understanding, the serenity that becomes a song in somebody, that becomes dance in somebody else, and the ultimate feeling of being grounded, centered, which makes you part of the universe. And unless a man is a part of the universe – not theoretically but experientially – he cannot get rid of problems. Mind will go on producing questions ad infinitum.

Rather than think, it is better to enter into silence. Just moments of silence are more valuable than years of your work, because the work can give you only something of the world. Silence can give you the opening into the other world, the first glimpse of godliness.

BELOVED OSHO,
WHILE I WAS AT RAJNEESHPURAM, IT WAS
DISCOVERED I HAD CANCER. MY ANGUISH WAS THAT
I WOULD GET LOST IN AN UNCONSCIOUS DEATH
AND NOT FIND THE WAY BACK TO YOU. I AM
BOUNDLESSLY GRATEFUL THAT YOUR PRESENCE AND
GRACE HAVE HELPED IN HEALING ME. THE OTHER
DAY, I HAD FOOD POISONING – AND AGAIN, THE
ANGUISH. IT WAS EASY TO BE IDENTIFIED WITH THE
BODY IN PHYSICAL PAIN. I HEAR THAT DOCTORS
GIVE MORPHINE TO DYING PATIENTS TO RELIEVE THE
DISCOMFORT. BELOVED MASTER, PLEASE SPEAK ON
MEDITATION AT THE POINT OF DEATH. IS IT POSSIBLE
TO MEDITATE UNDER MEDICATION? AND WHAT
ABOUT THE CONSCIOUSNESS OF THOSE DYING
UNDER ANESTHESIA, SLEEP OR COMA?

A few things... first, there is no death as such. Death is the great illusion, because it always happens to the other; it never happens to you, so you always see it from the outside. You don't know what is happening *inside* at the very innermost center. Something tremendously valuable is happening there, but all that you know is that the man cannot speak, cannot breathe, cannot walk. His pulse is gone, his heartbeat is lost — he is dead.

It is not true. It is almost as if somebody says he loves and you dissect the man's heart and try to find out where love is. I don't think you will find where love is, because love is not matter. It is a quality. You can experience it but you cannot catch hold of it.

Life begins in unconsciousness. It has to begin in that way, because the child has to pass through a very narrow passage from the mother's womb to the outside world. The passage is very narrow and the child finds it almost equal to death, because he has lived for nine months in a world which is being taken away from him, where he was immensely blissful, peaceful, without any worry, no problems of employment, of education. He has lived for those nine months in a paradise.

In fact, the psychologists say that the idea of paradise is nothing but a projection of the conditions in the womb. The womb is so luxurious that the child is searching his whole life for the same old golden days again, when he lived together with his mother, not even feeling any separation, not even knowing that he was separate from the environment he's living in. The environment and he were one, and now he's being thrown out into an unknown, strange world.

In the mother's womb he was in utter silence. Outside, it is so noisy, so maddeningly noisy. In the mother's womb he is in darkness. Darkness is very soothing, relaxing, very essential for growth — that's why the roots of plants hide themselves under the ground, in darkness. A child hides himself in the mother's womb to find darkness. Now he's being thrown into the world full of glaring lights. And he's being cut from all the connections to the mother; the shock is traumatic. There is a possibility of some truth in the idea that he goes searching for the womb again, that the search for the womb is the search for paradise.

As the child grows, he becomes more and more aware that the world is not what it is supposed to be. It is ugly, it is cunning, it is in every way deceiving, cheating. You cannot trust anybody, you cannot love anybody. Friendship is only an empty word. Love exists only in poetry. In life, everything is a pain.

But you cannot jump out of this vicious circle of life for many reasons. First, you don't have any idea that there is another possibility of life, an alternative way of living. You know only the way people are living and they are all suffering, they're all miserable.

Naturally, you start accepting misery and suffering as natural. By and by, you become immune to them. This immunity is very dangerous. It means now there is no hope for you, because now there is no possibility of any inquiry. You are not going to inquire into yourself, into your consciousness, because you have already believed what others have been telling you.

A person who really wants to go through a revolution.... And only a revolution can make you free from the fear of death. Otherwise, you have experienced death in your birth, so you have some idea of it. You lost your paradise. Your birth may have been a time of celebration for others but not for you. For you, it was a terrible experience.

And when you again think of death, it is very natural to infer that the coming death is going to be a bigger phenomenon than the death you knew in birth. You have lived only nine months in the mother's womb and what kind of life was it? Although it was comfortable, luxurious, there was no adventure, no change; you were almost vegetating. For seventy years you live, you experience many things, and then again comes death. That is the circle becoming complete – you are coming back to the same zero point from where you began your life.

This death looming ahead of you seems to be more dangerous, because now you are experienced. You have seen hunger, starvation, death, and it creates a deep anguish: "One day I will not be here to see the sunrise. The sun will go on rising and the flowers will go on blossoming and the stars will always be there in the sky waiting, waiting, but I will never come again." Death will erase all your senses.

You have tasted a few moments of beauty, a few moments of love, a few moments of joy – only a few moments, but a single moment of joy is enough, and equal to eternity because in the moment of joy you forget time.

Your fear is everybody's fear. And because you see death from outside, it creates the whole problem. The man is not dying, because nothing dies. Death as such has never happened. But you see it happening every day. Looking from outside, if you are told that these two persons are deeply in love, what will you find from the outside? Perhaps they are holding hands, but holding hands is not love. You can hold somebody's hand for your whole life and wonder: what is happening? Love is not coming, only the hands are perspiring.

And if you try such an experiment, don't do it in Bombay! In Bombay, love is not possible, only perspiration. Bombay lovers have to pass through very arduous gymnastics. Love in Bombay first means the perspiration, the body odor, mixed with the smell of deodorants, all kinds of powders, all kinds of perfumes....

But from the outside, what can you judge? Even if two persons are hugging each other....You can note immediately that hugging is love – but hugging is not love. I know it perfectly. I had to stop going to Punjab because of hugging... the Sikhs are a fire test. If you can hug a sardarji, you can hug any wild wolf! They were hugging with great love, but without thinking that they can give me fractures. When I saw that things were going too far, I simply stopped going to Punjab.

Watching from outside, whatever you note down – hugging, kissing, holding hands – or even if you see people making love, then too you will not find what love is. Love is an interior experience. Only those two persons know. And those two persons don't know about both; each knows only about himself; the other is out. He may be pretending, he may be a hypocrite, he may have other purposes and love may be just a bribe. You can be certain only about your own love. And you can be certain only about your own death.

All love outside is imagination for you. All death outside is fear, paranoia – not a reality for you. But as you grow old, the illusory death becomes bigger and bigger, because life becomes shorter and shorter.

In the great Emperor Akbar's court, it happened one day.... He came into the court. He used to have a blackboard in his court, just as you have blackboards in the universities, because he was himself a learned man and his court was full of learned people. He had collected from all over the country all the geniuses in different dimensions.

Drawing a line on the blackboard, he asked the wise men of his court: "Can anyone make this line small without touching it?"

Now how can you make it small without touching it? You will have to touch it to make it small; you will have to erase some part of it. So all the wise people were at a loss. Finally, Akbar said to Birbal, who was the most intelligent person in his court: "The court seems to be silent. Have you some idea, or have you also accepted failure?"

Birbal went to the board and drew a bigger line above the line that Akbar had drawn. He made it small without touching it; just with the bigger line, the whole context had changed. Now, in comparison to the bigger line, the first line has become small.

Your life goes on becoming smaller and smaller. You know every day that life is being cut short. Every breath, and you are less alive than you were before. Every day passing, and your life is becoming less and less. You don't know exactly when death will come, but one thing is certain: whenever it comes, you will be almost at the end of your life. And life is slipping away; hence, fear goes on becoming bigger.

And then, man has faculties which he can use wrongly or rightly. For example, imagination – he can use it in art, in creative works. He can contribute to the world something of beauty, something of joy, can make it more colorful, more musical, can make it a beautiful garden of human beings, blossoming in their consciousness. But imagination can do just the opposite, too. As a man comes closer to death, his imagination starts turning towards death. He thinks of death more – naturally, because that is the reality that he is going to face.

I have heard.... In a park, three old ladies were sitting on a bench and gossiping. One lady said, "My husband returned two days ago and he brought two beautiful motorboats, and a yacht big enough for twelve people to live on. I am very much excited. He's planning to go for a long journey on our own boats."

The second woman said, "My husband has not been here for a few months. He returned only last night, and he has brought me a beautiful Cadillac. He has purchased a house in the mountains, and I am dying to get into the Cadillac and go to the house as quickly as possible."

The third woman said, "My husband is not rich. He is a poor man, but a unique man. If I could swap husbands with you, I would refuse. You can have your rich husbands who bring yachts and motorboats, Cadillacs, mountain houses; you can keep your rich husbands. My husband is rare. You cannot find another person in a million comparable to him. I am so proud of him."

Both ladies became so excited. They said, "Tell us – what is the uniqueness?"

She said, "The uniqueness is that on my husband's cock, thirteen birds can stand side by side!" Of course, nobody believed it.

The first woman said, "Forgive me, I was lying. My husband has not come; only a telegram that he will be coming soon. There are no boats, no yachts. Just the other day I have gone on a motorboat ride; that much is true."

The other woman said, "If you are telling the truth, I cannot be left behind. I will tell you the whole truth: I have not heard about my husband since we got married. He simply disappeared when we were on our honeymoon. We had gone together; I came back alone. There is no question of any Cadillac, there is no question of any house in the mountains. Just to console myself, I go on imagining such things. It feels good at least for the moment when you forget that it is simply imagination. All that happened is that the day before yesterday, I went in a small boat which is not even a motorboat, you have to row it with your own hands. Now they both turned towards the third.

The third woman said, "Okay, okay. If you are telling the truth, then I will tell the truth also. The business about thirteen birds standing on the cock of my husband, side by side, is not right. The thirteenth bird has to stand on only one leg." People live in exaggerations.

And about death, everybody has a very dark, black, dangerous picture somewhere in the unconscious. And the strange thing is, death does not exist at all.

You have asked what happens to those people who die in coma, in unconsciousness, under some anesthesia. In fact – whether you are in a coma or under anesthesia, or in an accident, a sudden death – everybody except those who have realized themselves becomes unconscious before death. So it is not a question of only a small group dying in coma, dying under anesthesia, dying in unconsciousness on a surgeon's table or in an accident. *Everybody* dies unconscious. As death comes closer – and when I say as death comes closer, I mean as your life starts slipping out of your body, getting ready to enter into another womb – nature has an inbuilt program. The person becomes unconscious, because it is the greatest surgery that is happening. His whole being has to be taken from his body, in which it has lived, identified, for seventy or eighty years.

It is a natural phenomenon that before death, everybody goes into unconsciousness. In fact, Sushrut, the greatest surgeon the East has produced and the ancientmost, seven thousand years have passed since Sushrut was alive.... According to Sushrut – and he was perhaps the first surgeon of such great genius in the whole history of man – surgery learned the art of anesthesia from the common death.

Seeing that everybody becomes unconscious before dying, it became a clue. It means that such a great surgery is going to happen that the man may not be able to withstand it consciously. It is better to let him go deep into sleep, and in that sleep the transfer of the soul is easier.

That is why you don't remember your past life, because that gap of unconsciousness functions as a barrier. So it has two functions. It helps you to be moved from one body to another body. It has another function also: that gap of unconsciousness is so deep – the deepest possible – that it becomes a block to the memories of your past life. Because those memories are risky....

You are not able to make a beautiful life of what you have right now, and if your mind starts getting bombarded by your past lives and experiences, you are *sure* to go mad. You will not be able to figure out what is happening; it is almost like all the stations on your radio are turned on together. Life will become impossible, because as far as those memories of the past are concerned, when they open their doors it is not like a memory. It is not just in the mind, it is almost like reliving it. You forget completely that this is a memory; you start acting out your past life. And if you know many past lives, you are certainly bound to go mad – you cannot manage. Sushrut is right, that the first clue about operations.... He was the greatest surgeon, the first surgeon who wrote books on surgery, the first surgeon who described all the finest instruments that we have developed now.

But still, the East has a totally different approach from the West. In the West, surgery became more and more important, although it is only three hundred years old. It has been replacing medicine every day and taking its place. And its ambition is to create plastic organs so that whenever something goes wrong, there is no need to cure it – just replace it with a plastic mechanism. And the plastic mechanism never becomes sick; it is hoped that it will be lifelong.

For example, a plastic heart will not start beating harder if you see a beautiful woman. A plastic heart is, after all, a plastic heart, unless you have some special arrangements... a remote controller: "What are you doing? A beautiful woman is coming, go on!" Otherwise your heart will simply go on as usual.

In North Carolina, when they arrested me, they tried to show the whole world that they were treating me almost as a guest of President Ronald Reagan. They were afraid that if something happened, even accidental, then the whole blame would go to the United States government. So first they put me in the hospital section of the jail. I had six nurses, and one woman doctor. Before entering my name in the register, they examined my pulse, my heartbeat, my blood pressure. One nurse was taking my blood pressure and the head nurse just joked; she said, "Whenever a woman takes the blood pressure it goes a little high."

I said, "It will not be the case with me. It may go a little low but it cannot go a little high." She said, "What do you mean?"

I said, "It is better you don't ask me, because these nurses may feel hurt."

These nurses said, "No, we will not feel hurt; you just say it."

I said, "I have got so many beautiful women around me, and it is not so simple for me to decide who is a woman and who is a man. I have to look again to see that yes, she is a woman and this is a man."

A few of our sannyasins were also in the jail with me. The head nurse must have told them what I said: "I have so many beautiful women around me that you cannot hope to have a better and more beautiful nurse in your jail." Our sannyasins were very happy. She told me, "Your girls are very happy." I said, "They deserve to be!"

While I was there, one man died. And I felt his death in almost all of the six remaining inmates of the cell – they were all half-dead. I tried my best: "You are not dead! And I can give it to you in writing that you will never be dead. If it happens that by mistake you *are* dead, then come to me with the paper." He said, "But where will I find you?"

I said, "You are stupid. The first thing is not to find me, the first thing is that you are dead!"

He said, "My God, but you were persuading me that there is no death."

I said, "Yes, there is no death. But there is constant change in existence. It is a renewal; hence, there are seasons, hence there is childhood, youth, old age, death. Life goes on replacing better bodies, better minds, better consciousness. If we don't use it, it is our fault."

You are worried about death. You should be worried about meditation. Meditation is the only way you can know, while living, that there is no death. The other way, you ask me about people who are in coma, people who have anesthesia, people who are unconscious because of some accident – "What happens to these people?" Nothing special, it is the same business. They move into another body. The people who are left behind think they are dead.

They have simply moved into a new form, into a new sensitivity, into a new intelligence.

This life is a university. Here, we have to learn only one thing: that death does not exist, that life is eternal. But you have to experience it.

BELOVED OSHO,
SOMETIMES, WHEN I SUDDENLY BECOME AWARE OF THIS CLINGING MIND, WHICH IS ONLY CLAIMING TO BE AWARE BUT IS ACTUALLY MOVING OUT OF THIS VERY MOMENT, MY BEING STARTS TO LAUGH JUST FOR A FEW MOMENTS. THEN MY MIND TAKES OVER AGAIN. IT IS ALWAYS DESTROYING BEAUTIFUL MOMENTS WHERE IT MIGHT GET LOST. IT LOOKS LIKE I'M MISSING TRUST, AND NOW THERE IS SOMETHING I JUST CAN'T UNDERSTAND: I FEEL TRUST IN EXISTENCE BUT I CAN HARDLY TRUST HUMANS. MY BELOVED, BEAUTIFUL MASTER, WOULD YOU PLEASE SAY SOMETHING ABOUT THIS? COULD MY TRUST IN YOU BE A MIND GAME, AN ILLUSION, AS LONG AS I CAN'T TRUST IN SO-CALLED HUMANS? OR COULD IT BE JUST A BEGINNING?

It is certainly difficult to love and trust human beings, because they will create every kind of barrier. They will give you every opportunity to prove to yourself that nobody is worth trusting, nobody is worth loving; on the contrary, they are all taking advantage of your trust, your love, your friendship. One becomes hard, one becomes closed.

You love me. At least that is a good sign. If you can love one human being, you can love the whole of humanity. It is just that you have been expecting too much, demanding too much, asking human beings to be almost gods. When they cannot live up to your standards, then you are frustrated, then you are angry. It is not their fault. They are doing what they can do. You trusted them because you can trust and they deceived you because they can deceive. I don't see the problem. It fits perfectly well: for somebody to deceive, somebody is needed to trust.

Mulla Nasruddin had become an honorary magistrate and his first case came to court. He heard one party and he said, "Wait for the judgment."

The court clerk could not believe it, because the other party had not been heard at all. They were standing there with their attorneys. So he whispered in Mulla Nasruddin's ear: "Mulla, perhaps you are not aware of the procedure of the court. The other party is here, they are the defendants. Before listening to them, what kind of judgment can you give?"

Mulla Nasruddin said, "Be silent! Keep quiet! Don't disturb me! In fact, that is the reason why I am not allowing the other party to speak, because they will say things against the first party and the whole trouble will be on my mind – confusion, who is right, who is wrong. I am avoiding everything and finishing the case immediately! Right now, I am absolutely clear. I am not certain whether, when I have heard the other party too, I will be able to make the judgment or not."

Life is very simple if you are unprejudiced. If you are prejudiced, life becomes a continuously growing complexity. Every thread becomes entangled; it becomes more and more difficult to find a way out. But the way is one. Your problems may be different, your confusions may be different; that does not matter. The path is very simple. The path is to get out of the mind as many times in the day as possible. Whenever you have time, just get out of the mind.

A few things can be helpful. If you cannot be silent just by sitting, if you feel too much energy to do something and if you don't do it then the whole energy becomes a mind game, it is easier to begin with some creativity. If you are interested in music, play music, and get drowned in it. If you love dance, dance, and let the dancer disappear. Or anything – if you know pottery, make beautiful pots, bringing your total energy to it. Because when you bring your total energy to something, mind does not get any energy, and becomes silent on its own accord.

And it is only in the beginning that you have to do some work to keep yourself engaged, so the energy moves into that engagement and the mind becomes silent. Soon you will be able to sit silently, doing nothing, and the mind becomes utterly silent. In those moments you will know the eternity of life, you will know the beauty of this fragile existence around you, and also the great treasure of your own being.

Knowing these things, misery becomes impossible. You don't have any complaint, any grudge. You have only a deep gratitude towards existence. And if you love existence then there is no problem – just love it more. Love it so totally that your mind stops completely. The moment your mind stops completely, you will not find the problem that you are finding now, that you cannot love human beings.

It is not a question of loving human beings or animals or birds or trees. It is a question of being loving – even sitting in your room – just being loving, just being joyous, just being always in a singing mood. It is in your hands. And don't just go on asking questions.

Remember: when I answer you, try something of it in your life, because only your effort is going to transform you in such a way that all problems, all sicknesses, simply evaporate. And a man is not alive unless he is psychologically completely healthy. The body is going to be sick sometimes, because it has to become old, it has to die too. The burden of the body is big, but *you* are not going to be sick because consciousness cannot be sick, and consciousness cannot be old, and consciousness cannot be dead.

If you have been meditating in your life, at the moment of death you will remain aware. So very few people die with awareness. For those who die with awareness, this is their last death. Now they will not need to suffer the routine, boring, monotonous circles of life. If you are dying fully aware, you will be able to see the mystery of life and death separating – it is one of the great mysteries. And you will be able to enter into a new womb fully alert – your life has been a success. To me, this is the only success that is worth calling success.

BELOVED OSHO,
THOUGH I SEARCH, I CAN FIND NO OTHER.
EVERYTHING I FIND IS THIS ONE, ONLY THIS ONE.
THIS ONE ARISES AS A SENSELESS SENSATION, MORE
DELICIOUS THAN ANYTHING I'VE KNOWN BEFORE
AND GROWS INTO A BEAUTIFUL VAST ALONENESS. IT
IS AS IF MY EXPANSION WOULD HAVE NO END. THEN
SUDDENLY I JUMP OUT OF IT AND EXPERIENCE A
TERROR OF DEATH, AND I PANIC THAT TIME IS SO
SHORT AND I HAVE SO FAR TO GO. CAN YOU HELP
ME TO UNDERSTAND THIS JUMP BETWEEN ONENESS
AND SEPARATENESS, TIMELESSNESS AND TIME?

Surabhi, the experience you are going through is perfectly beautiful. You are on the right line... just a little more courage. You come to the point of merger, and that is the time when you jump off, because merger looks like death. It is just your interpretation.

You don't know merger, you don't know death, but you have heard: all around, death-oriented philosophies, religions, life-negative theologies, philosophies, are pouring as much crap in your minds as possible. You have to see one thing: that whatever you know is not your own. Put your knowledge aside – to brag about borrowed knowledge is not right. But man has a tendency to brag. He wants to have this, to become that, and he cannot. Then he starts bragging, and the danger is that he may start believing in his own bragging. Then he has no future.

I have heard... one old man went to his physician and asked for a thorough check-up. The physician said, "What is the need? You are so healthy. At this age," – he was eighty-three; tomorrow was his birthday – "why do you want a physical, a thorough examination?"

He said, "Doctor, I am going to marry an eighteen-year-old girl tonight. I want you to check my whole body thoroughly, because everybody is against it. My sons are against it, my neighbors are against it, my daughters-in-law are against it – even the small children are against it! And you are also against it. It seems nobody wants me to live a pleasant life. Are you my friends or my enemies? But even if the whole world is against me, I am going to do it!"

The doctor said, "If you are determined to do it, do it. Just one suggestion: you can keep a boarder also in your house. That may help your married life. He will have his wife also, not to become a trouble to you. Find a young, beautiful boarder."

The old man thought, and he said, "Okay, if you say so, I will do it."

After six months, the doctor saw the old man in a fund raising meeting. He was looking almost like a ghost – just a skeleton sitting on a wheelchair. Somehow, he managed to come to the doctor and he said to him, "Congratulate me, my wife is pregnant."

The doctor had difficulty to maintaining his poise, but he managed, he was a professional. And he asked, "That's very good, that's great news. And did you follow my advice?"

He said, "Of course, of course, I have a young boarder, too." The doctor said, "That's very good."

The old man said, "This is nothing, you have not yet heard the whole story – the boarder's wife is also pregnant!"

Now it would be very difficult to convince this man that he cannot make women pregnant – he even made two women pregnant! Man has such a subtle ego that he goes on claiming things he has not got, that he goes on knowing things that he has no knowledge of. He's not ready to listen to someone with his heart, nor with his mind. Unless you listen from the heart, the alchemy of love cannot transform you.

You are ready. Just a little push and your life will take a new turn, a new turn towards healthier values, more human qualities, more divine flowers.

19

Silence brings revelations, not words

BELOVED OSHO,
FOR TWENTY YEARS, I HAVE DONE FILM WORK. ALL
MY FIRST FILMS ARE WITHOUT SOUND. I NEVER
COULD FIND SOUND FOR THEM BUT THE MUTENESS
OF THESE FILMS, IN FACT, I COULD NOT ACCEPT. THEY
DID NOT SEEM COMPLETE AND ONLY SOMETIMES I
PRESENTED THEM TO PEOPLE. WORKING IN THIS
WAY, I COULD NOT BE SUCCESSFUL. SINCE I MET YOU
FIVE YEARS AGO, EVERYTHING HAS CHANGED. IN
THE LAST FOUR YEARS, I HAVE WORKED MORE AND
MORE FOR GERMAN TELEVISION – BUT MOST OF THE
PEOPLE WHO WORK IN TELEVISION ARE POLITICIANS
AND LAWYERS. THEY WORK ONLY WITH WORDS.
THEY CANNOT ACCEPT PICTURES IN THE PROGRAM
WITHOUT EXPLANATIONS OR COMMENTARY. MY
PICTURES ARE COMING FROM MY INNER SILENCE.
YOU HAVE SAID WORDS ARE CONTAINERS. WHAT IS
IN THE MEANING OF PICTURES? PLEASE OSHO, SPEAK
ABOUT THE DIFFERENCE BETWEEN WORDS AND
PICTURES.

There is a great difference between words and pictures. First, pictures are older. The child dreams, although he cannot speak. He can see, although he cannot say what it is. And the pictures in his mind are more alive, more vibrant, more radiant, more innocent.

It happened in a small school.... The teacher had been explaining to the students the Christian idea of the trinity. Her whole emphasis was on the life and teachings of Jesus Christ. After speaking for almost one hour, she asked the students a simple question: "Who is the greatest man on the earth?" It was an international school.

An American boy stood up and said, "Abraham Lincoln."

The teacher was shocked. After hammering for one hour on Jesus Christ, this boy had not heard a single word. But she said to the boy; "It is not absolutely right, although you are very close to the right answer."

An English boy said, "Winston Churchill," and so on and so

forth it went. And then a very small boy who never used to raise his hand or stand up or answer on his own initiative, suddenly started waving his hand, almost madly. He was afraid somebody else might say the right answer.

The teacher said, "You look really in a hurry, so you stand up."

When he stood, he said, "There is no question. Jesus Christ is obviously the greatest man in the world."

This was even more shocking because the boy was a Jew. All the Christians had missed – somebody was with Abraham Lincoln, somebody was with Albert Einstein, somebody was with Winston Churchill, somebody was with Karl Marx, somebody was with Sigmund Freud – strange, that a small Jew was the only one who would stand for Jesus Christ. He won the prize – there was a prize for answering this question.

After the class was over, the teacher caught hold of the boy outside in the corridor and asked him, "Are you not a Jew?" He said, "Certainly, I am a Jew."

She said, "Then, why did you say Jesus is the greatest man?"

The boy laughed. He said, "In my heart of my hearts, I know that Moses is the greatest man the earth has produced or will ever produce, but then business is business!"

Now, Jesus Christ is only business to this boy. And he is innocent and honest and true.

Man as such is covered with many prejudices. He thinks he thinks – that's a fallacy. He only repeats prejudices handed over to him by others. Unless a mind is completely vacated, unoccupied by all kinds of prejudices, you cannot understand anything of real, authentic value. Mind can understand only that which is mundane. But in a state of having an empty mind – fully alert and aflame but with no thoughts, no desires, no imaginations – you can see the reality as it is, because the word is no longer distorting your vision.

A picture comes from the object to you. If you are clean and clear, mirror-like, reflecting, your reflection can come very close to truth, to beauty, to bliss, to God. But the mind is so full of words, full of so many interpretations, so many explanations, that whatever you see is not seen exactly as it is.

A picture comes to you from the object; a word does not

come to you from anywhere. A word is a human creation. It is a soap bubble: while it is there, it may shine in the sun like a rainbow, but it is not there for long. Primitive people still think in pictures. Hence, they have a certain authority, a certain being, a certain centeredness. The modern man, compared to them, is uprooted. Children think in pictures. Thinking in pictures you bring with yourself; thinking in words is a social arrangement. Words and language are our manufactured commodities, and we have manufactured them for convenience, not for truth.

There are a few languages – for example, Chinese, Japanese and other far Eastern languages – which are pictorial. Because they are pictorial, they have more authenticity, more vitality, more resonance – but the language is very difficult to learn. Chinese needs at least thirty years to learn because it has no alphabet, it has only pictures – pictures for *everything* in the world. Now to remember those picture-grams... you need at least a million words, a million pictures to be a scholar. Just learning a few words will not do.

Other languages, which are no longer pictorial, which have found a new way, are alphabetical. Learning those languages is simple – twenty-six letters and the whole language is finished. All the words will be combinations of the same twenty-six letters. But in Chinese, there is no limitation. They have millions of picture-grams, and every day new things are happening, new discoveries are being made. China and Japan have to find new pictures for them.

It is closer to the heart, but certainly anything that is closer to the heart becomes automatically incapable of searching into the objective world. The heart cannot be just a bystander and go on watching the scientific experiment without interfering, without coming in.

For almost seven years, the Senate of America has been denying the fact that they have been supplying millions of dollars worth of weapons to the terrorists. Only just this week, they have been forced, simply by the facts, to admit that they had been supplying millions of dollars worth weapons to the terrorists. The question might not have arisen except that President Ronald Reagan asked that two-hundred million dollars immediately be sent to a country, to the terrorists there, because the country has become communist. So now the society has to be destroyed, order has to be turned into chaos. And it is none of America's business.

If somebody wants to be a communist, if some country *chooses* to be communist, it does not matter whether you agree with it or not. Your agreement is simply not the question. I may agree, I may not agree but on *this* point, I am absolutely certain: they should be given the opportunity to be, whatsoever they want to be. I can show my disagreement, I can place all the evidence against them, all the arguments against them – but terrorism is not an argument, it is a defeat. And when a great country, the greatest power in the world, starts using such third-rate strategies, then it seems there is no hope for humanity.

The day the German parliament passed an order that I could not enter Germany, they allowed on the same day.... And the reason given to the parliament was " because this man is dangerous." A man who has not even a paper knife is dangerous.... And in the same week, they allowed terrorists from around the whole world to have a world conference in Munich. It seems that just out of fear, they could not say no to the terrorists. And they are not dangerous!

One night I was denied a six-hour stay at the airport's first-class lounge in England – which is made for that. There is no opening from the lounge into the city; it is completely closed, you cannot get out of it. It is for passengers who have to change planes, for their rest. They did not allow me, and for the same reason. The officer had a file from the parliament saying that "this man is dangerous and he should not be allowed in England."

I said, "You are *not* allowing me in England, but six hours' rest *outside* England – this is an international airport."

He said, "I cannot argue with you. Perhaps you are logically right, but the problem is that the orders come from above – I have to follow them."

And the same English government, the next week allowed Ronald Reagan a base to bomb Libya – the base was in England. America bombing an innocent country, a poor country, and completely out of a misunderstanding. Is this not dangerous – is this something very cultured, civilized, something without which we cannot evolve?

People go on thinking in words, and then they become *heartless* because the words have no connection with the heart. Then they can do strange things.

In the last week, America has also admitted one great crime – and I simply cannot believe that the whole world simply remains silent. They were not admitting it for two years. And we never say to our politicians and leaders and priests that "You are continuously lying – how long we can trust you? You are demanding something inhuman and impossible. Your behavior does not allow anybody to trust you."

For two years they were saying that nothing like this has happened. How can it happen in a democracy? The problem was, there were rumors that the American Senate had given permission that on two hundred patients first, and then on five hundred more patients, a certain experiment could be done. It is part of the preparation for the coming atomic war. Seven hundred persons, without their permission – and this is democracy! – had their brains operated on! And all seven hundred patients died.

The government continued to deny that they had anything to do with it, but finally it has come to the light. And now, without any shame, they accept that yes, they have done it, because it is a question of saving the whole of humanity. Men have to be used as guinea pigs. This is the first time that any government has said that, and has already killed seven hundred people – without their permission. And the whole world goes on! Nobody raises a hand to say that "This is not democracy, and this is not even human!"

And if the government can do this, the government can do anything – every child's brain can be fixed with an electrode. He will never know, but because of that electrode, the government can know what is going on in his mind. The government can change gears, it can change the thinking that is going on in his mind. Government becomes all-powerful. Man is reduced to below the level of machines. And the whole thing has happened because we have been living for thousands of years in the head. The head cannot think in pictures. The heart cannot understand words. Both are needed – but the heart should be in power and the head should be in service, because love is the ultimate law. No law can be above it.

BELOVED OSHO, IS THERE ANYTHING LIKE DESTINY
IN LIFE OR DO WE CREATE OUR FUTURE MOMENT TO
MOMENT?

It all depends on you. If you behave mechanically, uncon-sciously, life has a destiny. Then you are simply following a certain program that your biology, your physiology, your chemistry, your hormones, have given to you. You *appear* to be free but you are not.

And you know – when you fall in love, you know you are not free. It is not your choice. Suddenly you feel you are in love and there is nothing that you can do either to improve upon it or to get away from it. In either case, you will destroy the delicate phe-nomenon of love. Almost everybody has done that. Either people are trying to do too much... and love is not something that you can do. You can be loving but you cannot be a doer. Loving is a relaxed state of non-doing. You simply are. You cannot increase it; you cannot have more love or less love – it simply happens.

In life, everything that is important only *happens*. Things that you have to *do* are unimportant things – utilitarian, needed, but not essential to your being. One of the greatest things to learn on the path is to discriminate between these two different worlds: the world of *doing* and the world of *happening*. They are all mixed up in your minds. There are things that can only be done – you can-not just wait for existence to do them for you. And there are things that, whatever you do, you are going to fail. Only in your utter failure, when you give up, they happen. They happen from the beyond.

A whole man is available to both, to doing and to happening. But remember: whatever you do is momentary; and whatever you do is lower than you, it cannot be higher than you. Action cannot be higher than the doer. And in *happening*, whatsoever happens is higher than you; it comes upon you from above. It showers on you as if it is a rain of flowers, blessings, benediction.

So if a man can sort out that which is *doing* and that which is *happening*, his life will have a clarity, a great intelligence, and a tremendous possibility of fulfillment. As you move towards happening, words will start disappearing. Pictures, visions, colors that you have never seen, fragrances that are unknown to you....

In doing, pictures are not needed, so pictures slowly, slowly disappear from the conscious mind. They start living in the underground, in the unconscious mind. That's why there are no words in your dreams. In your dreams, there are pictures. Those pictures are saying something but you have forgotten the language. You cannot interpret your own dream; you have to find a psychoanalyst, and that too is pure guesswork. If you go to a few psychoanalysts, analytical psychologists... psychosynthesis – and there are hundreds of schools of therapies – you will be amazed that they all interpret your dream in different ways, almost contrary to each other. And your dream cannot have so many meanings – your dream has only one meaning, and that one meaning has not been possible to discover through psychoanalysis, because psychoanalysis is basically a thinker's game, a word game. It is head-oriented.

Now, words cannot interpret pictures. What can you do if you see a beautiful sunset, so glorious in color, so silent and everything becoming more and more silent and still? You are enchanted with the beauty, you are overwhelmed, but what can you say about it in words? Just saying "a beautiful sunset" does not carry much meaning. And this sunset is something *outside*, so everybody knows – even if you say "a beautiful sunset," something is understood – but about the experiences of the inner world, which will all be pictorial, no word is capable to express them. Hence, beware of words. In silence you will have revelations, not words. You may have colors, you may have light, you may have beautiful darkness. You may have flowers, you may have the silence of the midnight sky. You may have all kinds of experiences, but the moment you start speaking about them, you will find yourself falling dumb. This is a good sign. This is a sign that what is happening to you is true.

BELOVED OSHO, THE IDEA OF YOU LEAVING THE
BODY MAKES ME VERY SAD AND SHAKY BECAUSE
EVEN NOW, I FEEL WANTING BUT NEVER REACHING
YOU COMPLETELY. SOMETHING INVISIBLE,
UNTOUCHABLE AND VERY BEAUTIFUL ALWAYS
HAPPENS BETWEEN YOU AND ME, BUT WHENEVER I
FEEL IT IS THERE, IT IS ALREADY GONE. THE JOY OF
THESE VERY BRIGHT MOMENTS CREATES MORE AND
MORE LONGING. THEN I FEEL YOU ARE THE ONLY
ONE WHO CAN TRIGGER THAT PROCESS AGAIN
UNTIL I FEEL REALLY FREE AND FLYING. I THINK I
HAVE TO HURRY. BELOVED OSHO, WHAT IS THE
RIGHT SPEED FOR OUR MEETING? WHAT IS NEEDED
TO MAKE IT LAST FOREVER?

It is a beautiful question. First, the right speed to meet me is no speed. Just sitting silently, doing nothing – let the spring come, and I will be there. It is not that you have to go somewhere. It is not an achievement. There is no goal. It is within *you*.

If you want to be acquainted with yourself, you have to learn the simple art of being silent. The moment you are perfectly silent, life goes through a radical change. Beautiful moments come to you even now, but they are only moments – you become aware and they are gone. You always see them going. You always see their backs; they are putting on their shoes. You have to be a little more alert. Events that will be happening to you and to everybody else – you have to be alert to see the face, not the back.

Once, Henry Ford was asked: "How did you become so rich?" because he was born a poor man and became the richest man in the world.

He said, "Very simple. I never missed any opportunity."

Those people said, "That kind of wisdom everybody knows, but the problem is how to recognize that this is opportunity? In our lives, by the time we recognize it, it is gone."

In fact, you have to recognize *before* it has come. You have to be a little prophetic, you have to be a little predictive. You have to see a little ahead, what is going to happen, so that you can be ready.

But the future remains unknown. You become aware of something only when it has become present. This is a very difficult and tough situation. By the time you can grab hold of it, it is gone, and you cannot bring any moment back.

Henry Ford said, "My method is different. My method is to go on jogging continuously so whenever the opportunity comes, you simply jump on top of it – but keep on jogging because one never knows. It is a little difficult, but it has worked for me. I hope it can work for you."

The man said, "But it looks crazy – the whole time jogging!"

Ford said, "I don't know any other method."

What he's saying is of some great value. He simply means you have to be *very* alert, as if your life is in danger.

A Hindu priest was tired of a man – not because he was creating any trouble for him, but because he was so obedient and was such a perfectionist that he was doing *everything* the Hindu monk was saying to do and nothing was happening. With others, it was easy – the monk could tell them, "You are not doing it rightly. You are not doing it totally; you are half-half, wishy-washy." But he could not say that to this man – he was so total, and he had never said no to anything.

Finally, the monk said to him, that "I am getting old and I'm sorry that I have not been helpful to you. You have to move to another master. Just one thing you should remember; this is my present to you: you have been such a rare disciple, that nothing else matters. What matters is your depth of awareness. If you are fully aware, you can change *everything*. Once something has happened, it has happened; you cannot do anything. If it has not happened, you are still the master. You can move it in any direction; give it any mold, any meaning – but only *before* it has happened. You have to be ready."

Painters are continuously ready for the moment when something will strike their intelligence, will open a door, a vision. Poets are continuously aware of when something clicks in them and they become silent and the beyond starts raining on them. All creative people are aware that only during moments of awareness, creativity happens. When you are not aware, you cannot create – you are just a driftwood.

The question about destiny, I said, depends on you. If you are living a somnambulistic life, almost asleep, then your life is predictable, because you are not using consciousness. You are being dominated by unconscious forces within you, and those forces don't have eyes – those forces are blind.

It is because of this that there are things like astrology, palmistry, the I Ching, and a thousand other methods and scriptures. They depend on your mechanicalness. Only a machine is reliable. A man, because he is conscious, can choose any moment a different direction, can choose to be something else than what the astrologers have predicted.

I was in Jaipur, and one famous astrologer there... he was the astrologer of the Maharaja of Jaipur, and I was staying in the Maharaja's palace. The Maharaja was very curious and wanted his astrologer to look at my hand.

His astrologer came, of course with great expectations of receiving a good reward. Before putting my hand into his hand, I asked him: "Are you aware, what kind of man you are going to encounter?" He said, "Of course, I am aware."

He looked into my hand. He worked out some charts, some arithmetic for half an hour, and then he was going to say what he had found.

I said, "Before you say anything, I want to say one thing to you: I will not give you any money because I think this is all nonsense. You are predicting my future and you don't know *your* future: that this man is not going to give you a single rupee. You should have let go of my hand, knowing that 'this man is not going to give me a single rupee.' That would have proved to me that there must be some validity in astrology, in palmistry. But you missed the chance. Next time, when I come again...."

Any action done unconsciously is a mechanical act, done under mechanical laws. Then you have destiny. Any action done with consciousness is beyond the powers of mechanical, robot-like functioning. Any act done with alertness is beyond the powers of destiny. And that's why we call the man who is enlightened, *liberated* – liberated from the chains of destiny.

BELOVED OSHO,
LISTENING TO YOU HAS CHANGED. I USED TO
REMEMBER WHAT YOU SAY; THE WORDS WERE
IMPORTANT. NOW I CANNOT FOLLOW ANYMORE. I
FEEL LIKE A CHILD WHOSE DADDY IS TALKING TO
SOME VISITORS IN A COZY ATMOSPHERE AND I AM
SITTING AT HIS SIDE – CONTENTED, AT HOME, NO
EXCITEMENT, BUT EVERYTHING IS AS IT SHOULD BE.
NO NEEDS, NO QUESTIONS. IS THIS CHILDISH,
BELOVED OSHO? AM I MISSING SOME INSIGHT GIVEN
IN YOUR WORDS?

No. You are not missing anything, because I am not in my words. I am just around my words. Go on throwing my words away and collecting the nothingness that surrounds my words. Collect that music. Collect that hum. You will become more and more like a child. The day you have become completely, entirely a child – that means you don't even remember that you are a child – you simply *are*. When innocence has reached its peak, the purpose of existence in you is fulfilled.

You were born a child; that's the way God has sent you into the world. You should go back more innocent than you came, more beautiful than you came, more silent, more ecstatic, more divine. Your life is a preparation for meeting the ultimate, and only a child is capable of meeting the ultimate. His truthfulness....

Remember one thing: even qualities are different. An old man may use truth in such a way that it harms somebody; he has been following his religion to be truthful, but a cunning man is a cunning man. He will speak the truth when it harms somebody; he will remain silent if *that* harms somebody. But the real criterion of a value is the ultimate flowering. A cunning man cannot flower. His cunningness is almost like a poison that he's taking slowly, slowly and committing suicide.

One woman had been out for two days with a friend who was sick. When she came back home her little boy ran towards the door and said, "Mom!" He was very much excited. "I have a surprise for you."

She pulled him aside and asked, "What is the surprise?"

He said, "The other day I was playing in your bedroom, inside the closet, when suddenly Daddy came in with the woman next door. Afraid of being caught, I stayed, breathing as slowly as possible but also looking from the keyhole at what was happening. Something was certainly happening. They undressed!

The mother said, "What? Say it just in my ear – undressed?"

He said, "Yes, they undressed – both. Not only that, they jumped into *your* bed and Pop was on top of the woman."

The woman said, "You wait. Just you wait, not a single word more. Just wait. Let that son-of-a-bitch, your father, come home. And when he comes, the first thing is that you have to relate the whole thing you have told me, word by word."

Finally the father came, and they were waiting at the door. The mother said to the boy, "I have packed everything," and to the husband, "I am leaving you. But before leaving you, I want you to hear what the boy has to say."

The boy said, "I was playing in your bedroom, in the closet. Daddy came in with a neighborhood woman. They undressed. They both went into your bed. Daddy was on top – and Mom, they were doing exactly the same thing you did last year with Uncle John when father went for a holiday! I don't know exactly the name," he said, "of what they were doing, but you must know, because I've seen you doing the same thing from the same closet where I used to play. Playing is just an excuse; that's the place from where I see great dramas."

The moment you become innocent, you have found a direct line to the divine. Your heartbeat synchronizes with the heartbeat of the universe. The world may condemn you as mad – don't be worried about the world. What you have to be always concerned about is what is happening within you. Blissfulness, peace, silence, tranquillity... ecstasy, an invisible dance in your energy. A song without words all over your body... every fiber of your body participating in it, as if in an orchestra. If you feel this, you are right – against the whole world.

You have to learn one simple thing: blissfulness is the criterion of your sanity. Miserableness shows your madness.

BELOVED OSHO,
WHILE I WAS SITTING QUIETLY THIS MORNING, AN
OVERWHELMING FEELING OF NOT KNOWING WHEN I
AM, WHERE I AM, OR WHAT WAS HAPPENING,
OVERCAME ME. WHILE FEELING SO LOST, YOU
APPEARED AS A GUIDING LIGHT IN MY HEART, NOT
SAYING ANYTHING, JUST BEING WITH ME. WITH
TEAR-FILLED EYES, I FELT A HAPPINESS I HAVE NEVER
KNOWN BEFORE. BELOVED MASTER, CAN YOU PLEASE
COMMENT?

Searching for the truth, seeking the eternal life, you will find many moments which are unbelievable. Even though you are in those moments, completely soaked – still the moment and its beauty is such, its golden glory is such that it seems too good to be true, and it is too good because it is too true. Many people have lost their path, stuck in a kind of fear. Anything overwhelming, like a great cloud surrounding you – if you don't know that it is a friend, you are going to be so much afraid that you won't allow the same experience to happen again.

Remember that every experience on the path, in the beginning is a great shock. Your very roots are shaken. Whatever you have believed to be true is no longer true. Whatever you have been thinking of as real, is dream stuff, and whatever you have never thought about seems to be the ultimate reality. The change is so much and so quick, that it is natural for human beings to be afraid. But the fear is only because you are ignorant of the experience. These are the moments when the master is needed to say to you that the overwhelming cloud of unknowing, of innocence, is a good sign, is indicative that greater things are going to happen. It shows that you are on the right path.

And you have to learn not to feel a stranger in a situation which is unknown to you, because now every day more and more unknown will open itself to you. That too, is a training for a further and final step: the unknowable.

Everything is very systematic. There is no chaos inside you. If you can pass one step, you will necessarily reach the second step.

The second step is going to be even bigger, because you will be melting into the unknowable. In the unknowable you cannot remain separate. You can have a separate flame of light, but in the roots you will be joined with the whole. Only the flame will be free, but in the roots you will be universal.

And the question of freedom is meaningless, because there is no one except you in the world. It is only you – in different faces, in different eyes, in different people, in birds, in animals, in trees. It is your consciousness. And unless one knows that he is the whole, he is not religious. He has not touched the nectar which makes him an immortal, which makes him a god, part of the innermost reality of existence. We have only forgotten. Nothing is lost – nothing *can* be lost; it is your very nature.

That overwhelming experience was not coming from outside, it was your own fragrance. Because you cannot see it, you felt it as outside yourself. It was your own joy, your own peace, your own silence that was radiating. It takes a little time to be acquainted with the inner territory of your being. But once you are acquainted with it, you have found the center of the world.

One great scientist, Archimedes, used to say: "If I can find the center of the world, I can revolutionize the whole existence." Unfortunately, it is very difficult now to find out where Archimedes is. Otherwise, his only fault was that he was looking outside for the center of the world, and the center is within him.

Your religion, your temple, your God, your holy book – all are within you. Go without fear. Go with fearlessness. You have nothing to lose, and you have the whole universe to gain.

20

The "other"... hell?
Or the door to the divine?

BELOVED OSHO,
I AM BECOMING AWARE MORE AND MORE HOW
MUCH I FOCUS ON THE OTHER, WHETHER IT IS A
FRIEND, A LOVER, A MOUNTAIN, OR MUSIC. ONE
THING REMAINS ALWAYS THE SAME: THE OTHER IS A
LONGING WITHIN ME BECAUSE WITHOUT THE
OTHER, I CAN NEVER FEEL COMPLETE, RECONCILED.
BELOVED MASTER, WHO IS THE OTHER? IS IT
IMAGINARY?

Surabhi, the other is one of the most significant questions to be solved in life. Millions of people with great intelligence have escaped from life, renounced life, just because they could not solve the problem of the other – and these were the giants of humanity.

Even in the twentieth century, a man like Jean Paul Sartre could say, "The other is hell." This assertion is an acceptance of failure: you have not been able to solve the problem; now you are calling names – "the other is hell." But who are you? – because for others, *you* are the other.

First see the real situation, because any solution that is going to work out has to arise out of the real. The other has become a problem – particularly, the more intimate the relationship is, the more problematic it is. The husband and wife, the children and the parents, the students and the teachers... wherever there are two wings, rather than having a beautiful flight under the stars, your wings are fighting with each other.

A man is a failure if he has not come to dissolve the other completely into himself or, in other words, dissolve himself into the other completely. But it has to be complete, entire, total.... If this is not the situation, then people are going to suffer in a hundred and one ways, because they are connected with so many others. And each 'other' is a problem for the simple reason that everybody is trying to dominate everybody else.

We have been raised as politicians. We have been filled with ambitions, desires – to possess, to become powerful, to have as much money as you desire, as you dream of. *These* are the problems, not the other – the other only reflects your problems because he's so intimate and close by.

The husband, if he is a human being, should stop calling himself a "husband." A wife, if she understands, should stop calling herself a "wife." More than friendship, you are bound to fall into a ditch; more than friendship, it becomes a bondage. Then both are fighting tooth and nail, directly and indirectly, with a single aim: to dominate the other, to reduce the other to the status of second. It is not possible. If it were possible, people would have solved the problem – although the solution would not have brought blessings. It would have stopped the continuous fight for monopoloy – although even if the fight stops, you will not be blissful. You will be almost dead, sad. At least before, there were excuses for your fight; now even those excuses are gone.

The very word 'husband' is ugly; it means a farmer. It was thought that the man is the farmer and the woman is the earth, so he sows his seeds in the woman and she goes on reproducing. He created the myth that he is the real producer, the farmer; and he pushed the woman – who is the real creative force – to a status that is almost to the point where it becomes inhuman and starts hurting.

In many countries, the woman has never been given voting rights. In many countries, the woman is not accepted as having a soul; she is just to serve nature. In almost all countries, the woman is not expected to enter certain temples, certain sacred holy places, because she is unholy.

For thousands of years continuously, the woman has been crippled, crushed, exploited – almost murdered. And yet, she is still the backbone of humanity. Without her, there *is* no humanity. Without man, there is a possibility for humanity to exist, because the function of man biologically is negligible. It is the function of a doctor's syringe. And the syringe can do it more hygienically than you could ever do it.

This situation for thousands of years has gathered too much revolt in the unconscious of the woman. That revolt comes out in small matters – in nagging, in fighting. The matters are almost immaterial, and people are continuously fighting for them. It seems the *fighting* is material. They need any excuse to fight, it doesn't matter what the excuse is. It is a painful stage, because half of humanity is not even accepted as human. The remaining half cannot be free, either.

One Sufi mystic, Junnaid, was going to the mosque with his disciples. On the road, they saw a man who was trying to move his cow. It was apparent, clear that the man was absolutely new at the job. He was doing hard work, pulling the cow with the rope, but the cow was stronger. She was backwards. He would manage somehow to pull her one foot, and she would back up two feet.

Junnaid and his disciples stood there... because that was the method of Junnaid, to use actual situations in life for teaching. He said, "This man has done no harm to the cow. He is taking her home, where food will be ready, shelter will be ready; a cozier, warmer place will be ready – but why is the cow reluctant? Why is she feeling annoyed, irritated, humiliated? Rather than going home with him, she's *fighting!*"

Junnaid said this to his disciples and the servant who was taking the cow was also listening. Junnaid said, "There is an art that, even in the smallest job like this, is needed. This man has good intentions but has no understanding of how the mind of man or animals functions. He's creating a reaction. He's making the cow an enemy."

He said to the man: "This is not the way. You are new; you just stand aside and I will show you what has to be done."

And he went into his house, brought out a bundle of green grass, and just walked ahead of the cow – not even a rope on the neck of the cow. He simply walked. Sometimes he went slowly, and when the cow would come too close he would go fast, almost running. The cow would start running.

When he came back, he said, "This is the situation of every human being. Society has created so many reactionary attitudes that he goes on doing things which are harmful to himself, and he goes on doing them the wrong way."

Each relationship first has to be based not on the choice of the parents, not by the situation of the stars when you were born, not by the lines of your hand... and there is no writing on your forehead! You come into the world completely clean, unburdened, ready to learn. You come with a self-respect. If your self-respect is crushed, your whole joy in learning and living and loving disappears. Women have lost the joy of life, and man is responsible for it. And he has already suffered, because if the woman is miserable, in suffering, the man cannot be blissful – it is impossible.

The woman is spread all over the house; she is the home. Without her, you cannot call it home, it remains only a house. It is the woman, with her song and dance and love, who transforms the quality of the house. From a material thing, it becomes something romantic, something poetic, something spiritual. It becomes, if everything goes right, a Kaaba, a Mecca, a holy land.

But things start going wrong. Perhaps they are wrong from the very beginning. Already when you meet a woman, you are wrong; the woman is wrong – both have been taught all kinds of superstitions and stupidities. Both have lived in a family, in a society, in a crowd which is almost insane. So naturally, one starts accepting one's life and its hell. One becomes tolerant, patient. One drops all great hopes of living in a beautiful way. One forgets all utopias. One accepts the desert of a life with not a single flower in it, not a single bird in it, not a single green plant in it.

But man is capable of adjusting to any situation. That is one of the great qualities in man. There is only one competitor, and that is the cockroach. She has the same qualities of surviving in any situation, anywhere. You may understand or you may not understand, but you are cousins, because wherever man is found, the cockroach is found. And wherever you can find a cockroach, man is not far away. This partnership in life is millions of years old, and scientists say perhaps it will remain forever, because something in their nature is similar.

I don't know much about cockroaches, but I know much about man and I agree: there *must* be much which is similar. I am saying it from the side of man. Those who understand cockroaches can say it from the side of cockroaches.

A man grows with dreams. He has a vision of his future, his life, the way he wants to live. But once he has found a woman... the woman also has her own dreams, her own hopes. The first problem is, their dreams and their hopes clash; they are not the same.

They cannot be the same, they are two different individuals.

Now, to keep peace, there are only two possibilities: either one becomes so dominant, so threatening, that the other simply becomes, out of fear, enslaved... that's what has happened with women. The other way is to see the situation and to change it completely. Our life is valuable and it is not to be wasted. And if you try to understand your life and the problems that arise with the other, you will find it hilarious, because all your problems are so tiny that to fight for them is possible only if you have a retarded head.

If the man has the right to fulfill his dreams, the woman has also the same right to fulfill her dreams. And when you have decided to be together, now it becomes something of a sacred duty to be careful that you don't trample on the dreams of the other. Nothing hurts more than when a dream is crushed, when a hope dies, when the future becomes dark, when all the great ideas that you have been thinking your life to be made of seem to be impossible because this woman, or this man, is continuously destroying your mood, destroying your peace, destroying your silence. And when these things are destroyed, you cannot be creative. You can only be destructive, you can only be violent.

Life has immense treasures, which remain unknown to people because they don't have time. Their whole time is engaged in some kind of fight with someone – the other. The other contains the whole world. And the greatest calamity that happens is that when you are fighting with the other, you slowly, slowly forget yourself. Your whole focus becomes the other, and when the focus becomes the other, you are lost. Then when are you going to remember yourself? When are you going to find your innermost source of life? When you are going to search for beauty and truth and poetry and art? You will miss everything, just quarreling with a woman or with a man! Are you together to quarrel? Perhaps... because to be alone and without anybody to fight is very difficult.

In madhouses, I have seen people fighting with themselves, boxing in the air! I have asked the superintendent, "What is happening?" And he said, "These people used to fight. They were brought into the madhouse thinking that when there was nobody to fight, they would stop fighting. But logic goes one way, life goes another. Instead of stopping fighting, they have started fighting with themselves. Now they don't need the other. They have divided themselves into two persons: they are themselves *and* the other."

In a way, in a very roundabout way, they have come very close to reality. Surabhi, your desire for the other, your longing that without the other you will never be complete, is absolutely true. And this is the insight of every human being; they are all right about this fact: that without the other you are not going to have a feeling of wholeness, of completion, of arriving home. This feeling is all over the world.

But why doesn't it happen? Because man needs a new psychology to understand himself. The old psychology does not give him much understanding. The new psychology will be based on the experiences of a certain, most ancient school – Tantra.

There are very few great discoveries in the world. Tantra can claim the greatest discovery. Even after nuclear weapons, Tantra's discovery has been standing there for ten thousand years unused; an insight of such great value.

The insight is that man and woman are not just one – man just man, woman just woman – no. They are both together: man is half man and half woman, and the same is true about women. And this seems to be very logical and very scientific, because every child is born of a father and a mother. The father contributes something, the mother contributes something, and that's how the child is – a combination, a synthesis between man and woman. If the child is a boy, then the man is on the top and the woman is in the unconscious layers of the mind. If the child is a woman, then the woman is on the top and the man is hidden just underneath.

And this is the great contribution of Tantra: that unless the man and woman inside you become one whole, you will remain discontented, with something always missing. And because you always look outside, you feel that feminine qualities are missing; you don't know that there is a world within you too. You know only one world, and that is outside you.

You start looking on the outside, finding a woman or a man

who can make a certain organic whole, a unity in your life, so that this constant gap, this something missing, this heavy incompleteness in your being will be removed. You go on looking for women outside, for men outside. But nobody has ever found any woman outside, or any man outside, to fulfill the desire, the longing to become one complete whole.

But the basic understanding is right, that somehow man and woman have to merge their energies into one. Just one thing is missing: that miracle can only happen within you, it is not something outside. It is something that as you become silent and peaceful and joyous, as you enter deeper into meditative states, as your intelligence becomes more sharp, you will see: the other that you have been searching for is within you.

And there is no problem with the inner woman, with the inner man. Once you recognize them, they start melting into each other without any effort on your part. Just your recognition is enough to trigger the process of merger.

Surabhi, you are too young perhaps for this experiment. It needs a certain background of frustration with the other who is outside. When you are utterly frustrated, when you have lost all hope – only then you close your doors and you close your eyes and you go in. Frustration also plays a tremendously valuable part in man's spiritual growth.

But meanwhile, before you meet your inner woman or man, find a man or a woman. You will learn much. This is not going to be the end; all men are experimental for women and all women are experimental for men. Experimenting with a few relationships, you will be mature enough to recognize your own woman or your own man. And that day is the day of great celebration, because you are free from the other. You have found the other within yourself; now there is no need to be dependent on anyone. The man is free, the woman is free – and this does not mean that you cannot love, you cannot have friends on the outside.

In fact, now you can very easily have very smooth-going friendships, very beautiful love affairs, because it is no more a necessity for you. As far as you are concerned, you are fulfilled. Now it is not a need such that you have to be dependent.

And remember: anybody who is dependent on somebody *hates* that person. Nobody likes dependence. Even though it is hidden behind the beautiful garb of love, obedience, belief, respect for the ancient, respect for the old, but behind everything is slavery. Once you are free from the slavery of the other, once you can live alone *and* joyously, you have entered into the world for the first time. Before it, you were only dreaming; now you will be facing the reality.

And the reality is just ecstasy. Now you can love, but love will have a totally different quality. It will be simply sharing because you have too much, an abundance, overflowing, and you would like to share it. And sharing is always unconditional. You are not giving it as a deal, as a business. You are not giving it to get something in return – you are simply giving it because your hands are too full. If you don't give it, it will fall by itself.

The day you are capable of sharing love, and being alone and absolutely blissful, the slavery of women is finished. And the bigger slavery of man is finished too.

It is strange that women are fighting for liberation and man is just standing, looking awkward. Do something! You also have to become free. A men's liberation movement is as much a necessity as a women's liberation movement. In fact, both movements should be two wings of one movement for freedom.

BELOVED OSHO,
HAVING READ RECENTLY SEVERAL BOOKS ON THE
MASTER-DISCIPLE RELATIONSHIP, I WAS STRUCK BY
THE IMMENSITY OF SUFFERING, PHYSICAL
ENDURANCE TESTS, DARK NIGHTS OF THE SOUL AND
HARDNESS OF TRAINING THE DISCIPLES HAD TO
UNDERGO. THERE SEEMS TO BE A TRADITION –
REGARDLESS OF SCHOOL – OF SUFFERING AND
HARDNESS. LOOKING AT MY ELEVEN YEARS WITH
YOU, BELOVED MASTER, IT HAS BEEN A BED OF ROSES
– THE AMPLE AMOUNT OF THORNS BEING PROVIDED
BY MY EGO ONLY. YOU CERTAINLY ARE NO BULLSHIT,

YET SO LIGHT, DELICATE, HUMOROUS AND JOYOUS
THAT I NEVER THINK OF YOU AS A HARD MASTER.
AND EVEN WHEN YOU WERE HITTING ME, YOU HAVE
NEVER BEEN AS HARD AS MY CONDITIONING HAD
TAUGHT ME TO BE ON MYSELF. YOU SEEM TO PREFER,
WHENEVER POSSIBLE, TO DISSOLVE AND MELT THE
THORNS AND CORNS RATHER THAN HACKING THEM
OFF. OVER AND OVER I HAVE THE FEELING THAT I AM
JUST STARTING. MY QUESTION IS: AM I JUST
EXTREMELY SLOW AND INSENSITIVE AND ARE THE
REALLY TOUGH TIMES STILL TO COME? OR, HAVE YOU
CREATED A WAY OF WORKING WITH US WHICH IS
VERY DIFFERENT FROM THE WAYS OTHER MASTERS
AND ENLIGHTENED BEINGS USED TO WORK WITH
THEIR DISCIPLES?

Purna, there is no need to fear, because no hard days are ahead; the hard days are behind. The masters in the past were working on their disciples, but at the same time they were making every effort so that their teachings, their disciples, their lifestyles, didn't come in conflict with the old society, with the old religion, with the conventions.

The journey to truth becomes very difficult if you are prepared to live a life which is unnatural. Truth is simply the experience of the purest nature. But if you are trained from the very beginning to be unnatural, then by the time you start your search for truth, you are in a dilemma: if you follow truth, you are going against your conditioning. And that is very difficult, because your conditioning is the conditioning of your society. If you follow truth without any fear of the consequences, then you will be crucified; then you will be given poison, like Socrates. Seeing this, most of the people forget all about truth. It seems to be very abstract, and the troubles and the antagonism of the society seem to be very real.

Very few people have the courage to go after truth even if life is in danger, because truth is a higher value than life. Truth means *eternal life.*

All the old religions have tried to make the path of the pilgrim as arduous as possible. Their whole scholarship has been devoted to a single point: that the path to truth should be very roundabout, full of difficulties, dark nights of the soul, ups and downs which drive you crazy. And you are alone. The society, the crowd, which has been a shelter for you – a subtle shelter which you may not have noted – the very feeling that so many people..."seven hundred million Catholics are with me"... one starts feeling that seven hundred million people, for two thousand years, cannot be wrong. The weight of tradition, the weight of time, the weight of conventions, the weight of your conditioning, is so heavy that to drop it, one feels afraid. You will be cut off from the society, from the parents, from the family. You will not be getting any more warmth from people; on the contrary, they will all become cold. They will suspect that you have gone crazy; they may even say it to you.

Why has this been done? because I see that the path to truth is just a single step. There is no question of any arduousness, any austerities, because they are absolutely irrelevant. You are fasting – what has your fasting to do with truth? Your fasting has nothing to do with love. Your fasting will not make you a better man, because your fasting is a psychological sickness, it is masochism. You are enjoying torturing yourself. And once a person starts enjoying torturing himself, it is very difficult to pull him out of the sickness in which he is caught. When somebody tortures somebody else, naturally, the other person defends himself, fights, and the whole society condemns it: "Why did you attack the person?" The police are there, the lawyers are there, the court is there, so that nobody is harmed.

The man who tortures himself is full of violence, but he starts attacking himself. One finds wonders and wonders in the history of man. I have been looking into books of law and books about laws and their evolution and I was surprised: there is not a single law that prevents a man from torturing himself. It is strange, because it does not matter who you are torturing – torture is torture. Whether I am torturing you or I am torturing myself, in the eyes of the law we should be equally criminal.

In fact, I am a greater criminal because I am torturing my own body which is dumb, cannot say anything, cannot go to the police station to report against me, cannot go to the court to appeal.

On the contrary, the more I torture myself in the name of religion, the more people worship me. That's how your saints are manufactured. These people are psychologically sick people, but they are worshipped by the society. They are part of the society, they support *everything* of the society. They support the whole past, without exception – remember my words: *without exception*. And they are not only saying those things, they are practicing those things.

People have the maxim that "Whatever you say, do it!" And the saints are doing things which look almost impossible to you. To avoid the feeling that you are inferior... just watch the delicate strategy of the mind. To avoid the fact of feeling yourself as inferior, you have raised these people to incarnations of God, sons of God, messengers of God; they are not ordinary human beings.

Do you understand the strategy? The strategy is that man is saying, "If we cannot do such things – lying down on a thorn bed, fasting for months, standing naked for years, not sitting, not sleeping"... because *you* cannot do it you certainly feel these people are superior. And as you respect them more, as you worship them more, and you call them saints and divine, their ego becomes bigger and bigger.

They enjoy only one thing: their ego. And they start torturing themselves more and more because they see that the more they torture, the more respectable they become. They are becoming almost part of history. Sick people have ruled over humanity.

Politicians are sick because they are nothing but the will to power – and the very idea of having power over somebody is mean, and it happens only in a very sick mind.

The religious saints are sick people – they are masochists, they are torturing themselves, and they are receiving so much respect and honor that they are ready to torture themselves as much as possible. Here, the ego is fulfilled – and in the other world God is waiting, with all the pleasures for them.

I am not a part of this old company of dodos. I am not psychologically sick. I have never felt myself inferior because I have never compared myself to anyone. I have never felt myself superior for the same reason. You can feel superior and inferior only when you compare. But how can I compare? I don't see another person who is like me. I see every person as unique. And if every person is unique then there is no question of comparison; then there is no question of equality either.

These people who have been torturing themselves... naturally, the question arises in your mind: with me, there is no self-torture. You are not told to stay awake for nights together, you are not told not to eat for weeks together, you are not given any discipline, any certain character. I cannot impose any character or discipline on you. I am not your enemy. I can only help your being to blossom. And unless it blossoms, we don't know whether it is a rose or a lotus. We will have to wait and see when it blossoms.

In the past, nobody had the patience to wait and see what happens when a person blossoms. They were all trying to force things – with all good wishes, but they have created this crippled humanity. Nobody is blossoming because nobody is accepted in his nature, whatever it is. You are told how you have to be to be accepted, to be respected, to be honorable in this society – how you have to be. But then, you may be the chief justice of the Supreme Court or the president or the prime minister, but you will never be happy. You will never smile with the heart, you will not have the quality of laughter and love and life. You can have all the money in the world and all the power in the world and still you will be only a beggar.

My effort here is totally different: I want you to be just yourself, and allow your hidden treasures to surface. It will be a surprise to others and it will be a surprise to you, too. And one of the most significant things is that whatever you have brought to the world, nobody else has brought and nobody else will bring it again.

It is the only worship which I can call religious – that whatever you have brought in your being, make sure that it blossoms, and you can shower those flowers in deep gratitude to existence. You have prayed, you have worshipped – remember, just once and it is enough.

Three or four hundred years ago, there was a great grammarian.... And Sanskrit is absolute grammar – it is just mathematics.

There is no other science, no other language which can claim such qualities. It is very flexible. One word may have twelve meanings. Because it is so flexible, the flexibility gives it a potentiality for being the best language for poetry, because poetry needs a flexibility of meanings, vagueness of meanings. Very solid meanings can only make prose. Sanskrit has the perfect grammar because for five thousand years at least, scholars have not been able to find any loophole, any way to improve upon it.

The grammarian looks at the same poem with a different eye than you look at it. And when a musician looks at it, he looks at it from a very different angle. If a dancer looks at it... certainly their visions cannot coincide. Each individual has a unique individuality. Once this is accepted, you will be able to be compassionate, to be human.

Whenever you are looking at the other, you will not be judgmental. Jean Paul Sartre *is*, when he says the other is hell. If you have experienced your inner, orgasmic unity, you may even say that the other is the door to the divine. It all depends on you.

BELOVED OSHO,
AM I A HYPOCHONDRIAC? I'M ALSO WORRIED
ABOUT MY SEX LIFE IN OLD AGE.

Milarepa, you are a hypochondriac! Just now you are not here because others in your bungalow have a cold. You are a very superior category of hypochondriac because I have heard about hypochondriacs who are continually having this trouble and that trouble. But I have never heard that just because *others* have a cold... what are *you* doing there?

He has raised a significant question, because hypnotherapy has come to the conclusion that thirty-three percent of people are very vulnerable, very suggestible. Thirty-three percent is not a small percentage – it is one-third of all the masses. One person in three is suggestible: somebody just says that you are looking very pale. You deny it immediately because you are not looking pale. You have seen in the mirror; you are not looking pale. You have met many people; nobody has mentioned it – this guy seems to be strange. You say to the person, "Perhaps you are suffering from jaundice, I am not pale. I am perfectly healthy."

The man says, "It is up to you. If you are feeling perfectly healthy, there is no problem," but he goes on looking back and starts creating doubts. Perhaps others did not say anything out of politeness.

And then another man comes and he looks and he says, "My God! What happened? You look like a ghost." Now you don't have the same courage to deny it, to say, "I am perfectly good; something must be wrong with you." That courage is gone.

Now you say, "Yes, I have not been feeling well for a few days... looking pale. I think I must go home and not to the office, because if I am looking like a ghost...."

The man says, "I will call a taxi, don't walk. Or if you are feeling too much difficulty, I can phone for an ambulance."

And you say, "That will be better; an ambulance will be better, because it seems I am at the last stage. Looking like a ghost and being a ghost is not very much different. You just call an ambulance because going home looking like a ghost... what will the children think? What will my wife think? It is better in the hospital, and if I can manage just to give some baksheesh to the doctors and to the nurses and to the pharmacist..."

And they all go on emphasizing: "You are finished!" And then the doctor says, "Listen, nothing can be done now; you are dead."

"I am dead? and I did not even feel it when I died." The doctor says, "Nobody feels it." You say, "Then where am I to go from here?"

The doctor says, "That is not my business. You go to the temple that is just nearby here and ask the priest where to go now. You are dead."

You go two, three steps, and think again: "Dead? And I am walking!" You come back, you say, "Listen, I want a second opinion. Is there another doctor in the hospital?"

They say, "There are many; you can have as many opinions as you want.

But about you, there is no problem. It is very simple: You are dead! Now, no sickness is possible for you, no infection, no tuber-culosis, no cancer, not even death is possible. Everything has happened!"

You ask the other doctor but they are all ready, so the other doctor looks at you and tries to escape from the room. "Where are you going?"

The other doctor says, "Listen. I am not an expert about ghosts. You have come to the wrong place. You go to some other doctor. Find out from the inquiry office, who the doctor is who deals with ghosts."

You say, "My God! I have never heard that in any hospital there is a department that deals with ghosts. I think it is better that I go to the priest and ask, 'Now show me the way: where is hell, where is heaven and where am I supposed to go? – some address? some phone number?'"

Thirty-three percent of his people are that type. Any disease, any epidemic and these thirty-three percent are the first to catch hold of it. They can't miss. These thirty-three percent of people are continuously having diseases, illnesses, and they are torturing doctors all over the world because you cannot cure them. They don't have any disease, so the question of curing them simply does not arise. And every doctor becomes fed up, because they go on and on... somehow you manage one disease and another disease starts....

There are many "pathies" in the world: allopathy, naturopathy, homeopathy, acupuncture; Chinese medicine and Greek medicine; ayurveda, Indian medicine, and they all work. I was puzzled... all *cannot* work; because their prognosis is different, their medicines are different. Still, *every* medicine succeeds with seventy percent of people. It is a shock that allopathy also succeeds only with seventy percent; homeopathy also succeeds only with seventy percent.

It has been found that seventy percent of illnesses are only in the head. They don't have anything to do with your physiology, with your biology, with your reality. They are hallucinations. But once you have them, once it has been emphasized again and again, then you are going to suffer.

There are millions of hypochondriacs. They need all these

medicines and they need all the miracle mongers because ordinary allopathy, which is the only scientific medicine, cannot help them. They don't have a real disease. They need as imaginary a medicine as their disease is imaginary. Milarepa, it is not only you, but almost everybody who suffers once in a while from imaginary sicknesses.

In my university, I had one student with me who had been in the same class for almost five years. I said to him, "It is too long and the course is too short."

He said, "What to do? I am constantly sick – and particularly at the time of the examination, I always fall sick." And when examination time came, he fell sick.

I went to the warden and I said, "This sickness seems to be just in his mind, because for five years he has been falling sick *exactly* on the date the examination begins. And I don't say that he is befooling anybody or that he's trying to cheat. He's *really* sick. If you show him to a doctor, he will find that he has fever, and that is enough proof. But for five years, exactly on the same day as the examination begins.... Yesterday he was perfectly okay, and now he's suffering from fever.

"I don't believe in this fever," I said to the warden, "and I don't want the doctor to be called. I am going to treat him. The doctors have treated him for five years, and what is the result?"

The old man said, "But you may put me into difficulty sooner or later, because if it is known that I have allowed you to treat him.... You are not a doctor – you are not even a student of medical science."

I said, "I am not a doctor and I am not a student of medical science, but I know man. And this disease is not a disease, this is only imagination. So you don't be worried. If we have to go to the court, I will manage to fight the case, so don't be worried. I am not treating the disease, I am treating the man; nobody can prevent me from that. And I am treating only an illusion. Is this criminal?"

That old man slipped away. He thought, "It is better to go from this place so nobody else sees him." I gave the boy a good cold bath. He shouted, he tried to escape, but I said, "You are too sick, you cannot. You just get into the bathtub."

He said, "What are you doing? By morning I will be finished!"

I said, "By morning you will be in the examination hall." He said, "But what about today's paper?"

I said, "I will manage everything, don't be worried. First, you get better. Either you get better, or you get into the bathtub."

It was ice cold. He touched it and he took his finger out. He said, "I think it's better I should leave this fever."

I said, "It is up to you; I have no preference. You can forget the fever and go to sleep. Tomorrow morning, go to the examination. I am going to the vice-chancellor to make arrangements for the one paper you have missed, so that this paper can be arranged at the end."

I told the vice-chancellor, "Five years is long enough. Now don't do anything that will force him to remain in the same class."

The vice-chancellor agreed. He said, "I was worried how it was going to happen, because *every* examination he is sick. I was always wondering how to get rid of him, and you have brought a beautiful plan. So he's not getting into the bathtub?" I said, "He's not getting in." He asked me, "Do you need some ice cubes?" I said, "That's a good idea! You send some."

When I was pouring the ice cubes in, the boy asked, "What are you doing?"

I said, "Preparing your whole night's rest in the bathtub." He said, "I will die!"

I said, "You are ready to die but you are not ready to drop your fever?"

He said, "I have dropped it – just look! When you were gone, I tried a few times, dipped my hand into the water... it is too much! It is better to drop the fever. I don't have any fever." I said, "Do you have any other disease?" He said, "What do you mean by other disease?"

I said, "I mean the *same* treatment. I'm not interested in your diseases – my treatment! I am determined to send you tomorrow morning to the examination, so if *any* disease happens, this is the cure!"

He said, "No, no disease will happen." And then he told me, "It is the fear of the examination" – he becomes paranoid, he starts having fever. "Now you have created a more dangerous thing." So now he will go to the examination. He cannot remain in this bathtub for a whole night. He will die. Certainly, he will die. "And I am too young," he said. "This is not the time for me to die."

I said, "This is time for you to pass the examination!"

Seventy percent of sicknesses can be cured by *anybody* who has your trust. It is your trust that cures. Only thirty percent of diseases – which are *true* diseases – need medicine, need surgery. Seventy percent simply need a doctor you trust.

One thing not to be forgotten: your sicknesses, your failures in life, your undeveloped intelligence, your messed up situation about everything is simply *your doing.* If you can understand just a simple thing: your life has an abundance of energy. You only need to know how to provoke that energy to function in your favor, how to make that energy a dance, not a destructive lifestyle. Meditating, watching your mind, you can get free of much that is only your imagination. The moment you are aware inside, no imagination can survive. It is bound to die.

And Milarepa, the second question you are asking... before I answer the second, I have remembered a small incident. A doctor was tortured by a hypochondriac, more so because he was very rich and he could not say to him, "Get lost!" For months he was treating him, but he could not find any sickness. But now it was becoming boring and the man was there every day. Finally, the doctor decided to bring things to a head – something has to be done, because this is not going to be a lifelong boring relationship with this man. So when the rich man came in, he asked, "Is there some trouble?"

He said, "Some? There are many, because they go on increasing and you have not been able to treat *any.*"

The doctor said, "I have found the treatment. See that cup there? Urinate in it."

The man looked around... because there were other patients, nurses, doctors... but what to do? If the doctor says.... He closed his eyes and urinated, somehow managed. And he was feeling very happy. At least he had done it! The doctor said, "Now defecate in the same cup." It was a little difficult, but he did that too.

And the doctor took a wooden ladle out of the drawer, mixed the concoction in the cup, and told to the man: "Open your mouth." The man said, "My God! For what?" He said, "Don't speak! Just open your mouth!"

And he poured the whole cup into his mouth. The man vomited.

The doctor said, "Ah ha! So now we know what the disease is! Upset stomach! For six months I have been trying and trying to find out what the disease is. Now there is no problem, you will be cured. Your medicine is ready."

The man said, "Now there is no need of any medicine. That shock was so much that I cannot afford to be sick anymore. You can keep your medicine for somebody else. But I have never heard," the rich man said, "that this kind of concoction is made."

The doctor said, "Finally, for a hypochondriac, that is the *only* medicine." So Milarepa, be aware!

The second question is: you are worried about your sex life in old age. First, I will tell you one story. An old man, must have been nearabout eighty-five years old, entered a reception room and said to the girl, with trembling hands: "Is this not Joe's Famous Mustang Ranch?"

The woman at the counter said, "Yes. What do you want? What are you looking for?"

He said, "Isn't this the place which has fifty beautiful girls, ready and able?"

The woman could not understand what... she said, "I don't understand. What do you want exactly?"

He said, "You don't understand what I want? I want a girl! I wanna be laid."

The woman could not believe it. She said to the old man, "Pop, how old are you?" He said, "How old? Must be eighty-five." The woman said, "Pop, you have had it." The old man said, "Had it? My God! So quick?" And he pulled out his wallet with trembling fingers.... I can imagine Milarepa opening his wallet, asking the woman, "How much do I owe you?"

In old age, Milarepa, you will forget all this nonsense – long before old age. People who are with me are going to become, before old age, mature enough so that sex becomes to them just a wastage. And the people who are meditating... their sexual energy starts moving in new dimensions. Up to old age, do you want to remain stuck where you are? If you go on growing, by the time you are eighty-five, you will have forgotten all about sex. People remember sex in their old age only if while they were young, their sexual urge was inhibited.

About another old man, I have heard that he went to his doctor and said, "You have to do something now. You have to bring my sexual urge a little lower."

The doctor said, "There is no sexual urge, nothing. It is all in your mind."

The old man said, "That's what I mean! Bring it a little lower – what the hell is it doing in the head?"

Either you remain in the dark bondage of biological energies... then sex continues to the very last breath. The last idea in most people when they die is of sex, and that is the great contribution your society has made to you! The last moments should be of peace, it should be of remembrance of one's own being. It should be of a deep experience with existence, so that death does not look like death but only a changing of the house.

And Milarepa's sex urge will disappear soon, so be quick! But don't complain to me later on that I did not warn you. Be quick! Your sexual urge will be gone nearabout the age of forty-two. If you want the exact date, I can give it to you.

21
This too will pass...

BELOVED OSHO,
WHO WAS THE MASTER WHO DISCOVERED OR
INVENTED THE LATIHAN MEDITATION TECHNIQUE?
WOULD YOU LIKE EXPLAIN THIS MEDITATION
TECHNIQUE?

Latihan is a unique method – unique in the sense that it is the only method that has come out of this century, and unique also because it happened to a man who was not searching for truth, who was not a seeker. It is also unique in that it has no parallel in any old methods of meditation.

Latihan was found by a Mohammedan in Indonesia, Bapak Subud. He was not in any way involved with the other world, with life beyond death, or with life herenow. He was just chopping wood on his farm and suddenly it happened: his ax fell from his hands and he started to make gestures, postures which he had never done. He himself could not believe what he was doing and why, but the force was so tremendous that in spite of himself, he *had* to do it.

He went into something almost like a dynamic meditation – shouting, running, jumping, just a pure play of energy for no reason at all. And then he fell into a deep silence, the deepest he had ever dreamt of, and when he woke up in the afternoon, just three or four hours afterwards, he was totally a new man. That happening changed him. He was no more a Mohammedan, he was no more his old personality, his old self.

He started teaching his close friends. To whomsoever he said this was a meditation, they laughed. But his intimate circle of friends were persuaded by him..."At least you should give it a try." A few tried, a few succeeded – and this happened just thirty years ago. After the experience, one feels utterly relaxed, no tensions in the mind, no tensions in the body. And a great joy arises from your interiority, not dependent on anything outside you. You are for the first time a universe unto yourself. For your happiness, for your joy, you are no longer dependent. You alone can live on a deserted star, joyously.

Slowly, latihan became a world movement. But there were a

few basic flaws in it; hence, the movement has disappeared – like a fashion that has come in vogue and now it seems to be some historical fact – and it has happened just within these thirty years.

First, Bapak Subud could not explain it, or why it happened to him. He was not religious, he was not philosophical, he was not interested in the esoteric side of life. The mysteries of life had never been a challenge to him. He was a very earthly man. He simply said, "It descended upon me from beyond. I don't know why – I have no explanation for why I was chosen."

But because it happened to a man who knew nothing about meditations, who never meditated – at least according to his conscious memory – it was natural that the method, the technique, must have some weaknesses, some loopholes. It is not a device created by a master; it is a very accidental thing.

Mohammedans cannot explain it for the simple reason that Mohammedans, Christians, and Jews don't believe in a series of lives; they believe only in one life. That cuts their wings, that cuts their time, and there are many things they cannot go into because of their religious conditioning. The past life does not exist; hence, to go into it for an explanation will be absurd – where are you going, there is no past life! And the wonder is, they don't have another answer. Why should it happen to Bapak Subud who has no qualifications at all?

The only explanation is in his past lives. Past lives and the theory of rebirth is not just a philosophical hypothesis in the East – it is based on the experience of thousands of years, because there were happenings which were impossible to explain without the hypothesis of a past life.

Bapak Subud may not have any religious qualities but he must have worked upon himself, his consciousness, in some past life. He must have come to a point very close to the goal. But unless you achieve something, when your death occurs all that you have learned will have to be learned from ABC. But if something has matured in you, if meditation has not been an abortion in you but you have given birth to yourself, then let death come. Your consciousness will carry the work on yourself from where you are leaving in this life, and you will remember it.

The method of latihan is simple: you have to stand in a room, just to stand loose as if you are just a coat hanging on the wall, so relaxed. And wait. You are not supposed to *do* anything, you have simply to wait. Things start happening to most people. Hands start moving, somebody starts rotating his head, somebody starts jogging, somebody starts dancing. Somebody starts singing. Somebody starts speaking gibberish, a language that does not exist.

After half an hour, they lie down and just rest – the exertion is great. They do latihan sessions twice a week, at the most thrice a week. It is a catharsis. You throw out all kinds of anger, jealousy, greed – all the muck that you are full of, you start throwing it away – and when you come out of latihan, you are clean; you feel the freshness of the early morning, the crispness of the air. Not only has it refreshed you, renewed you, it has given you a new sensitivity. The same roseflower looks so psychedelic... it is no longer ordinary, it is radiating with color. It has a certain aura around it. And in the same way, the whole of ordinary life suddenly takes a change, because you have a new pair of eyes, a new heart to feel, a completely clean mind to see as clearly as is humanly possible.

The movement died down because of faults in the method. And it was beyond Bapak Subud's capacity and understanding to find those faults, because this was his only experience; he had nothing else to compare it with. And to him, it *happened*; those faults were not a deterrent to him. But many people doing latihan have gone mad. That was the reason why the movement slowly, slowly died out.

The people who have not gone mad are just on the borderline. A few people, certainly, have attained to meditation, but of the lowest kind. They feel silent, they feel a certain togetherness; they are more rooted, more centered. But more than that... they have not experienced anything of the beyond. They have not come in contact with the gods, the god of truth, the god of love, the god of beauty, the god of bliss. They are absolutely ignorant of what spirituality really means.

They are in a kind of limbo. Latihan has created a certain space in them which makes it clear to them that this world is not enough. But remember: it is a negative feeling that this world is not enough. This world is denied, negated, but the other world is not visible yet. The person is in a difficult situation. This world does not appeal to him, he has seen something superior; but just to remain in the small space that latihan has created is boring. It has no excitement, because it is not like a river, continuously growing and becoming bigger, reaching the ocean to become the ocean itself. Latihan almost creates a pond which goes nowhere, which simply dries out, evaporates. And only mud, a muddy puddle is left behind.

Dynamic meditation has everything that latihan has – and more, because it is a device, deliberately made, considered from every possible angle, not to harm anybody in any situation. Latihan is almost a primitive thing in comparison to dynamic meditation, which has everything of latihan *plus*.

In latihan, you have to do it in a small group. Women and men are not allowed to do it together in one room. From this point the mistakes of the method begin. It is the old fear, the old Mohammedan mind – why can't women and men meditate together? In fact, they should only meditate together, because while you are meditating, you need the presence of the other which is your other half. It does not matter whether the woman you love is present. What matters is that feminine energy is available, male energy is available. If they are both available, the total effect is of wholeness, and the mind which starts feeling even a little bit of wholeness cannot go mad. Madness means you are in fragments, you are a crowd. There are many of you; even you cannot recognize who is the true one.

Latihan gives no idea of what is going to happen. You need not believe in that but you should be aware of it, because as it starts happening, if you have been aware beforehand, you will not be scared. You will know: this too will pass away.

Just the other day, one of my German sannyasins – a topmost model in Germany, Gayan – has sent her latest photograph. She has really a beautiful face, extraordinary in its innocence. That gives it its unique beauty. She must have felt I would like the picture. I have seen many pictures of her, but this was something different. Perhaps she was in a certain state of mind; perhaps the photographer was in a certain state of mind, but somehow the picture is far better, shows a state far higher than that in which Gayan is, in reality.

I have always wondered about her and about many other people. She looks so beautiful in her pictures – so innocent, so agelessly beautiful, agelessly young – but in reality, these qualities are not in her. It is possible that while she's being photographed as a model, she brings herself together. The camera, the studio... the photograph is going to be seen by millions of people. Perhaps all that creates the situation in which she becomes silent, just looking at the camera for a few seconds. But she realized that sending me the picture is not the full act, so she wrote by the side of the picture: "Osho, this too will pass." That is one of my old stories she is referring to.

I would like to remind you of the story because sometimes, if it hits the right place in your heart, it becomes a tremendous help in your evolution of consciousness.

A king was getting old and of course, worried and concerned about death. One day, he could not sleep the whole night long; he was continuously thinking of death. He has killed thousands of people himself; he has been a great conqueror – what has happened to him? Why has he become so cowardly? The death of the other does not matter to you, but your own death matters.

In the morning, he called his wise men and asked them: "If I fall into a situation where you are not available to advise me and I don't see any way out, I would like you to make a small suggestion that I can put under the big diamond in my ring." The ring was made with an opening device, so he could look underneath the diamond and read the message.

They were at a loss. This was something very difficult – just one sentence, for millions of situations. How can there be one answer for all the questions? Only a man like me can say, "Yes, not only that – there is only one answer for *all* questions; there cannot be even two."

They were worried and puzzled, but one old man suggested something and that appealed to them, so they brought it to the king. He was not to see it – the condition was that he was not to see it. He was not to open it just out of curiosity. He was to open it in a *real* danger, when there is no other possibility for him, when he cannot figure it out, when he's simply stuck and knows nothing about what to do. Only in such emergencies, when life is at stake should he open the ring and read the message.

And by chance, the time to read it came very soon, just after fifteen days. The neighboring country invaded. They had been invaded by this king many times, defeated many times. They were boiling with anger and violence and humiliation and insult. For ten years, they had been training their people and this time they were determined: "Either we take over the kingdom of the enemy or we are not going to come back home alive." And when somebody, even if he is beaten, has such an idea in the mind, he's no longer weak. He is far stronger than your strongest people.

They fought as the king had never seen anybody fight... because the king and his soldiers were just fighting to defend, but the enemy was fighting to gain self-respect. They had lost their integrity, and even at the cost of life it had to be regained – even if the whole country dies!

The king lost the war. Somehow he escaped to the mountains on his horse, but the enemies were following. He was alone and he could hear many troops of horses following him and the noise was coming closer and closer. He was running as fast as the poor horse could run, because he was wounded, almost at the point of death. But the greatest difficulty came when they reached the end of the road – that road was not going anywhere! It only came to this spot where tourists used to come. It was a very scenic situation, but it was death to the king – he could not go anywhere. Underneath, there was a rocky valley thousands of feet deep. If he jumped into it, he would be finished. And he could not return because it was a small road....

Then he suddenly saw the diamond shining in the sun, and remembered, opened the diamond, read the message. The message was very small but very great. The message was: "This too will pass away."

Just let the idea sink in your heart: This too will pass away. So there is no need to be worried. In life, there is nothing permanent.

Everything is changing. You could not have thought, fifteen days before, that you would be in this situation. You cannot think what your situation will be after fifteen days. Don't be worried: This too will pass. Everything passes by.

It had a great effect on the man. He relaxed, he forget all about those people following him. He said, "I have never come to this spot. It is perhaps one of the most beautiful spots around the capital and I might have missed it if I had not been defeated by the enemy. This beauty is worth losing the whole kingdom for." He enjoyed the beauty... and after a few minutes he became aware that the noise of the horses and the enemy coming was receding: "Perhaps they have moved into some other part of the mountains, but certainly they are not on this footpath."

He gathered his armies, he fought again. He won his kingdom back, and when he was received at the elephant gate of the capital, the whole capital was just festivity. Everybody was rejoicing the victory. Flowers were being thrown on the king from every house, from every place. People were dancing, singing, playing on their instruments. And for a moment the king said, just inside himself, "It is not so easy to defeat me." And he saw a subtle ego arising with all this reception and celebration.

Again, the big diamond was shining in the light and he remembered it. He opened it. He read it again: "This too will pass." He became silent. His face went through a total change – from the egoist he moved to a state of utter humbleness. If this too is going to pass, it is not yours. The defeat was not yours, the victory is not yours. The death was not yours, the life is not yours. You are just a watcher. Everything passes by.

This is what is missing in latihan. There is no place for the witness, for the watcher, and that is the essential part of meditation. Latihan prepares the ground, but never sows the seeds and then waits for roses and lotuses. And nothing comes up – just wild grass.

Meditation has two parts: one, a cleaning part. You are going to invite the greatest guest into your life. Clean the whole house, make it pure, fragrant, make it an aesthetic phenomenon inside you. Catharsis is perfectly good and right, but it is incomplete.

After catharsis begins the real work. When you have cleaned the ground of weeds and wild grass, then is the time to sow the seeds of flowers and wait for the spring.

Latihan is gone. It will be remembered in the footnotes of history but it has lost its grip. And the problem, the reason why it had to go was that it was only the beginning part of meditation. I have given you many meditations, but each meditation is complete in itself.

BELOVED OSHO,
THE OTHER DAY, I HEARD YOU SAYING THAT JESUS'
DISCIPLES ARE RESPONSIBLE FOR HIS CRUCIFIXION?
BELOVED MASTER, IT WAKES ME UP AT NIGHT TO
THINK THAT WE ARE RESPONSIBLE FOR YOU HAVING
BEEN DRAGGED AROUND IN PRISONS AND BEING
PERSECUTED AND THROWN OUT OF SO MANY
COUNTRIES. I LOVE YOU MORE THAN MY OWN LIFE.
HOW IS IT THAT MY AWARENESS AND MY
RESPONSIBILITY SEEMS SO FAR BEHIND MY LOVE?

Love is not far behind your responsibility and awareness. And if something like Jesus happens to me, which is probable, you will not be responsible for it. If it does *not* happen, then you will be responsible for it.

The people who can be responsible for it, I have been weeding out continuously. I have my own very simple ways so that the other person never becomes aware that he is being thrown out. I go on giving him the idea that *he* is leaving me. I don't want the poor fellow to feel guilty that he has betrayed. And if something happens to me then he will feel guilty his whole life, that he was responsible. Just to make him free of responsibility, I have never told anybody to leave. But it is very easy, without saying, to make someone leave. It is so easy that you will not believe me. There is no great esoteric principle behind it.

One old woman in the commune was a negative presence, and she was creating the same vibes around her. We tried our best here in India, in America, but the problem with the woman was first, that there was a language difficulty. She did not understand English or any language that I understand. Secondly, she was 70 years old – almost all her ideologies, Christianities... church... had all become so frozen that it seemed impossible to reach her. You could shout but her ears were full of prejudices, and something else would reach her.

Seeing that now she was being destructive to the commune.... I used to go every day for a drive, and sannyasins used to meet me on the road, both sides, dancing, singing. I stopped looking at her. The first day, perhaps she could not figure out why I had not looked at her. The second day, it was absolutely certain that I had not looked at her. The third day, she was certain that I was not going to look at her anymore, unless she changed. On the fourth day she left. But she left on her own decision; I had not said anything. So some small strategy has to be used for the person to go without feeling guilty.

Those who are with me are the reason why I am alive. I'm not alive for myself – my work is done. I'm alive only to see a few of my plants blossoming, a few of my trees bringing fruits. I have devoted my whole life. I have never bothered about respectability from the society, I have never bothered about anything. But one thing is very close to my heart: my only concern is to see you ecstatic, blissful, fulfilled. And if so many people love me, and feel their responsibility, it is the greatest security I have.

All the governments of the world are in conspiracy against me. All the religions, all the political parties are in the same conspiracy: to destroy me, to destroy my ideology, to destroy my people. But they will not succeed. If even a single person loves me unconditionally, I have more protection, more love, more friends, than nuclear weapons can destroy.

So you need not be sad about it. I am talking of those people who have not only left, but who were perhaps very happy that the US government and the Christian church together destroyed a small commune of five thousand people. They have all the forces, all the money. They have all the news media to spread whatsoever they want. It seems the people who have betrayed me are rejoicing that now, the commune will not be possible.

For the first three months after the closure of the commune, these people remained silent because they were weighing the possibilities: "Perhaps the commune continues. If it continues, then it is better not to say anything that may make it difficult for you to enter the commune again." So for three months, they were completely silent. After three months... and for these three months they were using their sannyas names, they were using the mala, they were using orange clothes, although I have freed you. But they were using them.

Once it was certain that America could not tolerate the commune, they all started changing to their old names. When they saw that the European countries, their parliaments, have decided that I cannot enter any European country, then they came out more clearly, saying that they are independent and they are doing the same work as Osho is doing. They are enlightened.

Just a few days ago, Santosh, one of the therapists in the commune.... I have worked on him twelve years to create a whole therapeutic science of dehypnotherapy. Hypnotherapy has been in existence, but a reverse process of hypnotherapy, so those who are hypnotized can be dehypnotized.... And everybody is hypnotized – by some culture, by some religion, by some politics – so everybody needs a deep spring cleaning, and dehypnosis can do it.

Now he is in California, and has started publishing a small newspaper. Even my name is not mentioned anywhere in the institute for dehypnotherapy that he has created there. And in this newspaper, just two days ago I saw: he has an announcement that all the European countries have prohibited the entry of Osho into their countries, so those who are waiting, hoping that sooner or later Osho will be coming to Europe, should drop the hope. "And we are already doing the same work." Now, their whole fear is, if I come back to Europe then they cannot go on being mini-gurus – just like mini-skirts, nothing much material. And Santosh is happy that I cannot enter America for at least five years. But they are wrong. It makes no difference whether I am in Europe or in America, Australia, or in India.

Those who have loved me and those who have drunk out of

my well, will not find another who will be satisfying. At least right now, there is nobody else. There used to be one – J. Krishnamurti. Unfortunately, he is dead.

These people, at least ninety percent of them, will come back. The ten percent, the very hard-core egoists, may find it difficult to come back – although they need not find it difficult, because I never even asked you why you left. That is your business. Why have you come? That too is your decision, and you have all the freedom to join or not to join.

I am not at all disturbed or annoyed by anybody. Because here, with me, you are not supposed to give anything in return for whatever you feel I have done for you. And in fact, I don't need anything to be returned by you because it is not a bargain, a deal, a business. It is simply my love. I love the truth – I have found it. I have loved you – I have found you also. Now my only remaining work is somehow to turn your eyes towards the truth. Once that happens, then there is no need for me to be here. But I am not a serious man, I can still be here. So you don't be worried; most probably I will be here.

BELOVED OSHO,
SITTING SILENTLY, SUDDENLY, SOFTLY, SLOWLY,
SOUNDLESSLY, PEACEFULLY, SOMETHING PEELED OFF
WHICH I COULD SEE WAS MY ILLUSION FOR A BETTER
WORLD AND GOOD PEOPLE. BELOVED OSHO, CAN
YOU SAY SOMETHING ABOUT THE DIFFERENCE
BETWEEN A VISION AND AN ILLUSION?

The difference between a vision and an illusion is very delicate and fragile, but the difference is very big. The dream is a mind phenomenon; it happens in your mind. It happens because you repress, and whatever is repressed comes up in the night when the conscious represser is asleep. Then the unconscious releases itself in dreams. Dream is the language of the unconscious.

Through the dream, the unconscious is doing many things: one is catharsis, second is giving messages to the conscious. If you don't hear, the same dream will be repeated again. It has happened in very rare cases that a dream was repeated almost every night for years. And it happened to a very intelligent, great creator – Leo Tolstoy. He used to have a dream – which was a nightmare, although there was no violence, no torture – but the set-up of the dream was such that he always woke up perspiring, breathing heavily, heart beating faster. And the dream was very strange, so he tried hard.... Perhaps he is one of the greatest novelists in the world. He has a very sensitive intelligence to find out even about others, but with his dream, he was simply helpless.

The dream was that he would see every night a vast, infinite desert – no greenery; just desert and desert, sand and sand, and it goes on and on in every direction. It is burning hot, and he sees a pair of shoes – his shoes – going away from him. They are walking. He's not in them. The shoes alone are going and going and going, and this continues. It can continue forever, there is no essential need for it to stop. There is no essential need for it to come to a conclusion. There is no question.

He told many of his friends, he told many psychoanalysts. They said, "Strange. We have heard thousands of people's dreams, analyzing them. We have read about the dreams of other people who have been analyzed, but we have never come across such a dream." Just the shoes go on walking and it is so tortuous, and every day you know; the whole day you know that the night is coming. Going to bed, you know: soon those two shoes... and how long it will continue nobody knows. Unless it comes to a peak, and just from the heavy breathing and perspiration, he wakes up.

One day, he was telling it to two of his friends, Chekhov and Gorky – both of the same caliber, both great novelists. He said, "I have asked psychoanalysts and others, and they don't seem to find any meaning in it."

Chekhov said, "You have said it – they cannot find the meaning – that is the problem. You also cannot find the meaning in your life. Your life is a meaningless life, just like those two shoes, going for no reason, not knowing where, not knowing why, but continuing in a desert where there is not even a tree to rest – it is all hot fire. But one has to reach, so they are going."

And suddenly Tolstoy became aware of the fact that it was true. His wife was from the royal family, he himself was a count. His wife was a sadist, a disciplinarian. And you cannot expect a man like Tolstoy – a painter, a musician, a poet, a novelist, a dancer – to behave the ordinary way people behave; they live in their own world.

Because Tolstoy could not manage, there was continuous fight... life was so miserable, and the dream was simply a representation, a very hidden, symbolic dream. But from that day, the dream disappeared. The meaning had been understood. It means that for ten or twelve years, the unconscious was trying to send a message to the conscious; the conscious could not get the message, so the unconscious went on and on and on until the day he understood. Then the message stopped.

Mind is full of repressions which need release. There is a certain capacity – you cannot hold more than that. Dreams are your unfulfilled desires, your repressed longings, your incomplete experiences, but they are all of the mind.

The vision is when the mind has gone, when the mind is in a state of silence and stillness, when there is not even a small stir of thoughts. The lake of the mind is absolutely calm and quiet. When the mind is absolutely calm and quiet, you can see – not through the mind but from a totally different source. In the East, we have called it the third eye. It is simply symbolic. When these two eyes which function for the mind are closed and the mind is no longer working, suddenly you start seeing with a clarity that you never had before. This is vision.

It has nothing to do with your repressions, nothing to do with your unfulfilled desires, nothing to do with your repressed instincts. It has something to do with the coming future. It is your clarity that has given you the opportunity to have a glimpse into the future. And if your meditation goes on deepening, your vision will go on becoming more and more clear, in detail.

The vision is possible any time – day, night, waking, asleep. The dream is possible only in sleep. The dream belongs to your small mind. The vision belongs to the universal mind. The vision is an indication that you are coming closer to home. The dream is an indication you are going farther from home.

One strange thing, it is simple to make the distinction: dreams are always in black and white; visions are Technicolor. So if you forget everything else, you can remember this much. Because dreams are very ancient, they don't know the new technology. They are still working with old photography and old plates, and everything is dim and dark. But visions are absolutely radiant and clear and full of color.

After dreams, you will find yourself tired. After seeing a vision, you will find yourself so full of energy... because the vision has been a contact with existence itself. Existence has refueled you, has given you more life because you have deserved it by going deeper in meditation. A dream is indicative of a sick mind, a sick psychology. Vision comes out of your inner health.

BELOVED OSHO,

FOR THE LAST TWO YEARS, I HAVE BEEN DOING
KARATE-DO AND I LOVE THESE AWAKE MOMENTS
WHERE ALL THOUGHTS DISAPPEAR OUT OF MY
HEAD. KARATE HAS THE ADDITION "DO", THE
JAPANESE MEANING FOR THE TAO OF LAO TZU. I ASK
YOU WHETHER THERE IS A CONNECTION BETWEEN
KARATE AND ENLIGHTENMENT.

There have been many mergings of different traditions, religions: Jews and Christians, Christians and Mohammedans, Mohammedans and Hindus. But except for the Buddhist, all the conversions and mergers have been through force of some kind or other. Mohammedans and Christians have been fighting – killing living people, burning living people in thousands. They call it holy war, *jihad*.

Of course if your life is at risk, very few people will be fanatic enough to die rather than be converted, because anyway you are not much of a Hindu – what does it matter if you become a Mohammedan? You will not be going to the temple, you will be going to the mosque. You will not be reading Gita, you will be reading Koran. But these are superficial things. For these superficial things, why lose your life? Even if these people are mad, you are not mad.

Mohammedans converted millions of people to Mohammedanism through the sword, and those who refused were killed. Christianity converts people by giving them bread, butter, houses, schools, hospitals. That is not very much different from the sword, because these people don't understand at all the religion in which they are, and neither are they going to understand anything of the religion to which they are converting. Their interest is in material things.

I had a friend, a principal of a Christian college. I asked him, "How do you feel about conversion?" because his father had become a Christian when he was a young kid.

He took me inside the house. In his bedroom, he had a picture and he showed me: "This is my father." I said, "My God! But he looks like a beggar!"

He said, "Yes, he *was* a beggar. This is my mother. They had to become Christians just to survive and just to take care of us. They were very much interested that their children should be educated but they could not manage it."

And he was in the same picture. You could not think there was any connection between those two old persons and this man. He is a principal, well-educated in the West, has the highest degrees, great respectability even among the Hindus. And then his son-in-law, who is an American, is a psychoanalyst. For six months he practices in America and six months in India. And his daughter is one of the most beautiful women I have seen. Just a small thing is wrong, but that has nothing to do with anybody except her husband. She has a small beard that she is continuously shaving. But the more she shaves it, the more it grows. Her husband was saying to me, "I feel a little embarrassed to go with her anywhere, because people immediately see the first thing – her beard." And she is such a beautiful woman... but perhaps nature was trying to see how a beard fits on a woman. It does not fit.

He said, "You can see what Christianity has done to us, what Hinduism has done to us. These are the Hindus – my father, my mother. In tatters... you can see they are hungry, you can see they have suffered their whole life."

"And then," he said, "you can look at me. You can look at my daughter, the doctor" – the daughter is also a doctor of psychology – "who also goes to America to practice. And she has married an American. Now they have cars, they have houses, they have bungalows in the hill station."

I said, "I can understand. It is perfectly right, there is no problem, but this is not religious conversion, because religion does not seem to play any part in it."

Conversion happens only when you experience something that you have never experienced before, and the experience is so radical that it does not allow you to continue, to remain the old self. It forces you to change your habits, to change your thoughts, to change *everything*, and be reborn.

The conversion that has happened through Buddhism is the only one that can be called religious. And because it was religious, there was no question of the sword, there was no question of bread and butter, or any kind of bribe. No violence... not even an invitation that you should become a Buddhist, but only sharing their meditations, their joys. And people seeing them, feeling them, became attracted, became followers of Gautam Buddha. But it was their own decision; no one has interfered in it. Because of this phenomenon, the same happened in Tibet and the same happened in Japan. The old religion of Shinto in Japan dissolved into Buddhism, just as a river meets an ocean – no conflict, just a welcome merger.

What I want to emphasize is that because of the difference in conversion, something very great has happened. And that is that many things are born out of the meeting of Buddhism with Confucianism, of Buddhism with Taoism, of Buddhism with Shintoism. Many creative things have happened which have not happened in Hindus becoming Christians, Hindus becoming Mohammedans, Mohammedans becoming Christians, Jews becoming Mohammedans or Christians – no change like that has happened. And that is going to be the criterion: the change that has happened is that they have all produced new methods that were inconceivable before. It was a friendship – nobody was higher, nobody was lower.

When a Hindu becomes a Christian, the Christian priest guides him in what to do. When a Taoist becomes friendly with Buddhism, nobody is going to guide him; they both have to share their experiences. And out of this sharing, a loving, friendly....

In China, Ch'an was the crossbreed between Buddhism and Tao – and Ch'an is certainly higher than both. Each child has to be higher than both the parents; otherwise, there would be no evolution. Evolution depends on the simple fact that every child has to defeat his father, his mother, in every possible way, in every possible direction. Ch'an is far superior to Buddhism and Tao both. It is not out of conflict and violence and blood; it is out of sheer love and joy. It is an inquiry: what you have found, what I have found... perhaps they can be one whole. And that one whole is Ch'an.

In Japan, the thing happened even on a bigger scale. Ch'an reached a higher form, even more delicate and more superior, when Buddhism and Tao became acquainted with the old Japanese religion of Shinto. When Shinto dissolved into Buddhism, they refined Ch'an because they had a few new experiences which Buddhists had never encountered, which Taoists had never known. Zen is the highest peak of meditation that has ever been reached.

Not only Zen... but in Japan almost a miracle has happened. Japan has tried the insights of Zen in other fields of life, for example, swordsmanship – a very faraway subject. Nobody can imagine what meditation has to do with a sword, but they developed swordsmanship in Japan. You learn it in the temple of Zen. And this swordsmanship is not the same as it is all over the world. It is totally different in Japan; it is a method of meditation, because with swords you have to be very alert. You are fighting with swords – you have to be very alert; otherwise you are gone. In such situations, you cannot afford to be sleepy.

Swordsmanship has been used to develop that quality of awareness, and in the same way, the other martial arts – aikido, jujitsu, karate. All these are arts of the warrior, but the Japanese have transformed them for the war that you are going to fight inside yourself with the darkness, with your own ego, with all that is ugly in you.

Karate is connected with Tao, is connected with Gautam Buddha, is connected with Confucius. But neither Confucius nor Gautam Buddha nor Lao Tzu were aware that their meditative techniques would bring such a transformation that even martial arts, which have been developed to destroy man, to murder, to commit suicide... but they can be used because the situation of death facing you in any form makes you alert, aware. And listening, and practicing jujitsu, karate, aikido... slowly, slowly you become more and more silent, more and more peaceful. The question of war and destruction disappears.

But this was possible because these religions met in a human way. The other three or four religions have met also, but they have met from the very beginning as enemies. So the Far East, where Buddhism has been the root, has been very creative. It is different from the rest of the world.

I would like you to understand meditation in such a way, that you can use it not only while you are meditating but while you are doing *anything*. Just do it more consciously, more gracefully, more lovingly and you have changed the very quality of the action. And once you know to change the qualities of your actions, your whole life becomes the life of a meditator.

22

The greatest discovery there is

BELOVED OSHO,
YOU HAVE NOT ONLY A PROFOUND
UNDERSTANDING OF HUMAN NATURE BUT ALSO
YOU HAVE THE KNOW-HOW TO TRANSFORM IT. YOU
ARE A PERFECT MASTER. HOW IS IT THAT WESTERN
AND EASTERN PSYCHOLOGISTS ARE NOT RECOG-
NIZING YOU? DO THESE HUMAN SCIENTISTS FEEL
JEALOUS AND OFFENDED BY YOU? PLEASE COMMENT.

There are many things to be understood. First, the psychology that prevails all over the world is Western psychology. Eastern psychology has been completely forgotten. Even in Eastern universities, everything is from the West – borrowed, second-hand – particularly with psychology. But the East has devoted thousands of years to human consciousness and it has come to very basic realizations about human evolution. To ignore Eastern psychology is to ignore man's future and his evolution. Because nature has completed its work. Nature cannot go beyond man; it has come to its ultimate production. Now, the whole burden of evolution is on human shoulders.

But unfortunately, Western psychology is materialistic, which means it denies man a soul, a spirit, a being which is immortal beyond this framework of your body. This happened because of a natural historical coincidence. All the sciences are about matter. Physics is about the most interior constituents of matter – so is chemistry, so is the whole panorama of human scientific endeavor. Psychology is in wrong company. All these sciences are studying *objects*. Psychology's world is the subjectivity of man, not the objects around him.

But because in these three hundred years sciences have been developing on a materialist basis... and they have been succeeding, the very word *scientific* has become prestigious. Just to say that something is "scientific" is enough to say that is *right*. Once you hear the word *scientific*, you have already agreed, there is no question of argument anymore. If science has established something, then there is no need to doubt it. The scientists themselves have doubted enough and have tried from every possible angle; if they have come to a conclusion, it must be so. In the midst of scientific progress, psychology was born. Naturally, it chose to be part of scientific growth.

Another thing has been happening for three hundred years: Christianity has been behaving with scientists and science in a very crude, primitive, superstitious, illogical, violent way. And because science went on succeeding in spite of the opposition of the religions, the religions lost their prestige, their credit, and science became the *only* rightful search for truth. In such an atmosphere, psychology was born.

Everybody was trying to prove that whatever he was doing was scientific; unless it was scientific, it would not be accepted by humanity at large.

And you can see the dichotomy in the very name of psychology. *Psychology* means the science of the soul. But the scientific attitude is to deny the existence of the soul, because there is no possibility of catching hold of it. There is no possibility of dissecting it, no possibility of taking it into the lab and doing all kinds of experiments before they can say yes, there is something like the soul, which is immortal. Because it is invisible. All forces are invisible, all energies are invisible. Energies and forces are known not by themselves, because they are not visible. They are known by their *effects*, because the effects are visible.

Nobody knows what electricity is – not even Thomas Alva Edison, who discovered it. But everybody knows how to switch it on, how to switch it off. Electricity, as energy, is not visible. You are seeing the light but the light is not electricity, it is an effect of its presence. We infer that electricity must be there because the light is on.

And there is enough evidence that the soul must be there in man because there are so many effects indicating towards it. Without a soul, man is a machine. But have you ever heard of machines revolting? going through a communist revolution? – machines throwing away one government, creating another government? No, machines are not concerned. They are not even prejudiced. They will work perfectly under communism, they will work perfectly under capitalism... to them, there is no question because there is no consciousness. A machine cannot say: "I cannot do this because this is immoral, criminal." If machines could do that, there would be no war – because no weapon will agree with your politicians.

If the atom bomb had been asked whether it wanted to destroy Hiroshima and Nagasaki, the bomb would have laughed: "Why should I destroy? They have done no harm to me. In fact, I don't know those people; there is no reason at all for me to destroy them. And I refuse to be a slave in an act which is irrational."

Machines don't think, don't have consciousness, don't have a heart, don't feel. It is certain that man is not a machine because he has qualities which machines don't have. Those qualities are indicative of a certain mysterious phenomenon inside, at the very center of our being – a flame of light, a flame of awareness. But science will accept it only if your consciousness can be put into their test tubes, if they can play around with your consciousness. But this, by the very nature of consciousness, is impossible.

Psychology accepted a very stupid definition: that it is a science. If I am allowed to rename it – and I have the right because I have renamed more people than anybody has ever done in the whole of history! so renaming is something which I have been doing continuously for years – I would call it *parapsychology*. In the East, it has been parapsychology: psychology of the beyond. And man has so much space beyond himself – the whole universe – that to give him a definition, to say that he is just matter, is to reduce him to the *lowest* denominator. Only his body is matter, the house in which he lives. He is not the body and he is not the mind: he is beyond both.

Western psychologists, thinkers and philosophers are very well acquainted with my thinking, but strangely enough, very few of them seem to have guts to stand against the vested interests.

One of my sannyasins, a world-famous economist, received the Nobel prize three years ago and naturally, when he received the Nobel prize and the honor, the first idea in his mind was: "Will it ever be possible for these people to understand Osho and recognize him?"

He asked the president of the Nobel Prize Committee... and

now that he is a Nobel prize winner he can propose anybody's name – only a member of the Nobel committee can propose a name. So he asked the president: "You have also been reading Osho, why is everybody silent about this man? We should take the matter in hand. His books should be considered for a Nobel prize."

The president of the committee said, "Say it in such a way that nobody else hears – at least, his *name* should not be heard by anybody. I love the man. I know you love the man, and I know a few more people love him; but it is almost impossible for the committee to decide to give him a Nobel prize because this committee consists of people who have already brought names given by their governments.

"Osho has no government. On the contrary, all the governments are against him; all the religions are against him. And these people here cannot gather enough courage to be against the religions and against the governments, to go against the rich people who are dominating and to propose Osho's name. But I would suggest you not get into trouble, because there will be international pressure not to give him the Nobel prize. I have received a few suggestions to give him the Nobel prize but I have received a hundred times more letters saying, 'Be alert! This man should not get the award!' And I don't want to get involved in a worldwide controversy.

"The moment you offer this man's name there will be a world-wide controversy about it. I am a non-controversial man." All politicians are non-controversial. They cannot afford to be controversial. It needs a lion's heart, and your politicians are simply rats.

There must also be some jealousy involved in it, because I am the only man, with the whole world against him, homeless.... They can manage to crucify me. And in fact, I belong to the category of people who have been crucified. I don't belong to the Nobel prize winners. My prize can be only like the poison to Socrates, crucifixion to Jesus, death to Al-Hillaj Mansoor – those are my rewards.

So they are unnecessarily jealous. Even if they decide to give me the Nobel prize, I refuse it beforehand – in advance. I don't want to take any chances. I don't have any respect for your rewards or your prizes.

I was a student in the university, participating in an all-India debate – almost fifty universities were participating. Knowing that I cannot speak very loudly, that if there are ten thousand people, I cannot reach them, they played a trick: they removed the microphone. At least one thing became certain: I am not going to get the first prize. Because only the first two or three rows in front of me could hear me, and the judges were sitting behind – they would not be able to hear a single word. The mike was there. When I arrived it was being used – the president, the vice-chancellor of that university, were speaking. And then they started whispering to each other.

I was sitting just behind them. I figured out that they are thinking to remove the mike so that at least I could not get the first prize. Anybody else could get it, that did not matter.

They had put my name first, so I said, "I am not interested in any prize, so include me out!" And I took the mike and I said, "I will use my time to talk to the students and to the staff. You need not be worried, just cancel my name on your list of people who are going to win the prize. I think now there is no problem for you if I use the mike."

I used the mike. I reached every judge and every person and in the end I said: "This was a conspiracy, because I speak slowly. I am not a street orator. I would ask *you* – the ten thousand people: students, professors, invited guests – what do you want? Should I remain on the list or should I drop the idea of the prize?"

They all raised their hands saying, "You should remain on the list." And the whole thing turned completely upside down because only I used the mike and nobody else used the mike, so the judges could not hear anybody.

One judge told me: "This has been so hilarious! What they wanted turned out just the opposite. We were very happy that you managed well. We wanted to hear you; we have come to hear you – not to hear all these childish debaters."

The same is the situation with awards all over the world: childish people, for reasons of politics, are getting Nobel prizes. These people may be famous intellectually but they are not people of genius. They are not people who have love in their hearts, justice, fairness. There is jealousy, and it takes such stupid forms that you cannot believe it.

One man has written a letter to the German parliament that I am a hidden Catholic and in fact, I am working to spread Christianity, Catholicism. Now even Christ must have laughed, although he is not a fellow who would even smile, but at this point he must have laughed. Because I am a hidden Catholic, I should not be allowed in Germany. This is the intelligentsia! But because I have been against our so-called intelligentsia too, the problem has become more complicated.

I am all for intelligence and not at all for intellect and I make a very clear-cut distinction between the two. Intellect is part of the mind – you can go on becoming bigger and bigger and more and more knowledgeable by accumulating information: you will be thought a great intellectual. These are the people who constitute our intelligentsia. All that they know is borrowed.

Intelligence arises only when meditation has blossomed. It is the fragrance of your silence – the song of your silence. It is a totally different thing because its source is different. Intellect functions as part of the mind, intelligence functions when mind stops functioning.

Intelligent people around the world are with me and that's what counts. I don't care about the crowd. My only concern is about those few people who have intelligence enough to enter deeper into their being, because as they open up more and more inside they start changing on the outside. One day, suddenly there is an awakened being and all his actions are full of the light, of the beauty, of the truth of what he has attained within himself.

They are with me. They have been coming from all over the world. All the governments are preventing them, but whenever there is something valuable, something so valuable that all those powerful people look like pygmies in comparison, they are naturally afraid. They would not like me to exist. But now it is too late. If they do any harm to me they will destroy their own society, their own economic structure; they will destroy their own prestige, their own credibility. And they will not harm my cause, they will help it immensely.

I don't want their Nobel prizes – just a small crucifixion will do. I would have preferred an electric chair but to carry an electric chair to the place does not suit me. And it is less dramatic too. A wooden cross is far more dramatic.

They are full of jealousy on *every* point because none of them has been able to answer all my criticisms of the past and its history. They are irritated also because they cannot find any way to somehow put a stop to my increasing number of friends and increasing number of enemies. Both are mine; they both relate to me. Without me, both would be at a loss. Somebody would lose a friend, somebody would lose an enemy – the whole world would be at a loss.

But my people are going to change the whole situation – not by any effort, but just by living the way I have been showing you. You are going to be my ultimate witnesses. Whether I was right or wrong will be decided by your actions, by your being.

BELOVED OSHO,
YOU SEEM TO MIXING TOGETHER ALL OF OUR
QUESTIONS. IT'S LIKE PUZZLE PIECES, WHERE ALL THE
PIECES FIT TOGETHER PERFECTLY IN THE END. IS THIS
ONE EXAMPLE OF THE ONENESS OF ALL?

The truth is, with numbers, at the most I can remember up to three. After that, I don't know what number comes. Secondly, all the questions that I choose have a certain coherence, a certain inner unity. It may not be apparent to you.

When I speak, if I go into one question in absolute detail, then I cannot deal with another question on that day. One question will be enough for two and a half hours. So I have my way; I introduce the first question, answer its essential points; then I take the second question, answer its essential points, and if there is any point there that can emphasize something in the first question, I bring in the first question again. And it is not done in any systematic way because I have not prepared it. It is just my sensitivity and my spontaneity. I simply go with whatever response arises in me.

So my answer to five questions is like a spiral: I may come to the first question many times but in the end, all those five questions and the answers given to them will make a whole answer. Perhaps those five questions were five aspects of one question that you are not aware of. Because in fact, there *is* only one question. We can ask millions of questions but the answer is one – there is no way to have many answers. Because the basic question is one, hence the basic answer is one – the remaining is just play.

Yes, they will all fit like a puzzle in a deep harmony – but while I am answering you, I'm more concerned with you than with your question. I am more concerned with the answer than with the questions. I am more concerned to bring all the questions to a certain synthesis so that the one answer can be acceptable.

And these problems are there: I cannot remember. I try my best... up to three I somehow manage. By that time, it is enough. Then I start using the wrong numbers. My memory is not very good.

So while I am answering a question – and your questions are not simply one question. Each of your questions can be divided into three or four or five questions. So I start answering one – by the time I have answered it, I have forgotten the other three or four. Rather than waiting for them to come back, I proceed to the second question.

Sometimes, while answering the second question, I start remembering what has been left incomplete in the first, so I have to complete it in the second. By that time, I have forgotten what the second question was all about. So I wait – perhaps in the third question, when I am answering it – some word, some sentence, some story, may remind me. It has been working perfectly well.

So you get all the answers – even those which are not visible on the surface. But this is not a prepared sermon. This is not a lecture in a university. I know professors who have been using the notes that they have taken in class when they were students. They have been using the same notes in teaching for thirty years. So much water has gone down the Ganges in thirty years, but they are not aware.

I also feel it's really amazing that by the end, slowly, slowly everything that has been forgotten anywhere comes to my mind, and I say okay to Maneesha only when I feel okay.

BELOVED OSHO,
SITTING WITH YOU, EVERY CELL IN MY BODY STARTS
DANCING AND SINGING 'HE IS HERE! HE IS HERE!'
AND I FEEL HOW LONG I HAVE BEEN WAITING. AND
THEN SLOWLY, SLOWLY MY DEEP LONGING AND THE
FULFILLMENT OF IT TOUCH EACH OTHER AND
SOMETHING VERY DEEP IN ME STARTS RELAXING.
STILL NOW, AFTER BEING A SANNYASIN FOR FOUR
YEARS, I SOMETIMES CAN ALMOST NOT BELIEVE IT –
THAT THIS IS REALLY HAPPENING, THAT THIS IS NOT
A DREAM AND THAT NOW, TODAY, I REALLY SIT AT
THE FEET OF MY MASTER AND MY HEART IS
OVERFLOWING, TEARS AND LAUGHING MELT
TOGETHER. BELOVED OSHO, I DO NOT KNOW IF I
HAVE BEEN WITH YOU OR ANY OTHER MASTER, BUT
I KNOW I HAVE BEEN WAITING, WAITING FOR SO
LONG. IF SOMEBODY HAS BEEN WITH A MASTER, CAN
HE FALL BACK AGAIN IN DARKNESS, LIKE I WAS IN
BEFORE TAKING SANNYAS? THANK YOU, BELOVED
MASTER AND FRIEND. EVERY DAY YOU ARE STILL
HERE IS A GIFT FOR ME.

The first thing: Anything achieved in any life as far as conscious growth is concerned, remains with you. And whenever you start the search again, you will start from the point where you had stopped in some past life. But it depends on a very subtle point – whether you have *achieved* something or just believed that you have achieved. If you have just believed, it is not going to be with you in the next life. You will have to start from scratch.

As far as you are concerned, because you feel this tremendous quality of waiting, that you have been waiting and waiting and waiting for long, that means you have never been with a master in the past but you have been a seeker, a long time seeker in the past. But you were seeking on your own, a lonely wanderer in search of the miraculous. Because you were not with any master, not with any school where many people were working together for their inner consolidation, you don't have any memory of such a thing. You have only one feeling, of waiting. That shows that for many lives you have been waiting.

And perhaps the time has come and now you may not need to wait anymore because I am ready to give you that which you have been seeking – whether you know or not. You may not know exactly, precisely what you are seeking, but one thing is certain: that you are incomplete, you are hollow, you are utterly, negatively empty. This much is certain: that you are not complete and entire. Hence, you are waiting for something to make you whole. That time has come.

Your love, your gratitude, your trust in me shows that unknowingly, you were searching for a master who does not belong to the old but belongs to the future. Every intelligent person is searching for the master who belongs to the future. Idiots are searching for masters in the past. The more ancient they are the more valuable they are thought to be.

Now you can relax. It may have taken many lives to come to me – now remember, going away from me will take even many more lives. So it is better now to settle. Wandering is good, but only to a limit. You have wandered enough. It is time to retire from this wandering.

BELOVED OSHO,
IT IS SAID "IF YOU MEET A MAN ON A HIGHER LEVEL
OF BEING THAN YOUR OWN, YOU WILL NOT
UNDERSTAND HIM." THE DISTANCE BETWEEN YOU
AND US SEEMS SO INFINITE. WHAT ARE WE DOING
HERE, OSHO?

It is true. If you meet a man of a higher development in consciousness, you will not be able to understand the man; communication will be almost impossible. But you are saying and seeing only one side of the phenomenon. You will not be able to understand a man of higher consciousness but he will understand you – *more* than you understand yourself. He has passed through the same stages that you are passing. He's well-acquainted with the whole territory and he is standing on a high place from where he can see far and wide.

On your part, if you can understand only this much – that understanding will be difficult because his consciousness is higher – then your question will be: "First raise my consciousness so that I am at a point from where communication is possible." You will not ask other questions because his answers will not make sense to you. The only question you can ask is: "I am here, *ready*. Give me a lift!" And this can be done. This is actually what is being done here.

Your meditations, my sittings with you, your own individual efforts – all together are creating only a higher consciousness in you. And whether *you* understand me or not is immaterial – I understand you perfectly well.

You may be blind, I am not. And I am holding your hand tight – so you may not be able to find the door yourself, but just don't try to escape! Allow me to hold your hand. I will take you out of the door into the open.

The greatest problem is not that you don't understand what comes from a higher consciousness. The greater problem is, you think that if you cannot understand him that means he is talking nonsense. You have closed the doors. The sun has come even up to your door – you close the door in the very face of the sun. The sun will come again tomorrow morning. People like me don't get tired because you have not been listening, you have been closing the door, you have been rejecting. The person with the higher consciousness understands it – that these are all childish ways of protecting one's ego. He is not going to be angry with you.

In these thirty years, I must have passed millions of people – talked about their problems, given them every help they wanted for their further growth: instructions, disciplines. But while the person was listening, I was also aware to what category the person belongs: Is he listening or is he just being polite, and deep down he thinks he knows everything? He need not bother about meditation. He need not think about changing his lifestyle so that the new consciousness becomes easier to grow.

With the old lifestyle it is difficult, it is almost like a rosebush growing in stones and rocks. Once in a while it happens, but that is not the rule – that is the exception. And you should always remember the rule, not the exception.

I can see while I am talking to you whether you are closed. If I see that somehow your closed doors can be opened, that perhaps you can be persuaded – if not for spiritual growth then for something else; perhaps for a Tantra group... just get caught in the net, then I will see – once you are caught things go on becoming easier.

There is a point of no return. And you all have to remember when that point comes in your life that you cannot go away from me, that it has become impossible. That even if I leave the body, it will not make any difference. You have found your master, and the master has found his disciple. And this is the greatest discovery there is.

BELOVED OSHO,
MY FATHER SAYS THAT YOU CANNOT BE AN
ENLIGHTENED PERSON BECAUSE YOU TELL SO MANY
DIRTY JOKES. DO YOU HAVE A JOKE TO TELL MY DAD?

Your father is right. That's why I have gone beyond enlightenment – now I can tell dirty jokes. Just because of enlightenment, I am not going to leave telling dirty jokes. But tell your father that to an enlightened man no joke is dirty. Either it is meaningful or meaningless, but no joke is dirty.

Why have jokes been called dirty? Just small things, but they carry so much past history. Because man's body below the belt is dirty. It is a stupid idea, because your whole body functions as a single unit, it is not divided anywhere. Your blood is circulating continually, twenty-four hours a day. The blood that was in the brain is now in the feet. In the brain, it was not dirty. In the feet, my God! And it is the same blood!

Because sex has become condemned by religions, any joke that has any relationship with sex has become dirty. It is their attitude about sex that makes the joke dirty. Otherwise, ask your father what is dirty in it. Ask him to pinpoint it.

And the greatest miracle in the world is that your father could give birth to you. Perhaps he has given birth to many others. He can make love but a joke about love becomes dirty. The action is perfectly alright, your father doing all kinds of gymnastics is right. Without those gymnastics you would not be here, but a joke about it is wrong. What kind of society are we living in? There seems to be no rationality.

A young boy went to the bathroom in the night. He had to pass through his parents' room and the boy saw the mother was performing fellatio on the father – look up in the dictionary what fellatio is, because I will not tell you the meaning – and the boy came out of the room scratching his head and saying, "These people sent me to the doctor because I was sucking my thumb!" And these are the people – in the morning they will be in church, all holy. But an innocent joke will be condemned as dirty.

Why are so many jokes related to sex? Why have they become dirty? Because sex has been suppressed and condemned. This condemnation and this continuous repression has made everything related to sex, dirty. But the whole condemnation is wrong.

And your father must have suppressed his sexual instincts, because in my books, he found only dirty jokes! He could not find any method of meditation? He could not find something that could give him more maturity, more integrity, more individuality?

It happened that Dr. Johnson wrote a very exhaustive dictionary of the English language. Of the old dictionaries, his is the best. The book was published and on the second day – it had just been in the stores for one day – on the second day, three old women, seventy, seventy-five, eighty, they reached Johnson's house and they said, "So you are the fellow who has written that dirty dictionary!"

He said, "Dirty? What do you mean by dirty dictionary? Everybody is praising it, saying that it is the best dictionary!"

The women said, "Those people don't know what is inside. There are three words which are dirty!"

A twelve-hundred-page dictionary.... Those three old women did a great search – the whole night it seems – and they found only three words!

Dr. Johnson said, "It seems you were looking only for these words. There are thousands of words in that dictionary, how did you manage to find these three words? Unless you were looking for them, there is no other possibility."

But why should a seventy, eighty-year-old woman look for some dirty word, some obscene word? It gives some kind of satisfaction. Even when old people become unable to experience love in the biological sense, still the urge is there. But that urge starts expressing itself in condemnation. So you remain holy, pure and you can condemn. But your very interest in it shows something deeper about your mind.

A joke for your father...*especially* for your father!

An old man went to a doctor and he said, "Do something! Give me some injections to make me sexually powerful." The doctor said, "Pop, how you old are?" He said, "I'm only ninety."

The doctor said, "Ninety?" He said, "Okay, let me first examine you. Show me your sexual organs." The old man took out his tongue and one finger.

The doctor said, "What is the matter? This tongue and this finger?"

He said, "Yes, doctor. These have been my sexual organs for forty years."

So tell your father that before such a condition comes, enjoy a little!

23

Being: The most beautiful flower in existence

BELOVED OSHO,

I'M OFTEN TORTURED BY THE IDEA THAT I HAVE TO
DO SOMETHING SPECIAL TO REALIZE MYSELF. A FEW
YEARS AGO, I WAS ON THE POINT OF BECOMING A
PSYCHOANALYST. FORTUNATELY, I DROPPED THIS
IDEA AND I TOOK SANNYAS. I TRIED TO WORK AS A
DOCTOR, BUT I WAS GETTING SO TENSE THAT I WAS
NO LONGER LOVING WITH THE PEOPLE WHO WERE
COMING TO ME. NOW I DO SIMPLE JOBS BUT STILL
THE IDEA IS THERE: AM I WASTING MY TIME? AM I
RUNNING AWAY FROM MY RESPONSIBILITY? ON THE
OTHER HAND, EVERY TIME THIS IDEA OF DOING WAS
DROPPED, I EXPERIENCED DAYS OF BLISS. CAN YOU
PLEASE TELL ME SOMETHING MORE ABOUT THE
DIFFERENCE BETWEEN DOING AND BEING?

It is one of the most significant questions for a seeker: the difference between *doing* and *being*. You are born as beings. In your mother's womb, you are just a being. Then life begins to teach you how to do things: how to be successful, how to be rich, how to be famous, how to be powerful. There are a thousand and one 'hows', and you see around you a whole world engaged in doing something or other.

And in a way, there are things which can only be *done*. For example, if you want money, you will have to work hard for it – or you can go the easy way, but that will be criminal. If you want to be a powerful politician, you will forget all about morality, humanity. You have to forget all great values of life, you have to concentrate only on one thing: your ambition for power. And you have to do *everything* – right or wrong, good or bad, anything that helps you to achieve your ambition. You are not to be worried about means and ends; once you are successful, whatever you have done will be known as right. Your success changes the wrong means into right means, and your failure changes your right means into wrong means.

Seeing the situation, one starts following the ways of the world. One starts running for goals, for recognition, for respectability –

one is ready to do anything. But the more one gets involved in doings, the more one starts going away from oneself. *Each* act takes you away from yourself, and the further away the goal is, the further away you have gone from yourself. No doing can help you to realize yourself, to know yourself, to *be* yourself. It is not a question of doing; you have to learn a totally different art than the arts which are based on doing. You have to learn just to *be* – silent, not running anywhere, no goal in the future, no desire to possess mundane things.

Relaxing into yourself – to such an extent that time stops, mind stops – you simply *are*. A kind of *isness*... this is your being. In its purity, it is the most beautiful flower in the whole existence. Lotuses and roses are very jealous of it. The moment you have tasted just a little bit the nectar of being silent, cool, centered... your whole life is going to change from this moment. Because this taste is not something that anybody has ever been able to forget; on the contrary, this taste of your own being makes you forget the whole world.

In fact, right now you don't have any inner world, or even if you have, you are not aware of it – which is almost the same. Whether it is there or not makes no difference to you; you know only the world of matter and objects. You know *everything* around you, except yourself. You are illusory and the whole world is real; money is real, power is real. You... even *you* don't know who you are. You have never come to encounter yourself.

I have heard.... In a train, two Englishmen were traveling. Then the train stopped and one of them got out of the train. His wife had come to meet him... but he looked very pale, sick.

She asked, "What is the matter, is something wrong with you?"

He said, "Yes. Whenever I have to sit, not facing towards the direction the train is going but facing the opposite way, then my whole body goes through a kind of feverish throbbing."

The wife said, "But you could have changed your seat rather than getting sick."

He said, "I wanted to, but another Englishman was sitting on the other seat."

So she said, "What is the matter in that? You could have told him your problem and he would have considered it; it is not a problem for everybody."

He said, "You are right, but how could I have said anything to him? because nobody has introduced me to him, and without an introduction...."

But it is not only about the Englishman – as far as the world of being is concerned, you have never entered it because nobody has introduced you to it. Nobody has given you a challenge to explore yourself. Man has accepted challenges from the moon, from Everest, from Mars... and man goes on and on without knowing himself.

Until the moment all action – even the movement of thoughts is action – stops, you will not be able to know what being is, because action functions like a thick smoke around you. There are so many thoughts, so many emotions, so many sentiments, so many moods... you are surrounded by an invisible wall, but very thick – almost as thick as the Chinese wall; a car can go on top of it, it is as wide as a road. But it is invisible. So you go on carrying all this weight for your whole life, getting more and more miserable and not knowing that misery is not the nature of existence. Misery is manufactured by man – existence is just playfulness, bliss. It is a song, it is a dance, it is a continuous celebration all the year round.

When you stop acting, doing, when you collect your consciousness at the very center of your individuality, you will be able to see a door opening into another world – the other world, the sacred world. Outside you is the world of action. Inside you is the world of being.

Action is mundane – it is necessary, but it cannot make your life a joy unto itself. It is necessary for survival – but just survival is not enough for a dance. For a dance, you need energy overflowing; you cannot contain it anymore. And one of the miracles of life is that by great action, you produce small things of no intrinsic value, and without any effort, *being* opens doors upon doors of treasures which you have never dreamt of. You have only heard the word – blissfulness, ecstasy, *samadhi*, nirvana, enlightenment – different names for the same situation. You have come home so totally that the outside world, which used to be very real, is almost like a dream that you had seen somewhere and forgotten. That's why the mystics have been calling the world illusory, *maya*, and they call the world of being the ultimate reality.

BELOVED OSHO,
YOU SAID A FEW DAYS AGO, "I LOVE YOU LIKE
NOBODY COULD EVER LOVE YOU." I KNOW IN MY
HEART THAT IT IS TRUE. I WOULD ALSO LIKE TO TELL
YOU THAT I LOVE YOU MORE THAN ANYONE I
COULD EVER LOVE. WITHOUT YOU, MY LIFE IS
ABSOLUTELY MEANINGLESS. WHEN I TOOK SANNYAS,
I USED TO SAY I WOULD DIE FOR YOU, I'M READY TO
GIVE MY LIFE TO YOU. NOW I SAY I WOULD LIKE TO
LIVE FOR YOU AND I'M READY TO GIVE MY LIFE TO
YOU. THANK YOU FOR THE LIFE YOU ARE GIVING ME.
I BOW DOWN TO YOU WITH INEXPRESSIBLE
GRATITUDE.

There is a great insight in your question. For the whole of the past, people have been told by religions, by politicians, by other kinds of fanatics, that if you are dedicated to any ideology – religious, political, social, philosophical – if you are *really* dedicated to an ideology, then you should be ready to die for it. The readiness to die is an indication from your side that your dedication is total.

This is not so, according to me. Your dedication is total if you are ready to *live* for me, not to die – because death is so easy, it is so simple to jump into the ocean. Even others can help. But to live, year after year, in an insane world, needs great dedication and great love and great devotion. Your love should be so great that it can tolerate the whole insanity of the world; it is still worth living because of your dedication, because of your love. Your love creates a small, cozy corner in this insane world, a cozy corner of your own life which is sane.

I teach you life, not death, because to me, death does not exist at all. If you have lived – and lived with intensity, lived with totality, lived with your whole being, not holding anything back – you will know not only life and its eternity, you will also know simultaneously death and its illusoriness.

In the past, the people who were teaching that your death is the only proof that your dedication is total were really exploiting you, destroying you, encouraging your suicidal instinct.

Man has a suicidal instinct – this is one of the latest discoveries by psychoanalysts and other psychologists – just as there is a deep lust for life. One wants to live – and people are living in such conditions; just go around Bombay and see the beggars, see the people living in slums. Somebody is blind, somebody is crippled, somebody is starving; somebody has no medicines, is sick; somebody is old and still dragging, there is no point in living. But why do these people go on? There is such a deep lust for life that one can tolerate *anything*.

It happened... in an Egyptian monastery, a monk went into a coma. But it was misunderstood by the other monks and the chief monk; they thought he had died.

The monastery had a graveyard, underground. They simply used to open the door... and it was a deep hole, sixty feet deep, with miles of tunnels inside, because the monastery had been there for thousands of years. All the monks who died were dropped into the underground tunnel.

This young man was also dropped – and the door was sealed, because it was not something to be opened every day. Once in a while, somebody dies... but the man was not dead. After a few hours, his consciousness returned. He could not figure out where he was. By and by, he became accustomed to the darkness, started groping, and then stumbled against corpses. Then he understood what had happened, they had misunderstood: "I have fallen in a coma."

It was a disease he had suffered since his childhood but it came only once in five or six years, so he had never mentioned it to anybody. But now it was too late. He tried his best – shouting, screaming – but in a sixty-foot hole, completely closed, who was going to hear him? It is difficult to hear even if the person is sitting in front of you; who is going to hear this dead fellow?

After a few efforts, he dropped it, but he could not drop the lust for life. But how to live in that graveyard? – no sunlight, no fresh air... it was disgusting. The smell of thousands of bodies which had become rotten... but man has the capacity to survive, to adjust in *any* kind of situation.

For a few days it was difficult, but slowly, slowly he started eating the rotten flesh of the corpses. The hunger was too much; it was not a time for being a snob, for saying "I cannot eat this."

From the gutters of the monastery, water used to leak down the stone walls of the graveyard. He knew it was from the gutters, the dirtiest water in the monastery, but there was no other way. He started drinking from that water. And slowly, slowly he forgot about the bad smell, he forgot that the water was dirty. He even forgot about the monastery and the world; he had found a new business, a new life. First his business was to find a corpse, in the early morning, for his breakfast.

And in Egypt, since the ancient days of the pharaohs, this has been the convention. You must have heard about the mummies of the queens and kings of Egypt. Their bodies are preserved, covered with gold. And when a king or a queen died, it was not a single death. It was the death of almost fifty persons, because all the people who were taking care of the king – his physician, his masseur, his cook – everybody who was taking care of the king had to be buried with him in the graveyard because he might need them at any time, and much money, gold, precious stones, so that he's never out of money. If he needs some money, he has enough.

Poor people did the same, in a poor way. Soon this man discovered... and it was not a smaller discovery than that of Archimedes when he jumped, naked out of his bathroom, shouting in the streets of Athens, "Eureka! I have found it!" He was solving a problem; the king had given him a problem and he solved it when he was resting in his bathtub. The joy of finding a new truth was so much, he forgot completely. He reached the court naked.

The prime minister was very angry, but the king understood. He said, "Don't be angry. I can see that the discovery means so much to him, he has forgotten everything – even right now he's not aware that he's standing naked."

Only then Archimedes saw. He said, "My God! I was in my bathroom!"

This monk's discovery was even greater. He also shouted, "Eureka! Eureka!" although nobody heard it. Because he discovered that all these corpses were very rich. They all had something – even the poorest had some money, some new clothes, some foodstuff – and he started collecting. He was hoping that, "One day I will get out, and then with all this money and gold and diamonds, I will be the richest monk in the whole country."

He lived in that graveyard for fifteen years. His only prayer was, "God have mercy on me. I cannot say exactly what I want but you know: one monk needs to die. Unless somebody dies, the graveyard will not be opened – and I cannot say it. Being a Christian, how can I ask you to kill some monk? No. But you know everything, you know my heart, there is no need to say it. You know what is right for me. Do it, and do it quickly, because I am growing very old."

One day a monk died and the graveyard's stone was removed. This old man – now he was old, his beard was touching the floor – shouted: "I am alive! Take me out!" They could not believe it, because for fifteen years, nobody had died and they had completely forgotten about him. Fifteen years is a long time, particularly in a monastery. It looks like eternity, boring... boredom makes time elastic. You can go on and on stretching it; it seems unending.

They pulled him out but they were surprised: he was bringing with him almost a great treasure. He had even collected clothes from the dead people; he had taken them off, because dead people are given fresh new robes, so they were perfectly good. He had pulled them out. He had nothing else to do... the whole day exploring, and it was a long, long tunnel. In thousands of years, so many people had died... and he found such antique things.

Nobody could recognize him. He said, "You can't recognize me?"

They said, "You look like a prophet from the Old Testament. Please tell us more about you – how did you manage to enter our monastery's graveyard?"

He said, "I was *here*, I know you all. Fifteen years ago, I died... and I shouted, but you did not hear. Then finally I had to adjust life according to the situation. And I cannot say that I have not been happy. In fact, I have never been happier than I have been for these fifteen years – no anxiety, no fight, nobody to insult you, nobody to humiliate you. And every day, new discoveries...."

What has been given by nature to man is a great faculty to adjust in different situations. It is a flexibility – nature has not made man rigid. But man has misused it: rather than going on a spiritual search for the secrets of life, the miracles of existence, he has become completely adjusted with the mundane, with the meaningless. He has misused his great faculty. Every faculty has that danger – you can misuse it.

A meditator has to remember: he has been given many powers and he has to be careful, watchful, alert not to misuse those powers. And what do I mean when I say not to misuse them? I mean if you are going outwards, it is misuse. If you are going inwards, it is the right use, because the ultimate joy is hidden within you.

Life is not just what it seems. It is tremendously much more, it is incalculably much more. But you will have to turn your face towards yourself. The day you are alone in your inwardness, you have come home. And the whole of nature and existence celebrates it, because even a single man's becoming enlightened is a celebration to the whole universe. A part of the universe has become enlightened – you are not apart, you are an essential part of existence. But don't waste your energies in futile things.

I was staying in a home. The man was rich, and he was very eager to show me something. I said, "In the morning. I have just come – forty-eight hours of train journey – you just let me take a bath and go to sleep."

He said, "First you have to see my collection of postal stamps."

That day I understood the proverb, "the last straw on the camel's back." I am dead tired, and this idiot wants me to see thousands of postal stamps that he has been collecting from all over the world.

I said, "What are you going to do with these? You have wasted money; you have wasted time. You go in search of postal stamps to faraway countries; you go to exhibitions where you can get extraordinary, unique postal stamps – but for what?"

He said, "I never thought about it... for what?"

I said, "Now you go to sleep and think about it, and let me also go to sleep – and I don't want the answer in the middle of the night! You can give me the answer in the morning." Life is simple if you have just a little clarity.

About doing... that is the extrovert side of your being. I am not condemning it. I am simply saying it has its uses but it is not what we are here to get. Inside you is your divinity – that's what we are here to get. This whole world is just an experiment, a training school to make you aware of your being.

Your being is the being of the whole existence. Your being and my being are not separate. Your body is separate, my body is separate, your mind is separate, my mind is separate, but your being and my being are one. To know oneself is to know the whole existence, is to know *all*.

BELOVED OSHO,
A BOY COCKROACH WAS TALKING TO HIS
GRANDFATHER. HE SAID, "GRANDPOP, MY TEACHER
SAYS IN SCHOOL THAT NO MATTER WHAT PEOPLE
DO, WE'RE ALWAYS GONNA BE HERE. HE SAYS WE'RE
GOING TO BE THE ONLY ONES AROUND AFTER THE
ATOMIC BOMB EXPLODES." THE GRANDFATHER SAID,
"WELL, SON. LET ME TELL YOU WHAT MY
GRANDFATHER TOLD ME. HE SAID, 'ROACHES WON'T
CROAK WHEN THE WORLD'S UP IN SMOKE AND
THOUGH THEY STEP ON US NOW, WE'LL HAVE THE
LAST JOKE.'"

It is really hilarious that even cockroaches are more intelligent than your so-called powerful politicians, priests. No animal in the world eats his own species except man; only man is a cannibal. However bad the situation may be, no animal eats his own brothers and sisters.

Man seems to be the most bloodthirsty animal. Without man, the earth will be more peaceful, more silent, more joyous, with more flowers, more birds, more songs. The sun will rise the same, the wind will bring fragrances the same.... I don't think anybody – trees or animals or rivers – is going to miss man, because man has not has contributed anything to the beauty of existence. On the contrary, he has been continuously destructive. All his science is nothing but manufacturing more and more destructive weapons. It seems we are here just to fight, as if in life there is no other blessing than fighting.

The cockroaches are far more intelligent. They have lived as long as you have lived, but not a single world war. There are different species of cockroaches. One species has a very developed sense of aesthetics. It has a very strange way of lovemaking: Each time a male cockroach makes love to a female – and remember, no male cockroach makes love to another male; no boyfriends, all that kind of nonsense has been left to man, and particularly to religious man, to churches, to monasteries, to monks – the male turns the cockroach on her back. And he has a small instrument – it looks like one of the hairs of his mustache; only two hairs are there, but one is not a hair, it is an instrument to dig a hole... just a screwdriver. He makes a new hole. First he looks... because how many other fellows have made love to the woman? Scars are there, but why should he be worried? he always finds fresh ground. What is the need of being worried that you should get married to a virgin girl? Those cockroaches are always on virgin ground.

Every time a cockroach makes love, it makes its own hole and then makes love. And until the hole heals itself, no other male will disturb the poor woman because she still has a wound. Unless that is healed, there is not going to be another lovemaking.

There are hundreds of species of cockroaches but they all have one thing in common: they have lived everywhere where man has lived. In Siberia, they are there; with the Eskimos, they are there. Once, a few explorers had gone to the South Pole and they were puzzled when they found cockroaches there. They were puzzled because there are no human beings. From where have the cockroaches come?

Their captain was an old, experienced man. He laughed. He said, "You are idiots! They have come with you in your shirt – it is full of cockroaches! And they are better explorers than you; they got down before you."

If man can show only qualities which are natural to animals, to birds, to trees, this earth can become a paradise. But how can you make this earth a paradise with nuclear weapons? Your nuclear weapons, if you knew where paradise was, may have destroyed it, because then for Russia to destroy your paradise would have been a priority. America would have been number two, because with the paradise, all your old saints and all your gods would be finished, and we could have an existence totally free from the domination of some unknown, unseen, unbelievable God. Man can change his qualities into creative forces. And my whole effort is to make religiousness the foundation of all our creativity.

Up to now, religion has been *against* life, *against* joy, *against* laughter. It has been in favor of a sick humanity – serious, sad. But no religion has supported life-enhancing qualities. They have not been creative, they have not added to man's intelligence. They have crippled man's intelligence, they have stopped his growth. They have left the whole humanity retarded – and you can see every day how retarded man is.

Just now I saw a clipping. In America, the churches were going to have conferences and meetings in churches all over America to find out ways and means to prevent the disease AIDS. They had declared their program; experts could explain, and how it can be avoided would be made more available to the public. But the archbishop of America has condemned this kind of thing, because in those programs of preventing AIDS, birth control is mentioned. Rubber condoms are mentioned. And he has taken it very seriously: "In a publication by the church, condoms are mentioned – not only mentioned, but pictures are shown to explain how they have to be used." He has declared, "No such conferences can be allowed to take place in my churches."

The church is absolutely against the condom. Strange... the condom is just a piece of rubber. Why should the church be against the condom? And just because of the condom, the whole program against AIDS is in jeopardy. AIDS can be prevented, but either the condom will have to be used... and the condom freaks out all the religious people of the world. Strange. Just a small piece of rubber, it is not harming anybody. The condom is not doing any harm to anybody. It has nothing to do with Christianity – it is a question of the whole of humanity's survival. But those idiots are not concerned about humanity and its survival, their strange interests are a rubber condom. But if you don't in some way stop the meeting of the sperm and the female egg, it is impossible to prevent AIDS. Even if you stopped that, then too, it is going to be very difficult to get rid of this disease, because you can kiss somebody and you can transfer it.

There are a few scientists who think it is possible that the disease and the virus may be infectious just by talking with a person who has AIDS; just the breathing can bring the virus to you.

In the commune, I was the first man in the whole world who proposed all the preventive methods. And in the commune, we managed perfect control. And I was criticized by Christians, I was criticized by all kinds of journalists, I was criticized and laughed at by the politicians, who said that I was unnecessarily creating fear. And now they are all thinking on the same lines. *exactly* the same program is being given to all the countries all over the world. And the dishonesty is such that not a single country has said that I was the first to tell the world that at least two-thirds of the world's population can die if immediate steps are not taken to prevent AIDS.

The steps that we have taken are now being accepted by *every* government in the world, and nobody is laughing and nobody is criticizing. And nobody is mentioning who the person was who first brought this whole program. We not only brought the program, we practiced it for three years, and the whole commune was perfectly capable of rising above the ordinary masses.

In five years' life of the commune, not a single child was born – and it was only out of sheer understanding that the earth is overpopulated. We had put condoms in every public bathroom, toilet, so there was no need for anyone to feel embarrassed. Because if you have to go to the chemist, to the druggist, to purchase a condom, you feel a little embarrassed. You might not be able to go openly into the market and purchase condoms and other things. We placed everything in all the public bathrooms for five thousand people. It was out of their understanding to pick them up – or if they were determined to commit suicide, then too, they were free. Nobody was forcing them.

But man seems to be very stupid. Now this archbishop declaring that condoms – even the *word* condom or the picture – cannot go into a church pamphlet. And these churches are responsible for all the pornography that exists in the world because they repressed sexuality, they forced people into unnatural ways of living, celibacy. Naturally, people started having unnatural relationships – and AIDS is just the culmination of all your religions and their teachings about celibacy. They have created this disease! The whole credit for AIDS goes to religious monasteries, it was born in religious monasteries.

Now it is absolutely clear that homosexuality is the cause, so there are governments who are making homosexuality a crime. But homosexuality is not the cause – the cause is the teaching of celibacy. No animal is homosexual, but teach any animal celibacy and see; he will start masturbating, he will start practicing homosexuality, he will start making love to chairs, furniture, shoes – anything! You have turned him into a Christian. And soon the poor fellow will be suffering from AIDS. And nobody sees the whole link.

I have heard.... A young man, who looked like a monk, was moving along the pavement in front of a shop, looking again and again into the show window. When every customer had gone and the time to close was near, he entered the shop. They said, "But we are closing now."

He said, "It won't take much time."

In the show window, there was a rubber cock in which he was interested. He said, "How much is that piece?"

They said, "It is very cheap." They were in a hurry to close the shop so they said, "What do you want? Should we pack it as a present or should we pack it just ordinarily to take home?"

The man said, "No, there is no need to pack it. Just give it to me; I will just eat it here. What is the need to take it home?" These insane ideas... however you repress them, they will come up.

One priest, a rabbi, went for his usual circumcision. He was given anesthesia and when he came back to consciousness, he saw that the doctors were a little disturbed, tense, and puzzled. He asked, "What is the matter?"

They said, "We are sorry, but a small mistake has happened." He said, "What mistake?"

They said, "First, we committed a small mistake. But when we tried to correct it, we messed up the whole thing. And before you came back to consciousness and could see what happened, our colleagues suggested that it was better to clean up the whole mess, so finally, instead of only doing a circumcision, we had to do a sex change operation. But you are a priest, and old" – he was seventy – "so it does not matter to you, although we *are* sorry. It was our mistake."

"But," the man said, "this is not right! It means I will never have the joy of erection."

The doctor said, "Well, you *will* have, but the cock will be somebody else's. It is a slight change, not much to be worried about. First, you used to have it on this side, now you will have to have it on that side. You will have it... but we thought you were a priest, and celibate."

He said, "Everybody thinks that. But the reality is not what is propagated to the masses."

Nobody can be celibate, it is unnatural. It is just as stupid as somebody coming and saying, "Here is a great saint – he never urinates!" Are you going to believe it, that he never urinates? And even if he manages it, then he's the man everybody should escape from. He must be disgusting; from every pore of his body, urine must be coming out.

That's what perversion is. You stop your energies at one point – they find some other way. But the other way is unnatural and is full of dangers. You don't know where you are going.

BELOVED OSHO,
SINCE I HAVE BEEN HERE WITH YOU THIS TIME, I
HAVE FELT A GREAT LONGING, A GREAT THIRST, A
GREAT URGENCY TO GO INTO MEDITATION. I LOVE
YOU AND I KNOW THAT THIS IS THE ONLY THING
YOU ASK OF US AND THIS IS THE ONLY REAL THANK
YOU I COULD GIVE – TO ONE DAY KNOW WHAT
MEDITATION REALLY IS. I SEE YOU SO ALIVE, SITTING
HERE RIGHT NOW WITH US IN THIS VERY MOMENT,
AND I LONG TO BECOME SO DRUNK WITH YOU THAT
THERE IS NO TURNING BACK. I'M DRINKING YOU AS
MUCH AS I POSSIBLY CAN. DOUBTS ARISE AND I FEEL
FEAR ABOUT GOING BACK ON WEDNESDAY. I'M
AFRAID I WILL NOT FIND YOU THERE AND WILL SLIP
BACK AGAIN. OH, MY BELOVED MASTER – WHAT
DOES IT MEAN TO RISK ALL FOR A SINGLE MOMENT
OF LOVE?

First, you will not be missing me wherever you are. We miss only our attachments, not our love. Attachment is to the physical body. Naturally, from far away you cannot touch the physical body, you cannot see the physical body. And you have never known anything more than the physical body. You have never known that which is there but cannot be touched – whether you are here or thousands of miles away. Only love reveals to you things which are immaterial, experiences which are immortal, spaces which are beyond time and mind.

So the first thing I want to emphasize to you: don't have any fear. Wherever you are, whenever you are silent, inside yourself, you will find me. And once that experience happens, then the question of separation disappears. Even death cannot separate us, because love is not of the body. And that which is of the body is only attachment, biological lust. Learn the secrets of love. Go into the depths of the poetry of love, move in the music of love, get centered in the consciousness of love, and there is no fear of losing *anything*.

And you have asked, "What does it mean to lose everything for a single moment of love?" It means exactly what it says. All things of the world can be put on one side and a single moment of love on another side – still, the side of love will be weightier, will be more valuable. The things – all the things that you have or you can have – only have prices on them, they can be purchased. Love has no price, it cannot be purchased; all those things can be purchased. Love is a prayer, not a commodity. You can offer it... and your being is full of it, you have just never looked at the inner springs of your life sources.

All the things of the world are nothing in comparison to one second of love, because that one second is enough to give you ultimate contentment – beyond which you cannot spread your ambitions and desires. Just that experience is enough to fill you with all that is beautiful, with all that is deathless, with all that is part of truth, part of bliss, part of benediction.

Just remember a small criterion. In life, there are two kinds of things – things which have prices on them and things which have no prices. Things that don't have any price are values.

This whole world is full of commodities. Only your hearts are full of a quality which is invisible, but is the most precious experience of life. A man who dies without knowing love has never lived. And a man who knows love needs no other lives anymore – he has passed the examination of life.

BELOVED OSHO,
DO YOU HAVE SOMETHING TO SAY ABOUT GANDHI'S
FOURTH MONKEY?

In China, based on almost twenty-five centuries of the teachings of Lao Tzu, some sculptor made a statue of four monkeys. Lao Tzu used to say, "Don't see anything wrong, because even by seeing it, you become in some subtle way a participant. And moreover, just by seeing it, it leaves an impression in you which may become a seed and some day it may explode into action. It is better not to see it."

It is not *my* philosophy, remember. My philosophy is to see it as accurately as possible from all sides, so you know it perfectly well and there can be no misunderstanding, and you are free of it – not because you have not seen it, not because you are ignorant about it, but because you have understood it, that it is useless. So this is not *my* philosophy. I'm simply explaining the four statues of monkeys to you.

One monkey is keeping his hands over his eyes; that is indicative of not seeing that which is not worth seeing. It is better to keep your eyes closed.

The second statue is: Don't hear that which is not worth hearing. So the second statue is putting its hands on both ears.

And the third statue is putting its hands on the mouth: Don't speak anything that is not absolutely necessary. Don't speak anything that is going to hurt somebody. It is better to be silent than to be unnecessarily in quarrels and fights and violence, because most of your violence begins with your words, with your mouth.

And the fourth was... all the monkeys are naked, as they have to be. The fourth was also naked. He was keeping his hands on his cock, hiding it. The message was that sex is a great energy, and you should not spoil it. It has to be transformed, it has to change from going downwards to going towards the highest center in your mind, the third eye. It has to move towards the third eye from the lowest center, in your genital organs.

When sexual energy starts moving upwards, you also start moving upwards with it. And the moment sexual energy reaches the third eye between your two eyes, you will be capable of seeing more clearly – without any distortion, without any possibility of any mistake – your path, your life, your achievements, your possibilities, your potentiality. Everything for the first time will be lighted up; darkness disappears. It was a beautiful statue – transformation of sex into spirituality. The same statues are made in Japan, more artistically, more beautifully.

One friend of Mahatma Gandhi sent him these statues, thinking that he would appreciate it. And he *did* appreciate it, but when the statues arrived, there were four monkeys and when the statues were cleaned and put on Mahatma Gandhi's table, there were only three monkeys. The fourth monkey had disappeared.

You are asking me about the fourth monkey. You will find him somewhere as a sannyasin, because I don't see any other place to escape to.

But it shows the level of understanding of Mahatma Gandhi. He was sex-repressive. He could not understand Lao Tzu. He was worried that people would see this naked monkey. So it is better from the very beginning if people don't know anything about it. In India, those statues don't exist; It is better to cut the fourth monkey separate. Now those remaining three monkeys Gandhi can manage: "Don't see what is not worth seeing. Don't speak what is not worth speaking. Don't hear what is not worth hearing."

But all these are nothing in comparison to the fourth. These three may make you a little more civilized, sophisticated, but these three will not transform you for the simple reason that you are not trying to understand. You are trying to avoid, not to look at. It is as if you have a cancer but you don't want to look at it, so you don't go to the doctor.

I used to know a man whose wife came to me, saying, "You have to come to my house, because my husband will not listen to anybody except you. We have tried our best. He has been sick for almost two weeks and we think something is seriously wrong. He's becoming weaker and weaker, but he is not ready to go to a doctor. And he is not ready even to say why he's not willing to go the doctor."

I went. I told everybody to go out of the room and I closed the door. I asked the man, "What is the matter? Why are you avoiding the doctor? If there is any problem, just tell me."

He said, "I can tell you. The problem is not with the doctor, the problem is with me – I am worried that perhaps I have cancer. My father died of cancer, my grandfather died. My wife, my first wife died of cancer, and I have seen so many cancer deaths in the house that it has become impossible to forget it. So I feel I have cancer."

I said, "Do you think not being examined is going to help you in any way?" He said, "No."

I said, "But there is a possibility – if the doctor says you don't have any cancer, you will be immediately cured. Secondly, if he finds there is something else, then medicines can take care of it. But fifty percent, the chances are that you may not have the cancer. You are missing a fifty percent chance. It is up to you, it is your life. I will not disturb you. Should I go or wait for your answer?"

He said, "Wait." After a moment he said, "It seems right. There is a fifty percent chance. It is only guesswork."

The doctor was brought, and he had the cancer. He told me, "Look!"

I said, "No harm. To know the enemy is always better than not to know, because knowing the enemy you can fight it better. Now we know it is cancer, we can fight it. There is no problem, you are not going to die."

There are people all over the world who are afraid – if a medical check-up turns up some calamity, a psychological check-up turns up some calamity... they go on living in fear. And out of their fear, they go on creating a thousand and one more fears. They may not have the cancer, they may not be *really* sick but their minds will create sickness – and their minds are capable of creating the cancer too.

One thing has to be remembered: you are, in your essential being, beyond all diseases, all old age, all deaths. In your non-essential parts – the body, the mind, the brain – you are vulnerable to all kinds of diseases, to all kinds of accidents. But they are not happening to *you*. They are happening almost as if in a dream, to somebody else.

The whole work of the mystery school is to somehow introduce you to yourself. That introduction is the introduction to existence itself. For centuries, man has lived in ignorance, in darkness. And in that darkness and ignorance he has been spinning and weaving dreams, nightmares, and he is suffering them. His nightmare may be just a dream, but his suffering is true.

To me, the definition of a religious man is one who has come out of dreams, one who has come out of sleep, one who is awake, one whose eyes are open. And he lives with this awareness. His every act is full of his awareness, is luminous with his awareness. Then nothing can go wrong.

I don't teach you any morality. I don't say "this is good, this is wrong, this is moral, this is immoral" – that is all childish. I teach you a single criterion: awareness. If in awareness you do something, it has to be right, because in awareness you cannot do anything wrong. And without awareness, you may be doing something very good, appreciated by everybody, but still I say it is wrong because you are not aware. You must be doing it for wrong reasons.

I am reminded of a small story. There is a big fair, somewhere in China. A man falls into a well, because in those days in China, wells were not made with a protective wall around them. So it was an ordinary, everyday accident – people falling into wells.

This man was shouting, hanging onto a root of a tree inside the well but the fair was so noisy that nobody heard him. By chance, a Buddhist monk was passing by the side of the well, and he heard. Perhaps because he was accustomed to meditation and silence... that may have been the reason he heard the man shouting from the well. He asked, "What is the matter? What is the trouble, why can't you be silent?"

The man said, "You seem to be strange. I am dying and you are saying 'Why can't you be silent?'"

The Buddhist monk said, "At the time of death, one *has* to be silent. Don't miss a single moment. Just close your eyes and be silent. If you die in this tense and anguished state, you will be born into a very ugly species. If you want to go higher, this is the moment – don't miss!"

The man said, "I don't want to go anywhere, I simply want to come out of the well."

The Buddhist monk said, "I know everything about higher consciousness. I can take you to the ultimate."

"But," he said, "who wants to go to the ultimate! Just take me out of the well!"

The Buddhist monk said, "That I cannot do, because it is forbidden to us for the simple reason that if I take you out and tomorrow you rape a woman, or a murder a man, then I will also be responsible for your act, because without me you would not have been able to do it; we are partners. Just excuse me."

And he went away! He said, "I don't want to become a partner to any kind of action. I am trying somehow to finish my own load, and I don't want to take on anybody else's load."

The man said, "Strange kind of people... I am dying, and he teaches me to be silent and die. He does not try to bring a rope and get me out."

Just at that moment, a Lao Tzu monk, a Taoist monk came by. He also heard. He looked in and he said, "Listen man – my master used to say that you should act in awareness, walk in awareness. Now you see? – you have not been aware."

The man said, "I will learn awareness but first – this time – take me out!"

The Taoist monk said, "That is beyond me, because nobody can save anybody else. That's what my master has said."

The man shouted, "It is said in a different context! It is not said in the context of a man dying in the well."

The man said, "If you talk about context and reference, then I will have to bring the scriptures and show you."

The man said, "I don't want to see any scriptures. And I am ready to take my words back – just bring a rope!"

He said, "No, neither can anybody save you nor can anybody destroy you. It is always *you*, deep down, who are responsible for every action. So take the responsibility, be brave. And... see you next life!" He said, "My God! All these religious people...."

And then came a Christian missionary with a bucket, with a rope... and he immediately threw down the bucket with the rope and told the man, "Sit in the bucket – it's a big bucket – and I will pull you out. Don't be worried."

He came out and he said, "You seem to be the only religious person in this whole crowd. What religion do you follow?" The man said, "I am a Christian."

The man who had been rescued from the well was very much impressed. He said, "This is real religion! Just one question: why were you carrying a bucket and a rope?"

The Christian missionary said, "We have to be ready for any emergency. And because so many people fall into wells, all Christian missionaries carry a bucket and rope and we always look into every well – 'Has somebody fallen or not?' – because our master Jesus Christ has said: 'Those who help the poor, the sick, the miserable, will be received with great honor in the house of God, in the kingdom of God.' Up to now, I have saved thirteen men from wells... but my number is not much. There are many other missionaries who have gone beyond sixty, seventy. It is very difficult to find a person in a well."

The man said, "This is a strange philosophy – even stranger than those two... the Buddhist, the Taoist. You are using us as stepping stones; you *want* us to be in the wells."

He said, "Of course, because unless there are poor, how can we help? Unless there are sick, how can we serve? Unless there are miserable people, we are out of employment."

The man said, "Anyway, I thank you that you pulled me out. I cannot agree with your philosophy, but whatever your philosophy, at least my life is saved."

The missionary said, "This is not enough, this is not the right gratitude. The right gratitude will be to fall as many times into wells as you can. And if you can, inform me in advance; that will be really wonderful."

We are living in an insane world, and you have to find some sanity within yourself. You cannot find it in the world, you can find it only within yourself. That sanity will be your ladder towards higher states of consciousness, bliss and ecstasies.

24

Charisma: A taste of the divine

BELOVED OSHO,

WHAT IS CHARISMA? ALL SORTS OF PEOPLE HAVE IT,
BOTH AWARE PEOPLE AND UNAWARE PEOPLE. ITS
SUCH AN INTANGIBLE QUALITY, I CAN SAY WHEN
SOMEONE IS CHARISMATIC BUT CAN'T DEFINE
WHAT IT IS.

Sudha, charisma is a mystery. It happens only to those people who have centered their being, concentrated their energies, who are no longer falling apart, who are consolidated, who have become *one* – the very meaning of the word, "individual."

Every individual has charisma. But individual means that which is indivisible. You cannot divide that person into fragments; you cannot say to that person that "this part is wrong in you, this part is right in you." You cannot create a schizophrenic psychology in that person; he's one and whole. This very phenomenon of being one, centered and whole, creates a magnetic pull.

Now, you cannot see a magnetic pull. You can see the magnet, you can see the small pieces of metal which are moving towards the magnet, but you cannot see magnetism, you cannot see any power. All power is invisible. All energy is invisible.

Charisma is the energy of the consciousness which is settled in itself – at ease, at home – which has arrived. Now there is nowhere to go. Utterly relaxed, with no tensions, with no anxieties, with no desires – in short, with no bickering, torturing the mind – one has arrived at the point called Being with a capital B. The moment you touch your Being, you are no more a separate entity from the universe – you have become part and parcel of this tremendously alive existence.

But the problem arises... if you see it in a Gautam Buddha, there is no problem. You can understand – the man has blossomed. You can see it. In his eyes you can see the depth; you can see in his gestures, the grace. You can see in his words an authority which can come only through experience, not through knowledge.

The problem arises when you find some charismatic qualities in an ordinary man who has never meditated, who has never gone inwards, who is as ordinary as everybody else. But sometimes it happens – you feel a magnetic pull. And because you have not arrived at your own center, it is very difficult for you to make a distinction between the man who is centered – hence, has a magnetic pull – and the man who is not so centered and yet you still feel a certain pull. You cannot make the distinction, for the simple reason that you have not experienced it in your own being.

The ordinary man sometimes has something similar to charismatic power, but you will be surprised to know it is not charismatic power at all. It is something just the opposite – it is overflowing sexual energy. In a charismatic experience, the energy in the person is at the highest center. It is at the seventh center, *sahasrar*, beyond which you enter into the infinite, beyond which you are no more *and* you are all. It is the same energy.

Man has seven centers, prominent centers. The energy is stored as a reservoir at the lowest center – naturally, because of gravitation. Water goes downwards because of gravitation; it pulls somewhere, but it is always the lowest place. Water cannot go upwards unless some effort is made. Unless some device is created to cancel the effect of gravitation, water is bound to go down and down and down.

The sex center is the lowest point in your being. All energy accumulates at the sex center. The moment the child is born, he brings all his life energy, stored at the sex center. But the sad thing is that 99.9 percent of people also die in the same situation – the energy is still at the sex center, although it is no more that overflowing energy of a child; it is the dying energy of an old man. But it is still at the lowest center.

The whole science of religion is nothing but an effort to create methods, devices, techniques to cancel the effect of gravitation and allow the energy a freedom to rise upwards. As the energy starts rising upwards, you will see changes happening on their own accord. Your behavior will change, your actions will change, your directions in life will change. You will be surprised, and others will be surprised, too. What has happened? – they have seen your anger, they have seen your rage, they have seen your jealousy, they have seen your hate – suddenly you are radiating love.

If the energy reaches to the heart center, which is the fourth, your whole life becomes so sweet, so fragrant, and so beautiful – and you have only moved half way. If the energy moves still higher, and as the energy goes on moving higher, your charismatic power will become more and more apparent – even to those who are deaf and cannot hear, even to those who are blind and cannot see, even to those who are heartless and cannot feel. But the charismatic energy is so powerful that the blind *has* to see it and the deaf *has* to hear it and the heartless has to feel it. It all depends how high the energy has reached. After the heart center, the charisma will be felt by many but not by all.

The fifth center is in the throat. When the energy moves to the throat center, your words start having something of the charisma of your being because they arise out of your heart, they come from your interiority, they bring with them some fragrance from your innermost being.

It was said about Jesus by his contemporaries.... Jesus was not educated, was not cultured – he was a poor man, a carpenter's son. His father could not afford to educate him. But people were amazed: he could not read, he could not write, but when he spoke there was no comparison. Then the greatest rabbis of that day, the great scholars, great orators, great religious leaders, even the arch priest of the great Jewish temple of Jerusalem – they were all pygmies before this young man. He was only thirty years of age when he started teaching and he was crucified when he was only thirty-three. He had not even reached the prime of his life. But whoever heard him, whether he agreed with him or not, had an absolute sense that when he speaks, you cannot disagree, at least in his presence. The idea of disagreeing does not arise. You cannot have doubts in his presence; something deeper convinces you. It is not logical. It is not his reason, it is his authority. It is the charisma that his words are carrying.

It was known all over Judea that no man had ever spoken like Jesus. It was said even by his enemies, that no man had ever spoken like Jesus. And he is saying nothing special – but the *way* he is saying it is certainly special, the state in which he is saying it is certainly special.

I have come across thousands of articles around the world in different languages, written for and against me — mostly against, but they all have recognized one thing which I was surprised that they all should recognize and yet not give a second thought to it.... And these are our intelligentsia. They all have mentioned — almost without fail — two things. One, that "You should not go to hear Osho. Because it does not matter what he's saying, when you are in his presence, it seems to be right. By the time you have reached home it may look suspicious, doubts may arise." A few have suggested: "You have been hypnotized." Only very few have suggested — and none of them has heard me — that the words have a charismatic influence.

I know only one thing — that I am not a speaker, that I don't know the art of oratory. All that I know is that if I have experienced something, I can convey it to you with my total authority, with my whole being behind it. And if you are open and available, perhaps the word may reach to your innermost shrine of being. And it may reach there with something of a charismatic energy.

As the energy goes on moving, the sixth center is the third eye — between the two eyebrows, exactly in the middle. It is when the energy is at the sixth center that the presence of the person... It is not just that he is here; it is not just a physical presence. There is no word for it, but we can manage... it is spiritual presence that you start feeling. His body becomes less important, his words become faraway echoes, but his *presence*, pure presence becomes such a tremendous pull that you know only one experience which can give you some idea of it, and that experience is falling in love — irrationally. You cannot give any explanation, but you know. You cannot say but you feel.

And if the energy reaches the seventh, that is the point where one becomes awakened. The energy has come to the highest peak of evolution. Then that person is pure charisma. Whatever he touches becomes gold. Wherever he sits becomes a holy place. Whatever he says becomes scripture. His actions take on a tremendous beauty. His inactions also open doors to the miraculous. He speaks the truth and even when he is silent, his silence also speaks. Those who can understand the language of silence rejoice, are blissful, know perfectly well that this is the man they have been searching for centuries, for many lives.

Charismatic power is the same sexual energy transformed, purified. It was poison at the lowest center; it has become nectar at the highest center. But at the lowest center also, it has a tremendous power. And you know that sometimes you feel a great attraction to an ordinary man. Remember, that attraction is sexual, and sexual attraction is blind. But ordinarily people only know that attraction, so when by chance they come across a man who has some charisma, they don't have any way to distinguish between the two.

That's why Sudha is asking why sometimes in people who are awakened, and sometimes in people who are not awakened, this power is felt. It is not the *same* power – although it arises from the same energy. But from the lowest center it is crude, primitive, animal. Its influence will drag you into lower realms of being.

But if you find really a charismatic person, you are fortunate. Just to sit at his feet is enough, because he's showering his energy whether anybody is there or not. If you are receptive, open, available, just being close to a charismatic person is the first taste of religion. I am calling it *taste*; I am not calling it understanding, I am not calling it knowledge. It is actually a taste. Your whole being feels it. Each fiber feels it – a nourishment, a nourishment which is divine. Let us summarize: The charismatic energy is divine nourishment flowing from those who have arrived home.

BELOVED OSHO,
I FEEL A STRONG URGE TO CREATE SOMETHING IN MY
LIFE. I WRITE SONGS AND WOULD LIKE TO SING
THEM. THEY EXPRESS MY FEELINGS AND MAYBE
BECAUSE I FEEL YOU INSIDE ME, THEY ALSO EXPRESS A
LITTLE BIT OF YOU. CAN YOU PLEASE SAY SOMETHING
ABOUT THE DIVIDING LINE BETWEEN EXPRESSING
NEUROSES AND THE CREATION OF SOMETHING OF
BEAUTY? IS IT GOOD FOR ME TO GO ON THIS TRIP?

The urge to create anything is the first ray of light in the dark night of your soul. The urge to create is the urge to participate in the work of God. There is no God as a person, but there is tremendous creativity going all over the place. God is not a creator to me, God is *all* this creativity – and whenever you feel some urge to create, it is an urge to meet God. It is an urge to be a small God in your own right. Only by creating something, you can feel fulfilled.

You write songs – it is beautiful. You want to sing. For whose permission are you waiting? – sing and sing madly! But remember only one thing, creativity has two possibilities. One is that it arises out of your silence, love, understanding, your clarity of vision, your intimate friendliness with existence – then creativity is healthy. But if it does not arise out of meditation, out of silence and peace and understanding and love, then there is a danger. It may be arising out of your confused mind. It may be arising out of your insanity.

Anything that comes out of your tense mind, helps you anyway. It gives a relief. Something that was going round and round inside you – you have released it, but it will torture somebody else. It may torture many... because the song that was imprisoned within you was a personal matter; you have made it public. And if the song has come out of some kind of madness, some kind of confusion, you will certainly feel good, but at a cost which is too big. Millions of people for thousands of years can be affected by it. You are relieved but you have not behaved responsibly. You have not behaved sanely, you have not behaved humanely. Your songs, your paintings, your dance will have all the qualities of your mind, from which they came.

Look at the paintings of Picasso. That poor fellow does not need worldwide recognition as a painter, as a creator – he needs psychiatric treatment. His paintings are like vomitings, he's sick. He *is* a genius; he has great insight into color. But he is not at ease. He is not feeling joyful. He's not feeling life as a gift. His paintings show his rejection of life. His paintings show his utter frustration, despair, anguish, confusion – you cannot figure out what the painting is all about. But because he is a genius, even though his creativity is not that of a Gautam Buddha, he has a great artistic, aesthetic sensibility. He has everything except a little meditation. Instead of a little meditation, there is a little madness.

Almost all the great painters of the contemporary world have been, one or two times at least, sent into psychiatric hospitals, and they lived – all of them – one year, two years, three years in madhouses. Great poets have been in madhouses. Great dancers, like Nijinksy, have been in madhouses. It is strange that the West is not yet aware that something is wrong.

Why do your scientists, your artists, your painters, your singers, your poets, your dancers – all creative geniuses – fall victim to madness? This has never happened in the East. And it is not that we have not created – we have created more than any other country in the world. But there has not been a single instance of a great artist, a great novelist, a great poet, a great mystic going mad. This is absolutely unknown in the East.

On the contrary, you will be surprised that in the Far East, particularly in Japan, mad people are brought into the Zen monasteries to be treated. They are given a beautiful place, a small cottage by the side of a pond, with swans in the pond, birds, flowers, trees, rocks, rock gardens – which is especially Japanese. Nobody has ever thought that rocks can make a garden. People throw away rocks to create a garden. In Japan, they *collect* rocks to create a garden! Unless you can create a garden out of rocks, what kind of an artist are you?

They put the madman in the most comfortable place. If he's a painter, they give him all facilities to paint... but he's not allowed to talk to anybody, he is not allowed to show his paintings to any-body. There is a fireplace – after painting, he has to put it into the fireplace. For three weeks he has to remain silent, and the master in the Zen monastery goes every day to look at his paintings – whether the paintings are changing, whether they are becoming more and more sane. The day he sees that a painting is perfectly sane, the man is released. They have used paintings to release his madness, but the paintings have all gone into the fireplace. They are not to go to the public – you are mad and you would be spreading your madness.

Before you start making your songs and singing and dancing, create the right consciousness, the right awareness, so whatever comes out of you is a blessing for humanity, not a curse. That is the criterion. Unless it can be a blessing, throw it into a fireplace. You are released, but don't burden somebody else.

I used to live in a city across from a homeopathic doctor. He was a Bengali. In India, Bengalis are addicted with homeopathy – strangely enough, because there seems to be no reason why Bengalis should be so interested in homeopathy. Homeopathy was discovered in Germany by a German scientist. So if in Punjab people are interested in homeopathy, we can understand – but Bengalis? They could not even run if somebody were going to kill them. They cannot run, their dress is such, their dhoti would fall down – it is so loose that how they manage is a miracle. Now these are not the people who fight.

This doctor was opposite me, so we became friends. But he was a torture. Usually, homeopaths don't get many patients, so he was torturing me as much as possible. But I used to take my revenge, and my revenge was: whenever my father would come to visit me, I would take him to the doctor.

He would say, "I am perfectly okay. Why do you always drag me to that idiot? I know more homeopathy than he knows." He was also a homeopathy addict.

But I would say, "No. Now you have come here, it is good just to have a check-up."

He said, "This is strange. I go on postponing coming to see you because of this doctor! Because I know you will leave me with the doctor and you will escape."

But that was my revenge. In homeopathy, they ask you... if you have a headache they will start asking you what diseases you have had since childhood, in what side of the body all your diseases were.

My father was a lover of homeopathy, and the doctor, seeing my father, would almost go through a nervous breakdown – because my father used to start from his grandfather's diseases. It took almost the whole day. And he may have had just a slight headache and the doctor would tell him, 'Wait, I have listened to all these things. I know! Three generations – I know everything. And you just have a slight headache? Take the medicine!"

But my father would say, "That is not right. Follow your cience. First listen to the whole thing, because everything is connected."

That's what homeopathy believes: that everything, every disease is connected with another disease; there is a pattern. A headache cannot come just from the sky, it must be coming from your grandfather! Although he is in the sky too.... But somehow it has to be connected. And after three or four hours describing it... and the doctor just pulling at his hair because he has heard all this so many times, naturally *he* will start having a headache. By the time my father had completed his story, he would tell me, "Now we can go."

I said, "But what about your headache?"

He said, "My headache is gone."

And the doctor said one day, "It is not gone, it has come to me! Whole hours listening to you – the same story! And I know no medicine can work because it has not come from *my* grandfather it has come from *your* grandfather, and in the whole literature of homeopathy, there is no mention of what to do if some disease from somebody else's grandfather comes to you. Now I have to suffer. How long will you be staying here?"

I said, "As long as you want," because he was free and there would have been no problem. But the next morning the doctor had left to a nearby hill station.

After seven days, he phoned. "Is your father still there? Because

I am a poor doctor and I cannot manage to stay in this hill station, it is too costly." I said, "He has gone, you can come back."

Life is an interconnected whole. Everything is interconnected. If you want to sing, just look into yourself – why? If you want to dance, just watch within yourself – from where is the urge coming and why? I am not preventing you. You can dance, you can sing, you can do whatever you want, but remember not to interfere in anybody's life – even with a song, even with a dance. Life is very delicate and very fragile. A small thing can become a great disturbance.

My suggestion is, your urge is beautiful. Just now, what you need is a little more silence, a little more peace, a little more relaxation, a little more no-mind, so that you can become just a hollow bamboo. And the song that wants to come out of you can come, and the dance can come, but they are not your creations. Your mind has not contributed anything to them, they are coming from the beyond. You have put the mind aside. Meditation simply means putting the mind aside, opening the door to your consciousness, an *immediate* relatedness to existence. Out of this, let the songs come, let the dances happen. They will be blessings to you and they will be blessings to the whole world. Share them. But share only when it has come out of silence, out of health, out of an integrated being.

BELOVED OSHO,

THE REAL QUESTION IS, AM I A COWARD IF I DON'T
JUST PUT EVERYTHING AT STAKE IN SPITE OF THOSE
WHO WAIT FOR ME BACK THERE? – MY GIRLFRIEND,
MY SICK OLD MOTHER WHO MAY DIE OUT OF GRIEF
IF I DON'T COME BACK, MY JOB AND MY COLLEAGUES,
WHOM I MIGHT PUT IN TROUBLE.... AND IN SPITE OF
THE UTTER INSECURITY I WOULD PUT MYSELF IN, AM
I A COWARD IF I DON'T JUST STAY IN THIS BEAUTIFUL
GARDEN OF YOUR PRESENCE, THE ONLY PLACE
WHERE I REALLY FEEL ALIVE? AM I MISSING ANOTHER
BEAUTIFUL OPPORTUNITY OR IS IT JUST NOT YET THE
RIGHT TIME STILL?

The old mother is waiting for you and she's so old that she may die if you don't return home. The woman you love is waiting for you. Your whole family, your friends, your job – you will be a coward if you don't return. But I can understand your longing to be here. You are not a coward in that sense, because if I say to you "Be here," you will be here. Mothers, after all, die – you cannot help it. Whether you go or not, the mother will die at exactly the same time, on the same day. Although if you do not go, you will feel guilty your whole life that you killed her. Do you think those people who never leave their parents... that their parents live forever?

Everybody dies. I am just trying to make it clear so that you are not burdened with guilt. Mothers will die, fathers will die. Everybody has to die. To me, the more important thing is that you are clean of guilt.

Your girlfriend is waiting there. If you stay here, you will feel guilty – you must have promised her you will be coming back soon, and you will going against your word. No, I will not suggest that. I will tell you: go back home, don't be a coward. Now... and it is not certain that you will find your girlfriend there. She may have already moved on. If she is intelligent, she will be enjoying her time there – with somebody, of course, hoping that you don't come back!

Staying here will be very cowardly at this juncture. You have to go and see what is happening. Where is the girlfriend? My feeling is, even if she has not left you yet, she will leave you. The average time for intelligent human beings to be together is three years. I don't know how many years you have been with her... in three years, you start getting utterly bored. Go back.

I have another suggestion to you: I am coming with you! This way, it is simple. Just your love for me, just your trust in me and your determination, your commitment to find out what this life is all about....

You can practice meditation anywhere you are. You need not be here. In fact, it is far better to go back into the world, and once in a while just come for a refresher course. In this way, you will avoid the feeling of guilt. If you reach home and the girl has eloped, you will not feel guilty. You will feel unburdened, relieved, free to move to another girlfriend.

You will find your mother also. Whatever has transpired within you here, if you love your mother, this is the time to be close to her. And just being close will not help. This is the time to help her to be silent, to be meditative, so that she can understand the beauty of death. So that she can disperse herself into existence without any resistance, without any fight, without any struggle. If she can welcome death, there is no death. Death is in your resistance. The moment you allow it, you are surprised: death has no reality. You are simply changing the house, from one body into another body.

So go and share your meditation with your mother. That is the greatest gift and present you can give to her before she leaves the world. And share your meditation with your girlfriend too, before she moves to another boyfriend. She is going to move, even meditation cannot stop that. On the contrary, meditation helps because meditation makes you clearly aware of things.

I have seen people living together for years, their whole life, thinking only of divorce – just thinking, but never being courageous enough to be alone without the wife. Because she is your whole misery – how are you going to live without misery? When you come home, it will look so empty, with nobody there to nag you.

I have heard, one man entered a restaurant and ordered lunch. The waitress was puzzled because the order was strange. The order was: "Four chappatis, all burnt." The woman looked at him.

"And two vegetables with no salt, finishing with a cup of coffee, completely cold, with no sugar, no milk."

The waitress said, "It is a strange order. I have been here...."

He said, "It is not a strange order. Look at the front of your restaurant, what you have written on the board outside" – on the board was written: Here you will feel completely at home. "I am trying to feel completely at home!" '

The woman said, "It is up to you."

She prepared his lunch, brought it, put it before him, stood nearby in case he needed anything more.

He said, "Why you are standing there? Sit in front of me!" She said, "Why?"

He said, "Nag me! Unless you nag me I will not enjoy my food!"

Just lifelong habits... it is not so easy to divorce. Rather, people become accustomed. That's why meditation is dangerous; it does not allow you to become accustomed. It keeps your intelligence always sharp and you can see when something has gone sour. It is stupid to bother about the spilled milk. That which has lost its joy, its beauty, its romance, its poetry – now why drag each other and torture each other? Most probably, the girl will have moved.

Man is not an unmoving property. Man is a movable, intelligent animal. You are meditating here. What will the poor girl be doing there? She must be eating, she must be drinking, she must be sleeping, she must be taking a shower. So what is wrong in having a boyfriend too? Just to continue the old habits, just to continue the routine smoothly.

But if she has not moved on yet, afraid that you may be coming any day, share with her also your meditation. That will help immensely to make both of you absolutely free. Then love is a free gift with no conditions attached to it. Teach your mother, teach your girl, teach your friends, and next time, those who can come, bring them. But if you stay here, then I will certainly call you a coward because you have not faced the reality.

Learn whatever is available here. Practice it anywhere. And whenever you feel that you need to be reminded of many things you are forgetting, come back – and next time don't come alone. It is not right that you have left your girlfriend there. If you love her and you have come in search of meditation here, you would have brought her because it would be a shared adventure.

Next time, this girl or another girl. Just remember one thing: that girls don't ask me whether it is courageous to stay here or to go away. They simply remain here! So be careful. If you want freedom from any woman, bring her here. No problem for you, she will make you free on her own accord. And a miracle is also possible, that your girlfriend and you may be able to enter into meditation together. And that will be the *real* meeting. Otherwise, only bodies meet – which is not a meeting. That is only a hit-and-run affair. If you can also be consciously together in silence, in meditation, in peace, then you are putting down the right foundations of a friendship that can last – not only this life, but that can last for lives together. And you can be immensely helpful to each other in understanding problems, hindrances.

So my suggestion is: be here, learn meditation. Go home, share your meditation, and whenever you can come, come back. This will be real courage: facing life, not escaping from life, and also making every effort to evolve your consciousness – not allowing life to create obstructions. You were thinking that courage is a simple matter – whether to stay here or go home. It is a little complex. Go home but don't forget me. I am coming in your heart with you. So whenever you start forgetting me, put your hand on your heart, close your eyes, and immediately you will be connected with me.

My sannyasins are all over the world. It is impossible to bring them together in one place. It would have been great to bring all of them into one place, one million sannyasins in one place, but all the governments consist of cowards. They are afraid of people. If they see one million people listening to one person, loving him to such an extent that even if their life is needed, they will give it.... Around the world this is the fear in the minds of all politicians: I have such a great strength around the world that it should not in any way be allowed to be in one place, because then it can become dangerous to the vested interests, to the governments, to the churches. And they are right!

But they are cowards. They should face it, they should allow me. They should help me to create an alternative society. They have failed – ten thousand years of continuous failure; what more do they want? They *have* failed, and now there is no possibility that their system can succeed. It can succeed only in destroying life on the earth.

They should think that if an alternative society can be created, then a chance should be given to it. People can live in a different way that perhaps is better. And perhaps other people would also like to live in this different way. But then again: the fear that in the

new life, they will not be powerful. In the alternative life, everything would be so different that right now the people who are
presidents, prime ministers, governors, senators, and are enjoying
their egos, will be simply nobodies.

In my vision, I don't see any place for these people. I see
singers, dancers, musicians. I see painters, poets. I see all kinds of
beautiful people living, loving and having a good laugh about
everything in life – because everything is hilarious, we have just
forgotten our sense of humor.

And these politicians, these priests, teachers... these are the people who have crushed man's sense of humor. To the people who
are in power, humor seems to be against them – people are laughing at *them*, so it is better that laughter should be destroyed. And
they have destroyed laughter. They have made man a long face,
sad, and they have convinced humanity that this is what life is.

Go into a church. It looks like a graveyard. In fact, it is a graveyard, because worshipping Jesus on the cross... and have you
observed that people – from the pope to the smallest priest – have
crosses, golden crosses, hanging around their necks, but Jesus is
missing. It is very strange. That cross is there because of Jesus, but
where is Jesus and why should the cross be given preference over
Jesus?

You could have a beautiful, smiling Jesus. But the society does
not want any smiles anywhere. Hence Jesus has been removed,
only the cross has been chosen. Now the cross is a symbol of
death, not of life. And crosses are not made of gold, and when you
are crucified the cross is not hanging around your neck, your neck
is hanging on the cross. What have these people been doing –
cheating the whole of humanity?

BELOVED OSHO,
THE OTHER DAY, YOU TALKED ABOUT PRIDE. IT FELT
AS IF YOU WERE TALKING ABOUT A LONG-LOST
FRIEND. THE WAY I HAVE BEEN BROUGHT UP, PRIDE
AND HUMBLENESS ARE CONTRADICTORY
CHARACTERS. MY HEART TELLS ME THAT I CAN ONLY
BECOME WHOLE WHEN THEY BOTH MEET. IS IT THAT
HUMBLENESS IS MY FEMALE PART AND PRIDE, MY
MALE PART? AND CAN THEY MEET IN A LOVING
HEART? PLEASE COMMENT, BELOVED MASTER.

You are born man and woman together – *aradhanarishwar*. We have the statues, five to seven thousand years old, of Shiva – half-man, half-woman. When the West came to know about those statues for the first time, they laughed. In fact, any idiot would laugh. But strangely enough, just in the beginning of this century, Carl Gustav Jung discovered that psychologically man is both, *has* to be both, because he is born of a man and a woman. Your father has contributed something, your mother has contributed something; you cannot be just a woman or just a man. You are both. But all the societies have been trying to enforce the idea that man is man, woman is woman, and they are separate.

Why are they insisting on this separateness? They insist on this separateness because unless the woman is separate, she cannot be enslaved. She cannot be exploited. She cannot be forced into prostitution. But because they were so concerned to keep the society in the hands of men, all power in the hands of men and *no* power in the hands of women, they did not allow a deeper search: What is in a woman that attracts a man – or vice versa, what is in a man that attracts a woman?

Carl Gustav Jung discovered that everybody is carrying the opposite sex in himself; half his being is made of the opposite sex. And it is this half of the opposite sex which creates the phenomenon of love – the love you are acquainted with.

Every man has his mother, her contribution, in his blood, in his bones, in his marrow. He is still carrying in the unconscious the idea of a woman: his mother. And whenever he finds a woman that in some way resembles his mother, he falls in love. That's why he cannot say why he has fallen in love. He does not know. In the unconscious is the ideal of the mother, but falling in love is a conscious thing. The unconscious knows the ideal, the conscious knows the woman he has fallen in love with.

And the unconscious and conscious are not on speaking terms. They don't talk with each other, they cannot – one is conscious, one is unconscious. While somebody is asleep, you may be sitting by his side but you cannot talk with him.

The woman within you and the man within you are already meeting. It is not that there is a partitioned wall; you are both together – every inch, every atom, every cell. So the question is not how to create the merger, the question is just to remember: the merger is already happening, you cannot live without the merger.

Sitting silently, just watch inside yourself and you will be surprised to see that feminine qualities, male qualities are all mixing without any effort on your part. In fact, their mixing is the very dialectic of life. You go on living a healthy life... it is healthier if the merger is close to perfection; it is not that healthy if the merger has been disturbed by your social upbringing.

Have you watched? The societies that are opposed to sex – their life span is small, their average life is not long. Societies which are not opposed to sex, their life is longer. And societies which are aboriginal, which have not yet heard of your great preachers and priests and philosophers, and are still living naturally – they live the longest.

There are even thousands of people who have passed the line of one hundred and eighty years. There are even more who have passed the line of one hundred and fifty years.

I may not have come to know about it, but a friend from Caucasus just sent me a picture. One man was going to marry a woman. The man was one hundred and eighty and the woman was one hundred and seventy-two – marrying! I love the idea. This is the time, the right time to marry! In life, there are so many other things to do – do everything, and when you are one hundred and eighty, get married! Prepare the grave and get married, because after marriage there is nothing. So have a good honeymoon. And because after the honeymoon is the grave, it is bound to be total, intense.

Why do people who don't have any condemnation of sex, live longer? Because the merger of their feminine and male qualities is more natural – unhindered, unobstructed, not condemned, not repressed. You don't have to do anything. Your chemistry is doing it. All that you have to do is be watchful, peaceful, and just see the miracles of nature that are happening in your body. You have the most miraculous thing in you – life, consciousness, love, and finally God – and you are searching here and there like beggars.

Each man is born an emperor; he just has to claim it. I want my sannyasins to be emperors, not beggars. And once you remember your glory, you can claim it – it is already there. It is within you. Nobody can prevent you.

So it is not a question of doing anything for the male and female within you to mix. You don't need a mixture, you need just a silent awareness of whatever goes on happening in you. And you will be surprised that everything is right, nothing wrong happens unless you interfere. Except for your interference, there is no sin.

BELOVED OSHO,

THE OTHER DAY YOU SAID THAT AS LONG AS WE ARE DEPENDENT ON THE OTHER, WE ARE BOUND TO HATE THEM. ARE YOU ALSO MY "OTHER"? I KNOW THAT RIGHT NOW I DEPEND ON YOU AND I SAY YES TO IT WITH ALL MY HEART, BUT IT DRIVES ME TO TEARS TO THINK THAT I SHOULD EVER HATE YOU BECAUSE I AM DEPENDENT ON YOU. CAN YOU PLEASE FILL MY HEART WITH UNDERSTANDING AND EASE THE PAIN?

Nobody is dependent on me. I am not creating a mob of slaves. My whole effort is just the opposite: to drag you out of the crowd of the slaves and to make you independent individuals. But from your side, I can understand. From your side, you may be thinking you are dependent on me. That is a misunderstanding. You are absolutely free. Free to be with me, free not to be with me, free to be for me, free to be against me – it is your joy. Don't make it heavy. Keep it light and playful.

You love me; hence the fear has arisen that one day you may fall into the opposite and you may start hating me. Don't be worried, because your love is not just love. You love me not for any biological reason, you love me for some spiritual growth. Your love is part of your meditation. Your love is nothing but a gratitude for someone who has opened a door to the beyond.

I don't think there is any necessity for your love to change into hate. I am ready to make you free at any moment without creating the whole drama of hate.

The drama of hate is a necessity – you love someone, then the natural process happens: you start getting bored, you start feeling stuck, you start looking all around. There are so many beautiful people and you are sitting with this woman, this man. You are the most unfortunate man on earth. Now, how to separate?

And you have been giving promises to the woman – "I will love you. Others love people only in life but I will love you even after life." Now what to do with all those promises? You cannot suddenly change. You cannot say, "I take my promises back." What about all those love letters? "I will die without you. I cannot live a single moment without you. You are my life, you are my soul."

So now you have to go back, step by step, from love to hate. Only when hate is ripe, will you be able to separate. Otherwise, how to separate from a woman without whom you cannot live a single moment? First you have to create just the opposite situation, that "I cannot live *with* you anymore, even for a single moment – enough is enough!"

But with me there is no problem, there is no need to create hate. You can love, that is your joy. You can turn off the switch, that is your joy. As far as I am concerned, neither your love affects me nor your hate affects me, it is just the same. So drop that idea completely. Don't get into unnecessary problems, because they take energy, they take time. That is the time, that is the energy that has to be put into meditation. And you are throwing it away all over the place. Remember only one word: if you love me, your love has to be for *meditation*. If you love me, that means you have fallen in love with yourself; for the first time you are making an effort to realize your potential. How can you hate yourself?

And if you are meditating then it becomes more and more difficult to hate. You cannot hate even your enemies; you will feel a deep compassion. So everything else is going perfectly right – just drop this idea that love may turn into hate. These are hypothetical questions, sheer wastage of time. Love while love is there. And when the hate comes, if you cannot manage to avoid it, then *hate*! But hate totally and intensely and you will still be following me, because my teaching is for totality and intensity. Who cares about love or hate?

25 Yes is the heartbeat of life

BELOVED OSHO,
JANOV SAYS THAT NEGATIVITY IS
ELECTROCHEMICALLY DRIVEN BY ENDOMORPHINS,
THE CHEMICAL EFFECT OF PAIN. HOW IS "YES"
POSSIBLE WITHOUT EXHAUSTIVE PRIMAL THERAPY?

Primal therapy has contributed something very essential and significant to human growth. But just as other therapies in the West are amateurish, primal therapy also belongs to the same category.

Sigmund Freud used to say that exhaustive psychoanalysis would free man from all tensions, all worries; would give him for the first time freedom from the past, and a tremendous energy to create the future – not as a continuity of the past but totally new, fresh, discontinuous with the past.

But the whole problem is that exhaustive psychoanalysis is impossible. There is not a single person in the whole world who has gone through exhaustive psychoanalysis, which means that now he does not need any psychoanalysis. People have been in psychoanalysis for fifteen years, twenty years, and yet they are exactly the same as they had begun. Only one thing has changed: they have now become full of psychological jargon. They have become knowledgeable. They can drive you crazy very easily, just by talking all the nonsense that they think is psychoanalysis.

Primal therapy is a simple method. It is helpful in releasing the deepest repressed emotions. And the person has to come to a point where he's not holding anything back – his scream becomes primal.

The moment the child is born, he goes through a great trauma. Changing from the mother's womb into the cold, strange world is a great shock, and that shock remains deep in your unconscious for your whole life.

Primal therapy is a process to release you from the trauma of birth. You have to scream for days together. Finally, the ultimate scream comes, as if your whole being – every cell of it – has screamed with totality, wholeness, intensity. And that scream leaves you so unburdened, so light, weightless... because with the primal scream, many other small screams that are in you are all released.

But Janov has failed the same way as Sigmund Freud has failed. Psychoanalysis has not been able to give man his spirituality, his being, his freedom. Of all that it has promised, not a single thing has been delivered, and millions of people have wasted their time and money for nothing. Now Janov has done the same number again.

One primal scream releases you, but only for a short time; tomorrow you will be the same. It was good, it gave you a good sleep because you were so relaxed. But your mind is accustomed to accumulating tensions, anxieties, worries. It will do its work. Tomorrow morning, you will find that you are the same person. Those few hours that you lived after the primal scream will become slowly, slowly faded, like a dream, far away.

Then he came up with the idea of "exhaustive primal therapy." Exhaustive means you go on doing it for ten years, fifteen years, twenty years. There is not a single person – many have tried – who is freed from all tensions through primal therapy. Even Janov himself has no experience of his own being, has no experience of relaxing into the universal life forces, merging, meeting, and experiencing the eternal, the endless, the deathless.

Primal therapy is just a toy. You can scream as much as you like. It is not going to be exhaustive for the simple reason that you don't have only one life. There have been hundreds of lives before, and an exhaustive primal therapy will mean that all the tensions, all the anxieties that you have gathered in thousands of years which are part of your deepest unconscious, are all released. Perhaps you will need a few lives just to scream, and go on screaming! More probable is that *you* will be exhausted but primal therapy will not be exhaustive.

Seeing the situation, now Janov does not talk about exhaustive primal therapy... because it is not possible, and Janov has no idea about past lives. If this were the only life, exhaustive therapy would be possible. It is only a question of twenty, thirty, forty, fifty years – you could throw all the rubbish that has gathered in you. But it is a question of *thousands* of years – it will take thousands of years to throw it. And all the while you are throwing it, your mind is collecting it. So you are in a vicious circle: by the time you are finished with ten thousand years of screaming and you look at the mind, he is ready with fresh problems – start primal therapy again!

These are childish approaches. And it is not a coincidence that all these therapies are born in California. Once you know that a thing is born in California, you can be absolutely certain that it is childish, and it is going to be only a fashion for a few days. Now in California, people are thinking about primal therapy as if it is something very ancient. They have gone to other therapies because there are other geniuses, and any type....

Now one of my sannyasins who is here invented a therapy – hugging therapy. The whole hour, the whole session, everybody is hugging everybody else... but in California, everything goes, and he was earning a lot of money. The strangest thing is, that you can tell the Californians any stupid thing and they will do it – and they will pay for it! Two hundred and fifty dollars at least. And when you have paid two hundred fifty dollars for screaming in a room for one hour – which you could have done for free – you come out smiling. You *have* to come out smiling; otherwise what will people say? that you are an idiot; you paid two hundred and fifty dollars and then you screamed for one hour, unnecessarily. You have to come out smiling – a big smile, spread ear to ear – and tell people, "Wow! It is far out!"

And people go on coming because they hear from others: "There is nothing like primal therapy. If you have not experienced primal therapy, your coming into existence is useless. You are here to do screaming."

The question is that Janov says man accumulates negativity, and that negativity is a chemical phenomenon. It is out of man's pain, misery, that certain chemicals start gathering in him which create the negative mind, which wants to destroy.

The miserable person always wants others to be miserable. The miserable person feels happy only when he sees somebody more miserable than himself. The miserable person becomes incapable of saying yes – to life, to love, to beauty, to poetry, to existence. He can only say no, he cannot say yes. Yes is impossible because in his life he has not felt anything for which he should be grateful.

Janov is saying that because it is a chemical reaction, the no.... The questioner is asking: if this is the situation, that the no inside us, the destructiveness is a chemical thing, then how can you expect sannyasins to say yes to existence, to love, to joy? It is something significant to understand. I accept the idea that misery, pain, anxiety, anguish, create certain chemical changes in your body. Just as love, joy, blissfulness, ecstasy, silence, peace – they also create tremendously great chemical, physiological changes in your body and mind.

The question will be difficult for Janov to solve, because these therapists do not believe that there is anything beyond mind, that there is anything more than the body. You are confined in a prison of physiology, chemistry, biology and you cannot be free from them just by meditating.

But neither Janov nor the questioner understand that meditation is not an effort that your chemistry which is ready to say no, should say yes. Meditation simply ignores mind. It bypasses mind; it reaches beyond mind, and once it is beyond mind it has a far superior power. And in that space beyond mind, pain has never entered.

Bliss is simply the very atmosphere beyond the mind. Once a person has touched something beyond, he has a new power. He can say yes, although his body chemistry is saying no. The body is a servant. Just wake up your master, and the body is a servant, the mind is a servant. And once the master is there... and the master is never negative, that is beyond its nature. It is intrinsic to your being to be creative. You are coming from the universal creativity, you are born out of it. You are part of it, you are still connected with it. You cannot live a single second without the connection.

Yes can be said, and the mind with all its chemistry will remain silent. Before the master, it has no power. All that power was derived from the master. But the master was asleep; now the master is awake and is not ready to give anything to destructiveness, to death. No represents death. Yes is the heartbeat of life. So I am not saying that your mind has to say yes. No, I am saying you have to go beyond the no-saying mind. And once you have gone beyond, it is not a question of *saying* yes – you *are* yes. Your very being is nothing but a totality of acceptance, with gratitude.

Out of this, the real prayer arises. All other prayers – in the synagogues, in the churches, in the temples, in the mosques – are just carbon copies. The original is within you, and the original has no words. It is absolute silence, but totally positive. Silence, but so full of music... silence, but so fragrant... silence, but so luminous.

Once you have entered your real being, the mind is such a small thing... it simply starts wagging its tail. No need to hold the tail and wag it – then perhaps it may get angry; the dog may start barking. Even a dog has a dignity of his own. He wags his tail out of his freedom – freedom of expression! Now you are holding his tail and moving it... he will start barking: "This is too much! You are going beyond your limits, you are entering into the territory of somebody else. It is interference." I don't want you to interfere in the mind.

That's what I have been teaching for thirty years continuously: don't interfere. Just be a witness, far above. To interfere, you have to be there – not far away, you have to be *within* the mind to interfere, to fight. Neither is fight needed, nor is interference needed. All that is needed is an aloofness. You are on the sunlit peak. The mind is in the dark valley. And because of your superior powers, the mind automatically follows you. You need not even give an order. It understands your new state of awakening.

You can say yes, but you will have to go into meditation. Through mind, you can force yes, but it will be superficial, hypocritical, forced. Underneath, there will be no – vital, stronger, and soon it will throw away your yes. Let the yes come from above, from a greater, bigger source of energy. The mind will automatically follow, and when mind follows on its own, there is a beauty and there is a grace. When mind says, out of its own understanding – because the master is awake, and now the mind cannot go on behaving in the old ways.... When the mind, out of understanding says yes, there is beauty.

One great Zen master, Hotei, was a strange man – beautiful, very loving, but a little bit eccentric. That eccentricity adds much spice to his life. It makes his life not ordinary and flat but very meaningful.

Each morning when he would wake up, this was his routine, only broken once. The routine was that when he would feel that he was awake, before opening his eyes, he would say, "Hotei," – that was his name – "are you still here?" And then he would answer himself, "Yes, master." He would say, "That's good."

His disciples thought that this seemed to be crazy. Many times they asked him, "Why do you do this?"

He said, "One day, I will wake up and Hotei will not be there. And Hotei has been such a beautiful servant – in good times, in bad times, in darknesses, in lights – the first thing is that I want to be sure, whether Hotei is around or gone. And the moment he says 'Yes, master,' I am filled again with great energy for the day's work. His 'Yes!' is such a beauty, such a grace."

"But," his disciples said, "there is nobody. You are saying both things. You ask the question and you answer it."

Hotei said, "From the outside, this is how it appears, but all that appears is not real. From the inside, I am asking: 'Hotei, are you here?' and it is my *mind* who says, 'Yes, master!' As far as I am concerned, the question and the answer are coming from different sources."

But in his whole life, only once... that was the day he died. He opened his eyes and his disciples were surprised. A lifelong habit... they have also become habituated to listening to it. Something was missing – what happened? There was silence.

And then one disciple asked: "Master, have you forgotten today? You have not asked, 'Hotei, are you still here?' Have you forgotten? Are you becoming old, losing your memory?"

Hotei laughed. He said, "I am not losing my memory and I cannot become old, I am eternally young. I am not asking because I don't want to put Hotei in an embarrassing situation."

They said, "We don't understand. What is the embarrassing situation?"

He said, "The embarrassing situation is that today, Hotei cannot say 'Yes, master!' This is my last day. In fact, I would have died in the middle of the night. I simply managed to go on breathing for the morning, so that you all can come and I can see you for the last time. And perhaps you can also see me for the first time."

He closed his eyes and said, "Hotei, okay – now we can go."

And he said, "Yes, master. I have been ready since the middle of the night, it is time."

Have you noted the beauty of Hotei's eccentric behavior? It looks eccentric... it is the sanest behavior possible.

BELOVED OSHO,
WHY DO I JUDGE SO MUCH?

It is a great disease. And we carry the disease from generation to generation. Everybody is brought up in a climate of continuous judgment, condemnation, criticism. This makes people hard, this makes people without compassion. And the society needs people who don't have compassion, who are hard, and who are always putting everybody down.

Your continuous habit of judging is nothing but an effort to put everybody lower than you. When you criticize something, when you judge someone, you have already taken a higher position. You don't know the other person. You don't know his life story, you may have known a little fragment. On that fragment, you judge the whole life of a man – unashamedly.

But the society wants you to be continuously struggling, competing; continuously putting others down, pulling on their legs and trying to raise yourself higher and higher in the world of power and position. This world is almost a battlefield. And there is cold war going on continuously; everybody is everybody else's enemy. Here there is no friend.

I was reading the Bible and a small child was sitting by my side. He was very curious and very cute. Whenever I used to sit in the garden, he would come and sit – and he was intelligent; he would ask questions. He would ask me to read something to him so he could also get some idea of what I was reading. He was the son of a principal who lived next door. I read him the sentence from Jesus: "Love your enemies as you love yourself."

And that little boy said, "This is very good. But I want to know... has he said anything about loving your friends?"

This is what only an innocent child can ask. A knowledgeable person will feel that it doesn't look right to ask such a question – why become a laughingstock? But he asked and I had to think it over. I told the boy: "Because there are no friends."

He said, "Right!" He said "This is the beauty of asking questions to you, because you say the truth. There are no friends, it is a friendless world. There are only enemies. That's why Jesus says, 'Love your enemies,' because there is no other kind available."

It is simple. Without becoming in any way superior... and one becomes superior only by having superior values. If you have infinite love, if you have unlimited compassion, if you have absolute fearlessness – with these qualities, you never think yourself superior, you *are*. Only those people who are *not* superior think that they are superior. Superior people never think, they never even become aware of the fact that they are superior. They are simply superior and they enjoy it. They really feel a deep pity for you, that you are capable of enjoying all these riches and you are missing – just collecting seashells and colored stones and wasting your life.

But to attain to superior qualities, to become a superman without any self-consciousness that "I am a superman...." The superman will know that "I am just an ordinary man." That will be one of the basic and fundamental qualities of the superman: that he cannot even dream that he is superior to anybody.

One of the mystics of India, Kabir, has a beautiful song. He was uneducated; he could not write, he could not read. All his songs are spontaneous outpourings. They may not be grammatical – they are not; they may not be linguistically correct – they are not; but they are so beautiful that after Kabir, there have been thousands of poets in this country who know language, who know grammar, who know the whole art of poetics, but they are pygmies. Kabir is a superman. His songs are simple but so full of meaning. One of the songs says:

"I used to think that I was a superior man, but then I went for a pilgrimage and came in contact with many, many people. When I returned home, the idea of being superior was dropped. Instead, I started feeling that I must be the most ordinary man in the world. My first idea was my ignorance about people. When I came to know so many people, I realized my utter ordinariness."

But this is the quality of a superman. Only a superman can say that, can have the *guts* to say it. But to attain to this superiority, you will need superconsciousness. You will have to climb to the sunlit peaks of your own being.

That is a little arduous. The cheaper way is – rather than making yourself superior; without any difficulty, the cheaper way is to judge others as inferior. Nobody can prevent you, it is just your inside idea. And because everybody is inferior, you are superior. Now this is the cheapest way. You don't move anywhere, you are the same person, but in your mind you have put others.... That does not change anybody else, it does not change you – but it gives a great consolation.

Winston Churchill, a great orator, was asked once: "You are one of the most important, articulate, impressive orators in the world. Do you remember the first day, when you faced thousands of people looking at you and you were standing on the stage – do you remember the stage fright?"

And you will be surprised at what Winston Churchill said. He said, "Don't be worried about the first day, that was sixty years ago. But even today, it is the same. When I stand up on the stage, the same fear – and I have been speaking for sixty years!"

He was the only person in the whole world who remained a member of the parliament for sixty years continuously without a gap. And he says that he feels afraid.

Then the person asked, "How have you been managing?"

He said, "I have my own strategy. My strategy is: before I stand up, I look all around and say to myself: All these are idiots; otherwise, why should they come to listen to me? And there is no need to be afraid of these idiots, because what can they do? Their opinion does not matter at all. Once I settle with the idea that all these people are idiots, then I start my speech without fear – what is the fear? who is there who can judge what I am saying?"

This is the cheapest way. But everybody's doing it – ordinary people and the so-called heroes like Winston Churchill – they are all doing this nonsense. That's why you judge. Your judgment about others is really an effort to feel satisfied that you are better: "This man is a thief. That man is a rapist. This man is crazy." And you can go on labeling anybody. Finally, only you are left. But judging is the quality of the inferior person. The superior person never judges. He feels compassion. If he sees something wrong in somebody, he feels compassion. He tries in his own way, without offending the person, to help him. But there is no judgment.

I was a professor in the university but I refused to examine people's answers in their examinations. The vice-chancellor called me and asked, "What is the matter? First you refused to make up some examination papers, question papers, and now you are refusing to examine the answer."

I said, "That's right! I will not ask questions for the simple reason that in my idea, your whole educational system is utterly wrong. Five questions, and you have judged the person's intelligence? It may be just accidental that he knows only those five answers and your judgment about his intelligence is wrong. It may also be possible that he does not know only those five questions and he knows everything else. Then too, your judgment is going to be wrong and inhuman. And I am not going to examine their answer copies, because whenever I see that somebody has not answered rightly, I feel great compassion for him. And because of my compassion, I give him higher marks than to those who have given the right answer, because they don't deserve any compassion."

He said, "What are you saying? The right answer gets less points and the wrong answer gets more?"

I said, "Yes! That's why I am keeping out of it, because then you will call me and ask. It is better – include me out. Don't put me in this game. There are many who are mad, who want to compose question papers because that brings money, who want to examine answer copies because that brings money. I am simply refusing money – anybody else will be happy to have it. Make somebody happy."

He looked at me and he said, "I have always thought that in your eccentricities, there is always something of truth. Yes, I agree. It hurts to give a zero to somebody, if you are not just mechanically judging but seeing the person behind the answer. With great hope he has given this answer – it may be wrong but his hope... what about his hope? His parents may be poor, he may be working in the night and studying in the day. He may not have the chance, the time, to rest which others have, and you are giving him a zero."

I said, "I simply refuse. And if you insist, then don't ask any question about what I do. I can compose question papers but you cannot ask, 'What kind of questions are these?' because I will be trying to figure out questions which don't depend on memory. I will cancel all those people who are depending on memory, because memory is not intelligence. I will compose questions which need intelligence – but intelligence is not found in the textbooks of the universities. Intelligence is not being taught. People are not being trained. Only memory is being filled, with more and more information.

"I will compose questions that will not ask information, they will be immediate questions. Whether the person has been reading or not, coming to the classes or not, if he has intelligence, he will find the answer. If he has no intelligence, then all his memory cannot help. Then don't tell me that I am disturbing the whole structure of the university. I can examine their papers, but I cannot be their judge. Everybody will pass first class, because as far as I am concerned, every human being is a first-class human being. What does it matter that he has not answered one question rightly? And what do you mean by not rightly – you mean that it is not the exact copy of the textbook! The student has not proved himself a parrot."

He said, "You simply forget all about it. From now on, you are free about question papers, answer copies...."

But he forgot one thing, and the superintendent of the examinations sent me a letter saying "You are appointed to supervise in the examination hall."

I said, "My God! I forgot to discuss this with the vice-chancellor."

So I went to the examination hall, and in the beginning I told the students: "You can take it for granted that I am not here, because I don't want to be an interference in anybody's life. You can do whatever you have planned to do. If you have brought notes with you, no harm. If you want to copy from other people, you can do it but don't disturb – so many people are here, so be silent. And there are professors outside in other rooms, so you have to be alert – not of me, but of all these people. I am absent and I will not disturb you at all; it is just some mistake that I am here."

They had never heard such a thing. And what I did was that I turned my chair facing towards the blackboard, with my back towards the students and I said: "When the time is up, wake me."

One of the students stood up and he said, "You trust us so much?"

I said, "It is not a question of trust or anything. I just love freedom and I don't in any way want to be in your way. You are mature enough. You must know what you are doing. Is it right? – then do it. If it is wrong, then it is up to you whether to do it or not to do it."

And you will be surprised. They brought their copies and their notes and they piled up everything in front of me. And they touched my feet and said, "Bless us."

"But," I said, "what is this big pile?" Even books, printed books they had in their pants... one boy brought his shirt. I said, "But you will be sitting without a shirt."

He said, "But I have to put this shirt here, because I have written notes on it."

"On the shirt?"

He said, "Yes, this is what I have done."

He showed me the other side of the shirt, the inside. He had written notes on it.

I said, "You can have it. I trust you that you will not look into those notes. But sitting without a shirt, and those professors... that will become a question mark, what is the matter?"

And all this pile in front of me... the vice-chancellor heard, because those professors were watching, listening to what I was saying. Everything was reported to him. In the evening, he came to my house and he said, "We forgot about this. And it was just out of a mistake, because another person is the superintendent of the examinations. It will never happen again. But the students who were in your examination hall have never been so happy. They have never been trusted, they have been never given their dignity." Judgment is an ugly phenomenon.

Rise in your own being – higher. Don't destroy that opportunity by judging people as lower. You are doing immense harm to yourself, not to anybody else.

BELOVED OSHO,
WATCHING THE MIND SEEMS TO BE ALSO
SOMETHING OF THE MIND. HOW TO FIND OUT
WHAT YOU ARE TALKING ABOUT?

Watching the mind, in the beginning, looks as if a part of the mind is watching the other parts. You are in the mind, so in the beginning it is absolutely okay. But remember that a real watching is not of the mind, in the mind, by the mind. The real watcher is far away from the mind. And to create the distance between the mind and the watcher is the whole art of meditation. So don't just get involved in intellectual questions; make a few efforts to experience whether you can be just a watcher of the *whole* mind. You can be, because I can be.

Thousands of mystics have been watching the mind from the outside. Because you *are* outside – it is not a question that you have to come out of the mind, you have never been in it. It is almost like a dream. You dream in the night that you are in Paris – but do you think that if somebody wakes you suddenly, you will wake up in Paris? You will still wake up here. You can dream of Paris, and in the dream you can be in Paris, but if awakened, you will be here. Awakened, you will not say, "Okay, I will try to find out about flights, how I can reach to Bombay because right now I am in Paris." If you say that, that means there is no more dream – you are mad!

There is a beautiful story about Chuang Tzu. The world has created many beautiful people, but Chuang Tzu is still unparalleled. He has something unique about himself.

One morning, he woke up. He was very sad. He called all his

disciples and he said, "I am very sad because for the first time in my life, I have come across a problem that I cannot solve. And I used to think that I had solved everything. For years, there has not been a single problem. I have lived in utter silence. But last night disturbed everything." One disciple asked, "Please tell us what happened."

He said, "In the night, I saw a dream that I had become a butterfly, flying over flowers, moving from this flower to that flower. Then I woke up and a question arose in my mind: in the night I had gone to bed as Chuang Tzu, and in the dream I became a butterfly. I still remember the colors, the flowers... and now I'm wondering: who am I? Is it not possible that the butterfly has gone to sleep and is dreaming that she has become Chuang Tzu? If Chuang Tzu can become a butterfly in a dream, then a butterfly can become Chuang Tzu in a dream, there is no problem. So who am I? – a butterfly dreaming to be Chuang Tzu? I am very much puzzled. You try to find out."

They all said, "This is only a *dream*. You are a great sage, you should not be concerned with these small things."

He said, "This is not a small thing. It is a very significant question."

And just then Lieh Tzu, his very intimate disciple, came in and he asked, "What is the matter? What is this whole crowd doing here?"

They gave him the way and they said, "Chuang Tzu, our master, is very sad."

He heard the whole thing. He went away and came back with a bucket of ice cold water and poured it on Chuang Tzu! Chuang Tzu said, "Wait! It is too cold. I am Chuang Tzu... no question, nothing! And where have you been? If you had been here from the very beginning, this whole morning could have been saved. All these idiots are trying to persuade me that this is not a significant question and only you have solved it. It *is* a significant question... but ice cold water?" He said, "A philosophical question is one thing... but Lieh Tzu, I'm getting old. You should be careful about it – this ice cold water."

Lieh Tzu said, "Nothing else would have brought you to your

senses. Anything more about the butterfly?"

He said, "No, nothing. Only butterflies have to bother about it. Why should I bother? I am Chuang Tzu again, it was just a small episode in the night. Forget all about it... but take your bucket!"

You have to grow. But never choose anything cheap, because no cheap thing can give you that which is the most precious experience in life.

BELOVED OSHO,
HOW CAN I DECIDE IF I HAVE REALLY ACHIEVED
SOMETHING, OR JUST BELIEVE I HAVE ACHIEVED?

It is very simple: Whenever you have a question about whether it is a real achievement or just imagination, then it is imagination. If you don't have any questions, even if the whole world says it is imagination but inside you there is no question, if inside you, you are absolutely certain that this is an achievement, then it is an achievement. Any authentic achievement brings with it a certainty, a guarantee that "I am true." And every imaginary achievement brings with it all kinds of doubts. So whenever you are in doubt, decide: it is imaginary. Whenever there is no doubt, you are in a doubtless certainty, then it is a real, authentic evolution. You have found something.

I have heard about a farmer who was coming home with his donkey. He found on the way a big diamond. He had no idea that it was a diamond but he loved his donkey very much, and the diamond was shining so beautifully... in the morning sunrise, it was throwing rainbows around. He said, "It will be good for the poor donkey. I have never given him a present." So he made an arrangement so that the diamond would hang around the neck of the donkey.

By coincidence, as he finished hanging the diamond around the donkey's neck, a jeweler came on his horse; he was going to some other place. He could not believe his eyes. His whole life he has been a jeweler, a prominent jeweler, but he has never seen such a big diamond. Even after cutting and polishing, it was still bigger than Kohinoor.

He said, "My God, and that is hanging around the donkey's neck!"

He got down from the horse. It was obvious that the farmer did not understand that it was a diamond, so he said, "A beautiful stone you have... how much you will take for it?"

He said, "How much? I have never sold any stone before – perhaps one rupee will be more than enough. If you are interested, you can have it. I will purchase something for my poor donkey."

But such is the greed of man... that diamond was worth millions of rupees, but the jeweler said, "No, one rupee is too much, just for a stone. I can give you half a rupee."

The farmer said, "No, then let my donkey enjoy it."

The jeweler went away. He thought that the man would think and would call him back. He went slowly on his horse, but by chance, another jeweler... he asked the price.

The man said, "One man was asking just before you. I said one rupee and he said he could give me only half a rupee. For half a rupee, I am not going to sell. My donkey is enjoying it so much." The man said, "I will give you two rupees."

The other jeweler, who was moving slowly on his horse, looked back and was shocked that some other jeweler had reached the man – "My God! Millions of rupees are gone!" He rushed back and he said, "Wait! Whatsoever he is offering, double! I will give you double."

The other jeweler said, "Then I will give you double that!"

And they went on doubling... the farmer stood there and said to the donkey, "What do you think? We should leave these two donkeys here and go home. I am not going to sell it anymore. Don't bother. You are jewelers, and you could not recognize that it is a diamond? You recognized it, but your greed is such that you are getting a diamond for one rupee and still you want to save half a rupee – and you are ready to risk millions. I was not aware that this was a diamond, but seeing the conflict between you, that you are now raising the price double.... I don't know what it is, but one thing is certain: it is not an ordinary stone. I am going to the jeweler's market, it should be auctioned there. You can come."

They said, "Wait!"

He said, "You have been stupid! You have both been stupid! Now I can understand why my donkey was smiling. I was puzzled – why was he smiling? He has never smiled before. But he had never seen jewelers before."

Life is very precious. You may not recognize the diamond that you are carrying within you, but the moment you enter into yourself and find it, its very presence, its very luminosity will be enough to convince you. There is not going to be any suspicion or doubt.

But if you are imagining things, certainly doubt will follow. Doubt follows only imaginations. For example, if you believe in God, doubt is going to be there. If you believe in heaven and hell, doubt is going to be there. But if you know from your own experience, then there is no doubt. When you fall in love, have you ever asked yourself, "Is this love REAL?" No. Nobody has ever doubted his love because his love is coming from his very heart, with a certainty.

You can doubt God but you cannot doubt love. That's why, to me, God has never had anything to do with religion. But love has much to do with it because it is the fundamental experience upon which your whole flight towards the unknown is going to be based.

BELOVED OSHO,
LATELY, I HAVE EXPERIENCED SOMETHING SOFT AND
CALM – A BEAUTY WHICH ARISES IN ME FROM
WITHIN. SOMETHING WHICH FILLS ME STRONGER
NOW THAN EVER BEFORE. I CAN'T SAY THAT IT
BELONGS TO ME, AND STILL IT FEELS AS IF IT IS ME. IS
IT LOVE?

Yes, it is love. And in other words, it is the beginning of a great pilgrimage which only begins and never ends, which goes on becoming bigger and bigger. Whatever you are feeling, go on deeper into it. Don't be afraid of anything because we have nothing to lose, and we have the whole universe to gain. You are right on the doorstep of the temple of God. Love is the beginning, God is the journey. God is not the goal, God is the pilgrimage.

I am reminded of Al Hillaj Mansoor, a great Sufi mystic. He was young, but very poor. He collected money, borrowed money, tried to earn, because he wanted to go to Mecca for a pilgrimage. For Mohammedans, one of the essential things is that at least one time in your life, you should go for a pilgrimage to Mecca, the place where Mohammed created the whole world of Islam.

Finally, after three years, he had enough money to go. The whole town had come to bid him farewell. As he left the people and was leaving the town boundaries, he saw an old man, sitting under a tree. It was a crossroad, so he had to ask him: "Which road goes to Mecca?"

The old man said, "Come here," and the way he said "Come here" was such that Al Hillaj Mansoor *had* to go.

The man said, "No road goes to Mecca! But if you are interested in the *pilgrimage*, that is possible, and there is no need to go anywhere. First, put everything, all your money and everything in front of me."

He was saying it in such a way... he had a certain charisma around him; whatever he said, Al Hillaj had to do. He hesitated a moment – "He is going to take all my money! Three years I have worked... but what to do? Looking at the man, money seems worthless. Looking into his eyes, it seems you have reached Mecca."

And the old man laughed, "Right! You are understanding it: Look into my eyes and you have reached Mecca. Put everything here!" So he had to put everything there – a bit reluctantly, but there seemed to be no other way. And then the old man said, "Now the pilgrimage begins – because God *is* a pilgrimage. Go around me seven times. Just the way Mohammedans go around the stone of Kaaba in Mecca seven times, go around me. And I promise you that you have reached Mecca; now start the real pilgrimage."

Mansoor went around the old man seven times. The closer he came to the old man, the more rounds he took around him... he felt so silent, so joyful. He started dancing, started singing.

The old man said, "Perfectly right! Now you can go anywhere, and wherever you go, it is the pilgrimage to God. Just remember the dance, the song – they should not only be outside, they should be inside, too."

He went back home. The whole town gathered. They said, "What happened?" Because Mecca in those days used to take at least four to six months, going and coming. "You are back! We have just reached home and you are back. What happened?"

He said, "Mecca came to meet me outside the town and asked me to give all my money. I took the seven traditional circles around the old man and he said, 'God is a pilgrimage and now your pilgrimage has started. Just sing, dance, feel the glory of existence.'"

The townspeople said, "You are a fool! Somebody has cheated you."

Al Hillaj said, "No, I have looked into the eyes of that man. I have looked into the face of that man. I have been around him, I have felt his presence. I am absolutely convinced that Mecca has come to receive one of its followers. There is nothing wrong. It has been said in the scriptures," he said, "that if your thirst is total, you need not go anywhere. Your thirst will pull the truth, God, to you, wherever you are. Mohammed has said that if mountains cannot come to Mohammed, then Mohammed will go to the mountains."

This is a beautiful statement. And Al Hillaj said, "He was right. You *are* on the doorstep of the divine. Just celebrate."

Enter into this feeling, into this beautiful mood you have arrived at. Merge, melt, disappear into it. It is love.

26

The Human Rights Declaration:
Hypocrisy of a barbarous society

BELOVED OSHO,
IT FEELS STRANGE WHEN THE ESTABLISHMENT,
WORLDWIDE, WHICH IS EVER BUSY WITH ALL ITS
EFFORTS AND RESOURCES TO MAKE SURE IN EVERY
POSSIBLE WAY THAT MAN CANNOT REMAIN MAN,
ASKS US TO CELEBRATE "HUMAN RIGHTS DAY."
GOODNESS, WHAT IS ALL THIS THAT'S GOING ON?
BELOVED MASTER, WOULD YOU CARE TO EXPLAIN?

One of the most fundamental things to be always remembered is that we are living in a hypocrite society.

Once, a great philosopher was asked: "What do you think of civilization?"

The philosopher said, "It is a good idea, but somebody has to change the idea into a reality. Civilization has not happened yet. It is a dream of the future."

But the people who are in power – politically, religiously, socially – are in power because civilization has not happened. A civilized world, a mature man, needs no nations – all those boundaries are false – needs no religions, because all those theologies are simple fictions.

The people who have been for thousands of years in power – the priests, the politicians, the super-rich, they have all the powers to prevent human evolution. But the best way to prevent it is to convince man, "You are already civilized," to convince man, "You are already a human being. You need not go through a transformation, it is unnecessary."

And man's weakness is that knowing perfectly well there exists no such thing as civilization, there exists no such thing as human sensitivity, still he starts believing in all the lies that the politicians have been speaking, the priests have been preaching, the educationists have been teaching – because it seems simpler to just believe, you don't have to do anything for it.

To recognize the fact that you are not yet a man creates fear. The very ground underneath your feet disappears. Truth makes you utterly naked – naked of all lies, naked of all hypocrisies. That's why nobody wants truth; everybody believes that he has *got* it.

Do you see the psychological strategy? If you don't want to give something to someone, convince him, hypnotize him, repeat again and again, "You have got it." And when thousands of people around you – your parents, your teachers, your priests, your leaders – are all believing it, it seems almost impossible for new arrivals in the world, small children, not to be convinced of this thousands-of-years-old idea. Millions of people have lived and died believing that civilization has happened.

So the first thing I want you to understand is that we are still barbarous. Only barbarians can do things that we have been doing for thousands of years – not human beings. In three thousand years, five thousand wars... and you call man civilized? In the twentieth century – exactly in the middle of the twentieth century – you can produce Adolf Hitler, you can produce Josef Stalin, you can produce Benito Mussolini, you can produce Mao Zedong, and still you believe man is civilized?

Adolf Hitler alone killed six million human beings, and killed with great sophistication. Science and technology have been used. One million Jews have been simply burned in gas chambers – within seconds thousands of people are nothing but smoke going out of the chimneys. He killed so many people that it was impossible to give each person the conventional grave.

Man has never been so poor – even beggars have graves, but he had killed so many people that to make graves for all of them... the whole of Germany would have became a graveyard. So he had deep ditches prepared, and people were simply thrown into the ditches and covered with mud. Before throwing their bodies in the ditches he destroyed even those dead peoples' dignity. Their clothes were taken away; their heads, their beards, their mustaches were shaved so you could not recognize the face of the person. Their heads were cut off; so you would find somewhere the head and somewhere the hand and somewhere the leg and somewhere the remaining parts of the body. And thousands of people – it was impossible to figure out who you were looking for. Why did he do that? So that nobody could be recognized. Even if somebody was found dead, he could not be recognized; he did not even have his whole body. And you say that man is civilized?

And this is not the end of the story. Seeing the second world war, one would have thought that just a little intelligence is needed and the second world war should be the last world war – seeing what man himself has been doing to man. But no, we are preparing for the third world war – and the last.

Albert Einstein was asked, "Can you say something about what is going to happen in the third world war?"

And Einstein said, "Excuse me, I cannot say anything about the third world war, but I can say something about the fourth."

The questioner could not believe it. He said, "You cannot say anything about the third – and it is so complicated – yet you are ready to say something about the forth, which will be even more complicated!"

Albert Einstein said, "You don't understand. I can say something definitively, categorically, about the fourth. And that is that the fourth is never going to happen, because the third will destroy all life – not only human beings, roses too. All that is living will disappear from the earth." And you say that humanity has become civilized? No, you have been deceived and this declaration of human rights by the United Nations is nothing but the same hypocrisy.

George Gurdjieff used to tell a small story – but it is about humanity. The story is that there was a magician. He lived deep in the mountains and the forests, and he had thousands of sheep. But the problem was that the sheep were afraid of the magician because every day the sheep were seeing that one of them was being killed for his breakfast, another was being killed for his lunch. So they used to run away from the magician's place, and it was a difficult job to find them in the vast forest. Being a magician, he used magic. He hypnotized all the sheep and told different sheep... to some, "You are a man, you need not be afraid. It is only the sheep who are going to be killed and eaten, not *you*. You are a man just like I am."

Some other sheep were told, "You are a lion – only sheep are afraid. They escape, they are cowards. You are a lion; you would prefer to die than to run away. You don't belong to these sheep. So when they are killed it is not your problem. They are *meant* to be killed, but you are the most loved of my friends in this forest."

In this way he told every sheep different stories, and from the second day, the sheep stopped running away from the house. They still saw other sheep being killed, butchered, but it was not their concern. Somebody was a lion, somebody was a tiger, somebody was a man, somebody was.... Nobody was a sheep except the one who was being killed.

This way, without keeping servants, he managed thousands of sheep. They would go into the forest for their food, for their water, and they would come back home, believing always one thing: "It is some sheep who is going to be killed, not *you*. You don't belong to this mob. You are a lion — respected, honored, a friend of the great magician." The problems of the magician were solved. I am telling you this story because it is literally true about you. You are being told things, and you accept them without even looking all around to see whether those things coincide with the reality or not.

The first thing... My first objection to the UN's Declaration of Human Rights is that rights exist only when there are duties. Duties are roots, rights are the flowers: you cannot have rights without duties. And to celebrate a day in the year for human rights... but they don't celebrate a day for human duties, which comes first.

Why are they not talking about human duties? Because they don't want to give you your human rights. Without duties, rights can only be talked about, but you won't have them in your hands. And about duties, these politicians who have made this declaration have no notion at all. I will give you a few examples.

They say that every human being is equal. And of course it satisfies the ego of every human being — nobody objects. It is one of the most dangerous lies to tell human beings. I say to you, equality is a myth. There are not even two human beings who are equal — in *any* way, in any dimension. I don't mean that they are unequal, I mean that they are unique, incomparable, so the question of equality or inequality does not arise. Are you equal to these pillars in the hall? The pillars may be beautiful, but you are not equal to them. But does that mean you are inferior to the pillars? It simply means you are not a pillar – pillars are pillars, you are you. Every human being is a category unto himself. And unless we recognize the uniqueness of each individual, there are not going to be any human rights, and there is not going to be a civilized world – human, loving, rejoicing.

In the declaration they emphasized the fact again and again that you should love all human beings; you are all brothers. But have you ever seen brothers being in love? Have you ever seen brothers being friends? The way brothers fight, nobody fights.

And just saying, "You are brothers," does not make it a reality. These people who declared these human rights – what authority have they got? Who are they? Politicians… and they are the cause of all the wars, they are the cause of all kinds of violence happening all over the world.

These are the people who have kept almost half of humanity – womankind – in a state of slavery. But looking at the declaration I had really a great time… because it does not talk about sisters, only brothers. Sisters don't count – yet they are half of humanity. They are not even mentioned.

These politicians are articulate, clever, cunning… mostly coming from the legal profession. They are saying there should be no discrimination between man and woman, between black and white. Between races, religions, political ideologies, there should be no discrimination. And who is making the discrimination? These are the same people who are making the declaration.

They have enslaved the woman for centuries, and they are not yet willing to give her freedom – which, according to their declaration, is a basic human right. The blacks are being treated as animals. Just at the end of the last century, the blacks were still be sold, auctioned in marketplaces like a commodity. And even today, they are not respected as the white people are respected.

And these are the white people – all these politicians are white. These white people have been driving the whole of humanity, for three hundred years, into slavery. They all had their empires. England had the biggest empire; it was said that the sun never set in the British Empire. Somewhere or other in the British Empire the sun was shining and it was day – all around the earth. But other white people were not far behind: the French, the Portuguese, the Spanish – they all had vast empires, exploiting the whole earth. They have been the parasites: and it is hilarious that all these parasites are now declaring human rights.

This is a deception. It is not meant; what they are saying they don't mean. It is just to give you an idea that you are equal to everybody, you are a brother to everybody, that you have all the human rights. But I know – all these human rights are just hypocrisies. I know by my own experience.

There is one human right enumerated in this declaration: Nobody can be arrested without a warrant. I was arrested exactly like that in America – without warrant, without any arrest warrant or search warrant. Not even verbally did they inform me what crime I had committed. And when I asked them, "What crime have I committed? I must know at least," the answer was loaded guns – twelve loaded guns surrounding my jet airplane. When guns are answers, then you can be certain civilization is far away.

They did not have any arrest warrant. The simple thing for the court would have been... but they not only arrested me, they were clever, they had deliberately arrested me at such a time that I would have to be in jail for at least two days. On Monday the court would open – only then could I be bailed out. They themselves were certain that I would be bailed out because there was no reason to hold me; they didn't have any proof, any evidence against me. They had chosen a certain situation in which for two days the court was closed – so at least they would have the satisfaction of torturing me for two days. On the third day... I was not amazed when the court refused to give me bail.

The magistrate, a woman, did not even allow my attorney's to question the fact that I had been arrested without any arrest warrant. In a democratic country which claims to be the greatest democratic country in the world, the court would not allow them even to discuss it, because to discuss it would be an exposure. There was no question of giving me bail. In the first place I had been arrested without any warrant, and even after three days they didn't have the warrant – the question of bail does not arise. The bail was not given. In the second court, in a higher federal court, again the question, What about my arrest? – which is the basic question – was not discussed. Everything else is secondary. First, you arrest somebody without even telling him why he is being arrested....

And in these human rights, these same politicians sitting in America, say that nobody can be arrested without an arrest warrant; this is a fundamental human right. If I was not arrested, I might not have known.

They say nobody should interfere in anybody's philosophy, religion, political ideology – that is every individual's birthright. But my commune in America has been destroyed for the simple reason that Christianity – my being not a white man, my commune being universal.... There were black people, there were people from all over the world. It was the only place where there was no discrimination of any kind. They destroyed a commune which was fulfilling human rights in every detail. On the surface man has become civilized, but deep in the darker parts of his unconsciousness he is still barbarous.

In the introduction to this declaration it says, We are determined to eliminate all forms of intolerance and of discrimination based on religion or belief. And this is not true in any country. Religions are fighting continuously, and if the government consists of fanatic, religious people, the minority is crushed and destroyed in every possible way. The desire is good, but the people who are desiring it are all wrong.

In the convention at which the UN declared these fundamental rights, the Soviet Union was absent; eight other communist countries were absent. America was present. Unanimously the declaration was adopted – all in favor and nobody against. I am mentioning it because it was basically an American initiative to make this declaration. And America is the first to be going against *every* human right.

Just now, America has given two hundred million dollars to the terrorists in Nicaragua, a small country which has become communist, just like Cuba. To destroy the country, America has flooded it with terrorists. Now millions of dollars are being poured in continuously, to support the terrorists with weapons and with everything. And in this declaration it says that every country is sovereign, and no other country should interfere in any other country's life, religion. That is *their* business – how they want to live, what they want to believe or not to believe. It is nobody else's business at all. If in some small country people have accepted communism as their lifestyle and their social structure, who is America? – and what right have they?

Nicaragua appealed to the world court; and the world court is full of American judges. Still the world court said to America, "Your act is against the human rights declaration, it is criminal." Ronald Reagan simply canceled it. He said, "We don't care about the world court or their decisions." Now these are the people who have made the declaration. They have created the world court to decide in situations where some conflict arises. And these same people are not ready to listen.

Do you see the politics behind it? The World Court, the declaration – all are facades to hide things. If some small country was doing it, then the world court would be right, and America would have taken action in favor of the world court to destroy that country because it was doing a criminal act. Now, because America itself is doing the criminal act, it simply can say, "We don't care about the world court."

And what can the world court do? It has no armies, it has no power. It has all the power that has been given to the politicians; but if those politicians themselves go against the law that they have made, what can the court do?

And the UN is silent. Its Court has been insulted. If the people in the UN have any dignity they will dissolve the UN and dissolve the world court – because what is the point? Today America is doing it tomorrow the other countries will. And the Soviet Union is far better, and is right, because it never participated in this declaration. It is not part of this declaration; no communist government participated in it. So at least they have shown from the very beginning that these things are all bogus: "Who are you trying to cheat?"

All the rights are, in a way, not very rational. For example, in this long declaration, the right to leave the body when one has lived enough and is now weak, sick, old, a burden, and of no use... One is suffering unnecessarily and waiting for death. Why wait? Why put this man unnecessarily in torture?

The society is responsible for thousands of people who are in torture – in hospitals or in nursing homes. They don't have any possibility of coming back to life healthy, creative, of any use. But they can go on vegetating; and medicine is developed enough – you can keep them in the hospitals for years. Artificial breathing... perhaps the man is already dead, but because of the artificial breathing you are deceived.

In this long list, one of the most important human rights is not included; and that right is the right to leave the world, to give the ticket back, to say, "I want to go back home? Who are you to prevent me or anybody?"

But that right, which is very significant today because in the advanced countries, the average life has gone to such lengths that more and more people will be in a situation where their sons and daughters are already old – eighty, ninety.... The fourth or fifth or six generation has already arrived, and that fifth or sixth generation cannot have any connection with a man one hundred and twenty years old, just vegetating in a hospital. Those new arrivals have no relationship, they don't have any respect.

Now, months pass and those old people are hanging around in the hospitals waiting, hoping that somebody may come – a friend, a child, an old acquaintance – to meet them. Nobody comes. People avoid them. They *are* boring, naturally. It is almost as if you are reading a fifty-year old newspaper. They don't have anything new; everything is fifty, sixty years old. If you go to them they will talk only about those golden days when they used to be young, and life was an adventure. You cannot connect with them, and you feel simply bored. Everything has changed in fifty years, and those people are not even aware of what has changed. But no government in the world accepts euthanasia, the right to die. In this long declaration it is not included.

Politicians are very, very cunning. They don't want to be controversial, so they say only things which you like or everybody is going to like. They are not concerned with the actual situation, and the changes it needs. Their whole effort is in how to make you happy just by giving you bogus words.

Nowhere in the world are any of the basic rights being applied. I will go through a few important rights.

> WHEREAS DISREGARD AND CONTEMPT FOR HUMAN
> RIGHTS HAS RESULTED IN BARBAROUS ACTS WHICH
> HAVE OUTRAGED THE CONSCIENCE OF MANKIND....

It has two implications in it. One is that the people who made this declaration have accepted that humanity is civilized. That's why once in a while if there is any barbarous act, those human beings in the world – the whole of mankind – suffers in conscience, feels the pain, the anguish. Both are lies, because I don't see humanity having any conscience.

When Mohammedans kill Hindus, no Mohammedan thinks that he has done wrong – the question of conscience does not arise. In fact, according to his religion he has done some virtuous act. He was trying to convert the Hindus to Mohammedanism, because if you are not a Mohammedan you cannot enter paradise.

He was trying to help you in every possible way, to smuggle you, rightly or wrongly, into paradise. From the front door or from the back door, it doesn't matter. But you are resistant, you don't want to go to paradise, you are determined to go to hell – that's why he prevents you, he beheads you: It is better to be killed by the hands of a religious Mohammedan. The Koran says, "The man who is killed by a Mohammedans will enter paradise, just as the Mohammedans who have killed him will enter paradise." So they are really trying to save people from going to hell – why should they feel any pain in their conscience?

No Hindu feels it, no Christian feels it. Christians have killed more people than anybody else, and particularly they have burned living people. Others have been killing and then burning; Christianity has a shortcut. Why make it in two parts? When the book can be published in one book, why make two volumes? First kill the man and then burn him? – burn him directly! Thousands of people have been burned alive. I don't see anywhere that anybody is outraged. If people are outraged things will change – because who is doing them? *We* are doing them.

This sentence in the beginning of the declaration is such a lie. First it says, "Barbarous acts...." In fact, in these fifty years we have done more barbarous acts than in the whole history of man. In ten thousand years we have not been able to do so many barbarous activities as we have done just within fifty years. We are becoming more and more barbarous – of course with a style and method.

Hiroshima and Nagasaki – what do you think? Are these barbarous acts, or an effort to send the beautiful people of Nagasaki and Hiroshima directly to paradise together? Whole cities, more than two hundred thousand people, entered within five minutes. I don't think there was ever such a crowd at the gates of paradise. And it was America that was responsible for Hiroshima and Nagasaki.

It is now absolutely confirmed by the people who understand military science that dropping the atom bombs on Hiroshima and Nagasaki was absolutely useless. Japan was already surrendering – Germany had surrendered and now there was no question that Japan could go on fighting; not for more than one week, or maybe not even that long. Seeing that Germany was finished, Japan could not fight alone. It is a small country of very courageous people, brave people but a very small country. It was fighting with the support of Germany, and when the main support disappeared.... Japan was going to surrender.

And this was the fear of President Truman of America: Japan may surrender tomorrow; then he will miss the chance to drop the atom bombs. And they had put so much money and energy and genius into creating atom bombs, they wanted to try them. Man is not important, but money.... Their bombs had to be tried.

And you say that because of barbarous acts, the civilized people feel a prick of conscience. Was President Truman a civilized man or not? Even his own military experts had told him that it was absolutely meaningless, unnecessarily destroying human life. But he went ahead.

The next morning hundreds of journalists had gathered at the White House to see President Truman, because world's greatest catastrophe created by man had happened. Their first question was, "Mr. President, did you have a good sleep in the night?" – because he had gone to bed only after he had received the message: "Hiroshima and Nagasaki are in smoke, they are no longer on the map of the earth." Then he went to bed; otherwise he waited for the news to reach him.

He said, "Yes, I slept more peacefully than ever, because our experiment has succeeded. Now we are the greatest power in the world." And you are talking about conscience?

More than two hundred thousand people died within three minutes, and the man whose order killed them, slept very 'peacefully,' as he had never slept before. And if this is the situation of President 'True-Man,' then what about the people who are not such true men?

As far as I am concerned, civilization is still a dream, a hope, a utopia. And if we don't get into the tricks of the magician, and start believing that we are civilized people, the hope can become a reality, the dream can become a concrete experience.

And conscience arises only after meditation, never before it. You are not born with a conscience. You can watch small children: if they see an ant they will kill it. Do you think the small child has some conscience? Do you think the small child is a criminal, a murderer? No, nothing like that. It is just out of curiosity, he's just exploring his world. He has entered into a new world, and he is exploring it. But there is no question of conscience. He does not feel that when he has been beating a dog for no reason, the dog also feels pain. Children don't have any conscience; they have only seeds.

All these politicians are trying to convince humanity: "You have a conscience." You *don't* have. You will have to grow it, you will have to work upon yourself. You will have to learn how to be silent, and how to listen to the still, small voice within.

I don't think any of the politicians who made this declaration have had any experience of what conscience is, of what consciousness is. It comes only after a long, long pilgrimage inwards. You are not given everything by birth. You are given by birth only the necessary things for survival; everything else is given only as a seed. If you are intentionally interested in evolving your consciousness to its highest peak, then it is up to you.

Nature provides only for survival – not life, not joy, not silence, not ecstasy, not love. Nature can manage itself with only lust – what is the need for love? Why create complications? Love you will have to find, consciousness you will have to grow. You will have to become a gardener of your own being – your being is your garden.

Your being is the Garden of Eden talked about in the Bible. That Garden of Eden is not somewhere else on some other star – it is within you. You have been thrown out of it, and you have been running all around but never going in. The moment you go in, you are back in the Garden of Eden.

But now, nobody has taken care for thousands of years. You have never been back inside. Everything has gone to seed; now nothing blossoms, no foliage, no greenery. But you can bring it back to life because everything is potentially there. These people don't understand what conscience is. They have learned only words.

I have heard... a psychologist was appearing for an oral examination for his doctorate. There were three examiners. The first question they asked was: "What are the most important qualities of the human mother's milk?"

The psychologist was a little puzzled: "What has psychology to do with mother's milk? I have not come here to be an expert in milk products or anything. But what to do, I have to answer...."

So he said, "First, it has all the nutrients for the child's growth – it is perfect food. Second, it comes from within the mother's body, so it is warm, easily digestible; and because it comes from within, it cannot be carrying any infection, any disease which may be around. The child is protected."

They said, "Right! Now, the third?"

There was a moment of silence because he could not figure it out – what is the third? The first two also he had made up. The third was coming up again and again in his mind, but he was repressing it. When he could not find anything else he had to say it. He said, "The third is that it comes in nice containers!" Now, these idiots are going to be psychologists! And that was the first thing that had come to his mind – "nice containers."

Looking at the declaration, my first feeling was that these people are articulate, they can play with words. They can use beautiful words which influence you and deceive you, and hide the reality.

ARTICLE ONE: ALL HUMAN BEINGS ARE BORN FREE.

This is absolutely nonsense. If all human beings are born free, leave a child in freedom: he will die within twenty-four hours. Man's child is the most helpless child in the whole world – what freedom can he have? He cannot walk, he cannot talk, he cannot fly....

In fact, one scientist had the idea – and I feel some sympathy with his idea – that human child is born earlier than he should be. He needs at least nine months more in the mother's womb because he is not complete, he's still growing. You see animals, kids – they are born and they start walking around and searching for food. They are more independent and they are more complete. For the human child it is impossible to survive without the support of the mother and the father and the family or other human beings. What freedom can he have?

This is what I say is the most cunning part of the politician's mind: He is giving you the idea that you don't need freedom. "Don't ask for freedom. You are born free; all human beings are born free."

All human beings are born utterly helpless and dependent. It may take years for them to be free. Then too, millions of people never become free. This declaration is saying that they are born free. I am saying millions of people die – even then they are not free. And you know it from your life: you are not free.

The husband is there, the wife is not free. The wife is there, the husband is not free. I have seen husbands and wives walking on the road – the husband is not even free to look here and there! He looks straight ahead, like a Buddhist monk, just four feet ahead. And his wife is looking out of the corner of her eye – where is he. What kind of freedom is this? The moment the husband reaches home, the first question is: "Where have you been?" – and you are a free man – "Why are you late?"

When I was in school, I was usually late. Life outside was so beautiful, and around my school there were so many mango trees. And when the mango season comes, just to pass by the side of mango trees – such fragrance, such sweetness in the air. The mango is certainly the king of all the fruits. There were other fruit trees too, and I was mostly in those trees rather than in class.

On the first day when I reached middle school, I was half an hour late. The teacher said, "This won't do. At least with me, this will not do. If you have to study my subject, you have to be here before I come into the class – five minutes earlier. Why are you late?"

I said, "Listen – just because of this question I am not going to get married!" He said, "What? The question of marriage?"

I said, "I will explain to you: I have been hearing it everywhere in my neighborhood; every wife is asking, 'Where have you been? Why are you late?' and I have decided that these questions I am not going to answer. So I am sacrificing my whole life – I'm not going to get married – because of this question, and you think I will answer it for you? I would rather change the subject. Good-bye!"

He said to the class, "This is a strange boy. Irrelevant things he brings in – marriage? What has marriage to do with my subject, geography?"

But he became interested in me. After school he caught hold of me and he said, "Now, we can sit. I want to understand what is the matter. Why?"

I said, "Nobody has the right to ask me why I am late, where I have been. It is *my* life: If I want to spoil it, it is my right. You are only a servant, to teach geography. You are not there to ask such questions to create dependence in me. I hate such questions. I can leave the school; I can completely forget about being educated, there is no need. Because if Jesus, without being educated, can experience himself; if Kabir, without being educated, can know the ultimate…. I am not interested in any business, in any service, in any employment. So if you want me in your class, you will have to be a little more human – not continuously interfering in my freedom."

This first article says: "All human beings are born free." These are the strategies of hypnotizing and conditioning humanity. They have given you the idea that you are born free – now there is no need to fight for freedom, there is no need to create an inner revolution which makes you *really* free – free from everything, free from the body... because the body is a bondage.

The East is far more truthful. It says you are born in bondage, not that you are born free. Your body is a prison and your mind and your brain are prisons. Your consciousness is confined in a very small space, and your consciousness is capable of spreading all over the universe. Because you don't know the potential, you think this is all you are.

These people, according to me, are criminals – greater criminals than those who go to the gallows – because they are deceiving the whole of humanity. But the deception is very clever: "You are born free." Naturally, freedom is not a question, not something to be created, to be deserved, to be earned, to be worthy of; you are already free!

George Gurdjieff is the only man in the whole of history who has said such a tremendously significant thing: "You don't have any soul." Now, throughout the whole world, all the religions believe that you have a soul, that you come with a soul. George Gurdjieff's voice is alone in the whole of history, saying that not all man are with a soul; the place of the soul is empty. There is a possibility – you can work, you can create the soul – but you are not born with it.

I know, and Gurdjieff knows that you are born with a soul – but the idea that we are born with a soul has not been helpful. It has made man more asleep: We are born with a soul, God is within you, the kingdom of God is within you, so what do you have to do? Things that are not within you, work hard to get them – money, power, respectability – because nobody says, "Every child is born with money, every child is born with political power, every child is born with respectability." Nobody will say that. These things have to be earned.

Freedom, consciousness, God, whatever you call it, has to be discovered. It is hidden, dormant; it has to be made dynamic, has to be made fully mature. It should be brought to flower and fruition. But to tell people, "You are born free – and equal in dignity and rights".... People can go on lying so smoothly, with such beautiful words – destroying those words. Nobody is equal. This is a psychological truth.

Neither in your body nor in your mind nor in your talents... nor among your geniuses – nobody is equal. A Sigmund Freud is a Sigmund Freud; a Bertrand Russell is a Bertrand Russell; a D.H. Lawrence is a D.H. Lawrence. There is not even one other D.H. Lawrence, and never will be. Each individual is unique.

This idea of equality is so ugly, but it has become almost the religion of the contemporary man – 'equality.' I say to you, it is the most destructive idea that has penetrated into the human mind. You have to be reminded about your uniqueness.

ALL HUMAN BEINGS ARE ENDOWED WITH REASON AND CONSCIENCE AND SHOULD ACT TOWARDS ONE ANOTHER IN A SPIRIT OF BROTHERHOOD.

These are all assumptions without any validity. All human beings are not born with reason, are not endowed with reason.

For example, there are people, very few... I have just named Bertrand Russell – he can be said to be endowed with reason. A J. Krishnamurti... but ordinary people are living with all kinds of superstitions. Unless you have dropped all your superstitions, you cannot be said to be a rational person. What does reason mean? For the Hindus, the cow is the mother. This is 'reason.'

I was talking to a *shankaracharya* – the equivalent of the pope to the Hindus – and I asked him, "Are you sure that the cow is your mother?" He said, "What do you mean?"

"Now," I said, "just entering your temple, I met your mother. So I was puzzled: who is your mother, this woman or the cow? Or perhaps one is your step-mother?"

He said, "What are you talking about? The woman is my biological mother, but the cow is my spiritual mother."

I said, "My God! What about the bull? You must have some relationship with the bull or not? – your spiritual father? And who are you? – just a bull; or perhaps castrated, not even a bull."

You live with superstitions, and you talk about reason. All Christians believe – and the whole group of politicians who have drawn up this declaration, ninety percent of them are Christians – they all believe that Jesus is born of a virgin mother. And they are rational beings....

It happened: One college girl got pregnant. She tried to hide it, but there are a few things you cannot hide. Truth is one, pregnancy is another! It is just impossible; it goes on becoming bigger and bigger. Finally her mother discovered it. She said, "What is the matter?" And the girl had to confess. The mother took her to the doctor.

The doctor examined her and said, "Even without examining her... she is pregnant – and eight months. Now abortion is not possible."

The mother started shouting and screaming at the girl: "You have blackened our name, destroyed our respectability in the society."

But the girl said, "Mom, I have not even touched the hand of a man. How can I be pregnant? This is impossible!"

Hearing this, the doctor got out of his chair, went to the nearby window and looked at the sky. The mother said, "Why you are looking there?"

He said, "I am looking for the three wise men from the East."

She said, "What do you mean?"

He said, "And I am also looking for the star because it happened once – when Jesus was born. The star came, leading three wise men. It seems it has happened again – a virgin birth!"

But ask these Christians, "Where is your rationality?" Jesus is born out of virgin mother. He is crucified and he's resurrected too, he makes dead people come back to life – and these are the fundamentals on which the faith of a Christian depends. You just take a few things out – it is very strange – and you will find Christianity to be the most irreligious religion, the poorest as far as religiousness is concerned.

The virgin birth – cancel it, if you have reason. Resurrection – cancel it, if you have reason. Walking on water – cancel it. Raising the dead back to life – cancel it. Changing water into alcohol – not only cancel it, but find the guy and give him to the police, because it is a crime, it is not a miracle. But if all these things are canceled, what remains in Christianity? That is the poverty of Christianity.

In Buddhism, you cannot cancel anything because nothing is based on superstition. Buddha himself has canceled anything that smells of superstition – it is just pure rationality.

But to say that man is endowed with reason by birth.... It doesn't seem so. Looking at the world, it doesn't seem that it is a rational world. We have not been living according to reason, we have been living according to all kinds of irrational things. But these are sweet words to believe: that you are *endowed with reason*. The more idiotic you are, the more you will believe it, and sooner.

... AND CONSCIENCE, AND SHOULD ACT TOWARDS ONE ANOTHER IN A SPIRIT OF BROTHERHOOD.

Conscience arises only after deep meditation – never before it. It is a flowering of meditation. Only very few people in the whole world, in the whole of history, have been conscious, have had conscience. Both the words mean the same, but because of religious people, in all the languages except French they have created different meanings for the two words. Only in French is 'conscience' and 'consciousness' one word, it means the same thing.

Religions around the world have tried to take conscience separately from consciousness for a certain reason: consciousness comes only after meditation. How long can you deceive people?

It is just like when you bring light into the room, and darkness disappears. The moment you are in a meditative state, you have consciousness, awareness. They created another word, 'conscience.' And conscience is what the priests, the church, the religion, teach you about what is good, what is bad, what is virtuous, what is sin – all these teachings make your conscience. It is a very clever trick to separate conscience from consciousness. There can be no conscience without consciousness. But they have created a false, artificial conscience.

For example, I was born in a very ancient religion – perhaps the ancientmost. It is a small religion as far as numbers are concerned, but they have their superstitions. Up to the age of eighteen I had not seen a tomato in my house. Do you think tomatoes are dangerous people? But because the color of the tomato is the color of meat, that was enough to debar it. Up to the age of eighteen I had never eaten in the night, because it is prohibited by that religion – you can eat only between sunrise and sunset. Eating in the night you may eat some insect, some ant: some violence may happen. So it is better to eat in light, in full light.

When I was eighteen my friends were going to see a beautiful castle very close by, a few miles away. I went with them. I had no idea, I had not even thought about it, but going up the hill to the castle... and it was so beautiful, so old, and there were so many things to see, that nobody was ready to prepare food.

I asked, "Do something – soon the sun will be setting and I am feeling very hungry, you are feeling hungry. The whole day long we have been moving on the mountain... it has been tiring, but it has been an experience."

They said, "As long as the sun is there, we don't want to miss. There are a few more things to see."

I was the only one who was not accustomed to eating in the night. They were all eating at night so there was no question. By nine or ten o'clock in the night, they had prepared such delicious food – and particularly after the whole day's hunger, starvation, and moving on the mountain, I was in a dilemma – what to do? Then I told them: "There is a great difficulty. I have never eaten in the night, and the religion in which unfortunately I have been born, thinks that if you eat in the night, you will go to hell. I don't want to go to hell just for one night's food, but I cannot sleep either. Moreover, the smell of your food is too much!"

They persuaded me, saying, "We will not tell your parents or anybody. Nobody will ever know that you have eaten in the night."

I said, "That is not the point – I will know. The question is not my parents or anybody. You can tell the whole world, that's not the problem. The problem is that I cannot conceive of myself eating at night, after eighteen years of continuous conditioning."

But they persuaded me – and I had to be persuaded. I ate, but I could not sleep; I had to vomit the whole night. Now, nobody else vomited. Twenty persons were with me; they all slept – they were tired, they had eaten good food. They slept well. I had to remain awake the whole night, vomiting. Unless I was completely clean of the food, I could not sleep. It was just in the morning near-about five that I went to sleep. That gave me the idea: perhaps eating in the night *is* dangerous. Just one time and the whole night became hell! And those who have been eating in the night for their whole lives... perhaps the idea that they go to hell is right. But the whole world is eating in the night. If it is true, then everybody will be going to hell. And these twenty friends are sleeping so beautifully – nobody has vomited so nothing was wrong with the food, and nothing is wrong with these people. Something is wrong in my conditioning; I have been brought up with a wrong idea.

But once you accept something, this creates a false conscience that goes on telling you, "Don't do this, do this." This is not consciousness. Consciousness simply *knows* what to do, what not to do. There is no question of choice. Consciousness is a choiceless state – you simply know what is right.

You are not born with conscience. It has been created by the religions, and they have exploited man through creating conscience. It is time that we should drop the word 'conscience' because it has become associated with a long past and has wrong connotations. You should use the word 'consciousness.' But consciousness is the fragrance of your becoming absolutely silent; it does not come with your birth. Yes, if you can attain consciousness, you will have a new birth; you will be reborn. That's what Jesus meant when he said to Nicodemus, "Unless you are born again, you will not understand me." He does not mean in your next life. He means that you will have to transform your being, rise in your consciousness: "Only then will you be able to understand me." If you have consciousness and silence and meditativeness, there is no need to say that the whole of humanity is one. It *is* – it is your experience. And it will not be only a brotherhood, it will be a brotherhood and a sisterhood! But it will be just a byproduct; there is no need to declare it as a fundamental right.

> ARTICLE TWO: EVERYONE IS ENTITLED TO ALL THE
> RIGHTS AND FREEDOMS SET FORTH IN THIS
> DECLARATION WITHOUT DISTINCTION OF ANY
> KIND, SUCH AS RACE, COLOR, SEX, LANGUAGE,
> RELIGION, POLITICAL OR OTHER OPINION, NATIONAL
> OR SOCIAL ORIGIN, PROPERTY, BIRTH OR OTHER
> STATUS.

All these are bullshit. The first question I was asked as I entered America was that I had to declare under oath that I am not an anarchist. If I am an anarchist, I cannot enter America. Anarchism is a political ideology. I cannot conceive that these people go on declaring these things. Who is going to ask them: "When are you going to practice them?" Everywhere there is discrimination – in different ways in different countries, but discrimination is there. Mankind needs a great uproar against these so-called humanitarians. They think they are doing a great service.

For example, in India, for the same amount of work the woman will be paid less. And in this declaration it is said that for the same amount of labor, the same rewards should be paid – whether it is man or woman, white or black does not matter. But it is not true.

In America, I was in six jails, and in all the jails there was not a single white man. In six federal jails – which were huge, six hundred people, seven hundred people in one jail... but all black people. And you say discrimination is not there. It seems strange – in a white country all the criminals are black. And that was not all. I inquired of a few black inmates – because they all loved me; they had been watching me on television every day for five years, and they had become involved in controversies themselves. They were reading my books, and they were happy that I had come at least for one day to their jail – they would remember this day for their whole lives. I asked them, "What is your crime?"

They said, "All these people you see have not committed any crime. They have been arrested the way you have been arrested – without any arrest warrant. And we have been told again and again: 'You will be taken to the court next week, tomorrow,' but that tomorrow never comes."

One man told me that he had been there for nine months without being taken to court. Now this declaration says nobody should be arrested without an arrest warrant, nobody should be kept in jail unless he is proved a criminal. Innocence needs no proof; you have to prove a person criminal, only then can you keep him in jail. Otherwise you cannot keep him in jail. But people have been there for nine months, eight months, six months in jail – and all young people.

So I started figuring out the reason: it is not that they have done anything wrong. The reason is that they are young and revolutionaries. They want rights for the blacks, equal rights for blacks. That is their crime. But they cannot be taken to court because the court will release them, so they go on keeping them in jail. But this is absolutely criminal on the part of the government of the US. I have seen only six jails and nearabout three or four thousand young black people. Perhaps thousands of people are in other jails.

They told me, "Because there is too much pressure from all over the world, that's why they are taking you to court. Otherwise, if the world had remained silent, if the news media had not spread all over the world that the whole government is doing everything criminal against an innocent person.... The pressure is too much and the eyes of the whole news media are focused on you. They are, under compulsion, reluctantly, taking you to court."

Still, they took twelve days. That too is against human rights. From the place where I was arrested, the court where I had to be present was only five hours' flight. My own jet was there. We offered them our jet; we said, "You can have your pilots; you can have your people, and you can take me to the court. What is the need to keep me here in your jail?"

They would only take me in their own airplane. The whole strategy was: "Today the airplane has not come... something is wrong with the airplane" – they had only one airplane, it seems. "The pilot is sick..." They took twelve days to make a five hours journey. But looking at other inmates I thought, "It is very quick, only twelve days...."

Every government goes on doing everything illegal and everything against human rights. And these people are the representatives of governments and without any shame they can make this declaration – perhaps without even feeling what they are doing. They are lying utterly – white lies!

ARTICLE THREE: EVERYONE HAS THE RIGHT TO LIFE, LIBERTY AND SECURITY OF PERSON.

But death is not included – and it is important. Because birth is not in your hands – you are born without your consent – now only death is there. And you have the choice: either to die without your consent or to die with a dignity of a human being, with your own consent – not to give death a chance, but to move, yourself, when you have lived. But they are worried about putting death into it because then all the religions and all the political parties will be creating havoc for them. Everything has to be consolatory: 'life' – but what kind of life?

Just in the last year, six months ago, in Europe the common market had accumulated mountains of butter and other foodstuffs. People were dying in Ethiopia – one thousand people per day – and they had a surplus but they would not give it to Ethiopia. That surplus had to be drowned in the ocean. Just in drowning it, two billion dollars were wasted – that was not the value of the food, it was just the labor of shifting and drowning it in the ocean. And they are doing it every six months, because every six months the surplus is there and you need more warehouses. And what will you do with it? – fresh crops are coming. But you will not give it to Ethiopia.

In India, fifty percent of the people are living below the medical standard of nourishment and twenty-five percent of the people are almost starving. Fifty percent of people in the villages are eating only one time a day – and when I say eating, don't think of the Taj

Mahal Hotel. It means just bread, salt, a little sauce from mangos or from other fruits – that's all. This is not food. Unless the world is one, we will not be able to give everybody enough nourishment.

And what does it mean to say that you have the right to life? Because people *are* there; and people are dying, people have died. America is doing the same, Stalin's Russia was doing the same. It is not something happening only in Europe. Every three months America drowns its surplus – and that is worth billions of dollars. In the days of Stalin, Russia was using wheat instead of coal in their railway trains because wheat is cheaper, it is surplus and coal is difficult and costly to obtain in Russia. People are dying – that is not important. People are starving – that is not important.

ARTICLE NINE: NO ONE SHALL BE SUBJECTED TO ARBITRARY ARREST, DETENTION OR EXILE.

I have been subjected, so I am a witness to it, that this declaration is not being used by any government – and particularly by America, which was the sponsor for this declaration. I have been in detention in England – not even for an *arbitrary* reason. I wanted just to stay for six hours at the airport in the first-class lounge because my pilots had flown their time and they wanted to rest. It is against their laws to fly more than twelve hours, so we had to stop.

My pilots said, "They may create trouble; they may say that the first-class lounge is for first-class passengers and you are not a passenger; you have your own plane. Now what class is it, how can they decide?"

So I said my people to purchase two tickets, two first-class tickets for the morning flight: "We will go with our plane, but purchase two tickets in case they bring up this point" – and they brought up that point. Then we brought up the tickets! The officer was shocked. He had not thought that we would have tickets too.

I said, "Now what do you think?"

He said, "I cannot do anything. I will have to ask the higher authorities." And who was the higher authority? It seems it was the prime minister herself. When the man was gone I looked into his file; he had left it on the table. The government had given him orders. I have never asked for any entry visa into England. They should not have bothered. But they decided in Parliament that I should not be allowed in the country – in case I should ask to enter.

When the man came back I told him, "I do not *want* to enter England, even if the whole of England wants me to enter England, I am the last person to do it. I have no business in England, I just want to sleep in the lounge. And from the lounge you cannot enter the country. It is closed; you will remain only at the airport. And the airport is international. It is not England."

But he said, "What can I do? The insistence is from the top: 'If he insists then put him in detention. That's the only way. He can remain in jail for six hours.'" I had to remain in jail for six hours – not even for an arbitrary reason. I had not committed any crime, I had the tickets, I had the plane, I just wanted to rest. But the politicians – because I have been exposing them continuously – now have become so frightened that even my sleeping six hours in the lounge at the airport is dangerous for the religion of England, its morality, its character. I can corrupt the youth just by staying in the lounge! These people are not lovers of human beings. Nor do they have any respect for human dignity.

> ARTICLE EIGHTEEN: EVERYONE HAS THE RIGHT TO
> FREEDOM OF THOUGHT, CONSCIENCE AND RELIGION;
> THIS RIGHT INCLUDES FREEDOM TO CHANGE HIS
> RELIGION OR BELIEF, AND FREEDOM, EITHER ALONE
> OR IN COMMUNITY WITH OTHERS AND IN PUBLIC
> OR PRIVATE, TO MANIFEST HIS RELIGION OR BELIEF
> IN TEACHING, PRACTICE, WORSHIP AND
> OBSERVANCE."

"Freedom of thought and expression" – I have never done anything except to express my thoughts. If that is a human right, then no government has anything against me. I am not active in any politics; I am not interested in any power. I am simply saying whatsoever I see more clearly than all these blind politicians.

What is the fear? Just now the pope has called a World Conference of Religions. All the chief priests and leaders of other religions have been called. My sannyasins from Italy have been writing to me: "We are insisting to the pope – and his secretary is very much interested in you and is willing to extend an invitation, but the pope is against it." In fact for eight months the Italian government has been thinking about whether to give me a three weeks' tourist visa or not. And the pope has been the cause of the whole delay. And these people go on saying, "We love freedom of thought, freedom of expression."

Nobody loves freedom of thought. It has to support *him*, then it is loved. "Freedom of expression...." The pope has put my books on the black list so that no Catholic should read them. They have a black list. In the Middle Ages, whenever a book appeared on the black list it was burned all over Europe. Now they cannot do that, but this much they can do: no Catholic should read it. And Catholics are not a small minority – seven hundred million people, a world in itself. Now, preventing them simply means you have accepted defeat; it simply means you don't have any answers to me. But then why all this nonsense about a declaration of human rights?

ARTICLE NINETEEN: EVERYONE HAS THE RIGHT TO
FREEDOM OF OPINION AND EXPRESSION; THIS RIGHT
INCLUDES FREEDOM TO HOLD OPINIONS WITHOUT
INTERFERENCE AND TO SEEK, RECEIVE AND IMPART
INFORMATION AND IDEAS THROUGH ANY MEDIA
AND REGARDLESS OF FRONTIERS.

This is not right. The Indian parliament has urged Indian journalists and news media people not to give any space to my ideas. The American government has been pressuring the Indian government so that no news media people from the West should be allowed to take my interview.

The American government has been doing two things: telling all the governments of Europe, and Australia, that I should not be allowed to reside in their countries, that I should be sent back from everywhere to India. So all the countries of Europe have passed resolutions in their parliaments that I cannot be allowed in their country even as a tourist for three weeks. The American idea is that I should not be allowed to enter any other country and nobody who wants to see me or meet me should be allowed to come to India. In this way they feel they can destroy the sannyas movement. This goes on in reality. And in words, beautiful and great slogans... but empty.

> ARTICLE TWENTY-TWO: EVERYONE HAS THE RIGHT
> TO THE FREE DEVELOPMENT OF HIS PERSONALITY."

I don't see that you are allowed to have freedom to develop your personality. In the first place, the people who wrote this don't know that personality is the false part of you, and it has not to be developed at all.

Your reality is your individuality, which has to be discovered. But they don't talk about individuality. They may not have ever thought of it. Because they are only personalities, they don't yet have their individuality awake, alert. Naturally, they are writing the word 'personality.' 'Personality' is an ugly word. It means a mask; the very root of the word is 'mask.' And we don't want people to have masks. People should be natural, spontaneous, themselves.

> ARTICLE TWENTY-FIVE: ALL CHILDREN, WHETHER
> BORN IN OR OUT OF WEDLOCK, SHALL ENJOY THE
> SAME SOCIAL PROTECTION.

Now, if this is true, it cancels marriage! If a child born from a marriage and a child born outside of marriage have the same rights, then marriage loses all meaning. What is the meaning of marriage? But they don't have the courage to say that. And this too is not true, because nowhere are children born outside marriage respected. They are condemned in every possible way.

I gave this much time to this rubbish because these are the people who are controlling the whole world, and these are the people whose heads should be hammered as much as possible.

They have kept humanity in slavery – this should not be allowed anymore. They don't have any right of declaration. *We* have the right to declare. We are the people.

As far as my people are concerned, we declare that we will live freedom, love, humanity. We will grow into our individuality and we will help anybody who is inviting and welcoming us. The only basic right is to become god. And unless you have found god within yourself, everything else is mundane. Finding godliness within you, everything else is found simultaneously.

27
Love is not something to get,
Love is something to give

BELOVED OSHO,

AS I AM AN ARTIST, I CAN EASILY PUT MY FEELINGS
OF LOVE AND BLISS INTO MAKING SCULPTURES. WHY
CAN'T I EXPRESS THE SAME FEELINGS TO HUMAN
BEINGS AND BE AS OPEN TO THEM AS I AM IN
MAKING SCULPTURES?

It is easy to be a sculptor because you are working with lifeless objects. You can create beautiful statues but those statues are dead. You cannot relate with them, you are alive. There is no dialogue possible between life and death. You can appreciate; you can enjoy – it is your creation. You can feel fulfilled – whatever you wanted, you succeeded in doing it. But remember one thing: on the other side, there is no one. You are alone.

Because of this situation, there are people who can love their dogs, who can love their gardens, who can love their cars, who can love anything in the world except man. Because man means you are not alone, the other is there. It is a dialogue. With a statue, it is a monologue. The statue is not going to say anything, is not going to criticize you, is not going to possess you. You possess the statue; you can sell it in the market. But that you cannot do with a human being. That is the problem.

When you start relating with human beings, you have to take into consideration that they are not things, they are consciousnesses. You cannot dominate them – although almost everybody is trying to do that, and spoiling their whole life. The moment you try to dominate a human being, you are creating an enemy, because that human being also wants to dominate. You may call it love, you may call it friendship, but behind the curtain of friendship and love and brotherhood there is a deep will to power. You want to dominate; you don't want to be dominated.

With human beings, you will be in constant conflict. The closer you are, the more the conflict will hurt you. There are thousands of people who have been so wounded by human relationship that they have dropped out of all human love, friendship. They have turned towards things. It is easier – the other party is always willing, whatsoever you want to do.

You are an artist, you sculpt. But have you ever thought about what you are doing? You are cutting chunks of the marble – that you cannot do to a human being, but people *are* doing that to human beings too. Parents are cutting their children's wings, their freedom, their individuality. Lovers are cutting each other continuously.

To be in love with a human being is not an easy affair. The love affair is the most difficult affair in the world for the simple reason that two consciousnesses, two alive beings, cannot tolerate any kind of slavery. When the parents say to their children "Don't do this!" even the small child feels hurt, humiliated, insulted. And he's going to *do* it if he has any guts.

Near the village where I was born, just ten miles away, every year there used to be a very big religious fair, by the side of the river Narmada. That is one of the sacred religious rivers in India. Perhaps it is the *most* sacred, for a mythological reason, because all other rivers are married – only Narmada is still virgin....

There is a beautiful place where Narmada comes out of the mountains and falls in a beautiful waterfall to reach the ground. I have seen many waterfalls but that waterfall has some uniqueness of its own. It is a very black stone, extraordinarily black, ugly ... and the Narmada falls in one thousand currents. It is not one fall, it is one thousand falls; it is the whole mountain.

Because of those one thousand rocks that the Narmada has cut, there is a mythology thousands of years old. There was a very monstrous king. He wanted to marry Narmada because, he said, "All rivers are already married. In my kingdom, I cannot allow Narmada to remain unmarried."

So he went to marry Narmada. But because of the purity of virginity ... a curse from Narmada turned him into stone. Those one thousand rocks are nothing but one thousand hands of that monster. He wanted to grab Narmada from everywhere; she's still falling out of those stone hands.

So a very beautiful fair happens every year. I wanted to see those one thousand hands, and how Narmada managed to remain virgin for millions of years. You will be surprised that the land where Narmada flows is the ancientmost land in the world. It came first out of the ocean – because in the mountainous regions from where Narmada comes, you can still find, very easily, dead sea animals. And from Narmada, the sea is thousands of miles away. Certainly one day the mountain was under the ocean, and then the ocean receded and the first piece of earth came out of ocean. It is the most ancient part of the earth.

I wanted to see the most ancient mountain ... but I knew that if I asked my parents, they would say no. The place is dangerous because of all those rocks; many people have died. The whole river is full of rocks and to swim in it is dangerous, and they had said to me, "You will not be able to resist the temptation of swimming there."

So I did not ask them, I simply went. They were very much concerned ... reported to the police, sent a few people to look around, inquired at the railway station, the bus station where I had been seen last. But they could not find me. After three days, I came back. They were *really* angry.

They said, "Where have you been?"

I said, "Where? I have been to the fair."

They said, "You should have at least asked us."

I said, "No, because I wanted to go. If I did not want to go, I would have asked. So remember, whenever I don't want to do something, I will ask you because I know the answer is no. And whenever I want to do something, I will simply do it. Now you can do whatsoever you want. If you want to beat me, you can beat me. If you want to punish me in some other way, you can do that. But this is going to be my whole lifestyle. I will never ask for a thing that I am going to do. I don't want anybody else's advice about it."

My parents said, "Are you crazy or what? You will ask us only about things that you don't want to do?"

I said, "It is very simple. It is so simple that even God missed it. It is so obvious that even God forgot about it. He said to Adam and Eve, 'Don't eat the fruits of wisdom and eternal life.' Every father has been doing that since then, and every Adam and every Eve has to rebel."

If you are interested in doing something, you can do it without any problem if there is no other consciousness. You are working on objects, on things. They cannot say yes, they cannot say no. Whatever you want to do with them, you can do, but not with man.

It is your fault that you have not yet become mature enough to understand that with human beings, if you want a loving relationship then you should forget all power politics. You can be just a friend, neither trying to dominate the other nor being dominated by the other. It is possible only if you have a certain meditativeness in your life. Otherwise, it is not possible.

To love a human being is one of the most difficult things in the world because the moment you start showing your love, the other starts going on a power trip. He knows you are dependent on him or on her. You can be enslaved – psychologically, spiritually – and nobody wants to be a slave. But all your human relationships turn into slavery.

No statue will make you a slave. On the contrary, the statue makes you a master craftsman, it makes you a creator, an artist. There is no conflict. The real test for love is with human beings. And a man is really intelligent if he can make a human relationship work smoothly. It needs great insight. Creating a statue or making a beautiful painting is one thing – those paints won't say, "I don't want to be put on this corner of the canvas, I simply refuse!" Wherever you want it, the paint is available. But it is not so easy with human beings.

Every human being has a birthright not to be dominated by anyone – but also a birth duty not to try to dominate anyone. And only then, friendship can flower. Love needs a clarity of vision. Love needs a cleaning of all kinds of ugly things which are in your mind – jealousy, anger, the desire to dominate.

I have heard ... in a marriage registrar's office, a couple came to get married. They filled out the forms. The woman looked at the man – they were lovers, and they had come to the registry office against their family, because in India, marriage is not done in the registrar's office. It is available. Legally you can do it but that happens only when you are doing something against the family, against the society.

Those two people must have been in deep love. They had revolted against the society, against the religion, against their parents, against the family. They had risked everything and they were going to be married. And the woman looked at the man who was filling out the form – because she had filled out hers – and then she suddenly said to the registrar, "I want an *immediate* divorce."

He said, "What happened? You are filling out forms for marriage. Even the honeymoon has not happened. In fact, even *marriage* has not happened because I have not sealed it. Why do you want a divorce so suddenly?" She said, "I hate this man!"

The registrar said, "This is strange – you brought him here?"

She said, "Yes, I brought him here. I *used* to love him, but when I saw his form ... he has signed in such *big letters*! He was watching when I was signing. I signed just the way I always sign, and he has signed in letters three times bigger – almost half of the form is his signature. I don't want to live with this man, he has shown his domination, his power."

The registrar said, "Then there is no need of any divorce. Just throw away your forms in the wastepaper basket, because I have not sealed them, and get lost."

Such a small thing, that the man was signing in big letters but it is indicative. It shows that he's a male chauvinist.

What about your whole life? Everything is a problem, everything is a conflict. And the reason is that we have accepted a false idea that we know how to love. We don't know. We are coming from animals. Animals don't love. Love is a very new thing in human life. Animals reproduce but they don't love. You will not find in buffaloes, Romeo and Juliet, Laila and Majnu, Shiri and Farhad, Soni and Mahival. No buffaloes are interested in such romantic things – they are very earthbound, they reproduce – and nature is perfectly satisfied with buffaloes, remember. Nature may be trying to destroy humanity but nature is not trying to destroy buffaloes and donkeys and monkeys, no. They are not problems at all. Love is a new phenomenon that has arisen with human consciousness. You will have to learn it.

Creating beautiful paintings, poetries, sculpture, music, dances – that is all in your hands. But when you come into contact with a human being, you have to understand that on the other side is the same kind of consciousness. You have to give respect and dignity to the person you love. This is the reason why you cannot relate with human beings.

Forget about human beings and love – you simply meditate. That will release in you the insight, the vision, the clarity, and the energy to share. Love is another name of sharing your abundant energy. You have too much, you are burdened with it. You would like to share it with people you like. Your love – what you call love – is not a sharing, it is a snatching. Everybody's trying to snatch more love. The wife goes on saying, "You don't love me enough!" The husband goes on saying, "It seems you don't love me!"

Mulla Nasruddin had gone with his wife to see a movie. In the movie, the hero kisses the heroine very tenderly, and the wife nudges Mulla Nasruddin ... "You never do that."

Mulla Nasruddin said, "Don't disturb me. That woman is not his wife."

But Nasruddin's wife said, "You are wrong! I know the couple; the woman is the wife of the hero."

Mulla Nasruddin said, "My God, then he's really an actor! Only an actor can do that. I am not an actor, you just forgive me. If it is his wife ... I was thinking it must be somebody else. I can also kiss somebody else's wife, but kissing one's own wife? This must be the greatest actor we have in our country."

You will have to change the meaning of love. It is not something that you are trying to get from the other. And this has been the whole history of love – everybody is trying to get it from the other, as much as possible. Both are trying to get, and naturally, nobody is getting anything. Love is not something to get. Love is something to give. But you can give only when you have it. Do you have love in you? Have you ever asked this question? Sitting silently, have you ever observed? Do you have any love energy to give?

You don't have; neither has anybody else. Then you get caught in a love relationship. Both are pretenders, pretending that they are going to give you the very paradise. Both are trying to convince each other that "Once you get married to me, a thousand Arabian nights will be forgotten – our nights, our days will all be golden."

But you don't know that you don't have anything to give. All these things you are saying just to *get*. And the other is doing the same. Once you are married, then there is going to be trouble because both will be waiting for a thousand Arabian nights and not even an Indian night is happening! Then there is an anger, a rage which slowly, slowly becomes poisonous.

Love turning into hate is a very simple phenomenon, because everyone feels betrayed. You show one face at the beach, in the movie hall, on the dance floor. It is perfectly okay for half an hour or one hour – sitting on the beach, holding each other's hands, dreaming about the beautiful life that is ahead of you. But once you are married, all that you have been expecting, dreaming, will start evaporating.

I have heard of one couple. They were entering a hotel with their suitcases, with the labels saying "Just Married." They were on their honeymoon. The man immediately went to the bed and covered himself with the blanket. The wife went into the bathroom to prepare for sleep.

The man said, "Please, put the lights off. I cannot sleep with lights on."

She said, "It is only a question of five minutes. I am coming, and then I will put them off."

He said, "First you have to put them off!"

And the quarrel started. The woman said, "Why, in the ... why can't you wait for five minutes? And you have been waiting for me for five years!"

The man said, "Forget about all that. You first put the lights off!"

The woman said, "I cannot do that. I will put them off when I come under the blanket." The man said, "Strange ... what is the reason?"

The woman said, "If you are so rational, first tell me your reason – what are you going to lose in five minutes?"

He said, "It is better to tell you the truth ... because now it is going to be twenty-four hours together. How long will I be under the blanket?" The woman said, "What do you mean?"

The man said, "The reality is, one of my legs is false, so I want darkness to remove it so you don't see it."

The woman said, "That relaxes me because my hair is false, my teeth are false, my breasts are false ... now there is no problem, light or no light."

Listening to this – that the hair is false, the teeth are false, the breasts are false, the man jumped out of the bed and escaped, and he has not been found since. And he was dying to marry this woman! Human relationship needs understanding.

My suggestion to you is: meditate. Become more and more silent, quiet, calm. Let a serenity arise in you. That will help you in a thousand and one ways – not only in love, it will also help you to create better sculpture. Because a man who cannot love human beings ... how can he create? What can he create? A loveless heart cannot be authentically creative. He can imitate, but he cannot create. All creation is out of love, understanding, silence.

BELOVED OSHO,
ALTHOUGH NOTHING IS REALLY CLEAR TO ME, HOW
CAN IT BE SO CLEAR TO ME THAT THE TRUTH IS IN
YOU? I DON'T KNOW IT, BUT I SEE IT IN YOUR EYES. I
FEEL IT IN YOUR BEING.

It is one of the most fundamental questions. One does not know what truth is. But when one comes across it, a few things become clear: that whatever he has believed up to now was not truth, because it has not given him this depth in the eyes, this silence in his presence, this authority in his words, this poetry to his life. The false is barren.

So although you do not know what is true, when you come across truth, you immediately know what is false. And if you understand what is false, a vague insight into truth starts arising in you. Because the truth that you see in *my* eyes is also in *your* eyes, just asleep. You have never awakened it. Let the false go, and your eyes will have the *same* truth. Your words will have the *same* music, your presence will have the *same* charisma.

Nobody comes to know truth first. Everybody comes to know first the false, and as the false is dropped ... because in the very understanding that it is false, it slips out of your hands. And when the false is not there, what remains is the truth.

You may not have seen beauty. But looking at a sunset with all the colors on the horizon ... you may not be able to say that this is beauty, but you feel an awe. You know *something* is there that touches your heart, and perhaps even reaches to your very being. Seeing this, you will start thinking – if this is so impressive, so deep-reaching in you, so touching that you want to dance and sing, then what was your whole life? Because before this, you have been dancing too, but it was only a sociality. The dance was not coming from you, it was only a social custom.

People were asking you to sing ... and you know the technical side of singing or playing music, but the technical side is not the real thing. You may sing, but your heart is not singing. You are simply being polite to the friends who are insisting that you sing. But when you see a sunset and you start singing ... nobody has asked. The sun has not asked, there is nobody around. Even *you* are surprised: from where is this song coming? Why are you feeling a tremendous urge to dance? Knowing this dance and this song, all your dances and songs will become false, and you will know for the first time something of the truth.

In the East, it has been the oldest tradition: people used to go walking thousands of miles just to look into the eyes of Gautam Buddha, or Mahavira. Just to sit for two minutes close to Gautam Buddha, holding his feet in their hands ... and people have traveled thousands of miles. All those people were not fools – just these two minutes transformed their life. Now they know what a true man, what an authentic man means. They have touched his feet, they have felt his vibe, they have been showered by his love and compassion. They have looked into his eyes and seen the whole universe opening up. Those one thousand miles, walking for months, were worth it.

The day Gautam Buddha died, ten thousand sannyasins had gathered from all over the country, because this was the last time they would be able to see this man. Once he is gone, people will not even believe that such a man ever existed. They will not accept that Gautam Buddha is a historical person.

Ananda was Gautam Buddha's constant companion for forty years, but he had not become enlightened yet. Many who came later on became enlightened, but Ananda was stuck somewhere. He asked about it many times.

Gautam Buddha said, "I know where you are stuck. I knew it the very first day you came to me."

Ananda was Gautam Buddha's cousin-brother and elder. When he came for initiation, he asked Gautam Buddha: "After initiation, I will be a disciple. Whatever you say, I will do it, there is no question of any doubt. So before I get initiated, I want you to promise me three things. As your elder brother, I demand it – right now, I am not your disciple."

Gautam Buddha laughed. He said, "Okay, what are your conditions?"

He said, "Not very great conditions, very small. One is that I will always be with you. You can not send me to spread the word, to faraway parts of the country, no. Twenty-four hours ... even in the night, I will sleep in your room. Granted?"

Buddha said, "Okay."

"And my second condition is that howsoever stupid a question may be, if I ask it, you will have to answer it. You cannot say, 'This is stupid, meaningless.' You cannot avoid it, you cannot change the subject. You have to answer it. And third, if I bring someone to meet you, even in the middle of the night when you are asleep, I am entitled to wake you up because I have brought a friend to see you and meet you."

Buddha said, "Perfectly okay."

Ananda was initiated. After forty years, on the last day, when he was dying, Buddha said, "Because you made conditions on your master – just because of an ordinary relationship of being a cousin-brother – that's where you are stuck. You cannot forget that you are the elder brother of Gautam Buddha. Although you are a disciple, deep down you are still older than me. And in India, old age is very much respected. But don't be worried. The moment I die, within twenty-four hours you will become enlightened. Only my death can help. For forty years, you have been trying – nothing has happened. But even if it were just for you that I had to die, I would have died." Ananda was crying.

Buddha said, "Don't waste time, don't waste your tears. Because of your egoistic idea of being an elder brother, you have not even seen into my eyes. Although you are holding my feet in your hands, I don't see that there is any communication."

Buddha died, and within exactly twenty-four hours, Ananda became enlightened. And for forty years, he had been sitting by the side of the river, thirsty.

If you can see me, not as a body ... if you can see into my eyes, if you can feel my presence, if something stirs in your heart, then certainly you will know that the life you have lived up to now is a life of falsity. But once you have known even a little bit of the truth, you cannot go back. Then, there is only one way and that is to go ahead. What you have seen in my eyes, others will see in your eyes soon. What you have felt in my presence, others will start feeling in your presence. Because whatsoever I have got, you have got. It is just that, you have not unpacked; your suitcases are locked.

BELOVED OSHO,

I HAVE BEEN EXPERIENCING SUCH AN ABUNDANCE OF YOUR BEAUTIFUL LOVE AND ENERGY THESE PAST TWO MONTHS. IT IS SO PRECIOUS TO EXPERIENCE YOU. DURING MEDITATIONS, ESPECIALLY DYNAMIC, IT HAS FLOODED ME WITH INTENSE FEELINGS OF ALL SORTS, BEYOND ANYTHING I'VE KNOWN. THE PURE ENERGY THAT TREMBLES THROUGH MY BODY LEAVES ME SINGING, DANCING, LAUGHING, CRYING, AND I FEEL SO SPACIOUS WITHIN. WHEN I EXPERIENCE MALE ENERGY, I FEEL VERY PLAYFUL BUT NOT SEXUALLY ATTRACTED. IS THERE SOMETHING WRONG WITH ME? COULD YOU PLEASE SAY SOMETHING ABOUT SEXUAL ATTRACTION AND THE MIND?

Something is right in you for the first time in your life. Energy is a playful phenomenon. If you are feeling joyous and happy with your own feminine energy – and you feel good, harmonious with the male energy; you love to play with the male energy and it does not turn into sexuality, it is a spiritual growth.

If men and women who are in deep love can be playful with each other's energies, there is no need of indulging in sex, because sex cannot give you anything – it simply takes something away from you. It brings your death closer. It is your life force. But if the woman and the man can just be playful, then they are enriching each other. Then the dialectics of life works, and they both are more than they were before. Both have gained; nobody has lost anything.

What is happening to you should happen, *has* to happen to every sannyasin. You just have to be aware of one thing: people are very much in a hurry, and they want to finish a job as quickly as possible – but it is not a job. In fact, people have completely forgotten the foreplay before making love, and they have absolutely no idea of afterplay when you have made love.

But one of the most insightful men into sexual energy is Vatsyayana, in his *Kamasutras*. He wrote them sometime three thousand years ago, and those people among whom Vatsyayana must have lived were really innocent, but intelligent – not knowledgeable, but wise. If I talk about sexual energy then the whole world condemns me – and Vatsyayana was the first person in the whole history of man to write a treatise on sex energy, *Kamasutras* – aphorisms about sex. But three thousand years ago, people called him a seer, a man who has realized himself. Because unless that realization had happened, he could not say what he was saying. His treatise, *Kamasutras* is exhaustive; he has said *everything* that is significant to be said about sex. And one of the things, in reference to your question, is that if a couple is in love and just goes on playing and is not in a hurry to finish, it then you will be surprised: The energy starts from a certain level where you are, moves upwards, and reaches to a peak without any sex. And it is so peaceful, so blissful, so silent, that you disappear into each other, that you become one energy. And then slowly, it becomes more and more absorbed, but no sex is involved. If it is happening, it is something to be greeted, welcomed.

I have heard.... A man went to a doctor, his friend, and asked him: "It is too much! I want to kill my wife in such a way that I am not caught; you have to advise me."

The doctor thought for a moment and then he said, "The easiest way is to make love to her so much that within six weeks she will be dead."

But the man said, "Six weeks and too much love? I will be dead before that! So you will have to give me some medicinal help."

He said, "Yes, I'm going to give you these tablets. Take six tablets, two at a time every day, and you can make love six times every day."

The man said, "My God! You had these tablets and you never told me? And you pretend to be my friend!"

He rushed home with the bottle. Just on the way, he swallowed two tablets. A month passed ... there was a fundraising campaign in the church one Sunday, and the doctor saw the man – he was in a wheelchair! Somehow, with difficulty, he was trying to reach the doctor. The doctor said, "What happened?"

He said, "Don't be worried, doctor. Only two weeks more and she will be finished!"

Sex is your energy, it is your life. If you can absorb it back into your system, you will have a new feeling of well-being. But if it is released, leaks out – that's what you call making love; energy leaking out – a plumber is needed. If you can – and a meditative person can – absorb the energy back, it rises to a peak and then subsides and goes to your blood, to your bones, to your marrow. It is a tremendous nourishment.

So don't say that something wrong is happening to you – people must be telling you that something wrong is happening to you. Something *right* is happening to you. Remember it and tell those people, "I am feeling so joyous and so full of love, how wrong can happen to me? You are looking so miserable, so British, hangdog British – something must be wrong with you!"

You enjoy your play. And once you have learned – with your

friend, with your lover – it is not a very big step. One day you may be able to play with your sexual energy alone – dancing, singing. There is no need of the other; you will absorb the energy yourself. Only in the beginning, the other is needed. That does not mean that you have to drop the other. He has been a great help, and there is no harm in being playful with anybody you feel loving towards. Sex has to disappear.

The moment sex disappears, the same energy starts rising in you, transforming you into a new man: the man who knows no death, the man who knows every mystery of life, the man who has come home.

BELOVED OSHO,
I HAVE HOPED TO BECOME MORE SURE OF MYSELF,
STRONGER AND MORE RELAXED THROUGH
MEDITATION. ON THE CONTRARY, ALTHOUGH I AM
LESS ANXIOUS, I FEEL MORE AND MORE EMPTY,
UNCERTAIN AND VULNERABLE. WHY DOES THIS
HAPPEN?

Every desire leads not to the goal it has promised you; it leads to just the opposite of it. You want to be special? you have already accepted your ordinariness. One who is special does not want to be special; he's not even aware that he is special. Whatever you want, one thing is certain: you are not that. And from where are these desires and wants coming? – imitation. All around, you see people: somebody is so rich, somebody is so intellectual, some-body is a wrestler, somebody is a boxer. And you are nothing – it hurts. It hurts because of your wrong conceptions about life.

So you have to note down a few things in your being: one, you cannot be anybody other than who you are. If you try to be somebody other than who you are, you will never be somebody else, but you will miss being that which you were destined to become. It is almost as if a roseflower wants to become a lotus. His whole energy will be in how to become a lotus; he will forget all about the roses. All his energy will become misdirected. He will never become a lotus because he has no seeds, no potentiality to be a lotus. Only one thing is certain: now he will not become even a flowering bush of roses.

And who said that a lotus is better than a rose? They are both beautiful and they are both needed. Even the smallest blade of grass is as much needed as the biggest star in the sky. This whole universe is one organic unity. Here, nothing exists that is not needed, and the most-needed persons are those who simply accept themselves as they are and enjoy themselves as they are – nobodies. But to be a nobody is the highest point of bliss in existence. Don't try to be special. Just allow nature, wherever it leads you. Don't go upstream; otherwise, your failure is certain. Go with the stream, let go. Don't even swim! And the stream will take you joyously, dancingly, to the ocean.

As far as I am concerned, from my very childhood I have been told ... how many times it is difficult to enumerate, because everybody was telling me: "The way you are behaving, the way you are living, the way you are doing things, you will turn into a nobody." And they were all right! I *have* turned into a nobody, but I don't want to be anything else. I never wanted that, because by being nobody, I don't have any worry, I don't have any tensions. I don't even have dreams, because nothing is repressed. I am living moment-to-moment, and life is such an ecstasy. And because I am nobody, I can contain the whole universe within me. Nobody, *nobodiness*, has no boundaries.

The more special you become, the more you shrink. The more special you become, the more hard you become. The more special you become, the more you are *against* existence – and nobody can win against existence.

There is only one victory, and that is just to be nobody, and the whole universe is within you. You are victorious. You will not know it, but birds will talk about it. Flowers will say, "Yes, it has happened." The whole universe will know it except you.

So it is good that you have failed in becoming special – you are blessed. Now try my way. And it is a shortcut – you have not to go anywhere, you can be nobody just sitting here right now. I don't promise you anything for tomorrow. I promise you only *this* moment. Just be silent, and nobody, and see the beauty of it, the truth of it, the glory of it.

BELOVED OSHO,
SHUNYO IS SEEING GHOSTS AGAIN.
ANY SUGGESTIONS?

Milarepa, she must have seen you! A few other people have also reported that a ghost has been seen around who looks like Milarepa.

28

The full stop never comes

BELOVED OSHO, WHENEVER I READ FRIEDRICH
NIETZSCHE, AND FEEL QUITE RELAXED, IT APPEARS AS
IF I HAVE A CONNECTION WITH A SPIRIT WHICH IS
ALIVE AND I TALK TO HIM. HE IS NOT DEAD BUT A
LIVING FRIEND AND IT DOESN'T SOUND ABSURD AT
ALL THAT ALL THE GREAT SPIRITS ARE IN DEEP
COMMUNICATION WITH ONE ANOTHER WHETHER
THEY ARE DEAD OR ALIVE. BUT WITH YOU, ALL
NAMES AND WORDS DISAPPEAR AND I FEEL BRIGHT
AND ENLIGHTENED. I LOVE THIS STATE OF BEING
WITH YOU LIKE THIS. WHAT IS YOUR SECRET?

My secret is simple: I don't have a name, I don't have a form, I
don't have any kind of identity. I am one with the whole. So the
moment you remember me, you will not find somebody appearing on the screen of your consciousness, but only an empty sky.

Friedrich Nietzsche or others are tremendously important, but
they are not one with the whole. On the contrary, they are super-
egoists – particularly Nietzsche. I love him, too. He has a tremendous insight into things; great revelations have come through his
mind. And he's the one most neglected all over the world – perhaps out of fear, because once you are deep into Nietzsche, you
cannot be the same person you have been before. Nietzsche is
going to change you. His thoughts are rational; his insights have
no parallel in the whole history of philosophy but still, he is not a
meditator. It is all mind.

And this is the distinction I would like you to remember: There
have been two types of influences in the world, people who have
changed millions of lives. One belongs to the mind – all the
philosophers, all the thinkers; they have great genius as far as mind
is concerned. They have impressed millions of people for thousands of years and they are still fresh. But there is an different line
of people like Gautam Buddha, Bodhidharma, Jesus Christ, Lao
Tzu – these are not philosophers. What they are saying is not
coming from the mind. It is coming from beyond the mind. They
have put the mind aside. To understand them, just intellect is not
enough. To understand them, you will have to go on the same

path as they traveled. Mind goes nowhere.

All philosophers are playing with words. Sometimes there is immense beauty even in words, great poetry, logic, that you cannot deny. Nietzsche, Hegel, Kant, Bertrand Russell, Jean Paul Sartre, Jaspers or Martin Heidegger are pinnacles of intellectuality. You are bound to be impressed – but you are not going to be transformed. And to be impressed is to be enslaved. Unless a transformation happens, your slavery goes on deeper and deeper.

You say that Friedrich Nietzsche, although dead, is still alive in spirit. Not only that, you talk with him. You have not said anything in your question but I assume that he must be answering too.

Both the things have to be done by you – the asking and the answering. But look at the *life* of Friedrich Nietzsche, not just his philosophical approaches towards reality. His life is one of utter misery. You would not like to be Friedrich Nietzsche if you knew his life. He lived absolutely alone, without friends, because he was such an egoist that to make friends with him was impossible. He was high above; you are just creeping on the ground. What friendship? – he does not consider you to be even a human being. He considers you as a subhuman species. And his whole philosophy is how to create the real human being which he used to call the 'superman.' But he himself was not even an ordinary man, what to say about a superman? – physically ugly... but that can be pardoned; he could not manage in his whole life to love a woman, because love to him was domination and nothing else. He wanted a servant, not a beloved – a slave to dance according to his tune.

Looking at his life, one feels deep compassion. He lived his whole life alone with his sister. The sister sacrificed her own life because somebody was needed to take care of Nietzsche. And finally, he went mad.

And remember, nobody goes mad suddenly. Madness is something that grows slowly until it is too much and everybody else becomes aware of it. He was mad from the very beginning, but it was not known; it was within the normal insanity of humanity. But soon, he crossed the line. In the end, even though he was declared mad, he had forgotten all his philosophy, he had not forgotten one thing – even in his madness. And you will be surprised: what is that one thing? That one thing was that he would always sign his signature as "Anti-Christ, Friedrich Nietzsche." That "Anti-Christ" was the only thing that remained even in his madness. Not a single letter has he signed without writing "Anti-Christ" before his name. If he had been born in India, he would have been anti-Gautam Buddha; if he had been born in China, he would have been anti-Chuang Tzu.

It doesn't matter, these names are not the point. Why was he anti-Christ? – because Christ is not a philosopher. Christ does not give any reasons for his assertions, he speaks on his own authority. He gives no arguments, there is no need. Because he feels the truth, he expresses it. He does not argue. In fact, only lies need arguments. You can see in any court, so many arguments....

Truth is naked. Its very presence is enough to convince you. And if truth can not have self-validity and depends on arguments, it is not truth. Arguments may change. Somebody may be more logical than you are....

I am reminded of one great logician, Keshav Chandra. Perhaps in this past century in India there has been nobody else with such a sharp mind and with such perfect arguments. He lived in Calcutta, at the time when Ramakrishna was also living outside Calcutta.

Keshav Chandra had a small following of intellectuals, but they were all puzzled: "Thousands of people go to Ramakrishna... that idiot! He's uneducated, he cannot even make his signature. Why are these people going to this madman?" Finally, Keshav Chandra could not resist the temptation to go and see with his own eyes – and he knew that a few arguments would finish this man forever.

He sent a challenge saying, "I want to argue with you. When can I come?"

Ramakrishna said, "Keshav is coming? There is no need to postpone; today is as good as any day. Go back and tell him: Come, and argue as much as you can!"

Keshav Chandra had forgotten. In giving the challenge, he had said, "I want to argue with you," but if the other person simply listens and tells you – "argue!".... You cannot force somebody to argue. But Keshav Chandra had no idea, because he had never come across such a man.

He went to Dakshineshwar where Ramakrishna used to live in a temple. His disciples were very much afraid. They knew – Keshav Chandra's arguments are like spears, they go directly to the heart. They can kill a man. And Ramakrishna is so simple... perhaps he does not understand the meaning of argument. Perhaps he does not understand the meaning of the challenge. But from the side of Ramakrishna – he was coming out of the temple again and again and asking, "Keshav has not come?"

Finally, Keshav Chandra came with a group of his intimate followers. Ramakrishna hugged him, although he could not respond to Ramakrishna's hug; he was withdrawing backwards. Ramakrishna said, "Keshava, you don't know how to hug people? You know only how to argue? You are missing much that is valuable – human warmth, human love – but it is good that you have come. I am so happy, I have always wanted to listen to your arguments."

Keshav Chandra could not make any sense of it. He started: "There is no God."

Ramakrishna said, "What a beautiful statement! Can I hug you again?" And he hugged him again.

Keshav was feeling very embarrassed. His following was feeling very embarrassed – what is happening? And Ramakrishna said, "Did you receive my answer or not?"

Keshav said, "You have not said anything. You have simply hugged me."

Ramakrishna said, "That is a way of saying things which cannot be said. You said, 'God does not exist.' And I say *you* are the proof that God exists; otherwise, from where such beautiful intelligence?" Now, how to argue with such a man?

After ten minutes, Keshav Chandra was at the feet of Ramakrishna – "Just forgive me, I had no idea of a man who is not in the mind but in the being. You have made it clear to me. You are not a man of logic, you are a man of love – but love is far higher, logic is mundane. Please accept me as one of your disciples."

Nietzsche is a great logician, a great philosopher, but he knows nothing of reality. All that he says is mind – guesses, inferences.

Assumptions supported by argument may befool people but they cannot befool a man who knows. Nietzsche does not know. But he writes beautifully. He writes very consistently, he reaches to the very heights of argumentation. But these are not things of real, authentic value.

The only thing valuable is *experience*, not argument. And Nietzsche is absolutely without any experience. He has never meditated, he has never been in his own being. He has never contacted the vast, beautiful universe that surrounds us. It is our womb. We are in it, continuously being nourished.

The West is rich as far as useless things are concerned and poor as far real values are concerned. Nietzsche was "Anti-Christ" for the simple reason that millions of people follow Jesus, and Jesus has not given a single argument to prove his philosophy. And to disprove his philosophy, Nietzsche goes on giving, one after another, hundreds of arguments – beautiful arguments, very refined arguments, but arguments are just arguments. You can go on arguing about love your whole life, but that will not give you the experience of love.

The West has produced only philosophers. The East knows nothing of philosophy, it knows only mysticism. And mysticism is based on the simple phenomenon that experience needs no argument. Experience is its own validity. Go inwards. Find your inner space, and suddenly, you will find an explosion of light, of beauty, of ecstasy – as if suddenly thousands of roses have blossomed within you and you are full of their fragrance.

You say that when you think about thinkers, philosophers like Nietzsche, you are almost in communication, as if they are not dead – but with me you feel a difference. Whenever you remember me you feel silence, you feel joy. You may burst into a song, you may start dancing or playing on a flute. But you will not find me there. You will find there the whole existence showering all its ecstasies on you.

This is the difference between the mystics and the philosophers: Philosophers live in words; mystics live in authentic experience. Philosophy has been a curse to the West. All the geniuses turn towards philosophy because the whole tradition is of philosophers

– from the ancient Greeks up to now. The philosopher seems to be the highest peak of human evolution. It is absolutely absurd! The philosopher is just playing a mind game. He's as poor in consciousness as you are.

The East never got into that trap. The East is poor as far as material things are concerned, but the East has touched the highest peaks of luxury as far as spiritual experiences are concerned. And that is the only thing that counts in the ultimate reckoning. You will not be asked how many houses you had, you will not be asked about your arguments. You will be asked, "Has your heart opened up and become a lotus? Have you blossomed? Has your spring come, or not?"

The East has seen the spring, people flowering. It is perfectly good to read Nietszche, Hegel, Kant, Feuerbach, Karl Marx... or you can go to older philosophers – Aristotle, Plato – but you will not get anything except empty words. And words mean whatever you want them to mean. They don't have any content of their own.

I have heard.... One masochist – a masochist is a person who enjoys being tortured and a sadist is a person who enjoys torturing. And there are a few very complicated people who are sado-masochists; they enjoy both. One masochist is sitting by the side of a beautiful lake. A sadist, his friend, is also sitting there but he has not said a single word. Somebody passes and asks the sadist: "You are friends, but you are sitting like enemies, back to back. And you have not spoken a single word."

He said, "That's what he enjoys – torture."

This is a subtle torture, that somebody is sitting with you and will not say a single word.

I have also heard that one optimist, who sees in everything, something beautiful – silver lines in the black clouds. And these are not just fictions. He was standing in a park with one of his friends who was a pessimist – a pessimist sees in the smallest silver line, a big, black cloud. They were friends.

The optimist said, "Our world is the best world out of all possible worlds."

The pessimist said, "You are right!" It is a little delicate... you will have to think over it in the middle of the night.

Just the same word, the same statement, in a different context, on different lips, takes a different color, a different meaning. Many philosophers have written beautiful sentences, but they are dead. When a man like Jesus or Buddha or Bodhidharma or Kabir speaks – ordinary words, but they are so full of juice. They are so full of truth that it is overflowing.

Read the philosophers – it is good exercise for sharpening your intelligence. But don't get too much involved with them. They are drowning, or they have drowned. In their own words, they have lost their light. Go deeper into mystics, because they are the people who have reached the sunlit peaks of consciousness. They are the people the world needs. I want my sannyasins to become a Noah's Ark. When the world is drowning, a Noah's Ark is needed.

You meditate. You experience your own life's sources, and only when you have experienced your own life's sources and juices, will you be able to see them all around. This universe is such a mystery, is such a miracle – if you can contact the miracle, you will also become part of it. Your life will become a dance, your every breath will become a joy.

I am not against the philosophers. I am simply making it clear that they should be kept in their place. Mystics have been forgotten, for the simple reason that they are not argumentative. They don't say much. They have nothing to say. They have something to *show* and those who are courageous enough to put their hands in their hands... they will take them to the place from where you can see the unbelievable.

After that, there is not going to be any misery in your life, any anxiety, any anguish, any death. You have become part of the eternal flow of life. No philosopher can give you anything.

BELOVED OSHO,
AFTER FIFTEEN YEARS OF TRYING ALL KINDS OF
DIFFERENT SPIRITUAL TECHNIQUES AND TWO YEARS
DOING GROUPS AND YOUR MEDITATIONS, I'VE NOW
DECIDED TO TAKE SANNYAS. EVEN SO, I DON'T FEEL
THAT ABSOLUTE INNER CERTAINTY WHICH I HAVE
BEEN WAITING FOR. OSHO, COULD YOU PLEASE SAY
SOMETHING ABOUT THE DIFFERENCE BETWEEN
BEING A SYMPATHIZER AND A SANNYASIN?

A sympathizer is on the way to becoming a sannyasin. There is no difference. The sannyasin has reached, the sympathizer is coming.

But your question is very interesting, that you had been waiting for so many years for an absolute certainty to take sannyas. Have you waited in the same way for other things? Getting married? Falling in love?... waiting for fifteen years, falling and falling and falling and falling.... Just watch your life – if you start waiting that long... fifteen years is a long time. You are hungry. Will you eat only when you are absolutely certain that this food is not going to give you food poisoning? Absolute certainty!...

You are sitting here – are you certain that this roof is not going to fall? Have you waited for fifteen years to see that the roof is okay? Now it is time to get in.

Life is so short that unless you start, even though you are not absolutely certain.... In fact, how can you be absolutely certain about something you have not experienced? In what way?

I have heard that Mulla Nasruddin wanted to learn swimming. He went to a teacher who used to teach swimming and they both went to the river. Just on the steps – he must have been very much afraid, because he was not absolutely certain that he wanted to enter this dangerous water, and who knows about this man with absolute certainty, that he is trustworthy? He must have been thinking fast, so he slipped just on the steps, got up and started running back towards his home.

The teacher said, "Where are you going? You had come to learn swimming."

Mulla Nasruddin said, "Forget all about it. I will come only when I am absolutely certain."

The teacher said, "But how are you going to be absolutely certain?"

He said, "First, I will try on my bed – no danger – and when I am completely satisfied, I will come to you." He never came, because nobody can learn swimming on the bed. You have to go into the water. And going into the water, you cannot go with absolute certainty. You have to go with an adventurous spirit, accepting that risks are there, dangers are there, failures are there.

In sannyas, you will be moving into deeper realms of existence – how can you have absolute certainty right now? You will have to trust somebody – somebody who knows the path, who has been traveling the path. And it is not difficult to find whether the man is authentic or not. Just look into his eyes. Just watch his movement, just listen to the authority of his words. Just feel his presence.

Otherwise, fifteen years or fifteen lives makes no difference; you will remain in the same situation. Absolute certainty comes at the end, not before it. The beginning... the beginning has to be not with absolute certainty, but with absolute *interest*. If you are interested to explore your own being and the secrets of existence, that's enough. Certainty will come as your experience matures. But if you are waiting for absolute certainty to come first, then forget all about it.

BELOVED OSHO,
SINCE GERMANS MAKE THE LARGEST NATIONAL
NUMBER OF YOUR SANNYASINS, WHAT IS HIDDEN
IN THEIR ROOTS THAT PUSH AND DRAG THEM TO
THAT CONTROVERSIAL RELATIONSHIP WITH YOU?

I am a German! And soon Germany will be the first sannyas land. No politicians can prevent it, it is just destined to happen.

BELOVED OSHO,
WHEN I AM WITH YOU, I FEEL LIKE A BOAT ON THE
WIDE OCEAN AND THE WAVES GO HIGHER AND
HIGHER. AND THEN THE QUESTION ARISES: ARE YOU
ME OR AM I YOU?

Two sides of one coin – both are right. You can see this side, you can see that side. The higher you go, the closer you come to me. At the highest point, certainly this question arises: Who are you? – me or yourself? In fact, those two entities have disappeared into one organic whole. This is what I call devotion, the ultimate state of disciplehood.

BELOVED OSHO,
I FEEL SO GUILTY WHEN WANTING TO EXPRESS
MYSELF AND WHEN I FINALLY TAKE COURAGE TO DO
SO, IT FEELS MORE LIKE A NO TO OTHERS THAN A YES
TO MYSELF. THEN THE GUILT RETURNS BECAUSE OF
THIS. POSTPONEMENT OR DEFIANCE ARE THE ONLY
WAYS I KNOW BUT THEY SEEM PART OF A CIRCLE
ANYWAY. BELOVED MASTER, IS THERE A WAY TO
TRANSFORM GUILT?

My God! Nobody has ever transformed guilt. It has to be simply dropped. Why transform it? Do you want to preserve it in some form or other? Guilt is not something that you are born with, it is not part of your nature. Guilt is created by the society.

For example, every religion creates guilt – in different ways, but the technique is the same. All the religions live, thrive, on guilty human beings. First make them guilty – once you have succeeded in making somebody feel guilty, you have almost killed his spirit. Now he will be a soulless slave to you. As far as I am concerned, my whole work is in how to *free* you from guilt – not to transform it.

I was born in a Jaina family. It is a very orthodox religion. You cannot conceive – small things become guilt. You cannot eat in the night, that is guilt. If you have eaten in the night, you have gone down towards hell; you have taken one step downwards.

I don't see any problem. The religion is very old – at that time, there was no light, no electricity, and it was understandable to prohibit people from eating in the night – but why make it guilt? Just a rational explanation is enough, but religions are not interested in rational explanations. They don't miss a single opportunity in which they can make you feel guilty. Guilt is their power over you.

If we can remove all guilt from humanity, all the churches will be empty, all the temples will be empty. There will be nobody praying, nobody carrying Holy Bibles. But anything can be made into guilt. Sometimes it is very hilarious....

Up to my eighteenth year, I had not eaten in the night, and I was praised for it and I used to feel higher and holier than all the Hindus who lived around me – they are eating in the night, poor fellows. They are all bound to go to hell. I was feeling tremendously happy that I was saved and these people were destroyed. But eating in the night... whenever you eat, *somewhere* it is night! So what difference does it make whether the night is here or the night is in London? The night is around.

In the Sikh religion, a Sikh is expected to follow five principles and each of those five is simply hilarious. A Sikh must have long hair... in the Punjabi language, these are called five "K's." The first K means *Kesh*, hair; you cannot cut any hair of the body. The second K is *katar*. Katar means a special kind of sword – now, what has a sword to do with a religion? – every Sikh has to carry a sword. The third K is even more strange. I have been trying to find the religiousness of it but I have not been able to yet. It is called *kachchha*. *Kachchha* means underwear – without underwear, you are finished.

My God! As far as I know, God himself has no underwear... because in no religious scripture is it described that God has underwear. But these poor Sikhs are having underwear. I was thinking, what is the matter? Why did underwear enter into it and become a religious principle?

Those were the days when Sikhism was born. India was under

Mohammedan rule. And in war, if you use something that falls – you are running and your dhoti falls away – then *kachchha* is needed. Otherwise, *katar* will not do anything and you will become unnecessarily a laughingstock. But now there is no war and nothing is a problem. You can put the *kachchha* to rest!

But a Sikh cannot cut his hair. If he cuts it, he feels guilty. You have never felt guilty – cutting your hair or shaving your beard, you have never felt guilty – not even a far away, faint idea of guilt. What is there to feel guilty about? But once the idea is put in your mind, and from the very childhood conditioned continuously, then it becomes difficult.

One Sikh driver used to drive me, he was my chauffeur. One night, when he was snoring, I cut his hair. In the morning he came running, crying, tears... he said, "I resign from the job."

I said, "What has happened?"

He said, "Can't you see? Somebody has cut all my hairs. He has destroyed my religion, my spirituality."

I said, "Just sit down. How, by cutting your hair, can your religion be destroyed?"

He said, "I don't want to listen to anything. It is written in the scriptures, and I don't want to listen to anything against my scriptures. So please, give me my *kachchha* and I am going."

Because while I was cutting his hair, I thought it would be good to take his *kachchha* also. So I pulled his *kachchha* out and he was so deeply asleep....

I said, "*Kachchha*? Who has taken your *kachchha*? You never take a bath – I can say that my chauffeur is within a one mile radius, your *kachchha* sends such disgusting radiations. If somebody has taken it, be finished with it!"

He said, "No, it is my religion! And first I want to know who the person is."

And he had his sword in his hand. I said, "Calm down. I will bring you a new *kachchha*."

He said, "What about the hair?"

I said, "False hairs are available." He said, "Then it is good."

These fools are all over the world, and they feel guilty. So you have to understand the psychology of guilt. Just understanding is enough, and it drops. You have to understand that people, to make you spiritual slaves, have put ideas in your mind that "these things are wrong." That "if you do these things, God will be angry and throw you into hell." And naturally, nobody wants to go to hell – except me, because I am immensely interested in hell. I don't want to go to heaven, for the simple reason that in heaven, you will find only dry bones, ugly saints, somebody holding his *kachchha*. In hell, you will find the best company possible. All great artists are there, all great poets are there. All great philosophers are there, all great mystics are there. In fact, anything that has happened on this earth and is beautiful, you will find in hell, not in heaven.

In heaven, you will find dusty old saints who are now suffering – why have they made so much effort to come to heaven? And remember one thing that shows the situation: from heaven there is no exit. You can only enter, and finished. From hell, there are both doors – entrance and exit. If you want to go, you can go. But nobody goes out. All the beautiful women, all the beautiful men – it is twenty-four hours a celebration.

So I told my chauffeur, "Don't be worried. If you are going into hell, I am coming with you. You can remain my chauffeur there too!"

He said, "But I don't want to go."

But I said, "You don't understand. In heaven, there is no car – what will you do?"

He said, "That is a real question – I know only one job. Are you *sure* there is no car?"

I said, "Never heard... you can look into all your scriptures, in all the religions' scriptures. There is no car."

He said, "My God! Then it is better – be finished with this *kachchha* and this *Kesh*, I am coming with you! If you are going to hell, then there must be something in it." Guilt has to be dropped. Simple understanding, that's all. You have been befooled, you have been conditioned. Just drop it.

The moment you understand that this is something absurd, drop it. Transformation is not needed. And transformation is not possible either, because guilt is not a real thing. It is just an idea enforced in your mind. It is like a person who by mistake has learned that two plus two are five. Now, do you think some transformation is needed? All that is needed is to tell that person: "Two plus two are not five but only four." Just put four chairs before him – two chairs on this side, two chairs on this side – bring them together and tell him to count, whether they are five or four. And do you think he will have much difficulty in dropping the idea of five? There is no question. The moment he sees that two plus two is four, the five is finished. Guilt is exactly like that.

It is the greatest crime against humanity done by your religious people. They cannot be forgiven.

BELOVED OSHO,
EITHER WAY, YOU HAVE FINISHED ME. THE PROSPECT
OF JOINING THE RANKS OF THE UNEMPLOYED
NEARABOUT THE AGE OF FORTY-TWO HAS GOT ME
INTO VERY HOT WATER WITH MY BELOVED. SHE'S
WANTING ALL MANNERS OF GUARANTEES AND
ASSURANCES, AND IN WRITING! ON THE OTHER
HAND, IF I REALLY DO HAVE NINE MORE YEARS TO
GO, THAT EXACT DATE YOU MENTION WILL NOT
ONLY BE THE END OF MY SEX LIFE, BUT THE END OF
ME, FULL STOP! BELOVED MASTER, YOU GOT ME IN
THIS DILEMMA; KINDLY GET ME OUT.

Milarepa, my business is to put people into dilemma. It is not my business to take them out. But for you, I will make an exception. You have only one misunderstanding in your question – the full stop. It is not a full stop, it is a semicolon.

Everything will continue but on a higher level, on a better level. The moment sex disappears it does not mean that you don't have life anymore, unless you have this wrong idea that sex and life are synonymous. They are not. The moment sex starts disappearing, a great spiritual revolution starts happening in you. The same energy that was moving downwards starts moving upwards. It is the same energy that has brought you into the world. It is the same energy that can take you to the other world – called by different religions, different names – nirvana, *moksha*, paradise, the kingdom of god... just different names. Sex energy is the only energy there is. Either you can destroy it, spoil it, throw it away, or you can be more articulate, more wise, and transform it.

I said guilt cannot be transformed because it is not part of your being, but sex can be transformed because you are nothing but made of sex energy. All the cells of your body are sexual cells. So don't be worried. Looking at me, you could have dropped your worries. I'm not dead. I have passed the full stop you talk about and I have found it was a semicolon. The full stop never comes. It is always a comma or a semicolon, but life goes on and on without any full stop.

And about your beloved – who must be freaking out that at just forty-two, you will be finished with sex? So give her all the kinds of documents she wants, in writing, because I know your beloved. She will be in the semicolon *before* you. In fact, *you* will be in trouble, not she. Your beloved is no one but Shunyo. You can give her any kind of guarantee, any kind of stamp, signature, writing – don't be worried. In fact, I have been forcing her to ask you – "give me in writing...." Poor Shunyo herself would not do such a thing, it is all my doing.

29

Human rights for the New Man

BELOVED OSHO,
ON DECEMBER 25TH, YOU SPOKE TO US ON THE
DECLARATION OF HUMAN RIGHTS. YOU EXPOSED IT
AS A POLITICAL DEVICE TO MAINTAIN MAN IN HIS
CURRENT STATE OF PHYSICAL AND PSYCHOLOGICAL
SLAVERY, AND TO ENSURE THAT HE REMAINS
IGNORANT OF HIS TRUE POTENTIAL FOR GODLINESS.
WOULD YOU, TONIGHT, MAKE YOUR OWN
DECLARATION OF HUMAN RIGHTS FOR THE NEW
MAN?

The Declaration of Human Rights basically means that mankind still lives in many kinds of slaveries. Otherwise, there would be no need for the Declaration. The very need indicates that man has been deceived for thousands of years. And he has been deceived in such a cunning way that unless you rise above humanity, you cannot see in what invisible chains humanity is living, in what bondage, in what invisible prisons everybody is confined.

My declaration of human rights consists of ten fundamental things. The first is life. Man has a right to dignity, to health; a right to grow, so that he can blossom into his ultimate flowering. This ultimate flowering is his right. He is born with the seeds, but the society does not provide him the soil, the right caring, the loving atmosphere.

On the contrary, society provides a very poisonous atmosphere, full of anger, hatred, destructions, violence, war. The right to life means there should be no wars anymore. It also means that nobody should be forced into armies, forced to go to war; it is everybody's right to refuse. But this is not the case.

Thousands of people are in prisons – particularly young people, sensitive and intelligent – because they refused to go to war. Their denial has become a crime – and they were simply saying that they don't want to kill human beings.

Human beings are not things you can destroy without a second thought. They are the climax of universal evolution. To destroy them for any cause – for religion, for politics, for socialism, for fascism... it does not matter what the cause is; man is above all causes, and man cannot be sacrificed on any altar.

It is so strange that the UN declares the fundamental rights of human beings and yet says nothing about those thousands of young people who are wasting their lives in prisons for the simple reason that they refused to destroy life. But it has deep roots which have to be understood.

The right to life is possible only in a certain, different atmosphere which is not present on the earth at the moment. Animals are killed, birds are killed, sea animals are killed, just for game. You don't have any reverence for life. And life is the same whether it is in human beings or in other forms. Unless man becomes aware of his violence towards animals, birds, he cannot be really alert about his own right to life. If you are not caring about others' lives, what right have you got to demand the same right for yourself?

People go hunting, killing animals unnecessarily. I was a guest in Maharaja Jamnagar's palace. He showed me hundreds of lions, deer – their heads. The whole palace was full, and he was showing them: "These are the animals I have killed myself."

I asked him, "You look a nice a person. What was the reason? What have these animals done against you?"

He said, "It is not a question of reason or a question of them doing anything against me. It is just a game."

I said, "Just look from the other side: If a lion killed you, would that be a game? Your wife, your children, your brothers – will any one of them have the guts to say that it was a beautiful game? It will be a disaster. If *you* kill, then it is a game; if they kill, then it is a calamity. These double standards show your dishonesty, insincerity."

He said, "I have never thought about it."

But the whole of humanity is non-vegetarian; they are all eating other life forms. There is no reverence for life as such. Unless we create an atmosphere of reverence for life, man cannot realize the goal of getting his fundamental right of life.

Secondly, because the UN also declares life to be a fundamental right for man, it is being misused. The pope, Mother Teresa, and their tribe are using it for teaching people against birth control, against abortion, against the pill. Man's mind is so cunning. It was a question of human rights – they are taking advantage of it. They are saying you cannot use birth control methods because they go against life; the unborn child also has the same right as you have. So some line has to be drawn, because at what point...?

To me, the pill does not destroy human rights; in fact it prepares the ground for it. If the earth is too overcrowded, millions of people will die of starvation; there will be wars. And the way the crowd is exploding it can lead humanity into a very inhuman situation.

In Bengal, there was a great famine in which mothers ate their own children. People sold their own children just for one rupee, two rupees. And do you think the persons who were purchasing them were purchasing human beings? No, they were purchasing food. The pope and Mother Teresa will be responsible for all this.

The pill simply does not allow the child to be formed in the mother's womb, so the question of human rights does not arise. And now, recently, science has found a pill for men too. It is not necessary that the woman should take the pill, the man can take it. The child is not formed in any way; hence, this fundamental right is inapplicable in that case. But these religious people – the *shankaracharyas* in India, Ayatollah Khomeini in Iran... and all over the world, all religions are against birth control methods. And they are the only methods which can prevent man from falling into a barbarous state. I am absolutely in favor of birth control methods. A child should be recognized as a human being when he is born – and then too, I have some reservations....

If a child is born blind, if a child is born crippled, if a child is born deaf, dumb, and we cannot do anything.... Just because life should not be destroyed, this child will have to suffer – because of your stupid idea – for seventy years, eighty years. Why create unnecessary suffering? If the parents are willing, the child should be put to eternal sleep. And there is no problem in it. Only the body goes back into its basic elements; the soul will fly into another womb. Nothing is destroyed.

If you really love the child, you will not want him to live a seventy-year-long life in misery, suffering, sickness, old age. So even if a child is born, if he is not medically capable of enjoying life fully with all the senses, healthy, then it is better that he goes to eternal sleep and is born somewhere else with a better body.

The right to life is a complex thing. Nobody is entitled to kill anyone, either, in the name of religion. Millions of people have been killed in the name of religions, in the service of God. No one should be killed in the name of politics. Again, the same has happened. Joseph Stalin alone killed one million people, his own people, while he was in power. Adolf Hitler killed six million people. And thousands of wars have happened.

It seems that on this earth we are doing only one thing: reproducing children because soldiers are needed, reproducing children because wars are needed. Even to increase the population, Mohammed said that every Mohammedan can marry four women or even more. He himself married nine women. And the reason is war, destruction of life. It is not out of love for nine women that he has married them, it is simple arithmetic. If a man marries nine women, he can produce nine children in one year. If nine women marry one man, this is okay but vice-versa, nine men marrying one woman may not be able even to produce one child. They will mess up the whole thing. Most probably they will kill the woman! It seems man is nothing but a necessary instrument for more destruction, more wars.

The population has to be reduced if man wants to be, to have his dignity, honor, his right to live – not just to drag, but to dance. When I say life is a fundamental right, I mean a life of songs and dances, a life of joy and blessings.

My second consideration is for love. Love should be accepted as one of the most fundamental human rights, and all societies have destroyed it. They have destroyed it by creating marriage. Marriage is a false substitute for love.

In the past, small children were married. They had no idea what love is, what marriage is. And why were small children married? For a simple reason: before they become young adults, before love arises in their hearts, the doors have to be closed. Because once love takes possession of their hearts then it will become very difficult....

No child marriage is human. A man or a woman should be

allowed to choose their partners and to change their partners whenever they feel. The government has no business in it, the society has nothing to do with it. It is two individuals' personal affair. The privacy of it is sacred. If two people want to live together, they don't need any permission from any priest or any government. They need the permission of their hearts. And the day they feel that the time has come to part, again they don't need anybody's permission. They can part as friends, with beautiful memories of their loving days. Love should be the only way for men and women to live together. No other ritual is needed.

The only problem in the past was what would happen to the children; that was the argument for marriage. There are other alternatives, far better. Children should be accepted not as their parents' property – they belong to the whole humanity. From the very beginning it should be made clear to them: "The whole humanity is going to protect you, is your shelter. We may be together – we will look after you. We may not be together; still we look after you. You are our blood, our bones, our souls."

In fact, this possession by the parents of the children is one of the most dangerous things that humanity goes on carrying. This is the root of the idea of possessiveness. You should not possess your children. You can love them, you can bless them, but you cannot possess. They belong to the whole humanity. They come from beyond; you have been just a passage. Don't think more than that about yourself. Whatever you can do, do.

Every commune, every village should take care of the children. Once the commune starts taking care of the children, marriage becomes absolutely obsolete. And marriage is destroying your basic right to love.

If man's love is free, there will not be blacks and whites, and there will not be these ugly discriminations, because love knows no boundaries. You can fall in love with a black man, you can fall in love with a white man. Love knows no religious scriptures. It knows only the heartbeat, and it knows it with absolute certainty. Once love is free, it will prepare the ground for other fundamental rights.

In fact, if you ask the scientists, people falling in love should be as different as possible. Then they will give birth to better children, more intelligent, stronger. We know it now; we are trying it all over the world as far as animals are concerned. Crossbreeding has given us better cows, better horses, better dogs. But man is strange. You know the secret, but you are not bettering yourself.

All the royal families are suffering. They create the greatest number of idiots, because they go on marrying amongst themselves. Royal blood cannot mix with a commoner's blood – even in the twentieth-century we think in terms of royal blood. Blood is simply blood. But if just a dozen families go on marrying amongst themselves continually, they create many kinds of diseases.

Retardedness is one. Just have a look again at the picture of the Prince of Wales and you will see what I mean by a retarded person. They are fed up, but they cannot go out of their small circle. I have never come across any person belonging to a royal family who has intelligence, and in India I have been acquainted with almost all the royal families. It is not only that their minds remain retarded, their bodies lose many things.

You must have heard the name of Rasputin. Before the Russian revolution he had become the most important man in Russia, for the simple reason that the child of the czar had a disease – if he wounded himself accidentally then the bleeding could not be prevented. No medicine could prevent it, there was no way; the blood would go on flowing out. And that is one of the symptoms of marrying close relatives.

Rasputin was a great hypnotist. He was not a saint and he was not a sinner, he was simply a great hypnotist. He managed with hypnosis to prevent the blood from flowing out of the child. What no physician was able to do... and the child was going to be the successor to the greatest empire of those days. Rasputin certainly became very important. Without him the child's life was in danger.

But still those royal families, although they have lost their kingdoms, their empires, continue to marry amongst themselves. It creates a very weak personality. Have you ever seen somebody from these royal families being declared as the beauty queen of the world? Do you think Queen Elizabeth of England can even be declared a beauty? All over England there is a rumor. I don't know whether it is true or not; hence I don't take any responsibility for it. The rumor is that Prince Philip, the husband of Queen Elizabeth, is a homosexual. I feel sorry for poor Philip. In fact anybody marrying Elizabeth would have been homosexual, so he should not feel worried about it. It is just natural.

And just two weeks or three weeks ago, one of the bodyguards of Prince Charles died of the disease AIDS. Now you cannot get AIDS from the sky. One does not know who the holy ghost is, but he must be in the royal family. And soon many more will die, because it is a chain disease.

There should be no boundaries – that a Hindu should marry only a Hindu, or a brahmin should only marry a brahmin. In fact, the rule should be that the Indian should never marry an Indian. The whole world is there; find your spouse far away, beyond the seven seas, and then you will have children who are more beautiful, more healthy, long living, far more intelligent, geniuses. Man has to learn crossbreeding, but that is possible only if marriage disappears and love is given absolute respect. Right now it is condemned.

The third most fundamental right... because these are the three most important things in life: life, love, and death. Everybody should be given the fundamental right that after a certain age, when he has lived enough and does not want to go on dragging unnecessarily.... Because tomorrow will be again just a repetition; he has lost all curiosity about tomorrow. He has every right to leave the body. It is his fundamental right.

It is his life. If he does not want to continue, nobody should prevent him. In fact, every hospital should have a special ward where people who want to die can enter one month before, can relax, enjoy all the things that they have been thinking about their whole life but could not manage – the music, the literature... if they wanted to paint or sculpt....

And the doctors should take care to teach them how to relax. Up to now, death has been almost ugly. Man has been a victim, but it is our fault. Death can be made a celebration; you just have to learn how to welcome it, relaxed, peaceful. And in one month's time, people, friends, can come to see them and meet together. Every hospital should have special facilities – more facilities for those who are going to die than for those who are going to live. Let them live for one month at least like emperors, so they can leave life with no grudge, with no complaint but only with deep gratitude, thankfulness.

Between these three comes the fourth: the search for truth.

Nobody should be conditioned from childhood about any religion, any philosophy, any theology, because you are destroying his freedom of search. Help him to be strong enough. Help him to be strong enough to doubt, to be skeptical about all that is believed all around him. Help him never to believe, but to insist on knowing. And whatever it takes, however long it takes, to go for the pilgrimage alone, on his own, because there is no other way to find the truth. All others – who think they are Christians, or they are Jews, or they are Hindus, or they are Mohammedans – these are all believers. They don't *know*. Belief is pure poison. Knowing is coming to a flowering.

The search for truth... you should not teach anybody what truth is because it cannot be taught. You should help the person to inquire. Inquiry is difficult; belief is cheap. But truth is not cheap; truth is the most valuable thing in the world. You cannot get it from others, you will have to find it yourself.

And the miracle is, the moment you decide that "I will not fall victim to any belief," you have already traveled half the way towards truth. If your determination is total, you need not go to truth, truth will come to you. You just have to be silent enough to receive it. You have to become a host so that truth can become a guest in your heart. Right now the whole world is living in beliefs. That's why there is no shine in the eyes, no grace in people's gestures, no strength, no authority in their words. Belief is bogus; it is making castles of sand. A little breeze and your great castle will be destroyed. Truth is eternal, and to find it means you also become part of eternity.

Fifth: to find the truth, all education systems from the kinder-garten to the universities will create a certain atmosphere for meditation. Meditation does not belong to any religion, and meditation is not a belief. It is a pure science of the inner. Learn-ing to be silent, learning to be watchful, learning to be a witness; learning that you are not the mind, but something beyond – the consciousness – will prepare you to receive truth.

And it is truth that has been called by many people, "God," by others, "nirvana." By others, other names have been given to it, but it is a nameless silence, serenity, peace. The peace is so deep that you disappear; and the moment you disappear you have entered the temple of God.

But strange it is, that people are wasting almost one-third of their lives in schools, colleges, and universities, not knowing any-thing about silence, not knowing anything about relaxation, not knowing anything about themselves. They know about the whole world – it is very weird that they have forgotten only themselves. But it seems there is some reason....

In India there is an ancient story. Ten blind men pass through a stream. The current is very forceful, so they hold hands. Reaching the other side, somebody suggests, "We should count ourselves. The current was so forceful and we cannot see – somebody may have gone with the wind, gone with the river."

So they count. Strangely enough the counting always stops at nine. Everybody tries, but it is always nine. One man sitting on the bank of the river starts laughing – it is hilarious! And those ten blind people are sitting there crying, tears in their eyes because they have lost one of their friends.

The man comes to them and he says, "What is the matter?"

They explain the situation. He says, "You all stand up in a line. I will hit the first person – he has to say 'one.' I will hit the second person – he has to say 'two,' because I will hit twice. I will hit the third person three times; he has to say 'three.'"

Strangely enough, he finds the tenth man who was lost. They all thank him, they touch his feet; they say, "You are a god to us. We were thinking we had lost one of our friends. But please, can you tell us... we were also counting; all of us tried, and the tenth was not there. How has he appeared suddenly?"

The man says, "That is an ancient mystery which you will not understand. You just go on your way."

What is the ancient mystery in it? One tends to forget oneself. In fact, one lives his whole life without remembering himself. He sees everybody, he knows everybody; he just forgets himself. Meditation is the only method in which you will start counting from yourself: "one." And because it is not part of any religion, there is no problem – it should be all over the world, in every school, in every college, in every university. Anybody who comes home from the university should come with a deep, meditative being, with an aura of meditation around him. Otherwise, what he is bringing is all rubbish, crap. Geography he knows: he knows where Timbuktu is, he knows where Constantinople is, and he does not know where he is himself. The first thing in life is to know who you are, where you are. Then everything in your life starts settling, moving in the right direction.

The sixth: freedom in all dimensions. We are not even as free as birds and animals. No bird goes to the passport office. Any moment he can fly into Pakistan; no entry visa. Strange, that only man remains confined in nations, in boundaries. Because the nation is big, you tend to forget that you are imprisoned. You cannot get out of it, you cannot get into it. It is a big prison, and the whole earth is full of big prisons.

Freedom in all dimensions means that man, wherever he is born, is part of one humanity. Nations should dissolve, religions should dissolve, because they are all creating bondages – and sometimes very hilarious bondages.

I was in a city, Dewas. For twenty years the Jaina temple there has not opened. There are three locks on the temple: one lock from the *digambaras*, one of the sects of Jainism, one from another sect, *svetambaras*, and the third from the police. For twenty years poor Mahavira has been inside – no food, no bath, no light. One wonders whether he is really alive or dead, because he does not make any noise... at least he could knock and shout, "Open the doors and let me out!"

When I saw it, I asked, "What is the matter?" I was just passing by and I saw three locks – big locks, bigger than you may have ever seen – and I came to know the story.

In Dewas, there is only one Jaina temple, and this was the temple. Jainas are few; they don't have enough money to make two temples, so they have made one temple and divided the time. Up to twelve o'clock in the morning, Digambaras will worship, and after twelve, Svetambaras will worship... but there was a fight every day.

The differences between Svetambaras and Digambaras are not very big – so childish and so stupid. Digambaras worship Mahavira with closed eyes and Svetambaras worship Mahavira with open eyes. This is the only basic difference.

Now a marble statue... either you can make the eyes closed or you can make the eyes open, unless you fix some mechanism, to switch on so he opens his eyes, and switch off.... But that much technology does not exist in India; otherwise it would not be difficult. You can find it in toys – a beautiful girl, you lie her down and she closes her eyes. You put her back and she opens her eyes. Something could have been arranged.

And they had something arranged – primitive, but they had arranged it. And it is being following all over India: When Svetambaras worship a statue which has closed eyes, they put false eyes on top; they just glue them on. That is simple, non-technical; not much technology is needed.

But every day the problem was there: at the time of twelve, exactly twelve, Svetambaras would be waiting. One minute more... and the Digambaras are worshipping – and they are worshipping *knowingly* a little longer – and the Svetambaras will come and start putting their eyes on the statue and the fight will start.

It happened so many times that finally the police locked the temple and said to them, "Go to the court and get a decision." The case goes on – how can the court decide whether Mahavira used to meditate with closed eyes or with open eyes? The reality is, he used to meditate with half open eyes.

No child should be given any idea by the parents what life is all about – no theology, no philosophy, no politics. He should be made as intelligent and sharp as possible, so when he comes of age he can go in search. And it is a lifelong search. People today get their religion when they are born. In fact, if you can get your religion when you die, you have found it early. It is such a precious treasure, but it is possible only out of freedom – and freedom in all dimensions, not only in religion.

There should be no nations, no national boundaries. There should be no religions. Man should be taken as man. Why confine him with so many adjectives? Right now he is not free in any way.

I was arrested in America. In one jail in Oklahoma, the US Marshal told me that I had to write my name as David Washington. I said, "This is the first time that somebody has told me my name. Do you read thoughts?"

He became a little puzzled. He said, "Is it really your name?"

I said, "Of course."

He said, "Then change it. Some other name will do."

But I said, "You know my name. David Washington is not my name. And why should I write David Washington? And you call this country a democracy! And not even the freedom to write one's own name. What other freedoms do you have? And on your coat there is written in big letters 'Department of Justice, US Marshal.'" I said, "At least take this coat off. David Washington is not my name and I am not going to write it." I said, "This is for the first time in my life that I am seeing how democracy works, how freedom works. I am not even free to write my name. What is the purpose?"

He said, "That, I don't know. From high above I have been ordered: 'David Washington should be his name and he should be called David Washington in jail.'"

I said, "Then you fill out the form" – and it was in the middle of the night, twelve o'clock. I said, "You fill out the form – I will not fill it out, I refuse – and then I will sign it."

He was in a hurry to go home, so he filled out the form. I signed *my* name. He looked at it and he said, "But it doesn't look like David Washington."

I said, "How can it? I don't look like David Washington." He said, "You are a strange man. You deceived me."

I said, "You are deceiving yourself. You know perfectly well what my name is. And tomorrow the whole world will know that the so-called democracies – free countries, talking too much of freedom – are not even able to allow people to write their own names." And I said, "You don't know the reason why your higher authorities have asked this?" He said, "I don't know."

I said, "This is strange, because I know. It is a simple, logical inference that even if you kill me in the jail nobody will be able to find out where I disappeared. Because in your forms, on your register, I never entered your jail, so the question of my being killed in your jail does not arise."

He was shocked. I said, "This is a simple thing. Otherwise, there is no need to change my name; you don't have any authority."

But in this world there is no freedom in any dimension. I was going to college. My parents wanted me to go to science college or to medical college. I said, "Am I going or are you going?"

They said, "Of course you are going; why should we be going?" "Then," I said, "leave it to me."

They said, "We can leave it to you, but then remember: we will not support you financially."

I said, "That's understood." I left my home without a single rupee. I traveled in the train to the university without a ticket. I had to go to the ticket checker and tell him: "This is the situation. Can you allow me to travel without a ticket?"

He said, "This is the first time in my life that somebody has come to ask me! People escape, people deceive me, cheat me. Certainly I will take you, and at the university station I will be at the gate so nobody bothers you."

I went directly to the vice-chancellor and told him the whole story. And I told him, "I want to study philosophy, but it seems there is no freedom even to choose what I want to study. So you have to give me all the scholarships possible, because I will not be getting any financial help. Otherwise I *will* study philosophy, fasting... even if I die."

He said, "No! Don't do that, because then the blame will be on me. I will give you all the scholarships."

From the very childhood we go on crippling, cutting free-doms; we try to make a child according to our desires.

I was talking to a Christian missionary and he said, "God made man in his own image."

I said, "That is the foundation of all slavery. Why should God make man in his own image? Who is he? – and to give his own image to man means he has destroyed man from the very begin-ning." And that is what every father is doing. Man's basic right is to be himself.

And in an authentic human society, everybody should be allowed to be himself – even if he chooses just to be a flute player, and he will not become the richest man in the world but will be a beggar on the streets. Still I say freedom is so valuable.... You may not be the president of the country, you may be just a beggar play-ing the flute in the streets. But you are yourself, and there is such deep contentment, fulfillment, that unless you know it you have missed the train.

Seventh: one earth, one humanity. I don't see any reason at all why there should be so many nations. Why should there be so many lines on the map? And they are only on the map, remember. They are not on the earth; neither are they in the sky. And the map is man-made. Existence has not created this earth in frag-ments.

I am reminded of one of my teachers. He was a very loving human being, and he had his own methods of teaching. He was a kind of rebel. One day he came with a few pieces of cardboard, placed them on the table, and said to us all, "Look, this is the map of the world, but I have cut it into pieces and I have mixed them. Now anybody who is confident that he can put them in their right places and make the world map should come up."

One tried, failed; another tried, failed. I went on watching him and watching the people who were failing and why they were failing. Watching five persons fail, I was the sixth. I went and I turned over all his cardboard pieces.

He said, "What are you doing?"

I said, "You wait, I am working it out. Five people have failed but I have found the secret."

On the other side of the map was a picture of a man. I arranged the man, which was easier. On one side the man was arranged and on the other side the whole map of the world was arranged. That was the key that I had been looking for, waiting to see if I could get some clue. And when the others were arranging the pieces, I saw that there was something on the other side.

The teacher said, "You are a rascal! I was hoping you would come first, but when you didn't come I understood that you were waiting to find out the key. And you have found the right key."

The world is divided because man is divided; man is divided because the world is divided. Start from anywhere; just let the whole of humanity be one, and the nations will disappear, the lines will disappear. It is our world – one humanity, one earth, and we can make it a paradise. Right now there is no need to describe hell. You can just look all around; it is here.

I have heard a story. A man died. He was a thief, a murderer, a rapist – you name it and he had done it. And when the angels started taking him away, he said, "Certainly you will be taking me to hell."

They said, "No."

He said, "What?"

They said, "Hell you have been in; now we are taking you to heaven. The old hell is empty because you have created a *better* hell, so all the sinners are sent here." And the story seems to be significant. Looking around the earth, man is in such misery and suffering that there seems to be no need for another hell.

But we can change the whole situation. This earth can become a paradise. And then there will be no need for any paradise; paradise will be empty.

Eighth: uniqueness of every individual. A very beautiful word has been misused so utterly that it is difficult to imagine, and that word is equality. A few thinkers say human beings are equal. To counter them, the UN declares that equality is man's birthright. But nobody bothers to see that man is not equal and has never been equal. It is absolutely unpsychological. Every man is unique.

The moment you are all equal you are a crowd, your individuality has been taken away. You are no longer yourself but just a cog in the wheel.

I teach not equality, not inequality – I teach uniqueness. Every individual is unique and needs to be respected in his uniqueness. Because every individual is unique, the birthright should be: equal opportunity for their growth of uniqueness.

It is such a simple and obvious fact. Two thousand years have passed and you have not been able to produce another Jesus. Twenty-five centuries have passed and you have not been able to produce another Gautam Buddha. And still you go on saying man is equal? Man is unique, and everybody should be respected as a world in himself. He is neither inferior to anybody nor is he superior to anybody; he is alone. In this aloneness there is beauty. You are no longer a mob, a crowd; you are yourself.

Ninth: a world government. I am absolutely against governments. I am for one government for the whole world. That means no war will be possible; that means there will be no need to keep millions of people in armies unnecessarily. They can be productive, they can be helpful, and if they are merged into humanity, all poverty will disappear.

Right now seventy percent of the national income of every country goes to the army and the rest of the country lives on thirty percent. If armies disappear, seventy percent of the income of every country will be available. There is no need to be poor, there is no need to have any beggars.

These beggars, these Ethiopias – they are our creations. On the one hand, we are creating great armies and on the other hand, we are killing human beings through starvation. And these armies are doing nothing. They are simply professional killers, professional criminals, trained criminals. We are giving them training in how to kill. And we talk about humanity, we talk about civilization, and still seventy percent of our income goes into killing.

One world government means a tremendous change, a revolution. The whole earth will be benefited by it. Secondly, if there is one world government it becomes only functional. Right now government is not functional, it has real power. The president of a country or the prime minister of a country... in a functional government things will be different. Now you have the postmaster general; he is a functional person, he has no power. He has work, he has no function, but he has no power. There is no need. The man who heads your railways, what power does he have? The man who is the president of your airlines, what power does he have? It is functional.

If there is only one government, it will automatically become functional. Right now it cannot be, because the fear of other governments keeps you afraid: "Make your leaders strong, give all support to the leaders." But if there is no war there is no need of anybody having power – war is the cause of power. And unless war disappears from the world, power cannot disappear; they are together.

A functional world government – like the post office, the railways, the airlines – will be efficient but without power. It will be a beautiful world where you don't know who the president is, who the prime minister is – they are your servants. Right now they have become your masters, and to keep their power they have to keep you always completely afraid. Pakistan is getting ready to fight with India, so you have to give all power to the Indian leaders. China is going to attack.... Adolf Hitler has written in his autobiography that if you want to remain in power, keep people always afraid. And he is absolutely right. Sometimes mad people are also right.

And tenth: meritocracy. Democracy has failed. We have lived under many kinds of governments – aristocracy, monarchy, city democracies – and now we have seen the whole world getting addicted to the idea of democracy. But democracy has not solved any problems; it has increased the problems. It was because of these problems that a man like Karl Marx supported a dictatorship of the proletariat. I am not a supporter of a dictatorship of the proletariat, but I have another idea that goes far ahead of democracy.

Democracy means government by the people, of the people,

for the people – but it is only in words. In India right now there are nine hundred million people. How can nine hundred million people have power? They have to delegate the power to somebody. So it is not the people who rule, but the people who are chosen by them. What are your grounds for choosing? How do you manage to choose? And are you capable of choosing the right people? Have you been trained, educated for a democratic life? No, nothing has been done.

The ignorant masses can be exploited very easily by very insignificant things. For example, Nixon lost his election against Kennedy and the only reason was that Kennedy looked better on television than Nixon; this is the analysis of the psychoanalysts.

Nixon improved. When he discovered this, before the next election, he improved; he learned how to stand, how to walk, how to talk, how to dress. Even the color of your dress will make a difference on television. If you go there in white clothes you will look like a ghost. Arbitrary reasons... somebody speaks well, is a good orator. But that does not mean that he will make a good president. Somebody makes good shoes – do you think that will make him a good president?

It happened when Abraham Lincoln was chosen president. On the day of his inaugural address to the Senate, people were feeling very angry and hurt – because Lincoln's father was a shoemaker, and a shoemaker's son has defeated the great aristocrats. They were offended. One arrogant aristocrat could not tolerate it. Before Lincoln started speaking, he said, "Wait a minute. Do you recognize me? You used to come with your father to my house sometimes because your father made shoes for my family. You used to help him." And the whole Senate laughed. This was an effort to humiliate Lincoln.

But you cannot humiliate people like Abraham Lincoln. He said, "I am very grateful to you that you reminded me of my dead father at this moment. Because my father was the best shoemaker in the whole country, and I know that I can never be the best president as he was the best shoemaker. He is still ahead of me." What criterion do you use? How do you manage?

That's why my idea is that the days of democracy are over. A new kind of system is needed, based on merit. We have thousands of universities all over the world. Why have ordinary, unknowledgeable, ignorant masses choose people who will be holding tremendous power for five years in their hands? And now the power is so much that they can destroy the whole world.

Meritocracy means that only people who are educated in a certain area should be able to vote in that area. For example, only the educationists of the country should choose the education minister. Then you will have the best education minister possible. For the finance minister, you should choose somebody who knows finance, somebody who knows the complexities of economics. But this choice is possible only for people who are trained in economics, in financial matters – and there are thousands of people. For every post, the person who is chosen should be chosen by experts.

The health minister should be chosen by all the doctors, the surgeons, the medical experts, the scientists who are working in the medical field. Then we will have the cream of our genius, and we can depend on this cream to make the life of all humanity more peaceful, more blissful, more rich.

This idea I call a meritocracy. And once you have chosen all the people, then these people can choose the president and the prime minister. They will be our geniuses; they can choose the prime minister, the president from the country, or they can choose from the members of the parliament. And for the parliament we should also make gradations.

For example, people who have at least a post-graduate degree should be able to vote. Just becoming twenty-one years old does not mean you are able to choose the right person. At twenty-one years, you don't know anything about life and its complexities. At least a post-graduate degree should be held by those who choose the members of the parliament or the senate or whatever you call it. In this way, we can make an educated, refined, cultured government.

Before the world government happens, each nation should pass through a meritocracy. And once we have enjoyed the fruits of a meritocracy then these people will be able to understand that if we can combine the whole world into one government, life can certainly be a joy, worth living – not to renounce, but to rejoice.

Up to now, whatever has happened has been accidental. Our history up to now is nothing but a history of accidents. We have to stop this. Now we have to decide that the future is not going to be accidental. It will be created by us; and to create our world can be the greatest creation possible.

30

The master only makes you
remember who you are

BELOVED OSHO,
YOU ARE FOR ME, THE MOST EXTRAORDINARY
PERSON I CAN IMAGINE. YET I KNOW THAT YOU FEEL
ORDINARY. WHERE IS THE DOOR FOR A TALENTED
AND GIFTED PERSON OR A GENIUS TO FEEL AND
BECOME ORDINARY? I SEE THAT EACH TIME I FEEL
SPECIAL, SOMETHING GOES WRONG. BUT I HAVE STILL
NOT FOUND THE DOOR TO REAL MODESTY AND
SIMPLICITY. COULD YOU PLEASE SAY SOMETHING
ABOUT THAT?

I do not feel ordinary – I am. The people who have talents, the gifted, the geniuses – they also suffer the same problem that you are suffering because they forget that the whole existence is ordinary. A sunrise, howsoever beautiful, is pure ordinariness. A sky full of stars does not feel in any way special. A rosebush full of beautiful flowers and fragrance is just part of the ordinary existence. The talented people get into trouble because they forget their relationship with existence. They become confined and imprisoned in their small talents.

What are your talents and what are your geniuses? Because you can paint, you are a genius? Look at the butterflies, look at the flowers, look at the sky when the sun is setting – the whole existence is so colorful. And because you have painted a small canvas, you have become special. And what have you painted?

The existence has to be remembered; then you will not get caught in the net of an egoistic feeling, that "I am special." The moment you feel you are special, you have lost contact with life, with love, with the totality of the whole – you are alone.

A true genius does not know, does not feel that he is special. That is the criterion whether he is a true genius or not. If he feels that he is special, he's not a true genius. The very feeling of specialness arises out of your inferiority. The more inferior you feel, the more you try to pretend, to pose your specialness.

Looking at the vastness, the infinity and eternity of existence, we are just dewdrops in the early morning sun. We may shine like pearls on the lotus leaves, but just a little breeze and the dewdrop slips into the ocean and is no more. The ocean always *is*. If you also want to be always here and now, don't get identified with a tiny dewdrop. Howsoever beautiful it looks, it is only appearance. Merge, melt, disappear into the ocean, and the ocean is no longer separate from you. It is not that the dewdrop has died. On the contrary, the dewdrop has become the ocean.

You are asking me how to attain, to achieve true humility, true simplicity – these things are never *achieved*. These things are not within your hands. If you understand, they happen. All that you have to do is to understand that we are part of a mysterious world. And the world is so vast, how you can be anything else but humble? It is not a question of attaining, achieving humility. It is a question of understanding: how can I be other than humble? One day, you were not. One day, you will not be again – and still you are trying to achieve humility? You want simplicity in your life?

But life *is* simple. If you want to make it complex, you can – you can stand on your head and life becomes complex! You can do all kinds of stupidities and life becomes complex. Don't do anything. Just try to be aware, alert, and see that you are related with such a miraculous, mysterious world. Suddenly, you will find that you are simple, just like a child. The child has simplicity not because he has achieved it, he has simplicity because he is still, in a subtle way, in tune with the whole. He was in tune with the whole in his mother's womb. He has not forgotten it yet.

Have you noticed a fact – if you try to remember backwards, how far can you remember? When you were four years old or three years old? More than that, you cannot go back. But when you were three years old, you were perfectly conscious. You were enjoying more than you will ever enjoy life. Everything was beautiful; small colored stones, sea shells on the beach were treasures.

The reason why you cannot remember backwards to the time when you were born is that in those three years you were simple – so simple that you had not even gathered memory. There was no need. You were just like a mirror – you reflected, enjoyed the moment, but you never collected. You were not greedy. Your ego had not come yet into being. It takes, for the society to bring the ego, at least three years in women and four years in men. I have been always puzzled: why three years in women and four years in men? It is because women are more self-conscious.

Mulla Nasruddin was trying hard for two hours to catch two flies. Finally, he got them and he told his wife: "I have caught them. One is male, one is female."

The wife said, "My God! How did you figure out who is male and who is female?"

He said, "Very simple. The female has been sitting continuously for two hours on the mirror, and the male was reading the newspaper for two hours. It was not difficult to find out who is who."

The woman is more body-oriented... becomes aware of her beauty, becomes aware that others are also aware of her beauty. That's why the ego is created one year earlier. The woman is more confined to herself.

The man looks around the world, forgetting himself completely; hence, it takes a little more time. But once the male ego is there, it is stronger, more poisonous than the female ego. Because the female ego is fragile – it depends only on her beautiful eyes, her beautiful hair, the beautiful proportions of her body. Its claims are not very big. But when the man claims, he becomes Alexander the Great, Napoleon Bonaparte, Ivan the Terrible. His scope of the ego is the whole world.

When the first group of mountain climbers, early in the century, tried to climb the highest peak of the Himalayas – Gourishankar, known to the world as Everest – they were asked: "Why are you putting your life in unnecessary danger?" Because there is nothing to be found... eternal snow, which has never melted.

And do you know, the leader replied, "It is not a question of finding anything there on the Everest. The question is that it is there, unclimbed, and it hurts our egos."

Strange – the poor Everest is not doing anything to you. Almost hundreds of people have died in climbing Everest, for a simple reason – because it is there. It cannot remain unclimbed, man has to defeat it.

What is there on the moon? But it is there, this is the difficulty. What is there on Mars? It is there. And those millions of stars are there. Man's ego has no limits. It is vast and it goes on growing.

The woman is satisfied with beautiful clothes, ornaments, a beautiful, small garden, a swimming pool – she does not ask much. And by the way, this is the reason no woman has been able to become a Gautam Buddha. You will be surprised. What can be the connection in it?

To become a Gautam Buddha, you need a very big ego so big that it becomes a mountainous burden on you. You have to get *rid* of it; otherwise it will kill you. But the woman's ego is so small, it never becomes a mountainous burden. There is no need to fight with it, to drop it. This is the reason why women have not been able to reach higher peaks of consciousness. They are easily satisfied with small things. Man knows no satisfaction, and this dissatisfaction becomes so troublesome, so painful, that he has to find a way out of it.

You are asking how to achieve simplicity. A simplicity that is achieved is phony, because deep down you know you are not simple. A humbleness that is achieved is false because in your heart of hearts, you know it is just etiquette, mannerism. It pays in the world to be humble, to be simple – these are your masks. But if you ask me, I will tell you: drop the idea of achievement. The very idea of achievement is egoistic. You *are* simple, you are humble. Just look all around. Look at the ocean, look at the sky. How can you manage not to be simple and not to be humble?

BELOVED OSHO,
WHEN I WRITE DOWN A QUESTION TO YOU, WITH
EVERY WORD, MORE AND MORE QUESTIONS ARE
ARISING WITHIN ME. IT IS ALMOST IMPOSSIBLE TO
WRITE DOWN A SINGLE SENTENCE WITHOUT
GETTING LOST IN THE JUNGLE OF QUESTIONS. BY THE
TIME I AM FINISHED WITH ONE QUESTION, I AM
COMPLETELY EXHAUSTED. I WANT TO KNOW IT ALL,
OSHO, SO DESPERATELY, THAT TEARS ARE COMING IN
MY EYES. IT MIGHT BE THE WRONG WAY TO START,
BUT I WANT TO KNOW IT ALL. I WANT TO ASK
EVERYTHING AND I WANT TO KNOW ALL THE
ANSWERS TO EVERYTHING. BELOVED ANSWER,
WOULD YOU PLEASE COMMENT?

Mind is just like a tree: questions grow on the tree like leaves. If you cut one leaf, the tree will replace it with three leaves, at least. That's how a gardener makes the tree thick, the foliage big. Mind is very productive as far as questions are concerned. It manufactures only questions. And each answer, mind will immediately change into hundreds of questions. No answer is going to stop the mind. So you are on a wrong track, completely wrong. And what are you going to do by knowing all? Do you want to become a god?

There are people who say that even God committed mistakes in making existence. There are people who propose that if God had taken their advice, the world would have been far better. And you cannot simply reject them, they have a certain validity. Just look at life and you will find how many mistakes God has committed. Just a few examples....

The biblical story is that first God created Adam and *not* Eve; Eve was the second woman that he created. He had created another woman before Eve. Christians don't talk about it, Jews are silent about it, because it will raise so many questions – what happened to the first woman?

But the very first night, the first mistake – he made only one small bed. It was not a double bed, king-size. What a foolish God, creating a man and a woman and giving them a small bed. The first night, the fight started that you are still fighting. The woman wanted to sleep on the bed. The man also wanted to sleep on the bed and there was a pillow fight. They could not sleep the whole night because nobody was ready to sleep on the floor. Even an ordinary carpenter would have been better. Adam went to God and said, "What kind of life have you given to me? This is going to be continuous trouble. Why have you made a small bed?"

And a second mistake: rather than making a big bed, which was a simple thing.... For a god who can make the *whole* universe, to make a king-size bed would have been very simple, but rather than doing that, he withdrew the woman. And that was the *right* woman because she was made equal to man – in strength, in body, in intelligence, in everything she was equal to man.

These thousands of years of torture all over the world of women by men, would have been avoided just by making a king-size bed! But he made another woman, this time not equal. The first woman was made out of the same mud as Adam was made. The second woman was made by taking a rib of Adam, and out of the rib, the woman was made. Naturally, she cannot claim equality – she's only a rib.

And I have heard that whenever Adam was late coming home, when he went to sleep the first thing Eve used to do was to count his ribs. Who knows? There may be some other woman some-where. But there was no need to ask him... just count his ribs.

Even the smallest intelligence can understand that to prohibit anything is to create interest, attraction – and God prohibited. Not only prohibited, he showed Adam and Eve two trees – one of wis-dom, one of eternal life – and said, "You are not to eat the fruits from these trees." And the garden was vast. If Adam and Eve had been left on their own, I don't think that even now we would have found those two trees.

God seems to be stupid: showing them the trees and telling them, "This is the tree of wisdom and this is the tree of eternal life. Never eat the fruits from these two trees. The rest of the gar-den is available." But naturally Adam and Eve must have become obsessed with those two trees. You would have done the same as

Adam and Eve did. And I say they did right. Wisdom is not something harmful – ignorance is harmful. Eternal life is not something to be denied to your own children. But it seems he had no idea of the basic principles of psychology. What are you going to do by knowing all?

It will be enough if you can eat the fruits of those two trees: the tree of wisdom and the tree of eternal life. And I am making available to my sannyasins *only* those two trees. Those two trees are not in the garden, those two trees are within you. As you meditate, as you become silent, as you become peaceful, wisdom arises. Wisdom is the light that radiates out of a silent consciousness. And once your inner being is full of light, *instantly* you know your life is eternal. Death is a fiction. God has prohibited man to go within himself. Go to the whole Garden of Eden – that means the whole universe – but don't go within yourself.

The devil who persuaded, seduced Eve to eat the fruit of wisdom... and just see, the story is not only a story. There is a perfect science hidden behind it. The devil did not say, "Eat first from the fruit of eternal life." You cannot eat from the tree of eternal life. You are blind, you cannot approach the tree. First, your eyes have to be opened.

Hence, he persuaded her for the tree of wisdom. And the reason he gave is worth remembering: the reason he gave was that "God has prohibited you because he is very jealous of anyone becoming *equal* to him, and if you are wise and have eternal life, you are a god. God does not have anything more than you. Because of jealousy, he is prohibiting you." The logic was perfect.

By the way, people all around the earth have asked me: "Why are there so many women interested in you? Why are there so many women sannyasins?" The reason is the same – why didn't the devil approach man first?

Man is argumentative, does not listen from the heart. He listens from the head. The devil would have convinced him but it would have taken a long time, and perhaps God may have come to know; the thing had to be done quickly. The woman listens from the heart, and the heart is quick. Mind is lousy, slow, needs all kinds of arguments, and then too there is doubt. Then too there are questions and questions and questions. If the devil had met the questioner, even by this time the questioner would have been asking because he wanted to know all.

Eve was ready because she was not interested in knowing all. This was enough, to have wisdom. Wisdom does not mean that you know all. It simply means pure intelligence, a heart full of light, no darkness in any corners of your being. Wisdom is a transformation of your whole being, knowledge is not. You are searching for knowledge. And you can memorize all the libraries in the world; still, more and more questions will be coming. The final result will be a madman. The woman, in this way, is simple. She listened to devil. The idea was perfectly clear.

One thing more to be reminded to you – that in Hebrew, Aramaic, the language that Jesus spoke, they don't have the idea that the word "devil" comes from Sanskrit. Devil and divine come from the same root. Never condemn the word "devil," because it simply means divine. Then the whole story takes a different color: God is against humanity. God is against your being wise, against your enjoying eternally the fruits of love and life. How can you call the person who was the *first* seer, the first sage... we owe to him everything. He is divine.

And as God became aware that they had eaten the fruit of wisdom, he immediately turned them out of the Garden of Eden. Because now he was afraid: the second step is absolutely necessary, and that is the fruit of the tree of eternal life. Before they eat that, they have to be turned out of the Garden.

You may have thought or you may not have thought, but it is significant to know that the whole of humanity has been searching for more life, longer life, better life, healthier life. Why? – because that wound is still not healed. We are still searching. All our sciences, all our philosophical endeavors are nothing but a search for the second tree.

Science perhaps may gave a little longer life, but it cannot give eternal life, because it works on the body and the body cannot be eternal. Philosophy may give you great ideas, but just ideas – soap bubbles. They cannot give you eternal life. There is only one approach and that is the approach of meditation. That goes directly to the tree of eternal life.

So rather than wasting your time in questions and answers, it is better to find the tree – and both trees are within you. And the methodology to reach to them does not need much effort. In fact, it does not need *any* effort, it needs an effortless relaxation. So whenever you have time, just relax, close your eyes and forget the whole world. Thoughts will go on just because of old habit. You have to learn a simple secret: the name of the secret is watching without any judgment. Let the thoughts move, just like on the screen of a movie. You simply watch, don't judge. And slowly, slowly the traffic is less and less and one day suddenly you see – there are no thoughts, you are utterly empty in your mind.

And that is the turning point in one's life, because the energy that was going towards thoughts, finding nothing there, turns back to the original source. The circle is complete. You must have seen – many secret societies of the world have used the symbol of a snake with his own tail in his mouth. That symbol is nothing but your own energy turning back to the source, becoming a circle.

You will not find any answer, so please don't call me "Answer." I am not your Answer. Although I discuss your questions, I never answer. My effort is just the opposite: I destroy your question, not answer it. In the name of answering, I am destroying it. I am taking it away from you, because I know that any answer given to you is going to become many questions. And I am not your enemy, and I don't want to burden you any more. You are burdened so much by your religions, by your philosophers, by your traditions. It is time that all your burdens should be taken away. You should be left alone in your silence. You will not find any answer, remember – but all questions will disappear.

And when all questions disappear, you have found something more than just a verbal answer – you have found your authentic reality, your being. And your being is rooted in the being of the whole universe. You have found the whole world. Just find your own center and you have found the center of the whole world. But beware of questions. They are not your friends. You will be lost in the jungle of questions. You will become very knowledgeable, but deep inside there will be nothing but darkness and death.

I want within you light and life and love. I teach these three L's, just like educationists teach three R's.

BELOVED OSHO,
DO ALL DISCIPLES BECOME DEVOTEES? IN YOUR
COMMUNES, I HAVE LOVED YOU, GOT LOST IN YOU,
BEEN EMPTIED OUT BY YOU. AWAY, YOUR PICTURE
HAS LIT ME UP WHEN I'VE GONE DARK. YOUR VOICE
ON TAPES HAS WOKEN ME WHEN I'VE BEEN
SNOOZING AND MADE ME SNOOZE WHEN I'VE BEEN
AWAKE. YOU ARE MY BLOOD, MY BONE AND
MARROW AND YET, AND YET OSHO, I DO NOT SEE
MYSELF AS A DEVOTEE. WHEN I SEE THOSE WHO CARE
FOR YOUR BODY, I CAN NEVER IMAGINE HOW I
COULD MANAGE SUCH A THING, SO GENEROUSLY
AND SELFLESSLY, EVEN THOUGH I USED TO DEEP-
DOWN DREAM MY ROLE SHOULD ONE DAY BE TO
SERVE, COMPLETELY LOST IN LOVE. IF I NEVER
BECOME WHAT YOU CALL A DEVOTEE, HAVE I A
DESTINY THAT SEPARATES ME FROM YOU?

Savita, every disciple grows into a devotee. There is no way to go anywhere else. But you have not understood the meaning of devotee. I have almost one million sannyasins around the world. If they all think that by being devotees they have to be close to me, then I will feel that to become enlightened was a mistake!

A devotee is just like the fragrance of a flower. The flower is the disciple, the devotee is fragrance. You can see the flower. You cannot see the fragrance. You can catch hold of the flower but you cannot catch hold of the fragrance. And the fragrance has no destiny. Only machines have destinies. You are conscious human beings. You don't have destinies because you are masters of your own being. Only slaves have destinies.

The fragrance is freedom of the spirit of the flower. The flower was the body, the fragrance is the soul. Now the flower has come to blossom, the fragrance is released. Now the fragrance belongs to the whole universe. Wherever the breeze takes it, it has no resistance. It simply goes with it.

The life of a devotee is the life of let-go, of absolute surrender to existence – not to me, not to anybody else. And when you are surrendered totally to existence, then all these beautiful mountains, all these beautiful trees, rivers, this whole universe becomes your home. A devotee is one whose ego is dead – in a certain sense, one who is absent as far as the ego is concerned and present for the first time, as universal consciousness.

Of course, I need a few people around me. Just being a lazy guy, it has nothing to do with devotees, it has something to do with me. I have never done anything in my life.

One friend has come from the Soviet Union. He said to me, "Never go to the Soviet Union."

I said, "In the first place, they will not allow me in anyway. If England cannot allow, if Italy cannot allow, if Germany cannot allow, the Soviet Union is going to be the last on the laundry list!" But I asked him, "Why are you saying this?"

He said, "Because of your hands. If anybody shakes hands with you, he will take his hand away." I said, "What is wrong with my hands?"

He said, "Your hands are bourgeois. You have never worked! And the Soviet Union is a dictatorship of the proletariat."

I said, "That's true, I have never worked. Even in the middle of the night, my cold drink is just by the side of my bed but I will ring the call bell – that call bell is also by the side of the bed – and somebody has to come to give me a glass of cold drink."

In fact, the people who take care of me insist: "Don't touch the glass, don't touch the bottle. You may break it!" So what can I do? I am simply lazy.

Savita, you need not be in despair that perhaps you are not growing towards being a devotee – you *are* growing but it takes a little time. Just wait a little, let the spring come and your buds will open and your fragrance will be released. This is *real* freedom, liberation, *moksha*. But every disciple sooner or later has to become a devotee. There is no way that you can go back. For one who has tasted the sweetness and the beauty of being a disciple, it is impossible to go back, to fall back. You have passed the line from where people can go back.

There is a point of no return. Thousands of my sannyasins have passed that point. Even if they want to, it is not possible. It is almost like a child is born... he was in paradise in his mother's womb. The outside world will look very strange. He might like to go back into the womb but it is not possible. He has crossed the boundary, the point of no return. He has to go only ahead.

A disciple has come a long way, has come very close to the ultimate explosion. That ultimate explosion is devotion, but it has nothing to do with taking care of my body. It has something to do with taking care of your meditation. Move with as much wholeness and totality as you can to the very center of your being, the center of the cyclone. And you have come home.

BELOVED OSHO,
WHEN WE REACH A POINT WHERE INSANITY CAN
OCCUR, AT THAT STATE, A BREAKTHROUGH IN
CONSCIOUSNESS CAN ALSO OCCUR. PLEASE TELL US
HOW TO SHIFT THE GEAR FROM INSANITY TO
CONSCIOUSNESS?

Radha, the question is very significant to every seeker on the path. There comes a moment where there are two possibilities: a breakdown or a breakthrough. Breakdown rarely happens because it needs certain conditions. For example: you don't have a master, you have been going on your own. You don't have anybody who knows the path. There is danger. Or, you may have a teacher, not a master, misunderstanding him as a master. Then there is more possibility of a breakdown. A teacher is without any experience. He himself has never traveled on the path, although he is knowledgeable. Perhaps he may be more knowledgeable than any master. And if you are impressed by knowledge, there is danger. Don't be impressed by knowledge, because knowledge can be accumulated from scriptures, from books, from thousands of other sources, but it is all borrowed, dead.

How will you discriminate between a master and a teacher? The line is very fine. I will tell you one story to make it clear.

One great philosopher, in the days of Gautam Buddha, came to Gautam Buddha to challenge him for a debate. He had been moving all over the country, defeating many, many famous, well-known teachers but he had not come across a master. He had no first-hand knowledge, of what a master is. He thought master and teacher were synonymous terms – they are not. They may be synonymous in the dictionary, but not in reality.

He was a famous man – five hundred disciples of his own always followed him. Buddha looked at him. There were ten thousand sannyasins of Buddha. There was a great silence because this was the first time that any man had dared to challenge Buddha for a debate. The man must be blind!

Buddha said to the philosopher: "You have been traveling all over the country. You have been asking questions, answers have been given to you. Have you received any answer?"

The man said, "No, my questions are still there."

Buddha said, "I can also answer you but your questions will still be there, because the questions are yours, the answer is mine – there is no bridge, no connection. Your question needs *your* answer."

The man said, "Then what am I supposed to do?"

Buddha said, "You are really in search of truth? Then for two years, sit by my side. No question – just be silent and watch whatever goes on happening."

The man was certainly sincere. And looking at Buddha, his charismatic presence, his authoritative words, his penetrating eyes... he said, "I am ready. Can I ask my questions after two years?"

Buddha said, "Absolutely! You will have to! If you don't ask, I will remind you."

He sat down by the side of Buddha. At that very moment, an old disciple of Buddha – Mahakashyap – sitting under a tree just nearby, started laughing madly.

The philosopher said, "What has happened to this man?"

Buddha said, "You can ask him; it has never happened before."

The philosopher asked Mahakashyap, "What is the reason? Why did you burst into laughter?"

He said, "The same is my story. I had also come here to challenge Gautam Buddha, but this man played a trick. He said, 'Sit two years by my side and then you can ask whatever you want.' I said, 'It is worth it.' But after two years, all my questions had disappeared! So I want to tell you, if you are really interested in asking your questions, this is the time. Ask! After two years, you are finished. You will be sitting under that other tree."

For two years he sat, and forgot all about time, that two years had passed. And watching, for two years continuously, the beauty, the grace, the sincerity, the authenticity of Gautam Buddha, he became more and more silent. He fell into a certain kind of love, in tune with the heart of Gautam Buddha – his heart also started dancing.

And exactly after two years, Buddha said, "Now it is time. You can ask your questions."

He had only tears of joy in his eyes. He touched Gautam Buddha's feet and he said, "Mahakashyap was right, I am going to the tree."

A master is a totally different phenomenon. He does not teach you anything, he transforms you. He does not give you doctrines, he gives you a totally new level of consciousness. He gives you a new birth. So if you want to become knowledgeable, this is not the place. But if you want to be awakened, to be enlightened, then you have come to the right place, perhaps accidentally.

A master imparts something invisible. His vibe enters your being. The teacher only plays with words which cannot reach beyond your mind. Your mind is only a mechanism. Your being is your reality.

The first thing you have to ask yourself is whether you want to become an Encyclopedia Britannica or you want to fall into the celestial music of existence and become an immortal part of it. You *are* already part of it, you just have to be reminded. The master only makes you remember who you are. The teacher gives you many theories, many philosophies, many doctrines. The master only gives you to yourself.

Knowledge in itself is useless, even parrots have knowledge. So don't bother about knowledge. You may be a better parrot... or perhaps not even a better parrot.

I have heard, a bishop had a parrot and he had taught him – with great difficulty – the Sermon on the Mount. Any guest who came was amazed – the parrot was so perfect, they could not believe it. Perhaps even Jesus was not so impressive as the parrot. But the parrot died and the bishop was in great misery. He went to the biggest pet shop. There were many parrots of different qualities, qualifications, but nothing satisfied him. His own parrot was so religious and so Christian.

He told the owner, "These parrots won't do," and he described his parrot who was dead.

The man said, "I have the right parrot for you but the price will be too much because it is far superior to your parrot who has died."

The bishop was ready to pay *any* price. The owner took him inside the shop to a special room where he kept that parrot, a beautiful parrot. The bishop asked, "What are the qualities?"

He said, "Just look closely and you will see two small threads – one tied to the right foot, another to the left. If you slightly pull on the right foot by the thread, he will repeat the whole Sermon on the Mount. The bishop said, "And what about the other leg?"

He said, "The other leg is for Jews, because sometimes some Jew may come."

The bishop said, "Jews come – they are my friends. The rabbi lives just opposite my house. He will be the first man to come and see it!"

The owner said, "Then that is the right parrot for you. If you pull the other leg, he will repeat the whole Song of Solomon." The bishop said, "My God! A double scholar!"

He paid whatever was asked. While he was paying the money, he asked: "And if I pull both the threads together, what will happen?"

Before the owner could say anything, the parrot said, "You idiot – I will fall on my asshole! Never do that!"

Teachers are simply parrots. A master is not knowledgeable but he knows his experience, his own experience. He does not depend on Gautam Buddha or Jesus Christ. He has entered into his inner subjectivity, and whatever he says is fresh – just born. Avoid knowledge; insist on experience.

Only experience can bring salvation to you, only experience can give you wings which can liberate you. Neither any book nor any religion nor any teacher – they cannot help. They can only deceive you, perhaps without any intention – they have been deceived, and this deception goes on from century to century. Our whole heritage is thousands of deceptions, and we go on passing them to our children. But if you are not just a curiosity-monger but really thirsty, then existence is very compassionate. According to your thirst, you will find the well. If your thirst is total, you will find the door of the master. And if your thirst is just in the mind, you are not really thirsty. You will be wasting your time, your life, your opportunity because there are thousands of teachers and rarely one master. Blessed are those who have knocked on the right door.

BELOVED OSHO,
I WANT TO DO A PERFECT JOB AND I DON'T SEE THIS
AS A PROBLEM BUT WHEN I CONDEMN MYSELF FOR
DOING AN IMPERFECT JOB, IT DOESN'T FEEL RIGHT. IS
THERE A WAY TO ACCEPT OUR FAILURES GRACEFULLY?

The perfectionist is sick, psychologically sick. He does not understand that in life, everything is imperfect because imperfection is absolutely needed for evolution. Without imperfection, there is no possibility of evolution. If everything is perfect, the whole world will be a graveyard, because after perfection, what will you do? Except enter your grave – of course, perfectly. Imperfection is the law. Nothing ever becomes perfect and nothing should ever become perfect, because you are driving it towards death. Imperfection is beautiful.

So your problem is first to understand that imperfection is perfectly beautiful. Do your best, hope for the best but always remember: nothing can be perfect.

I was staying in a palace of a Maharajah. It is one of the most beautiful palaces in India. His son was taking me around and I saw that on one side, a wall was only half-built. I inquired, "What is the problem? What happened?"

He said, "My father never made anything perfect. This palace is so beautiful, he was afraid it might come very close to perfection, so he left this wall incomplete. It is a protection – the palace will live long, it will not die soon."

The old man was dead, but I said to his son, "Your father was a wise man."

Once this is understood, that imperfection is the foundation of all evolution, you will be very easily capable of accepting your imperfections without any guilt – gracefully.

BELOVED OSHO,

THE WEST CONCEIVED INSTANT COFFEE. THE EAST
CONCEIVED INSTANT ENLIGHTENMENT. WHAT IS
THE DIFFERENCE?

Milarepa, the West has created the instant coffee, but the West does not know how to sip it. Enlightenment is nothing but the right, meditative way of drinking coffee or tea.

Enlightenment is to live gracefully, lovingly, moment-to-moment – not only being blissful yourself but showering your bliss all around – that is instant enlightenment. You can become enlightened this very moment. Because the East does not conceive anything more than *this* moment – who knows about the next moment? It may come, it may not come. If you want really to do something – coffee or enlightenment – do it *now*, immediately.

Instant coffee may take a little time, but instant enlightenment takes no time at all.

about osho

OSHO IS A MODERN-DAY BUDDHA whose wisdom, clarity and humor have touched the lives of millions of people around the world. He is creating the conditions for the emergence of what he calls the "New Man" – a completely new kind of human being who is aware, life-affirmative and free.

According to Osho, the spiritual traditions of the past have made a deep split within the individual, reflected in all the institutions of society. His way is to heal this split, to restore the unity of body and spirit, earth and sky.

After his enlightenment in 1953, the evolution of this New Man became his dream. In 1966, Osho left the academic world and his post as a philosophy professor at the University of Jabalpur and began touring India intensively and speaking to many hundreds of thousands of people. At the same time, Osho was developing practical tools for man's self-transformation.

By the late 1960s, Osho had begun to create his unique dynamic meditation techniques. He says that modern man is so burdened with the traditions from the past and the anxieties of modern-day living, that he must go through a deep cleansing process before he can begin to discover the thought-free, relaxed state of meditation.

By 1974, a commune had been established around Osho in Pune, India, and the trickle of visitors from the West had become a flood. Today, his Commune is the largest spiritual growth center in the world. Each year it attracts thousands of international visitors to its meditation, therapy, bodywork and creative programs.

Osho speaks on virtually every aspect of the development of human consciousness. His talks cover a staggering range – from the meaning of life and death, to the struggles of power and politics, from the challenges of love and creativity, to the significance of science and education. These talks, given over thirty years, have been recorded on audio cassette and videotape, and published in hundreds of books in every major language of the world. He belongs to no tradition and says, "My message is not a doctrine, not a philosophy. My message is a certain alchemy, a science of transformation."

Osho left his body in 1990 as a result of poisoning by U.S. government agents, while being held in custody for technical immigration violations in 1985. He asks always to be referred to in the present tense. The words on his Samadhi, which Osho himself dictated, read:

OSHO
Never Born Never Died
Only Visited this Planet Earth
between December 11, 1931 – January 19, 1990